RENEWAL
DATE

D0722465

THAILAND, INDONESIA AND BURMA IN COMPARATIVE PERSPECTIVE

The International Political Economy of New Regionalisms Series

The International Political Economy of New Regionalisms Series presents innovative analyses of a range of novel regional relations and institutions. Going beyond established, formal, interstate economic organizations, this essential series provides informed interdisciplinary and international research and debate about myriad heterogeneous intermediate level interactions.

Reflective of its cosmopolitan and creative orientation, this series is developed by an international editorial team of established and emerging scholars in both the South and North. It reinforces ongoing networks of analysts in both academia and think-tanks as well as international agencies concerned with micro-, meso- and macro-level regionalisms.

Other Titles in the Series

South Africa's Multilateral Diplomacy and Global Change
Edited by Philip Nel, Ian Taylor and Janis van der Westhuizen

European Union and New Regionalism
Edited by Mario Telò

Crises of Governance in Asia and Africa
Edited by Sandra J. MacLean, Fahimul Quadir and Timothy M. Shaw

The Politics of Economic Regionalism
David J. Francis

Reconstituting Sovereignty
Rory Keane

Thailand, Indonesia and Burma in Comparative Perspective

PRIYAMBUDI SULISTIYANTO
Southeast Asian Studies Programme,
National University of Singapore

Published by
Ashgate Publishing Limited
Gower House
Croft Road
Aldershot
Hampshire GU11 3HR
England

Ashgate Publishing Company
131 Main Street
Burlington, VT 05401-5600 USA

Ashgate website: http://www.ashgate.com

British Library Cataloguing in Publication Data
Sulistiyanto, Priyambudi
    Thailand, Indonesia and Burma in comparative perspective. -
    (The international political economy of new regionalisms)
    1.Comparative government 2.Burma - Politics and government
    - 1988- 3.Indonesia - Politics and government - 1966-1998
    4.Thailand - politics and government - 1988- 5.Burma -
    Economic policy - 1988- 6.Indonesia - Economic policy -
    1966-1998 7.Thailand - Economic policy - 1988-
    I.Title
    320.3'0959

Library of Congress Control Number: 2001099947

ISBN 0 7546 1932 X

Printed and bound in Great Britain by Antony Rowe Ltd, Chippenham, Wiltshire

Contents

List of Tables, Figures and Boxes   *vi*
Acknowledgements   *viii*
List of Abbreviations   *x*
Map of Southeast Asia   *xiv*

1	Introduction	1
2	Reform, Boom and Crisis: Contending Approaches	14
3	Thailand's Boom	45
4	Thailand's Crisis	81
5	Indonesia's Boom	121
6	Indonesia's Crisis	156
7	Burma's Unreal Boom	193
8	Burma's Crisis	222
9	Conclusion: Thailand, Indonesia and Burma Compared	246

Bibliography   274
Index   301

List of Tables, Figures and Boxes

Tables

1.1	ASEAN Economies, 1996-1999	3
1.2	Comparison of Basic Social, Political and Economic Data in 1999	6
3.1	Commercial Bank Deposits in Thailand	50
3.2	Businesspersons in Prem's Cabinets (1980-1988)	54
3.3	Major Business Conglomerates in Thailand	58
3.4	Election Results of the "Big" Political Parties (1992-1996)	65
4.1	Thailand's Economic Fundamentals	83
4.2	Commodity Structure of Thailand's Export Slow-down	84
5.1	Sectoral Contributions to GDP Growth, 1967-1992	129
5.2	Major Business Conglomerates in Indonesia	133
5.3	Major Foreign Investors in Indonesia, 1980 and 1992	136
6.1	Indonesia's Economic Fundamentals	158
6.2	Export Growth in Indonesia, 1994-1996	160
7.1	Foreign Capital Assistance, 1978	197
7.2	Growth, Investment and Savings in Burma, 1962-1988	197
7.3	The Results of the 27 May 1990 General Election	200
7.4	State-owned Enterprises and their Business Activities	204
8.1	Burma's Economic Fundamentals	223
8.2	Foreign Direct Investment Approvals, by Selected Countries	226
8.3	Changes in Basic Commodity Prices in Rangoon	234
9.1	The Politics of the Economic Reforms and Booms in Thailand, Indonesia and Burma	258
9.2	The Politics of the Economic Crises in Thailand, Indonesia and Burma	263

Figures

3.1	Commercial Bank Credit by Selected Sectors, 1968-1979	51
3.2	GDP by Sector, 1970-1993	53
4.1	Thailand's Short-Term External Debt, 1992-1996	85
4.2	External Debt Indicators	85
4.3	Average Baht/US$ Exchange Rate, 1997-1998	100
5.1	The Results of General Elections in Indonesia, 1971-1997	142
6.1	Total External Debt, 31 December 1997	159
8.1	The Budget, 1992-1993 to 1996-1997	224
8.2	Average Exchange Rates on Free Market (1997-1998)	231

Boxes

3.1	Political and Economic Policy Figures in Thailand in the 1990s	64
4.1	The Old and New Constitutions	106
6.1	Monopolies of State-owned Enterprises	162
6.2	Monopolies of Privately-owned Conglomerates	163
6.3	Profiles of 16 Troubled Banks	176
6.4	15 Mega Projects Allowed to Proceed in November 1997	178
7.1	Economic Reform Policies in Burma, 1988-1995	201
8.1	Trade Restrictions Imposed by Western Countries	227
8.2	The SPDC and the Cabinet Reshuffle	237

Acknowledgements

In many ways, this book reflects my personal and academic journeys over the past fourteen years. When I began researching for this book (which is based on the Ph.D thesis I submitted to the Politics Department at the University of Adelaide, Australia, in the middle of 1999), I was often confronted with questions as to whether I could compare the political economy of Thailand, Indonesia, and Burma (Myanmar). My answer to that question was, why not? I visited Thailand for the first time in July 1988 and at that time the country had just entered an economic boom period and also had a newly elected democratic civilian government led by the late Chatichai Choonhavan. From Thailand, I heard about the political uprising in Burma, news of which dominated the front pages of Thailand's media. My knowledge about both Thailand and Burma increased when I revisited Thailand in 1989 and, later on, when I lived in Bangkok from 1990 until 1991. Interestingly, during that time both countries experienced political crises: the Burmese military refused to honour the results of the May 1990 general elections and the Thai military staged a bloodless coup in February 1991. Being an Indonesian, who has lived in Thailand and carried out research on contemporary Burmese politics, the desire to compare these countries is challenging both personally and academically. Since only a few Southeast Asian scholars have undertaken comparative political economy study of this sort, I hope to make contribution towards filling this gap.

Much of the content presented in this book is based on my field research in Thailand, Indonesia, Burma and Singapore in 1997 and early 1999. The book would not have been written without help from many people. I would like to thank Bob Catley, Felix Patrikeef, Anton Lucas, Jim Schiller, Arief Budiman, Dan Lev, Harold Crouch, Chris Manning, Craig Reynolds, David Mathieson, Jonathan Ping, *Ajarn* Withaya Sucharithanarugse, Kavi Chongkitavi, Ji Ungpakorn, Myat Than, Michael Vatikiotis and Valerie Teo. I also thank my Indonesian friends Anggito Abimanyu, Alex Irwan, Edriana, Ifdhal Kasim, Nashrun Marzuki, M. Yamin, Rambun Tjajo, Agus E. Santosa, and Tati Krisnawati. Many thanks are due to my Burmese friends both in Burma and overseas whose names I cannot mention here. Special thanks to Mrs Lee Li Kheng from the Department of Geography at the National University of Singapore (NUS) for the map of Southeast Asia and to my friends at the Southeast Asian Studies Programme, NUS, for their intellectual contributions and friendship. Thanks are also due to the Vondies and the Sukardans in Adelaide and Yogya respectively for their loyal support over the years. Finally, I would like to thank my beloved wife, Rossi von der Borch, for her constant support and for editorial suggestions. Her companionship made the long journey of writing this book worthwhile. *Peace, Salam and Shalom.*

P.S.
Gillman Heights, October 2001

List of Abbreviations

ABSDF	All Burma Students' Democratic Front.
ABSU	All Burma Students' Union.
ADB	Asian Development Bank.
AFTA	Asean Free Trade Agreement.
AJI	*Aliansi Jurnalis Indonesia* (Alliance of Independence Journalists).
ALA	Arakan Liberation Army.
AMC	Asset Management Corporation.
APEC	Asia Pacific Economic Cooperation.
ASEAN	Association of South-East Asian Nations.
BAPPENAS	*Badan Perencana Pembangunan Nasional* (National Development Planning Board).
BBC	Bangkok Bank of Commerce.
BCA	Bank Central Asia.
BDN	Bank Dagang Negara.
BI	Bank Indonesia.
BIBF	Bangkok International Banking Facilities.
BII	Bank International Indonesia.
BIS	Bank for International Settlements.
BMS	Business Management Services.
BNI	Bank National Indonesia.
BOB	Bureau of Budget.
BOI	Board of Investment.
BOT	Bank of Thailand.
BPIS	Badan Pengelola Industri-Industri Strategis (Agency for the Management of Strategic Industries).
BPPT	*Badan Penelitian dan Penerapan Tehnologi* (Agency for Assessment and Application of Technology).
BRI	Bank Rakyat Indonesia.
BSE	Bangkok Stock Exchange.
BSPP	Burmese Socialist Programme Party.
Bulog	*Badan Urusan Logistik* (State Logistical Agency).
BUMN	*Badan Usaha Milik Negara* (State-owned Enterprise).
CAR	Capital Adequacy Ratio.
CBS	Currency Board System.
CDA	Constitutional Drafting Assembly.

CEM	Council of Economic Ministers.
CFD	Confederation for Democracy.
CGI	Consortium on Government of Indonesia.
CIDES	Centre for Information and Development Studies.
CPB	Communist Party of Burma.
CPP	Chart Pattana Party.
CPT	Communist Party of Thailand.
CSIS	Centre of Strategic and International Studies.
CTP	Chart Thai Party.
DAB	Democratic Alliance of Burma.
DDSI	Directorate of the Defence Service Intelligence.
DPR	*Dewan Perwakilan Rakyat* (Peoples' Representative Council).
DRN	Dewan Riset National (National Research Council).
EAEC	East Asia Economic Caucus.
EOI	Export-oriented Industrialisation.
EPB	Economic Planning Board.
FECs	Foreign Exchange Certificates.
FDI	Foreign Direct Investment.
FIDF	Financial Institution Development Fund.
Fordem	*Forum Demokrasi* (Democracy Forum).
FPKR	*Forum untuk Pemulihan Kedaulatan Rakyat* (Forum for the Restoration of Public Sovereignty).
FPO	Fiscal Policy Office.
FRA	Financial Restructuring Agency.
GATT	General Agreement on Tariffs and Trade.
GDP	Gross Domestic Product.
GNP	Gross National Product.
Golkar	*Golongan Karya* (Functional Groups).
HIID	Harvard Institute of International Development.
IBRA	Indonesian Bank Restructuring Agency.
ICMI	*Ikatan Cendekiawan Muslim Indonesia* (Indonesian Muslim Scholars' Association).
IDB	Industrial Development Bureau.
IGGI	Inter-Governmental Group on Indonesia.
IMD	Institute for Management Development.
IMF	International Monetary Fund.
ISI	Import-substitution Industrialisation.
IT	Information Technology.
JPPCC	Joint Public-Private Consultative Committee.
JSE	Jakarta Stock Exchange.

KIA	Kachin Independent Army.
KNU	Karen National Union.
LCT	Labour Congress of Thailand.
LDC	Least Developed Countries.
LIPI	Lembaga Ilmu Pengetahuan Indonesia (Institute of Indonesia Sciences).
MAPT	Myanmar Agricultural Products Trading.
MARDB	Myanmar Agricultural and Rural Development Bank.
MAS	Monetary Authority of Singapore.
MEB	Myanmar Economic Bank.
MFTB	Myanmar Foreign Trade Bank.
MICB	Myanmar Investment and Commercial Bank.
MITI	Ministry of International Trade and Industry.
MOC	Ministry of Commerce.
MOF	Ministry of Finance.
MOI	Ministry of Interior.
NAP	New Aspiration Party.
NCCC	National Convention Convening Committee.
NCGUB	National Coalition Government of The Union of Burma.
NEDB	National and Economic Development Board.
NEDCOR	National Economic Development Corporation.
NESDB	National Economic and Social Development Board.
NGO	Non-governmental organisation.
NIB	National Intelligence Bureau.
NIC	Newly Industrialising Country.
NLD	National League for Democracy.
NPKC	National Peace Keeping Council.
NU	*Nahdathul Ulama* (Islamic organisation in Indonesia).
NUP	National Unity Party.
OSS	Office of Strategic Studies.
Pakto	*Paket Oktober* (October Package).
PDI	*Partai Demokrasi Indonesia* (Indonesian Democratic Party).
PIBF	Provincial International Banking Facilities.
PKI	*Partai Komunis Indonesia* (the Communist Party of Indonesia).
PLMO	Property Loan Management Organisation.
PNI	*Partai Nasional Indonesia* (Indonesian National Party).
PPP	*Partai Persatuan Pembangunan* (Development Unity Party).
PRD	*Partai Rakyat Demokrat* (Peoples' Democratic Party).

Pyithu Hluttaw	People's Assembly.
SAP	Social Action Party.
SBI	*Sertifikat Bank Indonesia* (Bank Indonesia Certificates).
SBSI	*Serikat Buruh Sejahtera Indonesia* (Indonesian Welfare Trade Union).
SBSU	*Surat Berharga Pasar Uang* (Bank Indonesia Market Certificates).
SEC	Securities and Exchange Commission.
SET	Stock Exchange of Thailand.
SLORC	State Law and Order Restoration Council.
SOEs	State-owned Enterprises.
SP	*Solidaritas Perempuan* (Women's Solidarity).
SPDC	State Peace and Development Council.
SPSI	Serikat Pekerja Seluah Indonesia (All Indonesian Workers Union).
TDRI	Thailand Development Research Institute.
TTUC	Thai Trade Union Congress.
UMEH	Union of Myanmar Economic Holdings.
USDA	Union Solidarity and Development Association.
WTO	World Trade Organisation.

Map of Southeast Asia

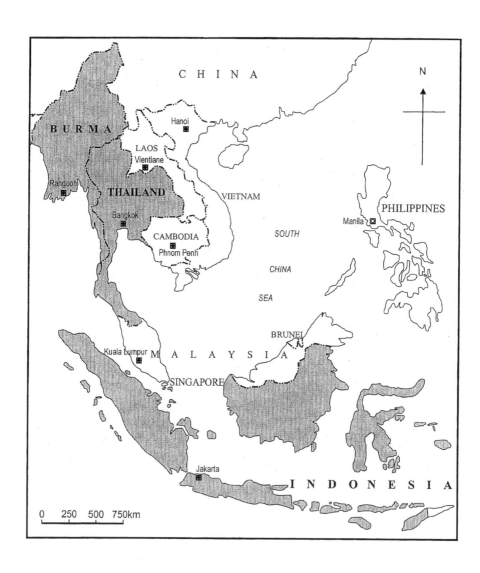

For Rossi, Aditiya and Mira-Srikandi

Chapter One

Introduction

This book is a comparative study of economic and political change in contemporary Thailand, Indonesia, and Burma (Myanmar).[1] It attempts to understand the similarities and differences in the ways these countries have experienced and responded to economic change and the political consequences. In particular, it focuses on a comparison of two interrelated economic and political events experienced by Thailand, Indonesia and Burma: firstly, the different factors which influenced the period of economic reform and boom and their political implications during the 1980s and 1990s; and secondly, the way in which these countries responded to the economic crisis, which occurred in 1997 and 1998, as part of a regional crisis.

In different ways, Thailand, Indonesia and Burma implemented economic reforms during the 1980s and 1990s. The governments and policy makers in these countries embraced market economies and aimed to give more opportunity to the private sector and foreign investors to invest in sectors that had been monopolised by the government.[2] These economic reforms changed the outlook and performance of the economies studied here. In the late 1980s and the early 1990s, respectively, Thailand and Indonesia entered a period of economic boom and became part of the "second generation" of newly industrialising countries (NICs), following the countries of East Asia.[3] Burma, despite the implementation of economic reforms, did not progress as much, although the Burmese economy was more open to the private sector and foreign investors than in previous decades.[4]

Politically, the pathways that these countries chose had both differences and similarities. In Thailand, the economic boom period was accompanied by a gradual transition toward the establishment of a representative political system and the strengthening of civil society. In Indonesia, the New Order government allowed a limited political openness in the face of strong demands for the replacement of the New Order's authoritarian system with a more democratic one. In Burma the military government continued to suppress opposition groups while it attempted to reform the economy. These different political systems faced increasing challenges until, in 1997-1998, the Asian region experienced economic crisis.

This economic crisis raised questions about the vulnerability of the existing economic and political systems that had been adopted by countries in the Asian region as a whole, and particularly by these three countries. The economic crisis had serious implications for economic and political stability in the region. It took everyone by surprise and was judged by some commentators and observers as the most serious economic and political crisis ever to have occurred in the region due to its far-reaching implications.[5] Although there has been much comment, analysis, and discussion of the causes and the consequences of this regional crisis, it is generally agreed that it began with the depreciation of the Asian countries' currencies by between 10-80 per cent against the US dollar in 1997.

Some interpretations of the causes of the economic crisis deserve attention here. There was a consensus among economists that the economic crisis resulted from a deterioration in the performance of the macroeconomics of the affected countries, evidence of which could be found in indicators such as the increasing current account deficits and debt, a decline in exports, overvalued exchange rates, the collapse of the property market, and low investment in education and human resources.[6] Some academics have attributed the economic crisis to the lack of good governance, meaning that widespread corruption, collusion and nepotism practices in these countries had produced economies that were inefficient and uncompetitive.[7] A few scholars pointed out that the crisis reflected a combination of bad economic policies and policy errors made by the government and the private sectors.[8] Others suggested the crisis occurred as a direct consequence of the globalisation process at work in the region and also from an economic model adopted by the affected countries which relied too heavily on infusion of foreign capital rather than on domestic resources.[9] In numerous ways and different perspectives, therefore, this event confirmed that those, including Krugman, who had argued in 1994 that the economic "miracle" of the Asia region was a myth, were now proving to have been close to the truth.[10]

Recent assessments and studies have confirmed that this was the most serious recent economic crisis the region had ever experienced.[11] It caused not only economic contraction in individual countries but also affected the region as a whole and, to some extent, other parts of the world. In the Southeast Asian region, Thailand and Indonesia were among the countries which suffered most, experiencing minus economic growth and high inflation for the first time in 1997 and 1998 (Table 1.1).

Table 1.1 ASEAN Economies, 1996-1999

	1996	1997	1998	1999
Indonesia				
Real GDP growth (%)	7.82	4.70	-13.13	0.85
Inflation (%)	7.94	6.70	57.60	20.50
GDP per capita (US$)	1,071	1,071	463	675
Malaysia				
Real GDP growth (%)	10.02	7.32	-7.37	5.80
Inflation (%)	3.8	2.64	5.28	2.74
GDP per capita (US$)	4,769	4,684	3,349	3,621
Philippines				
Real GDP growth (%)	5.85	5.19	-0.59	3.95
Inflation (%)	9.10	5.85	9.72	6.71
GDP per capita (US$)	1,156	1,129	891	1,030
Singapore				
Real GDP growth (%)	7.58	8.53	0.06	5.86
Inflation (%)	1.38	2.01	-0.28	0.03
GDP per capita (US$)	25,185	27,170	21,962	23,806
Thailand				
Real GDP growth (%)	5.88	-1.45	-10.77	4.22
Inflation (%)	5.85	5.61	8.10	0.29
GDP per capita (US$)	3,040	2,507	1,874	2,006
Vietnam				
Real GDP growth (%)	9.34	8.15	5.83	4.71
Inflation (%)	5.59	3.10	7.89	4.12
GDP per capita (US$)	328	349	357	364
Laos				
Real GDP growth (%)	6.88	6.92	3.99	7.28
Inflation (%)	13.00	27.50	91.00	128.37
GDP per capita (US$)	382	347	249	274
Cambodia				
Real GDP growth (%)	5.51	3.69	1.81	4.97
Inflation (%)	7.15	8.00	14.80	4.40
GDP per capita (US$)	310	296	262	275
Burma				
Real GDP growth (%)	6.44	5.74	5.77	10.92
Inflation (%)	20.02	33.90	30.00	15.60
GDP per capita (US$)	126	125	123	143
Brunei				
Real GDP growth (%)	1.00	3.60	-3.99	2.97
Inflation (%)	1.90	1.68	-0.41	-0.08
GDP per capita (US$)	17,328	16,565	13,870	14,094

Source: ASEAN Secretariat, ASCU Database, 2001.

The impact of the economic crisis, which will be described in detail in this book, also created social and political crises that had the potential to destabilise the whole region. A great deal of pressure was brought to bear on political leaders and policy makers who were forced to implement tough economic policies to end the crisis. From another perspective, there is some truth in the view that the economic crisis was a "blessing in disguise" because it created pressure for political change, even democratisation, across the region.[12] In Thailand the economic crisis was accompanied by strong demands from the civil society to create a more democratic constitution. It also led to the downfall of the Chaovalit coalition government in November 1997. In Indonesia, the economic crisis encouraged the take off of a widespread movement for political reform, which brought about the resignation of President Suharto in May 1998. In Malaysia, the crisis exacerbated tension within the Malay elites, leading Prime Minister Mahathir Mohammad to dismiss Anwar Ibrahim from the position of Finance Minister and Deputy PM in September 1998, which brought about the rise of the reform movement in the country.[13] The list could be extended. But these examples are sufficient to illustrate the point that the economic crisis created a situation in which demands for transparency and good governance in government and business were heard across the region. These demands mainly came from international financial institutions such as the International Monetary Fund, the World Bank, the Asian Development Bank, foreign investors and the Western countries, but they were supported by pro-reform groups in many countries in the region.

As explained above, one political consequence of the recent economic crisis was that pressure for political change emerged in the region as a whole. Although it is still too early to know just what the likely political features of the region will be in the near future, there is clear recognition that the existing economic and political systems in the Asian region failed to respond adequately to the economic crisis. For everyone, from political leaders, policy makers and specialists, to ordinary people, this requires a re-examination of existing views on the interrelation between economic development and political change in the region.[14] As the recent economic crisis has provided rich grounds for analysis and examination, so this kind of study must be carried out.

Having provided an overview of this study, several questions need to be posed here. First, in examining Thailand, Indonesia and Burma, we need to ask how the historical, social, political and other factors affected the formulation and implementation of economic reforms and contributed to the economic boom period during the 1980s and 1990s? What were the political implications of those economic reforms and the boom period in these countries? What were the causes of the economic crisis in Thailand,

Indonesia and Burma in 1997 and 1998, and how did these countries respond to the consequences of the crisis? Why did the crisis affect some countries more severely than others?

Comparing Thailand, Indonesia and Burma

Why Thailand, Indonesia, and Burma? There are a number of reasons why a comparative study of these countries is needed. First, in terms of basic social, political and economic backgrounds, a comparative study of these countries is illuminating (Table 1.2). These countries have had interesting and colourful histories. Burma and Indonesia experienced colonisation by the British and the Dutch and experienced politically and economically tumultuous post-Independence periods. Thailand was never colonised. Second, in all these countries the military has been the dominant political force. Third, these countries also have a history of struggle to establish democratic political systems to replace existing authoritarian ones. There have been successes and failures in this. Fourth, under a variety of circumstances, all these countries implemented economic reforms in the 1980s and 1990s. As a result, the governments of these countries entered into a situation where a private sector was emerging and the pressure for political change was growing steadily. Finally, research on the comparative political economy of the Southeast Asian region has been largely neglected when compared with the East Asian region.[15] More importantly, only few comparative studies of this sort have been done on these three countries. In previous decades a few scholars have written comparisons of two countries. Furnival pioneered a comparative study of the policies of the British and Dutch colonial governments in Burma and Indonesia;[16] K. Bandyopadhaya compared the foreign policies and economic developments of Indonesia and Burma;[17] Lissak studied military-civilian relations in Thailand and Burma;[18] and Silverstein compared the roles of the military and foreign policy in Burma and Indonesia.[19] Takashi Shiraisi, to the author's knowledge, is the only scholar who has compared the three countries, in his study on the political role of the military in Thailand, Burma and Indonesia.[20]

Although a good deal of analysis has been done on the economic crisis, surprisingly few comparative studies have been carried out. To name a few, for example, Thai specialists have recently written about the political dynamics of the economic crisis in Thailand.[21] Meanwhile, Indonesian specialists have also written about the political consequences of the economic crisis in Indonesia, with emphasis on the role of the state and the political patronage system during the crisis period.[22]   Indeed, there is no study that compares the contemporary political economy of these three countries.

Table 1.2   Comparison of Basic Social, Political and Economic Data in 1999

	Thailand	Indonesia	Burma
Social and Politics			
Population (millions)	61.7	207.0	45
Population growth rate (% pa.)	1.0	1.6	1.2
Labour force growth rate (% pa.)	0.6	2.7	1.5
Poverty (% of below poverty line)	16	20	-
Urban population (% of total population)	21	35	27
Life expectancy (years)	69	65	60
Infant mortality (per 1,000 births)	30	43	78
Illiteracy (% of population age 15+)	5	14	16
Official language	Thai	Indonesian	Burmese
Main ethnic group	Thai	Javanese	Burman
Main religion	Buddhism	Islam	Buddhism
Executive branch	Prime Minister	President	Prime Minister
Legislative branch	Parliament	Parliament	-
Regime type	Parliamentary	Presidential	Military
Economy			
GDP (% share):			
Agriculture	11.9	17.3	53.2 (1998)
Industry	41.7	43.3	9.0 (1998)
Manufacturing	29.3 (1998)	25.4	6.3 (1998)
Services	46.7	39.6	37.8 (1998)
Exports (US$)	71.5 bn	59.3 bn	1.6 mn (1998)
Imports (US$)	57.5 bn	41.9 bn	2.7 mn (1998)
Current account balance (US$)	11.3 bn	6.2 bn	-0.6 mn (1998)
External debt (US$)	95.6 bn	147.4 bn	5.6 mn (1998)
Currency	Baht	Rupiah	Kyat

Sources: World Bank, *Statistical Report* (Washington D.C.: World Bank, 1997 and 1999) and Clark D. Neher, *Southeast Asia, Crossroads of the World* (DeKalb: Southeast Asia Publications, Northern Illinois University, 2000), p. 8.

Before we proceed further, it is necessary to place this study in the context of a broader view of the dynamics of economic development and political change in developing countries. There is a consensus among those researching the political economy of the Asian region that there is a strong relationship between economic development and political change.[23] Related to this, there has been an increasing number of studies on the interrelationship between economic development and political change in the Southeast Asian region.[24] They have focused on the importance of historical and structural factors in the economic development that has occurred across the Southeast Asian region in the past three decades. The collapse of oil and commodity prices on the world market in the early 1980s caused economic crisis in Southeast Asia, which forced affected governments to implement a series of economic reforms with the aim of deregulating their economies and restructuring their domestic industries. Basically the reforms were intended to make these economies more export oriented and internationally competitive.

It was during this reorientation of economic policies in the 1980s that non-state actors emerged to influence government policies and, in some cases, to challenge government's domination of economic activities. The governments required the participation of non-state or society-based organisations in order to overcome failures in the economic development process. In the Southeast Asian region, the state was regarded by some as not being of the same calibre or capability as those states in the East Asian region, which effectively played the leading role in the economic development of that region in the 1960s and 1970s.[25] Two important points can be raised here. First, it can be argued that those countries which had already reformed their economies and political systems adjusted to the consequences of the economic crisis better than those which had not. Second, it can be argued that the economic and political changes which occurred during and after the economic crisis can be seen as a result of both the globalisation and the domestic-based political change that took place in the region during the 1990s.

Comparative Method and Research Strategy

Considering the importance of the above changes, this study will use a comparative political economy framework of analysis that combines the insights of the existing political economy approaches and of the globalisation and domestic politics-based approaches. Better understanding of the area of interrelationship between domestic politics and globalisation would help us to understand better the causes and consequences of the economic crisis in the region.[26] This study uses a comparative historical and structural analysis that has been widely used by scholars in the fields of political science, political economy, sociology, and international political economy.[27] In using this method, this study will do two things for each country: first, examine factors such as history and politics, the role of the state, domestic coalitions, policy-making institutions, external factors, and also non-state actors that shaped or influenced the reform and boom period of the 1980s and 1990s and second, examine the causes, responses and consequences of the economic crisis of 1997 and 1998. The study will use the "method of agreement", through which conclusions and generalisations can be made in comparing the similarities of the countries subjected to the study. This will be supplemented by the "method of difference", which looks at the differences in these countries and draws generalisations from them.

This study has been carried out through a combination of library studies and field research in Thailand, Indonesia, and Burma. The author originally set out to compare the political economy of economic reforms and booms in the three countries. The focus broadened when the author undertook field research in these countries from July to December 1997, when the currency crises were occurring. He revisited Thailand, Singapore, and Indonesia in early 1999 in order to gain up-to-date information. During the field research, the author developed this study by utilising primary and secondary sources and combining these with a series of interviews with politicians, businesspeople, bureaucrats, academics, journalists, activists, and ordinary people (not all of whom were willing to be quoted). However, it must be pointed out that this is a comparative political economy study and not an area study. Thus it relies very much on books, articles, and other information, which have already been written by country specialists. Access to information in Burma was more limited. As the economic and political events began to unfold the author decided to study the events related to the economic crisis in these countries in a comparative perspective. He finally decided to end the period of focus for this study with the Chaovalit coalition government collapse in November 1997 and Suharto's resignation in May 1998 and Burma's uncertain political outlook at the end of 1998.

The Structure of the Book

This book contains nine chapters. Chapter One provides an overview and the context of the study, the relevance, methodology and structure of the book. Chapter Two reviews the various approaches which may be adopted in a study of the political economy of economic and political change in the Southeast Asian region in the age of globalisation. By examining critically the existing approaches, this chapter argues that it is necessary to use a comparative political economy approach in understanding the politics of economic change in contemporary Thailand, Indonesia, and Burma.

Chapter Three examines the political economy of Thailand with emphasis on the historical, political, institutional, non-state and external factors that influenced the economic boom period of the 1980s and 1990s. It demonstrates that Thailand is a case where economic boom and political liberalisation occurred together. The implementation of economic reforms in the 1980s and 1990s opened the way for a gradual move towards the establishment of a representative political system. Chapter Four examines the impact of economic globalisation in Thailand in the 1990s. It focuses on the causes and consequences of the economic crisis which occurred in 1997 and 1998. The main aim of this chapter is to discuss the recent efforts of Thai policy makers to liberalise the financial sector and the implications of this for the performance of the Thai economy in the lead up to the crisis. The power struggles which occurred during the floating of the baht and during the events that led to the downfall of Prime Minister Chaovalit in 1997 will also be examined.

Chapter Five examines the political economy of Indonesia and, similar to Chapter Three, explores the historical, economic, political, institutional, non-state, and external factors that influenced the economic boom period of the late 1980s and 1990s. It suggests that Indonesia is a case where economic boom did not automatically lead to political liberalisation. It describes the way that the implementation of economic reforms in the 1980s and 1990s was not complemented by the establishment of a more representative political system. Chapter Six, similar to Chapter Four, focuses on the causes and consequences of the economic crisis which occurred in 1997 and 1998. It argues that Indonesia was a victim of contagion from Thailand's economic crisis, and that domestic factors deepened the economic crisis in Indonesia. In this chapter the political struggles which occurred during the floating of the rupiah and later leading up to resignation of President Suharto in May 1998, are also examined.

Chapter Seven examines the political economy of Burma and similar to Chapters Three and Five, discusses the various factors that influenced the transition period from a socialist to a so-called free market economy in Burma in the 1980s and the 1990s. It suggests that Burma is a case where the failure of economic reform has been accompanied by the maintenance of authoritarian politics. Chapter Eight focuses on the impact of the regional economic crisis on Burma. It suggests that despite the fact that the Burmese economy was not as open and globalised as those of

Thailand and Indonesia, Burma was not immune to the economic changes which occurred in the Southeast Asian region. In this chapter the responses of the military government to the economic crisis in Burma and their influence on the deepening political crisis in the country are examined.

Chapter Nine draws together the comparative political economy approach proposed in this study and the empirical evidences examined in the case studies. The comparison is made in two ways. First, a summary of the similarities between the factors that influenced the reform and boom period in each country and between the responses of each country to the economic crisis. Second, a summary of the economic and political differences between these countries, as they were observed during the reform, boom and crisis period. Third, a brief discussion on the relevance of the findings in the context of the globalised political economy and of the political change concludes the study.

Notes

[1] The Burmese military government changed the name of the country from 'Burma' to 'Myanmar' in 1989, but the name change has not been domestically and internationally accepted, many still preferring to use 'Burma', including this book.

[2] The core of policy reforms can be found in measures such as improved macroeconomic performance, reduced current account deficit, tightened monetary policy, reform of the financial sector and taxation system, adjustment of the exchange rate policy, liberalisation of the trade sector, reduced tariffs, and privatisation of the government-owned enterprises. For further discussion of the political aspect of economic reforms in the 1980s and the 1990s, see John Williamson (ed.) *The Political Economy of Policy Reform* (Washington D.C.: Institute for International Economics, 1994).

[3] For an interesting view on this issue, see Mitchell Bernard and John Ravenhill, "Beyond Product Cycles and Flying Geese, Regionalization, Hierarchy, and the Industrialization of East Asia", *World Politics*, vol. 47 (January 1995), pp. 171-209.

[4] John Wong, "Why Has Myanmar not Developed Like East Asia?", *ASEAN Economic Bulletin*, vol. 13, no. 3 (March 1997), pp. 344-358.

[5] See Steven Radelet and Jeffrey Sachs, *The East Asian Financial Crisis: Diagnosis, Remedies*, Prospects, a paper presented to the Brookings Panel, Washington D.C., 26-27 March 1998; and Suthad Setboonsarng, "Asean Economic Co-operation, Adjusting to the Crisis", *Southeast Asian Affairs 1998* (Singapore: Institute of Southeast Asian Studies, 1998), pp. 18-36.

[6] This view can be found in Manuel F. Montes, *The Currency Crisis in Southeast Asia*, updated version (Singapore: Institute of Southeast Asian Studies,

1998); and also Max Corder, *The Asian Crisis, Is there a Way Out?* (Singapore: Institute of Southeast Asian Studies, 1999).

[7] L. R. Rosenberger, "Southeast Asia's Currency Crisis: Diagnosis and Prescription", *Contemporary Southeast Asia*, vol. 19, no. 3 (December 1997), pp. 223-251; and Steven Radelet and Jeffrey Sach, "Asia Reemergence", *Foreign Affairs*, vol. 76, no. 6 (November-December 1997), pp. 56-59.

[8] Ross Garnaut, "The Financial Crisis: A Watershed in Economic Thought about East Asia", *Asian Pacific Economic Literature*, vol. 12, no. 1 (May 1998), pp. 1-11; and Linda Lim, "The Southeast Asian Currency Crisis and its Aftermath", *Journal of Asian Business*, vol. 13, no. 4 (1997), pp. 65-83.

[9] P. B. Rana, "Globalization and Currencies", *Far Eastern Economic Review* (11 September 1997); Walden Bello, *Addicted to Capital: The Ten-Year High and Present-Day, Withdrawal Trauma of Southeast Asia's Economies*, manuscript (Manila and Bangkok: The Philippine Center for Policy Studies, Focus on the Global South, and the Campaign Against Poverty 2000, 1997); and also Robert Wade and Frank Veneroso, "The Asian Crisis: The High Debt Model Versus the Wall Street-Treasury-IMF Complex", *New Left Review*, vol. 22, no. 8 (March-April 1998), pp. 3-23.

[10] Debate on the origins of the Asian "miracle", which will be explored more in Chapter Two, can be found in the World Bank report entitled *The East Asian Miracle, Economic Growth and Public Policy* (Washington D.C.: World Bank, 1993). For a critical perspective on this issue, see Paul Krugman, "The Myth of Asia's Miracle", *Foreign Affairs*, vol. 73, no. 6 (November-December 1994), pp. 62-78; and also A. Mommen, "The Asian Miracle, A Critical Reassessment" in A. E. Jilberto and A. Mommen (eds.) *Liberalization in the Developing World, Institutional and Economic Changes in Latin America, Africa and Asia* (London and New York: Routledge, 1996), pp. 28-50.

[11] International Monetary Fund, *World Economic Outlook, Interim Assessment* (Washington D.C.: The International Monetary Fund, 1997); World Bank, *East Asia: The Road to Recovery* (Washington D.C.: The World Bank, 1998); and Ross H. McLeod and Ross Garnaut (eds.) *East Asia in Crisis, From Being a Miracle to Needing One?* (London and New York: Routledge, 1998).

[12] This point has been suggested by Robert Garran in his book entitled *Tigers Tamed, The End of the Asian Miracle* (Sydney: Allen and Unwin, 1998), especially chapter 10.

[13] Greg Felker, "Malaysia in 1998, A Cornered Tiger Bares Its Claws", *Asian Survey*, vol. xxxix, no. 1 (January-February 1999), pp. 43-54.

[14] Garran, *Tigers Tamed*, pp. 205-206.

[15] Jamie Mackie, "Economic Growth in the ASEAN region: the Political Underpinings" in Helen Hughes (ed.) *Achieving Industrialization in East Asia* (Melbourne: Cambridge University Press, 1988), pp. 283-326.

[16] John S. Furnival, *Colonial Policy and Practice: A Comparative Study of Burma and Netherland India* (New York: New York University Press, 1947).

[17] K. Bandyopadhaya, *Burma and Indonesia: Comparative Political Economy and Foreign Policy* (New Delhi and Madras: South Asia Publishers, 1983).

[18] M. Lissak, *Military Roles in Modernization: Civil-Military Relations in Thailand and Burma* (Beverly Hills and London: Sage Publications, 1976).

[19] Josef Silverstein, "The Military and Foreign Policy in Burma and Indonesia", *Asian Survey*, xxii, 3 (March 1982), pp. 278-291.

[20] Takashi Shiraisi, "The Military in Thailand, Burma and Indonesia" in R. A. Scalapino, S. Sato and Jusuf Wanandi (eds.) *Asian Political Institutionalization* (Berkeley: Institute of East Asian Studies, University of California, 1989), pp. 157-180.

[21] Ammar Siamwalla, "Can a Developing Democracy Manage Its Macroeconomy? The Case of Thailand" in his *Thailand's Boom and Bust* (Bangkok: Thailand Development Research Institute, 1997), pp. 63-75; Prudhisan Jumbala, "Thailand, Constitutional Reform amidst Economic Crisis", *Southeast Asian Affairs 1998* (Singapore: Institute of Southeast Asian Studies, 1998), pp. 265-291; Kevin Hewison, "Thailand's Capitalism Before and After the Economic Crisis", a paper presented at the *Asian Studies Association of Australia Conference*, organised by the University of New South Wales, Sydney, 27 September to 3 October 1998; and for a good account on the crisis can be found in Pasuk Phongpaichit and Chris Baker, *Thailand's Crisis* (Singapore: Institute of Southeast Asian Studies, 2000).

[22] Andrew Rosser, "Surviving the Meltdown: Liberal Reform and Political Oligarchy in Indonesia", a paper presented at the *Asian Studies Association of Australia Conference*, organised by the University of New South Wales, Sydney, 27 September to 3 October 1998; M. Chatib Basri, "Indonesia: the Political Economy of Policy Reform" in Arief Budiman, Barbara Hatley and Damien Kingsbury (eds.) *Reformasi, Crisis and Change in Indonesia* (Clayton: Monash Asia Institute, Monash University, 1999), pp. 27-37; Donald K. Emmerson, "Exit and Aftermath: The Crisis of 1997-98", in Donald K. Emmerson (ed.) *Indonesia Beyond Suharto* (Armonk and London: M. E. Sharpe, 1999), pp. 295-343; and also Geoff Forrester and R. J. May (eds.) *The Fall of Suharto* (Bathurst: Crawford House Publishing, 1998).

[23] Discussion of this issue can be found in James W. Morley (ed.) *Driven by Growth, Political Change in the Asia-Pacific Region* (New York: An East Gate Book, 1993).

[24] See, for instance, Richard Higgott and Richard Robison (eds.) *Southeast Asia: Essays on the Political Economy of Structural Change* (London: Routledge and Kegan Paul, 1983); Richard Robison, Kevin Hewison and Richard Higgott (eds.) *Southeast Asia in the 1980s: The Politics of Economic Crisis* (Sydney: Allen and Unwin, 1987); Kevin Hewison, Richard Robison and Garry Rodan (eds.) *Southeast Asia in the 1990s, Authoritarianism, Democracy and Capitalism* (Sydney: Allen and Unwin, 1993); and Hal Hill, *Southeast Asia, Southeast Asian*

Economic Development: An Analytical Survey (Canberra: Economic Division, Research School of Pacific and Asian Studies, Australian National University, 1993); and also Garry Rodan, Kevin Hewison, and Richard Robison (eds.) *The Political Economy of South-East Asia* (Melbourne: Oxford University Press, 1997).

[25] Further discussion of this can be found in Richard F. Doner, "Approaches to the Politics of Economic Growth in Southeast Asia", *Journal of Asian Studies*, vol. 50, no. 4 (November 1991), pp. 818-849; and Garry Hawes and Hong Liu, "Explaining the Dynamics of the Southeast Asian Political Economy, State, Society and the Search for Economic Growth", *World Politics*, no. 45 (July 1993), pp. 629-660.

[26] Helen V. Milner and Robert O. Keohane (eds.) *Internationalization and Domestic Politics* (Cambridge: Cambridge University Press, 1996), especially chapter ten.

[27] On this comparative method, see Theda Skocpol, *States and Social Revolutions, A Comparative Analysis of France, Russia, and China* (Cambridge: Cambridge University Press, 1979), pp. 33-40; Stephan Haggard, *Pathways from the Periphery, The Politics of Growth in the Newly Industrialising Countries* (Ithaca and London: Cornell University Press, 1990), pp. 28-29; and Peter Gourevitch, *Politics in Hard Times, Comparative Responses to International Economic Crises* (Ithaca and London; Cornell University Press, 1986), pp. 35-68.

Chapter Two

Reform, Boom and Crisis: Contending Approaches

A growing number of studies of the Southeast Asian political economy in the past two decades have to some extent been influenced by the political economy approaches used to analyse economic and political change in the East Asia region. The debates on the Asian "miracle" and the globalisation process that took place in the Asian region during the 1990s have also influenced the way in which we understand and analyse the region. This chapter examines the various approaches that may be utilised in explaining the economic and political changes which occurred in Thailand, Indonesia and Burma in the 1980s and 1990s. It suggests that a comparative political economy approach is needed in order to understand better the politics of the economic reforms, booms and crises in these countries.

The Neo-Classical Political Economy

The neo-classical economics approach received serious attention among economists, particularly in coming to terms with the success of the newly industrialising countries (NICs) in East Asia in their transition from import-substitution industrialisation (ISI) to export-oriented industrialisation (EOI) in the 1970s.[1] According to this approach, the success of the East Asian countries in creating economic growth was the result of several factors. First, these countries were efficient in allocating government resources. In other words, "getting the right policies" was an important ingredient for success and this was found in the ability of these governments to implement market-oriented policies such as sound macroeconomic policies, a balanced budget, good fiscal and monetary policies, good exchange rates, trade liberalisation, openness to foreign investors and export-oriented policies. Second, their success was achieved by restricting the role of the state to provider of "public goods" (public infrastructure, law and order, and political stability) only allowing intervention into the market when there was a situation of "market failure".

Third, success was also achieved by allowing the private sector to operate freely in the economy.[2]

This approach influenced the thinking of scholars and policy makers in the East Asian region and also beyond, but there are criticisms of it, especially on the issue of the role of the state and the political dimension of this approach. So and Chiu consider the neo-classical economics approach to be too simplistic and too general in interpreting the success of the East Asian countries, arguing that economic development is not a linear process.[3] Every country has its own historical background, which shapes the course of economic development. Therefore economic development and its political consequences differ from one country to another. The government's primary role as provider of "public goods" is debatable. It is true that no one can question the importance of public goods in creating a conducive climate for economic activity, but as Dutt and Kim point out, the degree to which a government should or should not be involved in economic activities is problematic.[4] This also varies from one country to another. Thus, too, the issue of state intervention in the economy is certainly determined by differences in the social and political backgrounds of each country. In this respect, one can ask why it was that despite the fact that similar economic policies were implemented in the Latin American and some African countries, they were also experiencing economic crisis in the 1970s and 1980s? Therefore differences between countries' backgrounds certainly cannot be ignored.

On the political issue, the neoclassical approach assumed that the success of economic development and the creation of a market-based economy would create a democratic political system, like the pluralist political system which has operated for more than a hundred years in Western democratic countries. However, in reality the political systems in East Asian countries did not bear out this assumption. In fact, throughout the 1970s and the early 1980s political authoritarianism operated alongside rapid economic growth. For instance, South Korea was governed by a military government led by General Park Chung Hee and later by General Chun Doo Hwan, while Taiwan lived under the domination of a one-party government led by the Nationalist Party (*Kuomintang*).[5] Thus, the expectation of neoclassical economists that a democratic political system would emerge in the wake of economic development was not fulfilled in East Asia. In fact, political authoritarianism was maintained along with the economic development process.

Many governments in the Southeast Asian region took note of the success of the East Asian countries. As the world recession and the collapse in the price of oil brought economic downturn to the region during the 1980s, the economic policy makers or, as they are commonly known, the technocrats from Thailand, Indonesia, the Philippines, and Malaysia began to reorient their economies. With the advice of economists from the International Monetary Fund and the World Bank, and private economic advisers, these governments took on economic reform or economic deregulation, aiming to create export-oriented and internationally competitive economies.[6] The results of this were varied. Some countries succeeded and others failed. Malaysia and Thailand, for instance, were more successful than Indonesia and the Philippines.[7]

As was the case in East Asia, economic development in Southeast Asian countries did not produce democratic political systems as was expected by the proponents of neoclassical economics. Instead, political authoritarianism continued to be a dominant feature in Southeast Asia. Even those who advocated the neo-classical economics approach, such as the technocrats or economic policy makers, many of whom were educated in Western universities and influenced by liberal political views, worked as advisers to dictators such as Suharto in Indonesia, Ferdinand Marcos in the Philippines, and General Sarit Thanarat in Thailand. It is in this respect that the neoclassical approach falls short in explaining the diversity of the economic and political changes that happened in Thailand, Indonesia, and Burma. Globalisation and its economic and political impacts also cannot be fully understood using this approach.

The Developmentalist Political Economy

The origins of the developmentalist or statist approach are found in an influential book entitled *MITI and the Japanese Miracle* written by American scholar Chalmers Johnson.[8] In this book, he argued that the success of Japan in creating economic development in the post-war period was mainly due to the ability of the government and bureaucrats to pursue autonomy in formulating and implementing economic policies without being influenced by pressure from society-based groups or political parties. More importantly, the Japanese "miracle" was achieved because the Japanese government created what Johnson termed "a pilot agency", the Ministry of International Trade and Industry (MITI), which played an important role in the economic policy-making process.[9] In Johnson's view, it was above all the strong government and insulated economic policy-making institutions that were responsible for the success of the Japanese economy. Later, he applied this framework to an analysis of the economic success of South Korea and Taiwan in the 1960s and 1970s.[10]

Johnson's developmentalist approach was path breaking in terms of understanding the economic success of East Asian countries and thus it gained followers. The developmentalist approach expanded. For instance, Alice Amsden in her book *Asia's Next Giant: South Korea and Late Industrialization* argued that the economic success of South Korea was mainly due not to the work of market forces as was suggested by the proponents of neo-classical economics, but rather to the role of governments in guiding the industrialisation process.[11] Robert Wade developed a similar argument in his book, *Governing the Market: Economic Theory and the Role of Government in East Asian Industrialization.* He suggested that the South Korean and Taiwanese governments were actually "governing" rather than "being governed" by the market.[12]

The works of Johnson, Amsden, and Wade are important in the sense that they challenge the assumptions of the neo-classical economics approach, which argued for limiting the role of government in the economy. Amsden points out that in South Korea, the state intervened extensively in the market and the economy expanded rapidly. In addition, the state used big conglomerates known as *chaebol* to make major investments in targeted industries and also to expand Korean exports.[13] Wade also pointed out that the success of these countries was due to the heavy but constructive role of the state in the economy.[14]

What makes the East Asia developmentalist approach different from the neo-classical approach in explaining the success of these East Asian countries is the different view on the relationship between state and market. First, the developmentalist approach argues that the state can play a constructive role in stimulating economic activity and also, as Wade points out, can intervene in order to overcome "market failures" if necessary.[15] Accordingly, a free market economy as such never existed. In fact, the states in East Asia often deliberately "got the prices wrong" in markets in order to create economic competition and opportunities among economic actors.[16] Second, the states occasionally intervened in markets by "picking up the winners", particularly in infant or targeted industries. The states used "carrot and stick" policies, aiming to create a situation where market players could achieve government targets, particularly in export activities. Third, in order to establish the superiority of the state over the market, economic policy-making institutions were set up. These institutions employed high calibre public servants with expertise in the areas of economics and engineering. This was needed in order to match those working in the private sector. For example, South Korea set up the Economic Planning Board (EPB) and Taiwan the Industrial Development Bureau (IDB). Similar to MITI in Japan, these institutions were relatively free to formulate their policies and were insulated from political pressure from interest groups.

However, if we put this in a broader historical perspective, the East Asian developmentalist approach is not new at all. European countries like Germany, France, and Russia in the nineteenth century were the "late industrializers" trying to catch up with Britain, which had already experienced the industrial revolution. Alexander Gerschenkron in his important *Economic Backwardness in Historical Perspective*, argues, among other things, that state intervention was needed to make industrialisation policies successful and consequently, in the early stages of industrialisation a so-called "strong state" is needed.[17] Gerschenkron's view that to move beyond the early stages of the industrialisation process (including responding to market failures) the establishment of strong states was necessary, appeared to be born out in the experience of the East Asian countries.[18]

The developmentalist approach gained popularity during the 1980s as another way of explaining the success of the East Asian countries, but it also drew criticism from scholars. First, the point was raised that it was the geo-strategic location of East Asia and not the nature of states which mattered most; it was the geo-political configuration of the region during the post-war period that was the main factor in their success. At that time, the US government supported Japan, South Korea, and Taiwan financially and technologically. This was part of the Americans' geo-strategic strategy to counter the economic development of Socialist countries like China and North Korea. The US played a crucial role in creating economic opportunities for Japan, South Korea, and Taiwan and it was in the interests of the US that these countries be more prosperous than their socialist neighbours.[19]

Second, the idea that the "strong state" is an important factor in the economic success of East Asian countries is debatable. The new "post-statist" approach argues that it was not necessarily the "strong states" in East Asia that were the main factor in the successful economic development of that region.[20] South Korean's industrialisation in the 1970s and 1980s was a good illustration of this. Jong-Chan Rhee in his book, *The State and Industry in South Korea: the Limits of the Authoritarian State*, argued that the strong state of South Korea was a myth and that indeed the state had limitations in intervening in market forces.[21] The evidence of this was that despite the fact that the state had all the resources and capacities that were needed, South Korea failed to implement industrial restructuring policies in the heavy and chemical industries during the 1970s and early 1980s which forced the government to end their interventionist policies. Rhee's study and others were important because they challenge the East Asia developmentalist approach, which throughout the 1980s was very popular among scholars in the field of East Asian political economy. Here was evidence that the strong state in East Asia could also fail and was not always successful in guiding economic activity.[22] Therefore to overcome the limitations of government in guiding the economy, non-state actors were needed. As other proponents of the post-statist approach argued, the success of the East Asian countries, in fact, relied very much on a close cooperation between the state and private sectors, rather than on the domination of one or the other.[23]

In further criticism of the developmentalist approach, it was pointed out that this approach accepted that political authoritarianism and economic success were the reality of the East Asian countries in the 1960s and 1970s. The political repression of labour, students, and opposition groups were the price that the East Asian countries had to pay in their economic development process.[24] As mentioned earlier, from the 1960s until the 1980s the East Asian countries were governed by either military or one-party governments which ruthlessly repressed their own people in the name of economic development. This development ignored also the human cost of environmental damage caused by state-led economic activities.[25]

In Southeast Asia, the East Asia developmentalist approach also had supporters. For instance, Indonesia was interested in the idea of using state intervention to finance heavy and strategic industries. The proponents of this idea came from the nationalist and protectionist groups which dominated the economic policy-making institutions during the 1970s. At that time Indonesia had entered the oil boom period, which convinced the elites and policy makers that state-led industrialisation was the best way to catch up with the Western industrial and East Asian countries.[26] But the collapse of the oil price and the world recession in the early 1980s forced Indonesia to re-orient its economic policies. A similar reorientation of economic policies happened in Malaysia, Thailand, and the Philippines during this time.[27] Subsequently, the interest in applying the developmentalist approach disappeared.

Indeed, it can be argued that, despite that fact that the East Asia developmentalist approach attracted policy makers in Southeast Asian countries, it is not an adequate tool with which to analyse economic and political change in Southeast Asia. Again, as with the earlier case, this approach does not allow for the differences in capacity of the states of Thailand, Indonesia, and Burma in the economic development process. There are also different degrees of state intervention in these countries and this is reflected in different stages of economic development. More importantly, this approach does not encompass the economic and political changes that have emerged from the globalisation of these countries.

The Southeast Asian Political Economy

The Southeast Asian political economy can be divided into the state and society-based approaches. The state-based political economy approach is mainly found in the works of Marxist or structuralist scholars such as Robison, Hewison, Rodan, Sundaram, and Hutchinson.[28] This approach focuses on the importance of historical and structural factors in the economic development process in Southeast Asian countries. According to this approach the state plays an important role in shaping the development of domestic and international capital in different countries. It is argued that over a period of time, the state becomes very strong and relatively autonomous from society. This approach is useful in explaining the "big picture" of economic and political change in Southeast Asia.

This approach differs from the East Asia developmentalist approach in that the state-based political economy approach of Southeast Asia suggests that the state is a product of the unique historical context of its country and therefore no two or three states are the same. In this approach, the phenomenon of East Asia's strong states belongs to East Asian countries because the states reflect their own socio-historical backgrounds. The state-based political economy approach differs from the neo-classical economics approach, in that it is the state, and not the private sector, which is responsible for economic development in Southeast Asian countries. However, the state-based approach, which dominated the thinking of Southeast Asian political economists in the 1980s, was complemented by the society-based political economy approach, which emerged in the early 1990s.

Studies utilising the society-based political economy approach (also known as the institutional approach) have been done by Anek,

MacIntyre, Bowie and Doner.[29] This approach gives emphasis to the role of non-state actors over that of the state. It emerged as a result of the collapse of the oil price and the world recession which occurred in the early 1980s, forcing the states in Southeast Asia to readjust their role. Many Southeast Asian countries re-oriented their economic policies at this time, aiming to make their economies more export-oriented and competitive internationally. While the state retreated from economic activity, an increasing number of non-state actors, such as business groups, interest groups, and professional associations, emerged to play a role in influencing the economic policy-making process.

It can be argued that the society-based political economy approach complements the state-based approach, because it is useful in explaining the "micro picture" of the contribution of non-state actors to the growth of the economies of Southeast Asian countries in the 1980s and 1990s. This approach recognises that because the Southeast Asian states are weak and less efficient than those in East Asia, non-state actors could have helped to overcome state failures in the economic development process.[30] In comparison with East Asian countries, this approach questions the usefulness of the East Asia developmentalist approach in analysing economic development in Southeast Asia. There are a number of reasons for this. Hawes and Liu explain that the capacity of the Southeast Asia states to guide the economic development process is not as great as that of the East Asian countries.[31] The Southeast Asian states are often categorised as "weak states" compared to their counterparts in East Asia. It is also significant that Southeast Asian economic policy-making institutions, except those in Singapore, have not been of the same calibre as those in East Asia. In addition to this, state intervention in Southeast Asian countries often did not produce the good results that East Asian countries experienced. MacIntyre summarises it thus:

> The Southeast Asian states have either not attempted to involve themselves in governing the behaviour of firms to a similar extent, or, if they have (as in Indonesia), intervention has generally been poorly coordinated and subject to extensive manipulation by business people with powerful patrons in government...In Thailand, Malaysia and Indonesia the swing towards an export-led high growth trajectory which began in the mid-1980s was accompanied, not by extensive state intervention, but by a marked reduction in the economic role of the state...Government failure through inefficient or unproductive intervention in markets has been a significant problem in Southeast Asia, particularly in interventionist Indonesia.[32]

Lastly, the society-based political economy approach challenges the assumption that it is the state which creates economic and political change. Instead, it argues that in reality the economic and political change which occurred in Southeast Asian countries during the 1980s, was a product of the combined influence of state and non-state actors. Nonetheless both the state and society-based political economy approaches also fail to recognise the diversity of the economic and political changes which have resulted from both domestic factors and the globalisation of the Asian region. Therefore, the causes and consequences of the recent economic crisis in Thailand, Indonesia and Burma must be analysed using an approach that is beyond the state and society-based political economy approaches.

The Political Economy of the Asian "Miracle"

Criticism of the neo-classical economics approach did not cause this approach to disappear. To some extent, the publication in 1993 of an influential report by the World Bank entitled *The East Asian Miracle*, rejuvenated neo-classical economics.[33] This report suggested that the success of the East Asian countries in achieving an economic miracle (which means high growth and equity) was due to these countries implementing what it called "market-friendly" policies; economic policies that bridged the gap between the neo-classical economics and the developmentalist views.[34] The report suggested that the governments "got the fundamentals right" by implementing policies of macroeconomic stability, low inflation, competitive exchange rates, effective financial systems, limiting price distortions, opening up to foreign technology, limiting bias against the agricultural sector, creating credible policy institutions, improving human resources, and creating export-pushed programmes.[35]

The publication of this report expanded debate on the nature of economic growth and public policy in Asia. The debate mainly focused on two aspects: the economic "miracle" itself and politics-related issues. One scholar who was critical of the report was Paul Krugman, an American economist, who argued that the Asian miracle was a myth.[36] He pointed out that there were shortcomings in the Asian countries which made the economic miracle and boom unsustainable. These were found in Asia's paradoxical conditions, in areas such as low wages, slowness in transfer of technology, low productivity and capital, and widespread protectionism.[37]

Krugman also questioned the authoritarian political foundations of the majority of the Asian countries, finding them unsustainable and problematic in the long-term. A similar argument was also put forward by Mommen, who raised doubts as to whether the Asian miracle would last long.[38]

Nonetheless, the report distinguished the East and Southeast Asian countries in respect of the role of the state and public policy. It described the states in Southeast Asia as less competent and less efficient in economic development than those of East Asia.[39] The report also suggested that the effectiveness of the Southeast Asian states often was circumscribed by corruption and widespread rent-seeking activity in the bureaucracies, making it hard for the governments to formulate, to implement and to reach the goals of economic policies. Like other reports published by the World Bank, this one did not discuss regional political change in any depth. It mentioned briefly the importance of implementing credible public policy and good governance. But it did not elaborate on how to achieve this in the context of the diverse historical and political backgrounds of the countries concerned.

After the Asian region experienced the economic crisis of 1997 and 1998, one has to ask whether the optimism inherent in the report was well founded.[40] The report failed to acknowledge the possibility that the economic boom enjoyed by the Asian countries in the 1990s suddenly could be replaced by economic crisis. It also failed to mention early signs that the globalisation process that had begun to take place in the Asian region in the 1990s could make the region more vulnerable to sudden changes in the global economy. In other words, we need to understand more deeply the political economy of globalisation in the Asian region.

The Political Economy of Globalisation

Globalisation has become a "buzzword" among government leaders, policy makers, journalists, business people, academics, and ordinary people in the Asian region. Arguably globalisation has no single meaning. The literature on globalisation is immense, and some scholars suggest that globalisation consists of a wide range of aspects such as internationalisation of trade, finance, and services and also the relocation of "forms of production" across the world.[41] What does globalisation actually mean? According to Charles Oman in his book, *Globalisation and Regionalisation: The Challenge for Developing Countries*, globalisation refers to "a multilateral lowering of policy impediments to the movement of goods and services across national and regional boundaries".[42] Meanwhile, Dickens points out that there are three basic characteristics of the globalisation process: first, the operation of economic actors and capital between countries; second, through this process, those companies can take advantage of each country's national endowments; and third, there is also flexibility in moving resources and operations across the globe.[43] Although there is acknowledgement that the internationalisation of trade started almost a thousand years ago, modern forms of globalisation should be seen in the context of rapid changes in the contemporary global economy and the development of new information technology during the 1990s.

Given this, we can explore the international and domestic factors which accompanied the process of globalisation in the Asian region during the 1990s. First, globalisation took off at the end of the Cold War, when ideological rivalry between the US and the Soviet Union in the region came to an end. This affected the ways in which international economic activities were carried out. The level of economic cooperation between countries inside and outside the region increased. More and more countries formed economic organisations or even trading blocks. This phenomenon was seen by leading Japanese scholar Kenichi Ohmae as a sign that globalisation would bring about interdependence between countries, and at the same time create regionalisation.[44] Thus, the creation of the Asia Pacific Economic Cooperation (APEC), the East Asia Economic Caucus (EAEC) and the Asean Free Trade Agreement (AFTA) during the 1990s was evidence of the globalisation process in the region.[45] With those changes, restrictions on the movement of goods and capital in the Asian region were gradually reduced. Thus, capital could flow easily between countries without restriction.

The end of the Cold War also brought new prominence to the concepts of democracy and human rights in the Asian region. These concepts were promoted particularly by the US and the Western democratic countries, which encouraged broad public debate within countries in the region about the merits of adopting them. At the same time, the globalisation process and the pressure for political change gained momentum with the emergence of civil society and non-state actors in the Asian region. This interrelationship resulted in what Held and McGrew called "political globalisation", where "political decisions and actions in one part of the world can rapidly acquire world-wide ramifications".[46] A further point to make is that the development of new information technology also brought enormous changes to the Asian region, particularly in the financial and telecommunications sectors. More people used telecommunications equipment such as mobile phones, tele-videos, fax machines, and the internet to communicate within and between countries. As argued by Yam, this technology also facilitated the movement of different forms of capital and portfolios (bonds, stocks, or blue chips) from global financial centres in the US and Europe into the Asian region faster than before.[47] Thus, the spread of these new technologies deepened the integration of the Asian region into the global economy. The world became more interconnected than ever.

The globalisation process has not occurred without criticism. Its opponents argue that globalisation will ultimately eliminate the existence of nation-states and destroy nation-based economic activities.[48] Capital mobility, which has expanded rapidly, will also threaten the sovereignty of any country in the world. The implication here is that individual countries will no longer be able to control their own destiny, and in the economic arena the, will lose control over the flow of capital and other financial transactions. As in other places, in the Asian region the globalisation process has produced winners and losers.[49] An illustration of this can be seen in the economic crisis which occurred in the Asian region in 1997 and 1998. As will be explained in more detail in this book, the magnitude of the economic and political impact of that economic crisis has been widely recognised. It was clear that the economic crisis had the potential to destabilise the Asian region and to destroy the economic achievement of the Asian region, which only a few years earlier had been hailed by the World Bank as a "miracle". One has to ask whether the economic crisis was not able to be detected in advance and what were the causes of the economic crisis.

After experiencing at first-hand the economic crisis in part of the Asian region in 1997 and 1998 and also by examining empirical evidence from some affected countries, it can be argued that that the economic and political changes resulting from the globalisation cannot be underestimated, nor can the dynamics of domestic politics in this process. A study carried out by Milner and Keohane is useful to consider.[50] They argue that the internationalisation of the world economy could be influenced by the domestic politics of individual countries. They write:

> ...the internationalization of the world economy has had important effects on domestic politics. The clearest effect of internationalization has been to undermine governments' autonomy in the domain of macroeconomic policy, and this has resulted largely from rising capital mobility...the effect has been to create the "political space" necessary for leaders to

embark on major domestic political reforms. Rising internationalization has increased the portion of the economy susceptible to external economic shocks. It has thus triggered domestic economic crises – usually either in the balance of payments or in currency values – which in turn have sparked major political changes.[51]

In addition, they argue that, despite the fact that the autonomy of any government to formulate and implement its own economic policies has been undermined by the rapid changes in the global economy, this does not mean that individual countries have no role to play. They also recognise the way in which individual countries' responses to the internationalisation of the world economy differ because of differences in history and in social and political conditions. This point is also made by scholars such as Wade and Weiss who argue that, to some extent, individual countries are still able to adjust their own domestic politics to the rapid changes caused by globalisation.[52] The importance here is that both globalisation and the dynamics of domestic politics could influence each other in the course of political change in individual countries.[53] In this respect, globalisation could also create both crises and also opportunities for any country.

Towards a Comparative Political Economy Approach

This comparative political economy approach utilises the insights of a variety of previous approaches and applies them all as far as they are relevant to this study.[54] The reasons for this are clear. First, it must be acknowledged that there is some merit in each approach. Second, the Asian region in general and the three countries which are the subject for this study in particular, have experienced rapid economic and political change in the 1980s and 1990s. These events cannot simply be seen as the result of neo-classical economic policies, and the state intervention style of East Asia. They are the result of a combination of globalisation and the dynamics of domestic politics in different countries. No single approach is adequate to explain these events. Lastly, the examination of these countries requires many variables that have accompanied economic and political change in them.

Before doing this, it is necessary to describe a number of variables that influenced the economic reforms and economic booms of the 1980s and 1990s (history, state and regime types, domestic coalitions, policy-making institutions and economic ideologies, the international factor and the role of non-state actors during the reform period). Then the responses of these countries to the consequences of the economic crisis of 1997 and 1998 will be examined as will the dynamics of the globalisation process and domestic politics in these countries in the 1990s. Here we need to explore the causes of the crisis, which were linked to external and domestic factors such as the internationalisation of the financial sector, the effectiveness of policy-making institutions, the credibility of economic policies, rivalry between elites and policy makers, the role of new market players, governance issues, and domestic political conditions.

Historical Setting

Historical background is an important factor that contributes to the ways in which countries pursue their varying economic policies and political systems. The experience of colonisation and periods of political instability in post-Independence years have influenced the formulation and implementation of economic policies. For instance, the struggle between the economic nationalist and populist camp and the pro-market camp over economic policy in Indonesia is rooted in the colonial and early Independence period. Strong nationalist sentiment also influenced economic policy in Burma and, to some extent, Thailand in the early twentieth century.

The history of ethnicity and ethnic relations in these countries has also influenced the configuration of economic actors and the organisation of economic activity. Ethnic relations is an important issue because these countries are regarded as multi-ethnic societies, which contain different cultures and languages. The influence of this cannot be ignored and every country has its own approach to the issue. This explains why the role of the ethnic Chinese in Thailand is different from the cases of Indonesia and Burma. These similarities and differences deserve attention.

The State, Policy-Making Institutions and Regime Type

The state is seen as the whole system of governing bodies such as the bureaucracy, the parliament, the judiciary, and other related institutions.[55] Each of them has its own role and contributes significantly to the formulation and implementation of economic policy and in establishing the political system. Haggard suggests that there are three factors in the policy formulation and implementation process: the ability of policy makers to be insulated from societal pressures, the capacity of policy institutions to formulate economic policies, and the availability of policy choices which make it easy for the political leaders and elites to implement the policy reforms.[56]

It was the belief of the political leaders and policy makers in East Asia that economic policies needed to be able to be implemented free from political pressures from groups in society. As Williamson argues, the implementation of reform by East Asia's authoritarian governments was successful particularly when "the level of social conflict over economic policy [was] high and democratic institutions [were] weak".[57] Evans stresses the role of "embedded autonomy" in states in East Asia that contributed to the growth of economy in that region.[58] Haggard argues that the institutional arrangements that link the state and society are important in the process of economic development.[59] Over the long-term, society-based groups might collectively agree to sacrifice during the economic development process, but in the short-term these groups often challenge the policy-making process. Thus, in his view, the creation of institutional arrangements that can facilitate communication is necessary to overcome the complexity of the reform processes.

The cohesiveness of economic policy-making institutions is also important in the economic development process. These institutions are generally located within the bureaucracy. Haggard and Webb argue that a high degree of insulation from political pressures from political parties or interest groups must be maintained, especially during the reform period.[60] If necessary, institutional reforms that could aid the cohesiveness of economic policy-making institutions are needed in order to sustain the reforms. The policy makers are also responsible for formulating credible policies in response to economic crisis or external shocks. This means that the availability of policy choices that could be implemented in the event of an economic crisis is important.[61] In other words, a wide range of credible economic policies must be available for policy makers and political elites when making political decisions about problems such as the deterioration of balance of payments, high debt, fiscal problems, budget deficit, high inflation, and overvalued currency. Unlike Burma, Thailand and Indonesia have capable economic policy-making institutions, which played an important role during the economic reform and boom period in the 1980s and 1990s. They provided economic policies for their respective governments and political leaders and aided the survival of these countries in facing economic crisis prior to boom period.

Regime type refers to forms of government: military government, dominant party regime, or coalition government.[62] It is not simply a matter of authoritarian and democratic governments. Authoritarian governments have been able to undertake economic reform because they suppress any group which opposes the reform process. This observation is based on the experiences of the success of military governments in Latin America and South Korea and the one-party governments in Taiwan and Singapore in the 1970s in generating economic development. But in contrast, there is also evidence that economic reforms can be successful under democratic governments, as evidenced in the transitions to market economies in Eastern European countries.[63] In these countries the implementation of economic reform has often gone hand-in-hand with political reform. A study carried out by Haggard and Kaufman showed that there was no evidence that one regime type was better than another in making a success of their economic reform policies.[64] Both authoritarian and democratic governments have experienced failure and success.

We can observe that Thailand was in a democratic transition period when it implemented economic reform, while Indonesia and Burma maintained different types of authoritarian political systems. As a result, these countries experienced different levels of economic and political change in the 1980s and 1990s, which will be examined in greater detail in chapters three and four. The point to be made here is that the state and regime type are significant factors to include in this analysis.

Domestic Coalitions and Interest Groups

The success or failure of economic reform is not merely in the hands of the state and policy-making institutions but also depends on wider support from domestic interest groups.[65] Not every interest group supports the reform process. Generally they can be categorised into two camps: pro-reform and anti-reform. The pro-reform camp contains those who support the reform process and believe that the reforms could benefit them, while the anti-reform camp opposes the reform on the grounds that they will be losers in the reform process.

Haggard and Webb point out that interest groups such as business, labour and farmer groups play an important role during the reform period.[66] Business groups represent the interests of those predominantly urban people who have capital. This group often has mixed views on reform. Those who enjoy and benefit from government protection and subsidies regard reform as a threat to their business interests. Therefore they ally themselves with others who want to safeguard protectionism. Meanwhile, there are also business groups who would see the reform process as an opportunity to expand their business activities in both the domestic and international markets. In exercising their influence, these business groups use their resources to argue their views so that the reforms will serve their business interests. For instance, they can use business representatives to influence policy makers. They can also lobby government leaders and politicians to influence the reform process so that it suits the interests of business groups. Labour groups represent the workers in the industrial sector who are frequently affected negatively by reform and economic crisis. When a government is implementing industrial reform, organised labour groups may resist this. Their protests are often focused on demands for better wages and conditions and protection. Labour strikes and acts of civil disobedience have the potential to create political uncertainty, which consequently influences the outcomes of reform.

In the Asian region organised labour groups are not as powerful as those in the Western industrial countries. Many authoritarian governments in the region still do not guarantee the right to assembly and to strike. During the 1970s and 1980s, South Korea, Taiwan, and Singapore suppressed the political activism of organised labour groups in order to make certain the transition to export-oriented industrialisation went smoothly.[67] Similar conditions prevailed in Indonesia under the New Order government.[68]

Farmer groups represent the interests of the majority of people in rural areas. Their position is often weak economically and politically, especially during the implementation of economic reforms. In developing countries farmers and their organisations provide most agricultural and primary products. The government provides subsidies and financial incentives to protect farmers from the uncertain prices of agricultural products in both domestic and international markets. However, during a period of reform, urban dwellers generally benefit at the expense of rural areas. In other words, the agricultural sector becomes a less important source of government revenue, compared to the manufacturing or other industrial sectors, which are usually located in cities.

Again, Haggard and Webb argue that the success of economic reform depends very much on the ability of political leaders and policy makers to create a broad coalition among these interests groups.[69] Building institutional arrangements which can accommodate the different interests of each group is crucial. In the context of this study, Thailand created a government-business forum in the 1980s, which brought policy makers and business leaders together frequently in order to overcome some of the problems which emerged during the economic reform process. To some extent, Indonesia's New Order government also relied very much on prominent business leaders to expand the economic activity of the private sector.

Economic Policies and Policy Makers

The success or failure of economic development can also depend, according to Haggard, on the availability of so-called "economic ideologies", which are "more or less coherent frameworks of policy-relevant knowledge".[70] They are not ideologies in the real sense, but rather a selection of economic ideas and knowledge in which policy makers can find inspiration in formulating reforms. These ideas often come from both domestic and international sources. They circulate among the economists, political economists, policy analysts and other experts who occupy positions in international organisations, universities, think tanks and research institutions.

A range of ideas has influenced economic policy in developing countries in the past three decades. As mentioned earlier, the neo-classical economics-based policies were the most popular and were mostly advocated by American university-educated economists. In Indonesia these economists were known as the "Berkeley Mafia" (as they were educated in the University of California at Berkeley in the 1960s). In Chile they were the "Chicago Boys", in Mexico the "MIT Connection", in Poland the "Harvard Connection", and in Australia the "economic rationalists".[71] Most of them also had strong links with or had been economists at the World Bank, the International Monetary Fund (IMF), or other international financial organisations in the US.

During the 1990s there was widespread support for what was known as the "Washington Consensus". The term was introduced by a leading American economist, John Williamson, who outlined a set of a broad-based reforms containing several measures: fiscal discipline, scrutinising public expenditure, tax reform, financial liberalisation, exchange rates reform, trade liberalisation, foreign direct investment, privatisation, deregulation, and property rights.[72] With the support of the World Bank and the IMF, both of which had their headquarters in Washington, the "Washington Consensus" was seen as a continuation of the widespread American concept of liberal economics and the neo-classical economics. According to Williamson, the "Washington Consensus" was not simply about economics, it also had a political dimension.[73] The implementation of these policies had to be accompanied by good government and capable policy makers. He argued that any government would need more than just technocrats (those who have expertise in economic matters and advise governments on economic policy), but also what he called "technopols", technocrats who are willing and ready to take political positions and therefore act as politicians.[74] With their economic and political skills, "technopols" would be in a better position to initiate and implement reform policies.[75]

In Thailand, Indonesia, and to a less extent in Burma, competing groups fought over the formulation and implementation of economic policies. In these countries, there are also policy makers who advocated nationalist and populist-inspired economic policies. We find that pro-market economists are often at odds with the pro-protectionists or nationalist policy makers. Nonetheless, it must be pointed out that economic liberalisation became strong in the 1990s. More and more countries implemented economic policies aimed at opening up their economies to foreign investors and becoming more competitive internationally. The globalisation process that took place in the Asian region made the economic liberalisation agenda, which was advocated by the US and other Western countries, expand faster than before.

External Factors and Changes in the Global Economy

The role of external or international support has also been important in the formulation and implementation of economic policies. Haggard and Webb point out that there are many forms of external support, including ideas, technical and financial support.[76] This support can involve international advisers or consultants who share expertise and advise policy makers on economic matters. There is also financial assistance from international or regional financial organisations like the World Bank, the International Monetary Fund (IMF), the Asian Development Bank and donor countries. However, it can be argued that external support can be ineffective, particularly if it comes with conditions. For those countries with a strong history of nationalist and populist traditions, external conditionality can create problems that have the potential to affect the implementation of economic policies. The recent involvement of the IMF in the economic crises in Thailand and Indonesia is a good example of how external support was needed but also opposed by certain groups in these countries.

As far as this study is concerned, it can be observed that the external factor has played an important role in contributing to economic growth and boom in Thailand and Indonesia, but not Burma. The growth in foreign investment and capital has also helped economic growth in the region as a whole. The creation of international and regional economic groupings such as the Asia Pacific Economic Cooperation (APEC) and the Asean Free Trade Agreement (AFTA) has promoted regional interdependence. Indeed, change in the global economy is also a factor that has influenced economic growth and economic crisis in a number of countries. The economic boom and crisis in the Asian region cannot be separated from developments in other economies. For example, the growth of the US economy since 1992 meant US interest rates lowered and the US dollar rose, encouraging American investors to move their capital offshore, including to the Asian region. The stronger US dollar against other currencies created difficulties for those countries that had foreign debts in US dollars. At the same time, the rise of the Euro market, the economic downturn of the Japanese economy and the rapid growth of the Chinese economy in the 1990s also influenced the direction of the Asian economies.

Capital Mobility and New Market Players

One of the results of the globalisation process that occurred in the 1990s was that it internationalised the financial sectors of countries in the region. The development of new information technology and financial liberalisation in individual countries also facilitated the movement of capital within and between countries in the region and with other regions. More than US$2 trillion worth of capital moved around the world daily.[77] For instance, there was a rapid increase in capital inflow in Asia from US$33.8 billion in 1990 to US$101.9 billion in 1996 and this was more than half the total of the international capital inflow movement into developing countries, which amounted to US$196.9 billion in 1996.[78] This increase contributed to ongoing economic growth for years and transformed the region into an emerging market. But it also made the region more vulnerable to external shock. Capital could enter and withdraw from any country on a large scale with potentially disastrous results. The economic crisis in 1997 was a result of capital withdrawal and panic among investors.[79] As Bhagwati points out the Asian crisis confirmed that the economic policy makers of individual countries had became powerless in reasserting their authority in managing their economic policies and they were replaced by the powerful so-called "Wall Street-Treasury-IMF Connection" in influencing economic direction in the global arena.[80]

The increase in capital inflow in the region also created "new market players". This term refers to those who work in the capital market, such as fund managers and hedge managers, many of whom became involved in trading foreign currencies, stocks, portfolios, bonds, and securities. Among those of international reputation is George Soros, who operates from his base in New York. There are similar market players from the region, mainly operating from Tokyo, Hong Kong and Singapore. They operate beyond their own countries, making a large amount of transactions. These new market players became powerful not only because they could influence the market but also because they could change the direction of economic policy in individual countries. Evidence of this was found in the economic crisis of 1997, when money speculators and fund managers played a significant role in destabilising several currencies including Thailand's baht and Indonesia's rupiah.

Governance Issues and Non-Economic Factors

Good governance, a code of conduct for government and business when engaging in economic activities, is an important factor in determining the image and integrity of government and the confidence of investors in any country. Corruption is an important issue in any country. According to the World Bank, corruption, which manifests itself in forms such as bribery, collusion and nepotism, weakens the ability of government to implement economic policies and increases the cost of "doing business", which in turn can make a country's economy less competitive internationally.[81] Although corruption can be found everywhere, for the developing countries corruption is a serious problem because it is entrenched in the political systems established in these countries. Corruption is widespread where there is a lack of checks and balances, rule of law, independent judiciary, free media, and civil society. Many countries in the Asian region share this problem.[82]

As pointed out in a recent study carried out by the IMF, in a more globalised world, non-economic factors such as political "rumours", mass demonstrations, riots, military coups and environmental disaster are increasingly important in determining investors' choices and preferences in making business decisions.[83] Although these factors cannot be measured quantitatively, they influence the business climate of any country. This is clear in the capital market where the direction of the stock market index and the stability of the currencies reflect the confidence of domestic and foreign investors in a country's economic and political situation. The experiences of Thailand and Indonesia in defending their currencies and economies in 1997 proved that non-economic factors also played a crucial role in determining economic stability.

Civil Society and Non-State Actors

It can be observed that the rapid economic change which occurred in the East and Southeast Asian region in the 1990s also created pressure for political change. There have been studies debating as to whether this economic change itself encouraged the growth of a middle-class which was committed to the establishment of democratic political systems similar to those of Western industrial countries.[84] Nonetheless, in the 1990s there was also recognition that the civil society and non-state actors emerged and continued to put pressure on their governments to open up the political system.[85]

Civil society and non-state actors are those independent and autonomous organisations outside formal political institutions, and representing people from a variety of backgrounds including artists, lawyers, businesspeople, academics, and students. Every country has different forms of civil society and non-state actors because they have different historical, social, economic and political backgrounds. Putnam pointed out that democracy could only flourish when the civil society is strong.[86] Those countries in the Southeast Asian region that, in recent years, moved from authoritarian politics toward a more representative political system are in a slightly better position in terms of the growth of civil society. The best example is Thailand where the civil society plays an important role in influencing government policy and in national politics. Indonesia and Burma have not yet seen the birth of a civil society of this sort.

Cox also argued that the globalisation process, to some extent, has contributed to the strengthening of civil society and the emergence of non-state actors.[87] The liberal ideas of democracy and human rights which are advocated by the US and the Western countries have gained support among a wide range of people in the region, including workers, the middle class and opposition groups.[88] Modern telecommunications facilities such as satellite antennae, mobile phones, fax machines, modems, computers and the internet have facilitated the spread of these ideas. The influence of this modern technology is very significant. For civil society and non-state actors in the Southeast Asian region, the need to have alternative information to that provided by the state is crucial to their effort to challenge the domination of the state.

Conclusion

This chapter has examined the various political economy approaches which have been used in analysing the economic and political changes which occurred in the East and Southeast Asian region in the 1980s and 1990s. The neo-classical political economy was widely accepted during the 1970s as an appropriate approach in analysing the economic success of the East Asian countries. This approach suggests that these countries were successful economically because they had implemented market-based policies, imposed restrictions on the role of the state in the economy, and allowed market forces to operate freely in the economic arena. However, this approach was criticised on the grounds that it interprets economic development in a linear way and does not take into account the different social and political backgrounds of countries, and their different ways of developing their economies. This approach does not adequately explain why, although Thailand, Indonesia, and Burma all implemented various forms of market-based economic policies during the 1980s, the results differed for each country. Some were successful and others failed. More importantly, these countries also pursued different political systems.

The developmentalist approach opposed the assumptions of neo-classical economics on the issue of the role of the state in the economy. It argued that the economic success of the East Asian countries mainly resulted from the strong state and effective and insulated policy-making institutions. The state intervened in the market extensively to foster economic activity. The proponents of this approach argue that state intervention is needed to overcome market failures. Criticism of this approach is based on the issue that the economic success of the East Asian countries took place in a particular geo-strategic location and social and historical background. Therefore, this could not be repeated in other countries. Criticism also focuses on the role of the "strong" state and it is argued that this was not always the case with the East Asian countries. Recent studies have pointed out that non-state actors have also played an important role in the economies of East Asia. In addition, the Southeast Asian states are generally "weak" and not as effective as those of East Asia. This is particularly true of Thailand, Indonesia and Burma where the role of the state varies from case to case and does not always fit the assumption of the East Asian developmentalist approach.

Rapid economic and political changes in the Southeast Asian region saw the emergence of the state and society-based approaches. The first recognises the importance of the historical role of the state, and not the private sector, in creating economic growth in the region. The latter argues that the changes in economic policy in the 1980s gradually reduced the role of the state and allowed society-based actors to help in overcoming state failures in the economic arena. These approaches, in combination, are useful in analysing what happened during the 1980s, but are not adequate to explain the changes of the 1990s. The 1990s saw a rapid economic boom in the region which was hailed by many as the "Asian miracle". This interpretation failed to foresee that the economic boom was unlikely to be sustainable in the long-term, and also failed to address the importance of the issues of good governance and public policy in the implementation of economic reform. The sustainability of the "Asian miracle" could also have been questioned on the grounds that the Asian region had undergone rapid economic and political change as a result of the globalisation that took place during the 1990s. Clearly, another way of understanding and analysing those changes was needed.

This chapter proposed a comparative political economy approach towards this study. This approach incorporates the insights of existing approaches in a comparative historical and political economy analysis and also takes into account the significance of domestic politics and globalisation. Factors such as historical setting, state and regime type, domestic coalitions, policy-making institutions, economic ideas, external factors, capital mobility, good governance, and civil society and non-state actors are incorporated into the analysis.

Notes

[1] Jagdish Bhagwati, *Foreign Trade Regimes and Economic Development: Anatomy and Consequences of Exchange Control Regimes* (Cambridge: Ballinger, 1978); and Anne Krueger, *Foreign Trade Regimes and Economic Development: Liberalization Attempts and Consequences* (New York: National Bureau of Economic Research, 1978); Bella Bellasa, *The Newly Industrialising Countries in the World Economy* (New York: Pergamon, 1981); and also see Helen Hughes (ed.) *Achieving Industrialization in East Asia* (Melbourne: Cambridge University Press, 1988).

[2] The summary of this argument can be found in Anis Chowdhury and Iyanatul Islam, *The Newly Industrialising Economies of East Asia* (London and New York: Routledge, 1993), pp. 42-46.

[3] Alvin Y. So and Stephen W. K. Chiu, *East Asia and the World Economy* (London and New Delhi: Sage Publications, 1995), pp. 5-6.

[4] Amitava K. Dutt and Kwan S. Kim, *The States, Markets and Development, Beyond the Neoclassical Dichotomy* (Aldershot and Brookfield: Edward Elgar, 1994), pp. 4-6.

[5] For an interesting comparative political economy of both countries, see Yun-han Chu, *Authoritarian Regime Under Stress: The Political Economy of Adjustment in the East Asian Newly Industrializing Countries*, unpublished Ph.D thesis (Minnesota: University of Minnesota, 1987).

[6] See, "Introduction", in Andrew MacIntyre and Kanishka Jayasuriya (eds.), *The Politics and Economics of Economic Policy Reform in South-east Asia and the South-west Pacific* (Singapore: Oxford University Press, 1992), p. 3.

[7] For a recent assessment of the comparison between the Asean countries, see Alasdair Bowie and Danny Unger, *The Politics of Open Economies, Indonesia, Malaysia, the Philippines, and Thailand* (Cambridge and Melbourne, 1997).

[8] Chalmers Johnson, *MITI and the Japanese Miracle: The Growth of Industrial Policy, 1925-1975* (Stanford: Stanford University Press, 1982).

[9] Ibid, pp. 10-11.

[10] Chalmers Johnson, "Political Institutions and Economic Performance: The Government-Business Relationship in Japan, South Korea and Taiwan" in Frederick Deyo, (ed.), *The Political Economy of the New Asian Industrialism* (Ithaca and London: Cornell University Press, 1987), pp. 136-164.

[11] Alice Amsden, *Asia's Next Giant: South Korea and Late Industrialization* (New York: Oxford University Press, 1989).

[12] Robert Wade, *Governing the Market: Economic Theory and the Role of Government in East Asian Industrialization* (Princeton: Princeton University Press, 1990).

[13] Amsden, pp. 8-9.

[14] Wade, pp. 26-27.

[15] According to Wade, market failure is "a situation in which the market system produces an allocation of resources which is not Pareto-efficient – it is possible to find ways of changing resource allocation so as to make some consumer(s) better off and none worse off.   Hence individual self-seeking behaviour by consumers and firms will not achieve the highest level of welfare for society as a whole in so far as market failure is prevalent. It is predicted to occur in the presence of monopoly and oligopoly, externalities, public goods, and common property resources, in each of which individualistic behaviour leads to sub optimal results." Wade, *Governing the Market*, p. 11.

[16] Heather Smith, "Industry Policy in East Asia", *Asian-Pacific Economic Literature*, vol. 9, no. 1 (May 1995), p. 20.

[17]Alexander Gerschenkorn, *Economic Backwardness in Historical Perspective* (Cambridge, Mass.: Harvard University Press, 1962); and also Herman M. Schwartz, *States versus Markets: History, Geography, and the Development of the International Political Economy* (New York: St. Martin's Press, 1996), pp. 92-95.

[18] This point was also made by Amsden, *Asia's Next Giant: South Korea and Late Industrialisation*, pp. 3-4.

[19] So and Chiu, *East Asia and the World Economy*, pp.15-16.

[20] For example, see Linda Weiss, "Governed Interdependence: Rethinking the Government-Business Relations in East Asia", *The Pacific Review*, vol. 8, no. 4 (1995), pp. 589-616; David C. Kang, "South Korean and Taiwanese Development and the New Institutional Economics", *International Organisation*, vol. 49, no. 3 (Summer 1995), pp. 555-587; and also H. J. Chang, *The Political Economy of Industrial Policy* (London: St. Martin's Press, 1994).

[21] Jong-Chan Rhee, *The State and Industry in South Korea: The Limits of the Authoritarian State* (London: Routledge, 1994).

[22] Ibid, especially chapter 1.

[23] Weiss, "Governed Interdependence: Rethinking the Government-Business Relations in East Asia", pp. 601-602.

[24] For further discussion on the authoritarian politics in East Asian countries, see Frederic C. Deyo, *The Political Economy of the New Asian Industrialism* (Ithaca and London: Cornell University Press, 1987).

[25] Walden Bello and Stephanie Rosenfeld, *Dragon's in Distress: Asia's Miracle Economies in Crisis* (London: Penguin, 1992).

[26] Ali Moertopo, *The Acceleration and Modernization of 25 Years' Development* (Jakarta: Centre for Strategic and International Studies, 1973).

[27] Alasdair Bowie and Danny Unger, *The Politics of Open Economies*, 1997, especially chapter conclusion.

[28] Richard Robison, *Indonesia: The Rise of Capital* (Sydney: Allen and Unwin, 1986), Kevin Hewison, *Bankers and Bureaucrats: Capital and the Role of the State in Thailand* (New Heaven: Yale University Southeast Asian Studies, 1989); Garry Rodan, *The Political Economy of Singapore's Industrialization: National State and International Capital* (London: Macmillan, 1989); Jomo Kwame Sundaram, *A Question of Class: Capital, the State and Uneven Developments in Malaysia* (New York: Monthly Review Press, 1988); and Jane Hutchison, "Class and State Power in the Philippines" in Kevin Hewison, Richard Robison and Garry Rodan (eds.) *Southeast Asia in the 1990s, Authoritarianism, Democracy and Capitalism* (Sydney: Allen and Unwin, 1993), pp. 193-212.

[29] Studies that use this approach include Alaisdair Bowie, *Crossing the Industrial Divide: State, Society and the Politics of Economic Transformation in Malaysia* (New York: Columbia University Press, 1991); Anek Laothamatas, *Business Associations and the New Political Economy of Thailand: From Bureaucratic Polity to Liberal Corporatism* (Boulder: Westview Press, 1991);

Andrew MacIntyre, *Business and Politics in Indonesia* (Sydney: Allen and Unwin, 1990); also Richard Doner, *Driving a Bargain, Automobile Industrialisation and Japanese Firms in Southeast Asia* (Berkeley: University of California Press, 1991).

[30] Further discussion of this issue can be found in Garry Hawes and Hong Liu, "Explaining the Dynamics of the Southeast Asian Political Economy, State, Society, and the Search for Economic Growth", *World Politics*, vol. 45 (July 1993), pp. 656-657.

[31] Ibid.

[32] Andrew MacIntyre, "Business, Government and Development: Northeast and Southeast Asian Comparisons" in Andrew MacIntyre (ed.) *Business and Government in Industrialising Asia* (Sydney: Allen and Unwin, 1994), p. 12.

[33] World Bank, *The East Asian Miracle: Economic Growth and Public Policy* (Washington D.C.: The World Bank, 1993).

[34] Ibid, pp. 84-85.

[35] Ibid, pp. 348-360.

[36] Paul Krugman, "The Myth of Asia's Miracle", *Foreign Affairs*, vol. 73, no. 6 (November-December 1994), pp. 62-78.

[37] Ibid, pp. 77-78.

[38] Andrew Mommen, "The Asian Miracle: A Critical Reassessment" in A. E. Jilberto and Andrew Mommen (eds.) *Liberalization in the Developing World, Institutional and Economic Changes in Latin America, Africa and Asia* (London and New York: Routledge, 1996), pp. 28-50.

[39] See "Introduction" in Richard Robison, Garry Rodan and Kevin Hewison (eds.) *The Political Economy of South-East Asia* (Melbourne: Oxford University Press, 1997), pp. 7-8.

[40] Robert Garran, *Tigers Tamed, The End of the Asian Miracle* (Sydney: Allen and Unwin, 1998), pp. 12-14.

[41] Few studies on this issues deserves attention here, for example, Paul Kennedy, *Preparing for the Twenty-First Century* (London: Harper Collins Publishers, 1993); Malcolm Waters, *Globalisation* (London: Routledge, 1995); and Paul Hirst and G. Thomson, *Globalisation in Question* (Cambridge: Polity Press, 1996).

[42] Charles Oman, *Globalisation and Regionalisation: The Challenge for Developing Countries* (Paris: Development Centre of the Organisation for Economic Cooperation and Development, 1994), p. 27.

[43] Paul Dickens, *Global Shift: The Internationalization of Economic Activity*, 2nd Edition (London: Paul Chapman Publishing, 1992), p. 27.

[44] Kenichi Ohmae, *The End of the Nation State: The Rise of Regional Economics* (London: HarperCollins, 1996).

[45] For an interesting discussion on this issue, see Richard Higgott and Richard Stubbs, "Competing Conceptions of Economic Regionalism: APEC versus EAEC in the Asia Pacific", *Review of International Political Economy*, vol. 2, no. 3 (Summer 1995), pp. 516-535.

[46] David Held and Anthony McGrew, "The End of the Old Order?, Globalization and the Prospects for World Order", *British International Studies Association*, vol. 24, special issue (December 1998), p. 232.

[47] Joseph Yam, "The Impact of Technology on Financial Development in East Asia", *Journal of International Affairs*, vol. 51, no. 2 (Spring 1998), pp. 539-553.

[48] This point is suggested by Robin Brown, "Globalisation and the End of the National Project" in Andrew Linklater and John MacMillan (eds.) *Boundaries in Question: New Directions in International Relations* (London: Pinter, 1995), pp. 54-68.

[49] For an interesting study on the impact of the globalisation in the Asia-Pacific region, see Peter J. Rimmer (ed.), *Pacific Rim Development, Integration and Globalisation in the Asia-Pacific Economy* (Canberra and Sydney: Department of International Relations and the Department of Human Geography, Australian National University and Allen and Unwin, 1997).

[50] Robert O. Keohane and Helen V. Milner, *Internationalization and Domestic Politics* (Cambridge: Cambridge University Press, 1996), especially chapter conclusion.

[51] Ibid, pp. 256.

[52] Robert Wade, "Globalization and Its Limits: Reports of the Death of the National Economy are Greatly Exaggerated" in Suzanne Berger and Ronald Dore (eds.) *National Diversity and Global Capitalism* (Ithaca and London: Cornell University Press, 1996), pp. 60-88; and Linda Weiss, *The Myth of the Powerless State, Governing the Economy in a Global Era* (Oxford: Polity Press, 1998), especially chapter six.

[53] There are several studies examining the impacts of globalisation in the region. For instance, in Australia, see Bob Catley, *Globalising Australian Capitalism* (Melbourne: Cambridge University Press, 1996); Stephen Bell, "Globalisation, Neoliberalism and the Transformation of the Australian State", *Australian Journal of Political Science*, vol. 32, no. 3 (November 1997), pp. 345-367; and in Japan, see T. J. Pompel, *Regime Shift, Comparative Dynamics of the Japanese Political Economy* (Ithaca and Cornell: Cornell University Press, 1998).

[54] See, for instance, Stephan Haggard and Robert Kaufman (eds.) *The Politics of Adjustment: International Constraints, Distributive Politics and the State* (Princeton: Princeton University Press, 1992); Joan M. Nelson (ed.) *Fragile Coalitions: The Politics of Economic Adjustment* (Washington D.C.: The Overseas Development Council, 1989); Anne O. Krueger (ed.) *Political Economy of Policy Reform in Developing Countries* (Cambridge: The Massachusetts Institute of Technology Press, 1993); Robert H. Bates and Anne O. Krueger (eds.) *Political and Economic Interactions in Economic Policy Reform* (Cambridge: Blackwell Publishers, 1993); Andrew MacIntyre and Kanishka Jayasuriya (eds.) *The Dynamics of Economic Policy Reform in Southeast Asian and Southwest Pacific* (Singapore: Oxford University Press, 1992); and also John W. Langford and K.

Lorne Brownsey (eds.) *Economic Policy-Making in the Asia Region* (Halifax: The Institute for Research on Public Policy, 1988); and James Morley (ed.) *Driven by Growth, Political Change in the Asia-Pacific Region* (New York: East Gate, 1993).

[55] Theda Skocpol, pp. 29-30; and Hawes and Liu, "Explaining the Dynamics of the Southeast Asian Political Economy", p. 637.

[56] Haggard, *Pathways from the Periphery*, p. 43.

[57] John Williamson (ed.), *The Political Economy of Policy Reform* (Washington D.C.: Institute of International Economics, 1994), p. 569.

[58] Peter Evans, "The State as Problem and Solution: Predation, Embedded Autonomy, and Structural Change" in Stephan Haggard and Robert R. Kaufman (eds.) *The Politics of Economic Adjustment, International Constraints, Distributive Conflicts, and the State* (Princeton: Princeton University Press, 1992), pp. 139-181.

[59] Ibid, p. 44.

[60] Stephan Haggard and Steven B. Webb, "What Do We Know about the Political Economy of Economic Policy Reform", *The World Bank Research Observer*, vol. 8, no. 2 (July 1993), p. 152.

[61] Ibid, p. 156; and for further discussion on this issue, see Peter Hall, *The Political Power of Economic Ideas: Keynesianism across Nations* (Princeton: Princeton University Press, 1990).

[62] Hawes and Liu, "Explaining the Dynamics of the Southeast Asian Political Economy", p. 637-638.

[63] Alice Amsden, J. Kochanowicz and L. Taylor (eds.) *The Markets Meets Its Match: Restructuring the Economics of Eastern Europe* (Cambridge, Mass.: Harvard University Press, 1994); and Adam Przeworski, *Democracy and the Market: Political and Economic Reforms in Eastern Europe and Latin America* (New York: Cambridge University Press, 1991).

[64] For an interesting comparative study on this relationship, see Stephan Haggard and Robert R. Kaufman, *The Political Economy of Democratic Transitions* (Princeton: Princeton University Press, 1995), pp. 15-16.

[65] For further discussion on the politics of domestic coalitions during the reform process, see Stephan Haggard and Steven B. Webb (eds.) *Voting for Reform, Democracy, Political Liberalization, and Economic Adjustment* (New York: Oxford University Press, 1994), pp. 1-36.

[66] Ibid, pp. 16-19.

[67] See Frederic C. Deyo, *Beneath the Miracle: Labour Subordination in the New Asian Industrialism* (Berkeley: University of California Press, 1989); and Haggard, *Pathways from the Periphery*, p. 39.

[68] Vedi R. Hadiz, *Workers and the State in New Order Indonesia* (London and New York: Routledge, 1997).

[69] Haggard and Webb, *Voting for Reform*, p. 20.

[70] Haggard, *Pathways from the Periphery*, p. 46.

[71] Williamson, *The Political Economy of Policy Reform*, p. 565; and Bob Catley, *Globalising Australian Capitalism* (Cambridge: Cambridge University

Press, 1996), especially chapter four; and also see Stephen Bell, *Ungoverning the Economy, The Political Economy of Australian Economic Policy* (Melbourne: Oxford University Press, 1997).

[72] Ibid., pp. 26-28.

[73] Ibid., pp. 35-36.

[74] Ibid., p. 12.

[75] There are several criticisms of the "Washington Consensus" which deserve attention here. First, the reform policies are not always suited to the diversity of countries who undertake the reform process. The failure of the Latin American and the African countries in creating economic growth during the 1980s despite implementing similar policies, demonstrated the need to take into account the diversity and local ideas or knowledge in the reform process. Second, the role of the so-called "technopols" in implementing the economic policies has to be clarified. There is no guarantee that because someone obtains a political position that they can implement economic policies effectively. It can be argued that having expertise in economics is not necessarily helpful in the political process. In other words, being an "economist" is one thing and being a "politician" is another. Third, not every country would have technopols, which requires economic and political skills. See Barry Gills and George Philip, "Toward Convergence in Development Policy? Challenging the 'Washington Consensus' and Restoring the Historicity of Divergent Development Trajectories", *Third World Quarterly*, vol. 17, no. 4 (1996), pp. 585-591.

[76] Haggard and Webb, *Voting for Reform, Democracy, Political Liberalization, and Economic Adjustment*, pp. 25-32.

[77] Roy E. Allen, *Financial Crises and Recession in the Global Economy* (Aldershot: Edward Elgar, 1994), p. 2.

[78] International Monetary Fund, *Developing Countries and the Globalization of Financial Markets* (Washington D.C.: International Monetary Fund, 1998), p. 6.

[79] On the logic of capital withdrawal and panic, see Steven Radelet and Jeffrey Sachs, "The East Asian Financial Crisis: Diagnosis, Remedies", Prospects, a paper presented for the *Brookings Panel*, Washington D.C., 26-27 March 1998.

[80] Jadish Bhagwati, "The Capital Myth, the Difference between Trade Widgets and Dollars", *Foreign Affairs*, vol. 77, no. 3 (May/June 1998), pp. 7-12; and also see Robert Wade and Frank Veneroso, "The Asian Crisis: the High Debt Model Versus the Wall Street-Treasury-IMF Complex", *New Left Review*, vol. 22, no. 8 (March-April 1998), pp. 3-23.

[81] World Bank, *World Development Report 1991, The Challenge of Development* (Washington D.C.: The World Bank, 1991), pp. 131-132.

[82] See Robert Garran, *Tiger Tamed, The End of the Asian Miracle* (Sydney: Allen and Unwin, 1998), pp. 13.

[83] International Monetary Fund, *The Relative Importance of Political and Economic Variables in Creditworthiness Ratings* (Washington D.C.: International Monetary Fund, 1998).

[84] For instance, see Richard Robison and David S. G. Goodman (eds.) *The New Rich in Asia, Mobile Phones, McDonalds and Middle-Class Revolution* (London and New York: Routledge, 1996); and Anek Laothamatas (ed.) *Democratization in Southeast and East Asia* (Singapore: Institute of Southeast Asian Studies, 1997).

[85] Garry Rodan (ed.) *Political Oppositions in Industrialising Asia* (London and New York: Routledge, 1996).

[86] For comparison in Italy, see Robert Putnam, *Making Democracy Work, Civic Traditions in Modern Italy* (Princeton: Princeton University Press, 1993).

[87] Robert Cox, "Civil Society at the Turn of the Millennium: Prospects for an Alternative World Order", *Review of International Studies*, vol. 25, no. 1 (January 1999), pp. 3-28.

[88] On recent democratisation debate, see Samuel P. Huntington, *The Third Wave: Democratization in the Late Twentieth Century* (Norman: University of Oklahoma Press, 1991); Bob Catley, "Hegemonic America: The Arrogance of Power", *Contemporary Southeast Asia*, vol. 21, no. 2 (August 1999), pp. 157-175.

Chapter Three

Thailand's Boom

Thailand is a case in which it can be observed that economic success and political liberalisation occurred together. Economic reform policies during the 1980s were implemented along with a gradual move towards the consolidation of a representative political system. This transformation evolved from economic and political crises, involving both domestic and external influences. This chapter examines the historical, economic, political, institutional, and external factors that contributed to the economic boom in Thailand in the 1980s and the 1990s.

Historical Setting

Three important factors influenced the political and economic climate in Thailand in the early twentieth century. First, Thailand was the only country in the Southeast Asian region which was never colonised. Although without a formal political colonial master, the other face of colonisation, that is economic colonialism, had begun in the 19th century. This was initiated in 1855 when King Mongkut (Rama IV) agreed to sign a trade agreement with the British Imperial government, represented by Sir John Bowring.[1] The agreement, which was known as the Bowring Treaty, was a part of the British ambition to establish trade and economic links across Asia, from India-Burma, to Singapore, Hongkong, and China. This marked the beginning of the integration of Thailand into the world economy.[2] In this period Thailand was ruled by an absolute monarchy. It was known as the *sakdina* society; a society in which political power solely rested in the royal families and the elites.[3]

As Girling points out, in the early twentieth century Thailand experienced further economic, political and social change.[4] The Bowring Treaty did indeed expand economic activity in Thailand. Thailand was exporting primary products, such as rice, sugar, rubber, teak, tin and others. The expansion of economic activity also effected change in the social life in urban areas, especially in Bangkok. Foreign traders from

Europe and China poured into the country to expand their trading activities while the Thais, mostly the small Thai elite, also began to participate in a variety of economic activities.[5]   This change forced the then King Chulalongkorn to modernise the Thai bureaucracy along the lines of those in European countries.[6] In doing so, he sent many Thais to study in Europe and he also invited foreign advisers to work in Thailand. One of King Chulalongkorn's achievements was the creation of a modern Treasury department to oversee economic and monetary policies in Thailand.[7]

The second factor which influenced Thailand's political and economic climate early this century was the fact that the integration of Thailand into the world economy led to the domination of the economy by one small group.   This group was comprised of Europeans, Chinese immigrants, and Thai royal families. The Europeans and the immigrant Chinese dominated the financial sector. For instance, the Britans introduced a branch of the Chartered Bank, the French the Banque de l'Indochine, and the Chinese the Hongkong and Shanghai Bank.[8] These banks played an important role not only in strengthening the economic power of the European traders but also in becoming a source of money for the business activities of the immigrant Chinese. During this time the Europeans also controlled foreign exchange transactions.[9] And in order to break up the domination of the foreign banks in Thailand, the government, the royal families and the rice traders opened the Siam Commercial Bank in 1904.[10]

The third factor was the rising economic power of these groups which contributed to the decline of the ordinary Thais' business activities. This caused widespread disappointment among educated Thais and created a strong nationalist sentiment among the Thai people.[11] Despite the fact that King Chulalongkorn-led reforms had successfully modernised the Thai bureaucracy, the economic integration into the world economy created fertile grounds for the growth of the nationalist movement led by progressive elements in the bureaucracy and educated urban people. Eventually, in June 1932, the People's Party staged a *coup d'etat* to replace the absolute monarchy.[12] This coup was masterminded by a group of high-ranking military officers and elite bureaucrats, most of whom had been educated in Europe. It marked the end of the absolute monarchy and the beginning of the constitutional period, which lasted until 1957.

Factional rivalries within the People's Party, however, meant that the 1932 coup was followed by a power struggle among the political elites to influence the direction of economic and political policies in Thailand. The moderates advocated gradual change, while the hard-liners proposed more radical changes. In 1938, the hard-liners' camp led by General Phibun Songram (who was then the Prime Minister) and Pridi Phanomyong, the Minister of Finance, won the political battle and launched more nationalist and interventionist policies in politics and the economy.[13] Economic nationalism was the order of the day under the Phibun regime (1938-1957). Under the banner of "Thailand for Thais", the government launched nationalisation programs by placing the European and the Chinese immigrants' companies under the control of state-owned enterprises. As a result, the government's economic activities increased and contributed significantly to the national economy. For instance, the production of basic commodities such as sugar, paper, cement, alcohol, cigarettes, tobacco, rice, and soap increased by the end of the 1940s.[14] More importantly, the government's interventionist policies in the economy also forced the policy makers to upgrade the existing economic policy-making institutions.

The irony was that despite the fact that the spirit of "Thailand for Thais" discriminated against the ethnic Chinese, the domestic financial sector gradually expanded as more banks (mostly owned by the ethnic Chinese) were established.[15] For instance, the Wang Lee Bank and the Bank of Asia were founded during the 1930s; and the Bangkok Bank (owned by the Sophonpanit family), the Bank of Ayudhya (the Rattanarak family), the Bangkok Metropolitan Bank (the Taechaphaibun family), the Thai Farmers' Bank (the Lamsam family) and the Union Bank (the Mahakhun family) were established in the 1940s and the 1950s. It was in this period that the Chinese immigrants began to expand their economic activities in Thailand.

From the Sarit Regime to the Prem Regime

Thailand experienced various types of political systems after 1932: absolute monarchy, militarist authoritarianism, and, in the 1970s a parliamentary democracy. Because of this the state has always been a focus for competition among Thai elites and powerful economic actors. Between the 1950s and the 1980s the power struggle to control the state intensified. As a result, Thailand experienced cycles of political crisis from the 1960s until the end of the 1970s. Ironically, during this period of political turmoil the Thai economy expanded rapidly. In the early stages of this expansion, Thailand was governed by a strong and authoritarian military leader, General Sarit Thanarat. Later, during the 1980s, General Prem

Tinsulanonda was in power. It was these two military leaders who laid the foundations for the expansion of the Thai economy.

The Sarit Regime and the Early Stages of Economic Development

During his reign from 1957 to 1963, General Sarit drastically changed the direction of political and economic policy in Thailand. In the economic arena, General Sarit abandoned Phibun's nationalist and interventionist policies and opened up Thailand to foreign investors. He also encouraged the participation of the private sector in the national economy. In politics, General Sarit established an authoritarian regime by abolishing the constitution and replacing it with martial law, concentrating power in his own hands and among his close advisers. He also dissolved the parliament, banned political parties, controlled the press and the unions, and arrested many left-wing figures.[16]

In the area of foreign policy, General Sarit allied himself with the US government. Muscat points out that the US actually had a good relationship with Thailand at this time and supplied economic and military assistance from the end of the 1940s, but not until the end of the 1950s did the American leaders begin to pay serious attention to the domestic situation in Thailand.[17] As the Cold War began to spread into the Southeast Asian region, the US government was searching for an ally who could help to stop the spread of communist movements in the region, and especially those from Vietnam.[18] General Sarit was indeed the right person at the right time for the US. The result was a flood of foreign investment (led by the US and other Western countries) which has continued to pour into Thailand ever since.[19] As noted by Riggs, the Sarit regime brought to birth the "bureaucratic polity" in Thailand which means that power was concentrated in the hand of the bureaucracy and the regime did not allow extra-bureaucratic forces or political parties to assert themselves in influencing the policy-making processes.[20] This phenomenon of the bureaucratic polity continued to shape political developments in Thailand until the 1980s.

With this authoritarian political system and the support from the US, the Sarit regime undertook the establishment of import-substitution industrialisation (ISI) in Thailand which started in the 1960s and lasted until the 1970s. Government institutions such as the NEDB (National Economic Development Board), the Board of Investment (BOI), the Ministry of Industry, the Ministry of Finance, and the Bank of Thailand were the core supporters of the ISI policy. As Hewison points out, the desire of the Sarit regime to implement the ISI policy was based on the deterioration of the balance of payments and trade deficits inherited from the Phibun regime, and on pressure from the domestic industrialists camp who demanded protectionism in order to insulate them from international competitors.[21]

The effect of the ISI policy can be seen in the influx of foreign capital as well. The Bank of Thailand's official data shows that the annual foreign capital inflow from 1965 to 1975 was about 1.25 billion baht (with 38 per cent of it coming from the US, and 30 per cent from Japan).[22] In addition, the structure of the Thai economy, especially in sectors such as industry, manufacturing and finance, was changed at the expense of the agriculture sector. Between 1960 and 1971, the manufacturing sector share of the gross domestic product (GDP) rose from 12.5 per cent to 17.5 per cent, while the share held by agriculture decreased from 39.8 per cent to 29.8 per cent.[23]

During the Sarit regime, the financial sector was dominated by the "big five" banks consisting of the Bangkok Bank, the Siam Commercial Bank, the Bangkok Metropolitan Bank, the Thai Farmers' Bank, and the Bank of Ayudhya. Collectively, these five banks increased their share of the total commercial banks' deposits from 32 per cent in 1962 to 59 per cent in 1972 (Table 3.1). The domination of these banks was possible because the owners, mostly ethnic Chinese, had been able to build a close relationship with General Sarit and other members of the military elite. This political patronage was useful because it allowed them to lobby the policy makers not to liberalise the financial sector in Thailand. As a result, under the 1962 Commercial Banking Act, the government only allowed a few foreign banks to open branches in Thailand.[24] The expansion of these banks was also a result of the increase in demand for capital in the domestic manufacturing industries during the ISI period. This strong demand from the manufacturing sector contributed to the expansion of credit allocations channelled through domestic banks (Figure 3.1).

After General Sarit died in 1963, his closest advisers, General Thanom Kittikachorn and Field Marshal Praphat Charusathien, continued to govern Thailand until 1973. In the early 1970s, at which time Thailand was in the middle of its second six-year social and development plan, policy makers began to contemplate change to the export-oriented industrialisation (EOI) policy.[25] Pasuk and Baker point out that in the early 1970s there was a strong consensus among the technocrats and policy makers (working with the National Economic and Social Development Board [NESDB], the BOT, and the BOI) that the ISI policy no longer suited Thailand, as its export commodities had begun to lose their competitiveness in the international market.[26] Consequently, the technocrats and policy makers argued for export-promotion policies.

Table 3.1 Commercial Bank Deposits in Thailand (in million baht)

Name of Bank	1962	1972	1981
Bangkok Bank	1,578	16,991	103,269
Bank of Ayudhya	475	3,288	14,489
Thai Farmers' Bank	431	4,151	40,912
Bangkok Metropolitan Bank	253	2,530	12,032
Bank of Asia	304	1,365	6,082
First Bangkok City Bank	248	648	8,532
Siam Commercial Bank	557	2,956	16,719
Krungthai Bank	1,723	8,637	40,589
Wang Lee Bank	7	14	1,067
Siam City Bank	348	2,256	10,050
Bangkok Bank of Commerce	494	2,077	14,956
Laem Thong Bank	179	448	1,779
Union Bank of Bangkok	248	1,182	4,672
Thai Danu Bank	154	2,006	2,741
The Thai Military Bank	288	1,781	9,226
Asia Trust Bank	-	835	5,049
14 foreign banks	1,167	3,738	6,913
Total	8,454	54,904	299,077

Source: Akira Suehiro, "Capitalist Development in Postwar Thailand: Commercial Bankers, Industrial Elite and Agribusiness Groups" in Ruth McVey (ed.) *Southeast Asian Capitalists* (Ithaca: Southeast Asia Program, Cornell University, 1992), p. 49.

As the technocrats and policy makers began to dismantle the ISI policy, the authoritarian regime, led at the time by Generals Thanom and Praphat, began to lose its power base among the Thai people, and especially those who lived in the urban areas. At the end of the 1960s and in the early 1970s, a coalition of political parties, students and business groups began to put pressure on General Thanom to end his authoritarian rule. This resulted in political crisis which triggered popular protests in Bangkok and other cities. These finally brought down the Thanom regime in 1973.[27] From October 1973 until 1976, Thailand was governed by democratic regimes headed by two elected politicians, Kukrit Pramoj (the leader of Social Action Party or the *Kitsangkhom* Party) and Seni Pramoj (the leader of Democrat Party or the *Prachathipat* Party). This period was known as the "open politics" period because it was a period of freedom of the press, freedom of assembly, and the establishment of constitutional rule in Thailand. During this democratic period, the power of the military was gradually reduced, and especially after the 1974 Constitution was enacted, restricting the appointment of active military officers to political positions. As suggested by Chai-anan and Morrell, this period symbolised the beginning of the end of the dominance of the military and the bureaucracy in national politics.[28] The democratic period transformed the political institutions of Thailand. More people with business backgrounds (about 35 per cent) were elected to the parliament and more than half of the Kukrit cabinet, which was formed in 1975, came from a similar background.[29] Ockey in his study on Thai politics suggests that there were two ways in which business people began to influence national politics: directly, by entering into politics as politicians, and indirectly by supporting the financial needs of certain politicians or factions within political parties.[30]

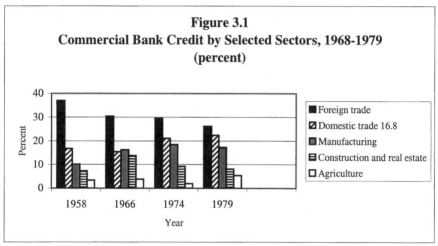

Figure 3.1
Commercial Bank Credit by Selected Sectors, 1968-1979
(percent)

Source: Richard Doner and Danny Unger, "The Politics of Finance in Thai Economic Development", in Stephan Haggard, Chung H. Lee and Sylvia Maxfield (eds.) *The Politics of Finance in Developing Countries* (Ithaca and London: Cornell University Press, 1993), p. 105.

Thailand again experienced a military coup in October 1976. This military coup, which caused the death of hundreds of students (mostly from Thammasat University) and civilians, created political instability in the country as a whole. From 1976 until 1978 Thailand again entered a period of authoritarianism and was governed by a civilian leader Thanin Kraivichien. With the support of the military leaders, Thanin abolished the 1974 Constitution, declared martial law, repressed democratic rights, and banned political parties. However, the Thanin regime was unpopular among the Thai people and struggles among the military and political elites for the control of the state intensified. During this period, economic performance deteriorated, as the external foreign debt increased rapidly, while at the same time the current account deficit and the trade deficit per cent from the gross national product (GNP) increased from 2.7 per cent in 1976 to 5.7 per cent by the end of 1977 and from 3.3 per cent in 1976 to 6.5 per cent in 1977 respectively.[31] This economic downturn was also influenced by external factors such as the uncertainty regarding oil prices in the international market and the withdrawal of the US from Indochina.[32]

In an attempt to avoid further economic and political crises, General Kriangsak Chomanan replaced Thanin in 1978. Although he came from a military background, General Kriangsak began to ease the political restrictions in Thailand by allowing the limited participation of political parties in national politics. In 1978 General Kriangsak facilitated the birth of a new constitution which allowed political parties to contest the 1979 general elections in which the Chart Thai Party (led by Praman Adireksan) and the Social Action Party (led by Boonchu) gained a significant number of seats in the parliament.[33] But General Kriangsak's efforts to restore political stability failed due to his indecisiveness in the political and economic arena. As noted by Girling, two factors were at play here: factionalism within the Thai military and dissatisfaction among the business community with the Kriangsak regime.[34] Finally, pressure from the progressive young military officers' faction known as the "Young Turks" forced General Kriangsak to resign in early 1980. He was replaced by the then Chief of Army, General Prem Tinsulanonda.[35]

The Prem Regime and the Foundation of the Economic Boom

As mentioned earlier, until the end of the 1970s, Thailand's economy still relied very much on the export of primary products (mostly rice and agricultural goods) and pursued an import-substitution industrialisation (ISI) policy. In the early 1980s all this changed, due to worldwide economic recession and the collapse of the price of oil which plunged the Thai economy into a severe economic crisis. Thus, the continuation of Thailand's economic development was one of the major issues which General Prem Tinsulanonda had to tackle during the 1980s.

As General Prem stayed in power until 1988, he was able to implement a series of economic reforms such as the readjustment of the exchange rate, changes in tariffs and taxes, export promotions, and other sectoral reform efforts, and to do so at a rapid pace. One of the most controversial reforms was the devaluation of Thailand's currency. Between 1981 and 1987, the government devalued the baht several times with the aim of improving the worsening economic situation in Thailand.[36] Although there was opposition to it, the effect of the devaluation policy was an increase in the level of exports of manufactured and agro-industry products. It also boosted the tourism industry in the 1980s. Although it is true that the agricultural sector's share in GDP declined from 27 per cent to 12 per cent between 1980 and 1993, the manufacturing sector grew from 16 per cent to 26 per cent in the same period (Figure 3.2).[37] But the growth of the manufacturing sector was also caused by an increase in foreign direct investment (FDI) entering Thailand, mainly from Japan. The Japanese investors' share of the manufacturing sector in Thailand rose rapidly from 32 per cent in 1984-1985 to 72 per cent in 1988.[38] By the end of the Prem period in early 1988, Thailand's economic performance was ahead of other countries in the region, with economic growth reaching almost 7 per cent.[39]

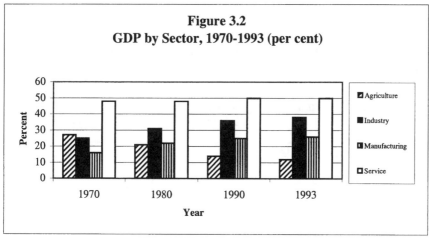

Figure 3.2
GDP by Sector, 1970-1993 (per cent)

Source: Pasuk and Baker, *Thailand, Economy and Politics* (Singapore: Oxford University Press, 1997), p. 153.

On the political arena, General Prem gradually enhanced the democratisation process in Thailand by restoring democratic institutions and, at the same time, by maintaining a balance between the political differences of the military, the bureaucrats, and the politicians. Unlike in the 1960s and early 1970s, when power was concentrated in the hands of the bureaucracy and the military, during the Prem period political players such as the career politicians, the technocrats, the business community, and other non-bureaucratic forces began to have their own channels to power.

General Prem held general elections in 1981, 1986 and 1988 and initiated a series of constitutional reforms aimed at strengthening public participation in the decision-making process. This is why Thailand, under his premiership, came to be known as a "semi-democracy" (known in Thai as the *prachathippatai khrung'ng bai*).

It is true that the conflict of views and interests over economic reform caused some problems. General Prem reshuffled his cabinets several times in order to please the opposition parties, but the support of King Bhumipon Adulyadej kept him in power longer than anybody in Thailand's modern history. The Prem period saw the end of the "bureaucratic polity" that had dominated Thai politics since the 1960s and 1970s, and its replacement with a more democratic political system. The end of the "bureaucratic polity" followed by the rise of the non-state actors in Thai politics. During the Prem period business groups began to exert political influence in national politics. Many businesspersons and urban middle class representatives entered parliament.[40] The rise of elected politicians (with business backgrounds) in national politics was at this time very impressive, representing almost half of the total number of cabinet members (Table 3.2). This trend continued to shape the Thai politics in the 1990s.

Table 3.2 Businesspersons in Prem's Cabinets (1980-1988)

Cabinet	From	To	Business persons	Total	Per cent
Prem I	3/80	1/81	17	37	45.9
Prem II	1/81	12/81	12	40	30.0
Prem III	12/81	4/83	17	41	41.5
Prem IV	5/83	8/86	21	44	47.7
Prem V	8/86	4/88	21	44	47.7

Source: Anek Laothamatas, *Business Associations and the New Political Economy of Thailand* (Boulder and Singapore: Westview Press and Institute of Southeast Asian Studies, 1992), p. 34.

Thailand's Policy-Making Institutions

The origins of the Thai economic boom cannot be separated from the role played by economic policy-making institutions in the previous few decades. Two important institutions deserve attention here: the Bank of Thailand (BOT) and the Ministry of Finance (MOF). The BOT was established in 1939, with the primary aims of maintaining price stability, managing loans, supervising the commercial banks, and controlling foreign exchange transactions in the country.[41] Later, under the 1942 Central Bank

Act, the BOT had its own first governor, Prince Viwat. As a highly respected economist and graduate from Cambridge University in the UK, Prince Viwat's urgent task was to defend the baht which had lost value and to protect the foreign reserves during the Second World War.[42] From this time, Prince Viwat came to be known as someone who played a crucial role in laying the foundations of the independence of the BOT and, more importantly, in establishing the tradition of monetary conservatism in Thailand.

The desire to maintain the independence of the BOT started during the 1950s. This created conflicts among policy makers. For instance, on several occasions the BOT disagreed with the government for adopting budget deficits and for the expansion of credit to finance industrialisation programmes. Often these disputes resulted in the forced resignations of the BOT's high officers such as Dej, the Governor of the BOT in 1952 and the deputy governor Puey Ungphakorn in 1953.[43] During the Sarit period in the early 1960s, the tradition of monetary conservatism and the independence of the BOT remained strong. The central bank was then run by very capable and disciplined technocrats who were mainly concerned with maintaining macroeconomic stability in Thailand. One of those who played an important role in continuing this tradition was the BOT's governor, Dr. Puey Ungphakorn, who occupied this position from 1959 until 1971. Under his leadership, the BOT was relatively free from political intervention, and especially that from the military elites.

The Ministry of Finance (MOF), the other important policy-making institution in Thailand, was dominated by a group of economists educated in American universities. They became known as the "technocrats" group who advised General Sarit on economic policy. It was the MOF which formulated macroeconomic policy in Thailand in the next three decades. General Sarit also appointed technocrats from various occupations to important ministries, such as the Ministry of Interior (MOI), the Ministry of Finance (MOF), the Ministry of Commerce (MOC) and others.[44] In addition, both the National and Economic Development Board (NEDB) and the Bureau of Budget (BOB) were directly accountable to the Office of the Prime Minister which allowed General Sarit to oversee the economic policy-making process in Thailand.

However, the rise of the civilian politicians during the democratic period of the mid-1970s challenged the autonomy of the economic policy-making institutions. This occurred when Boonchu Rojanasathiem, a former banker and an elected politician from the Social Action Party, was appointed as the Minister of Finance. Under the influence of the Party's attempt to gain popularity in the rural areas, Boonchu implemented a rural credit programme aimed at reducing the widening gap between the rich and the poor and developing the agriculture sector in Thailand. This programme was opposed by the then central bank Governor, Dr. Snoh Unakul, because it created fiscal constraints and therefore led to an expansion of the budget deficit.[45] Despite this, it must be pointed out that Boonchu's rural policies successfully transformed Thailand's agribusiness sector into one of Thailand's main exports in the 1980s.

Under the Prem regime in the 1980s, economic policy-making institutions were more independent and insulated from political pressures. This was needed because the technocrats had advised then Prime Minister Prem to implement a series of economic reform policies. General Prem created centralised and insulated policy-making institutions which were part of what Muscat termed a "technocratic policy structure".[46] In this technocratic structure, Prem himself and the Prime Minister's Office were involved in the process of formulating economic policies. As occurred during the Sarit regime, General Prem was helped by a group of capable technocrats who occupied important positions in bodies such as the National Economic and Social Development Board (NESDB), the Bureau of Budget (BOB), the Fiscal Policy Office (FPO), the Ministry of Finance (MOF) and the Bank of Thailand (BOT). During the Prem period, the NESDB (led by well-known technocrat, Dr. Snoh Unakul), as an important planning agency, played a vital role in preparing budget proposals and financial allocations to each ministry.[47] General Prem also set up the Council of Economic Ministers (CEM) which was responsible for making strategic decisions on economic and political issues. The membership of the CEM comprised Cabinet Ministers, representatives of the coalition parties, PM's advisers and prominent technocrats.[48] This type of policy-making body meant General Prem and his cabinet were relatively free of political pressure from political elites and business groups. Arguably, it was these kinds of economic policy-making institutions that brought Thailand into a period of economic boom at the end of the 1980s.

These insulated policy-making institutions, however, did not necessarily make it easy for the Prem regime to implement economic reform policies in the 1980s, including that of the structural adjustment programme funded by the World Bank.[49] Tienhcai points out that the implementation of this programme created a political struggle among the principal players within Thai politics.[50] Each of them pursued and protected their own interests and agendas in an attempt to influence the formulation and the implementation of the economic reform policies. This was particularly clear in the case of the resistance of the military and several political parties, who supported the import-substitution industrialisation policies and even in the case of the Ministry of Industry which preferred the continuation of trade protection policies which were at risk of disappearing once the structural programme was implemented.[51]

Domestic Coalitions

The success of Thailand's economy cannot be separated from the existence of a domestic-based coalition between business groups, bureaucrats and the military. On this point, we cannot underestimate the role that the ethnic Chinese business community played in this process. Why, despite the fact that the Chinese were discriminated against during the nationalist period of the Phibun regime in the 1930s and 1940s, did they survive? Riggs explains ʰat to protect their business activities, the banks' owners developed a close relationship with powerful figures in the military and in the bureaucracy.[52] This was done by offering directorships or shareholdings to political leaders (and their family members). In return, these business groups often received preferential treatment where credit or loans from the government (usually through the BOT) or administered government projects were concerned.[53] For instance, the owner of the Bangkok Bank, Chin Sophonphanich, appointed General Phao Sriyanond, a key figure in the Phibun government, as advisory director; the Bank of Ayudhya associated with the National Economic Development Corporation (NEDCOL), a holding company controlled by the "Soi Ratchakhru" military faction (belonging to the General Phao Sriyanond and General Phin Choonhavan groups); and the Thai Farmers' Bank had close ties with Pridi Phanonyong's political faction.[54] This kind of relationship successfully protected the business interests of the ethnic Chinese in Thailand and in the following decades transformed them into the engine of, to borrow Yoshihara's term, "ersatz capitalism" in Thailand.[55]

These relationships shaped the success of the Thai economy under the Prem regime in the 1980s.[56] At that time General Prem needed to create a domestic coalition to support the implementation of national economic reform policies. To do this, he invited the assistance of Boonchu Rojanasathian, the leader of the Social Action Party (SAP), who was then a supporter of trade liberalisation and export-driven strategies in Thailand. Throughout the 1980s, Boonchu was a champion of the so-called

Table 3.3 Major Business Conglomerates in Thailand

Company name	Principal owner	Principal activities
Bangkok Bank	Sophonphanich family	Banking, investments
Thai Farmers' Bank	Lamsam family	Banking, manufacturing, investments
Bangkok Metropolitan Bank	Techaphaibun family	Banking, whisky
Bank Ayudhya	Ratanarak family	Banking, manufacturing, lighterage
Wanglee Bank	Wanglee family	Banking, rice milling, property development
Bangkok Metropolitan Bank	U Chu Liang	Banking, importing
Betagro	Hong Yiah Seng	Rice trading, textiles, importing and manufacturing
Thai Roong Ruang	unknown	Sugar and related business
Kwang Soong Lee	Mitr-Pol	Sugar and related business
Laem Thong	Yongsak Kanathanavanich	Rice and jute export, animal feed etc.
Metro	Prasert Tangtrongsakdi	Fertiliser importer and manufacturing, flour mill
Central Dept. Stores	Chirathiwat	Retail trade, property development
Siam Motors	Taworn Pornprapha	Motor distribution and assembly (Nissan), property development
Saha Union	Damri Darakanda	Wholesale trade, manufacturing (household goods)
Thai Wuthipat	Sukree Phothirattanangkun	Manufacturing (textiles)

Source: Jamie Mackie, "Changing Patterns of Chinese Big Business in Southeast Asia" in Ruth McVey (ed.) *Southeast Asian Capitalists* (Ithaca: Southeast Asia Program, Cornell University, 1992), pp. 185-186.

"Thailand, Inc" and had a close relationship with business organisations such as the Thai Chamber of Commerce, the Association of Thai Industries, and the Thai Bankers' Association.[57]   Boonchu engineered the birth of the Joint Public-Private Consultative Committee (JPPCC [*Kor Ror Or*]), a forum through which the business community could actively participate in the economic decision-making process in Thailand.[58] Of course, many business leaders in the JPPCC and other business associations were second generation ethnic Chinese businesspeople. They controlled sectors such as finance, telecommunications, property, transport, retail, tourism and others (Table 3.3).

This generation was more sophisticated and more "Thai" in the sense that they were already integrated and accepted by the rest of the population as Thai people. By the 1980s there was not much animosity against those of Chinese descent. This climate had aided General Prem in reforming the Thai economy because he did not have to deal with the ethnicity issues that plagued Indonesia or Malaysia.[59] There was a consensus that those of Chinese descent in Thailand had already played an important role in contributing to economic growth and that they would continue to play a crucial role in the future. It was in this context that General Prem created a coalition among the military, bureaucracy, technocrats and business community to reform the Thai economy in the 1980s.

External Factors

External factors also played a key role in the creation of Thailand's economic boom. It is important to mention the role of the US at the end of the 1950s in assisting the Sarit regime through the involvement of US economic and technical advisers in the economic policy-making process. Through the US aid programmes, General Sarit and his team implemented economic reconstruction programmes in Thailand, building up the infrastructure of the country (roads, ports, bridges, and railways), training public servants, giving scholarships, running poverty alleviation programmes, and combating the narcotics and drugs business. The total amount of US aid given to Thailand between 1951 and 1975 was about US$2.5 million.[60] The US also assisted General Sarit to establish government policy-making institutions such as the National Economic Development Board (NEDB), the Bureau of Budget (BOB), the Board of Investment (BOI), and the National Statistical Office.[61] In addition, the World Bank and the International Monetary Fund (IMF) were involved in the early process of drafting Thailand's first long-term economic strategy known as the First National Economic Development Plan (1961-1966).

Besides the US, Japan also played a significant role in fostering the growth of the Thai economy. Japanese investors actually started to come to Thailand from the end of the 1960s, to set up joint venture activities with local companies. Later on, this also coincided with the Plaza agreement in 1984 in which the Japanese yen was overvalued, causing many Japanese manufacturing companies and Japanese investors to move their operations into the Southeast Asian region. As Hewison points out, Japanese investors contributed to the growth of Thailand's domestic manufacturing conglomerates such as Siam Cement (owned by the royal family), Charoen Pokphand (agribusiness), Saha Union (textiles), Siam Motors (automotive), Bangkok Industries (steels), and also Mahboonkhrong (retailing).[62] By the 1990s Japanese investment in Thailand had moved from foreign direct investment to more diverse types of investment such as shares of portfolios, bonds, and securities.

Political Pluralism and the Civil Society in the 1990

The economic boom also changed the dynamics of Thai politics in the 1990s. Thailand became more pluralist politically, in the sense that power was no longer in the hands of the bureaucracy, the military, or a single political party. Instead, it was distributed among a number of political actors, whose alliances shifted and changed from time to time. After Thailand returned to parliamentary democracy in 1992, the political parties themselves became important players in Thai politics. But the return of parliamentary democracy did not come without a price. To understand Thai politics in the 1990s, we must look closely at the factors that contributed to the return of parliamentary democracy. These were the rise and fall of Thai democracy, the emergence of coalitional politics, the widespread nature of so-called "money politics", and also the retreat of the Thai military from politics.

Weak Governments, Strong Politicians

The departure of General Prem in 1988 was followed by the return of parliamentary democracy in Thailand. The Chart Thai Party or the Thai Nation Party (led by Chatichai Choonhavan, a former general and diplomat), won the general elections and Chatichai became the first elected civilian prime minister since 1976 (when the military launched a coup to overthrow a civilian government). There were three political and economic aspects to the early policy lines of the Chatichai government. First, from the outset, Chatichai restored democratic institutions such as the parliament, the press, the court, and non-governmental organisations

(NGOs) and allowed them to participate freely in national political discussion.[63] Second, Chatichai gave the political parties more say in the economic policy-making process. Unlike General Prem who allocated a number of cabinet positions to non-elected persons with military backgrounds and to the technocrats, Chatichai appointed elected politicians to occupy all cabinet positions. Important ministries such as the Defence Ministry, the Ministry of Interior, the Ministry of Transport and Communications and the Ministry of Finance were all held by elected politicians.[64]

The Chatichai government lasted less than three years. In February 1991 the Thai military (led by a group of military leaders from the Chulachomklao Military Academy Class V) launched a coup to overthrow the Chatichai government and established the National Peace Keeping Council (NPKC).[65] The military coup in 1991 marked the re-emergence of the military in Thai politics and once again led to the fall of democracy in Thailand. It is true that Chatichai's aggressive stand in promoting the political parties precipitated a conflict with the military. Before the coup, the relationship between the Chatichai government and the military leaders had been strained because the military felt they were being alienated from decision making especially on sensitive national security issues. There was deep suspicion among the military leaders about the integrity of certain elected politicians occupying ministerial positions.[66] In order to please the Thai people and the international community, the military leaders appointed Anand Punyarachun, a diplomat-turned-business leader, as caretaker Prime Minister. Without wasting time, Anand formed a caretaker government and invited technocrats, former government and military officers, and business people to fill the cabinet positions. The Anand caretaker government was built from a coalition of the military, technocrats and businesspeople. It, in many ways, resembled the coalition during the Prem period in the 1980s. With the support of these people, Anand and his economic team acted to restore the confidence of foreign investors by implementing economic reforms.[67]

These economic reforms were aimed at maintaining the macroeconomic stabilisation policy, which involved keeping the budget under control, monitoring low inflation, and the balance of payments; reviewing the big project spending of the Chatichai government; liberalising trade barriers and tariffs; continuing the privatisation policies; reforming the tax system; reforming the financial sector; and continuing the drafting of the anti-monopoly and intellectual property laws.[68]

Following the coup, there was intensification in the rivalry between the political players in Thai politics. The coup leaders tried to influence the drafting of a new constitution by putting forward the idea of appointing military personnel to the upper house (Senate) and also by proposing clauses that would give the military more political power in Thailand.[69] This move by the military triggered protests from some political parties and from other pro-democracy groups such as students, lawyers, the non-government organisations (NGOs), and unionists. At the end of 1991, the new constitution was passed in parliament, but it provoked widespread protests against the military. This situation brought a deepening political crisis which finally forced Anand (with the agreement of the military leaders) to call general elections in March 1992.

The political parties viewed the March 1992 general elections as an opportunity for the return of parliamentary democracy. Meanwhile, the military leaders who had masterminded the coup, formed a new political party, the *Samakkhitam* Party (led by Narong Wongwan), just a few months before the elections and used it as a political vehicle for maintaining power. Indeed, the *Samakkhitam* Party won the March 1992 general election but the overall results from the elections fell into two camps: *pro-military* and *pro-democracy*. The former comprised the *Samakkhitam* Party, the Chart Thai Party, the Social Action Party and other small parties, while the latter comprised the Democrat Party, the Palang Dharma Party, the New Aspiration Party and the Solidarity Party.[70]

The division between the two camps widened when the military leader, General Suchinda Kraprayoon, was appointed Prime Minister, after the nomination of Narong Wongwan (the leader of *Samakkhitam* Party) was dropped because of his past involvement in drug trafficking in Northern Thailand. The pro-democracy camp regarded the appointment of General Suchinda as undemocratic, and with the support of the urban middle class launched mass protests in the streets in Bangkok, which became known as the May 1992 Uprising.[71]   Only after hundreds of protesters died, were injured, or disappeared during the clashes, and also after the intervention of King Bhumipon, did General Suchinda finally agree to resign from his position. The pro-democracy camp saw the resignation of General Suchinda as a strong sign that the people had chosen democracy rather than authoritarianism.[72] And the desire of the Thai people to support the return of democracy in Thailand was proven when the pro-democracy parties (especially the Democrat Party) won the September 1992 general elections.[73]   Chuan Leekpai, the leader of the Democrat Party, was elected as the new Prime Minister and he governed

Thailand with a strong resolve to protect democratic institutions. He was criticised as an indecisive leader but nonetheless he provided the political stability which Thailand needed to provide a good climate for economic and business activities.[74]

In 1995, the Chuan government collapsed after its main political partner, the New Aspiration Party, withdrew from the coalition. In that year Thailand held further general elections and brought in a new government led by a powerful provincial-based politician, Banharn Silapaa-archa, the leader of the Chart Thai Party. The Banharn government only survived for eleven months, and in November 1996, Chaovalit Yongchaiyuth, the leader of the New Aspiration Party, was elected as the new Prime Minister. Indeed, Thailand had no less than six governments with different leaders, political parties and policy makers in the ten years to 1997, making change a feature in modern Thai politics (Box 3.1).

The 1990s saw the political parties play a more active role in national politics and the policy-making process. The general elections held in Thailand from the end of the 1980s and through the 1990s failed to produce a majority of votes for a single party.[75] Instead, voters' choices frequently changed, their votes being distributed in varying ways between the main political parties (Table 3.4). Perhaps a factor in this was the way in which the return of the political parties to national politics also increased the incidence of "vote buying" and other corrupt practices in Thai politics.[76] For the political parties, electoral politics was a means to power. The political parties did many things, including buying votes (especially rural ones), to boost their popularity and so increase their chance of election or re-election. Because the political parties and their candidates spent so much money during elections, the elected politicians, once in government, would then attempt to recoup their money by delivering government projects to their constituencies.[77]

The magnitude of this problem is discussed in recent studies. In a study of corruption in Thailand, Pasuk and Sungsidh point out that vote buying and other corrupt activities increased as this country enjoyed rapid economic growth and the political parties again controlled the ministerial positions at the end of the 1980s and early 1990s.[78] Their study shows that the Ministry of Interior was known as the most corrupt government institution, followed by the ministries of Agriculture, Education, Public Health, Communications, and Defence.[79] According to the Thai Farmers' Bank Research Centre, the political parties spent about 20 billion baht (1 billion) on vote buying during the 1996 general elections, which was an increase of 20 per cent from the 1995 general elections.[80]

Box 3.1   Political and Economic Policy Figures in Thailand in the 1990s

Prime Minister	Finance Minister	BOT Governor	Coalition-led Party	Regime Type
Chatichai Choonhavan (1988-Feb.1991)	Pramuan Sabhavasu	Vijit Supinit (1988-1995)	Char t Thai Party	Democratic
Anand Panyarachun I and II (1991-September 1992)	Virabongsa Ramangkura		Military and Technocrats	Military-dominated government
Chuan Leekpai (1992-July 1995)	Tarrin Nimmanahaeminda	Rerngchai Marakanond (1995-July 1997)	Democrat Party	Democratic
Banharn Silapa-archa (1995-Nov.1996)	Surakiat Sathienthai (1995-May 1996) Bodi Chunnanda (1996-Oct.1996) Chaiyawat Wibulswasdi (caretaker)		Chart Thai Party	Democratic
Chaovalit Yongchaiyuth (1996-Nov.1997)	Amnuay Virawan (1996-June 1997) Thanong Bidaya (June 1997-Oct.1997) Kosit Panplemrat (Oct.-Nov.1997)	Chaiyawat Wibulswasdi (July 1997-May 1998)	New Aspiration Party	Democratic
Chuan Leekpai (Nov.1997-2000)	Tarin Nimmanahaeminda	Chatu MongolSunakul	Democrat Party	Democratic

Another negative aspect of contemporary Thai politics, as pointed out by Christensen, is the division between the Bangkok-based politicians and the province-based politicians.[81] The rivalry between the two camps is a contributing factor to political instability in Thailand. For instance, when the Democrat Party-led coalition government was in power from 1992 to

1995, its policies were biased towards the middle class in Bangkok and other urban areas while when the Chart Thai Party (led by Banharn Silapa-archa) governed in Thailand from 1995 until 1996, followed by the New Aspiration Party (led by Chaovalit Yongchaiyuth) until November 1997, policies were biased towards people in the rural areas outside Bangkok.[82] These governments, so concerned with their own survival, had difficulty in setting policies based on long-term needs and for the benefit of the whole population.

Table 3.4 Election Results of the "Big" Political Parties (1992-1996)

Party	1992a	1992b	1995	1996
Democrat	44	79	86	123
New Aspiration	72	51	57	125
Chart Thai	-	60	92	38
Social Action	31	22	22	20
Chart Pattana*	-	60	53	53
Samakkitham**	79	-	-	-
Palang Dharma	31	22	23	1
Prachakorn Thai	4	1	18	18

* This party was formed only few weeks before the September 1992 general elections and led by Chatichai Choonhavan, a former leader of the Chart Thai Party.
** This party was formed in mid-1991 led by Narong Wongwan and the pro-Suchinda military leaders.
Sources: Surin Maisrikrod, *Thailand's Two General Elections in 1992* (Singapore: Institute of Southeast Asian Studies, 1992), appendix I and also James Ockey, "Thailand, The Crafting of Democracy", *Southeast Asian Affairs 1997* (Singapore: Institute of Southeast Asian Studies, 1997), p. 312.

The Decline of Military Power

During the 1990s, the military-civilian relationship in Thailand underwent considerable changes. Where during the Prem period, military leaders restricted the freedom of elected politicians on the grounds of protecting national security, during the Chatichai period elected politicians did not hesitate to reduce the budget allocation for the military in both 1989 and 1990.[83] However, under the Chuan coalition government, which was elected in September 1992, the military was placed under civilian supremacy.[84] When the Democrat coalition government returned to power in October 1997, civilian Prime Minister Chuan Leekpai occupied the powerful position of Minister of Defence, usually reserved for former generals.

Civil Society in the Making

The rapid economic growth that Thailand experienced from the 1980s until the mid 1990s, and the return of parliamentary democracy from 1992, created fertile ground for the flowering of civil society. Although arguably this civil society is not a replica of that in the Western democracies, autonomous and independent organisations outside the formal political institutions are growing extensively and have already had a considerable influence on national politics.[85] These organisations encompass business, media, non-government organisations (NGOs), intellectual/academic groups, unions and independent think tanks.[86] Some of these deserve our attention here.

Business

Traditionally big business groups have always been close to, and enjoyed political patronage from, the political leaders in Thailand. This kind of relationship is constantly evolving on the basis of the changing nature of Thai politics. During the Prem period in the 1980s, business representatives such as the Thai Chamber of Commerce, the Association of Thai Industries, and the Thai Bankers' Association played an important role in influencing the policy-making process. These business representatives and their leaders mainly represented the interests of the large, established business groups, which supported the economic reforms of the 1980s for the expansion of their business activities both in Thailand itself and abroad. In the 1990s a new generation of businesspeople emerged in the diverse and more sophisticated business areas of computing, telecommunications, property, and the finance/banking industry.[87] The political involvement of these new businesspeople changed after the May 1992 uprising. At that time many young businesspeople became active politically and some of them joined other pro-democratic forces.[88] A well-known example is the Business Club for Democracy, which comprised bankers and businesspeople who were concerned with the restoration of the democratic system and the establishment of a clean government in Thailand.

This new breed of businesspeople was less dependent on government money as a source of investment, particularly after Thailand introduced the Securities and Exchange Act in 1992. Through the Bangkok Stock Exchange (BSE), it found new sources of capital to expand its business activities, one being through the capital market. These businesspeople set up their own securities companies or participated actively as "market players" in stock exchange activities.[89] In this new business environment they also started to voice their concerns in debates on the direction of economic policies.[90] The political and economic changes of the 1990s arguably brought business leaders and business representatives out of a situation in which they were passive partners of the government and into one in which they began to play a more active role in pursuing their own views and ideas. Indeed, they began to exercise considerable influence on the policy-making process in Thailand.

Media

Thailand's media is relatively free from government censorship and political interference. According to Thitinan, Thailand's media has operated in a variety of ways.[91] In the past, the media was under the control of the elites, namely the military leaders and bureaucracy. During the democratic period of 1973-1976 the media became more liberal and critical in reporting political and social events. The economic boom made publishers more independent financially, especially with the increase in revenue from advertising. The desire among journalists to uphold the freedom of the press was strengthened with the return of parliamentary democracy in 1988. Under the Chatichai government the media gained more freedom in reporting news and, more importantly, it began to show political muscle by scrutinising and monitoring the way in which the government and its leaders ran the country. For example, corruption was one of several issues that the media focused on during the Chatichai period.[92]

The media played a crucial role after the military coup in 1991 and during the May uprising in 1992.[93] During this time, the Confederation of Thai Journalists continued to defy the restrictions placed upon them by the military leaders.[94] Several newspaper journalists were intimidated by the military, including the prominent editor-in-chief of *The Nation* daily, Suthichai Yoon.[95] Several liberal newspapers such as *The Nation*, *The Bangkok Post*, *The Manager*, *Thai Rath* and *Matichon* as well as private radio broadcasters and television channels took a leading role in defending the freedom of the press and also in criticising the military leaders for their intention to return Thailand to authoritarian rule. When Chuan Leekpai's Democrat Party-led coalition government came into power in September 1992, the media made the radical decision to join the pro-democracy camp. Since then, the media has been an opposition voice in Thai politics.[96]

Non- Government Organisations (NGOs)

The non-government organisations (NGOs) as a social movement came into being in the late 1960s.[97] During the democratic period of 1973-1976, university activists worked to expand the activities of the NGOs. However, this political activism was interrupted by the military coup of 1976 when many students and NGO activists were arrested or left for the jungle of Northern Thailand which was controlled by the Communist Party of Thailand (CPT).[98] During the 1980s the NGO movement gained momentum again, especially after many of those students who joined the CPT were given amnesty by Prime Minister Prem Tinsulanonda.[99] Many of those who returned to the cities, particularly Bangkok, set up non-government organisations on rural development, legal aid, and environment issues.[100] During the 1990s the NGOs continued to play an important role in strengthening the democratic movement in Thailand. During the May 1992 uprising, NGOs along with other pro-democracy groups such as students, unions, business groups, and politicians, formed the Confederation for Democracy (CFD), a broad-based coalition which organised mass demonstrations in the streets of Bangkok against the appointment of General Suchinda as Prime Minister.[101] The NGOs also initiated the establishment of the new election-monitoring body known as Poll Watch, which aimed at addressing voting fraud and vote buying during the September general elections in 1992.

Recently, NGO activists also set up the Assembly of the Poor, a coalition of NGOs, rural-based organisations and academics aimed at putting pressure on the government to change policies that discriminate against people in rural areas.[102]   The first and the biggest public rally took place in April 1996. About 10,000 people, mostly from rural areas, protested and camped in front of the parliament building in Bangkok and demanded that the Banharn government improve economic conditions in the rural areas of Thailand. The Assembly of the Poor held further protests in April 1997 and made similar demands of the Chaovalit government.[103]

Environmental Groups

The environmental movement is a new phenomenon in Thailand, emerging as a consequence of the rapid economic change that took place during the 1980s. The environmental movement transformed into a political body after a coalition of several NGOs, students, academics, and rural-based organisations successfully forced the Prem government to abandon the construction of the Nam Choan Dam in Kanchanaburi Province in 1988.[104] Since then the environment groups have continued to campaign on and raise the profile of environmental issues such as the logging of Thai forests, pollution and eucalyptus plantation projects. Hirsch points out that during the 1990s the environment movement gained increased support from some elements within Thai society.[105] A number of environment-based organisations have been formed, using a variety of approaches in promoting environmental issues. The environment movement joined a broad alliance of pro-democratic groups during the May 1992 uprising. As Thailand currently faces increased environmental problems as a result of industrialisation, it is likely that the environment movement will continue to play an important role in influencing policy in Thailand.[106]

Intellectuals/Academics

The role of intellectuals or academics in Thailand is very important and widely recognised. Political activism among Thai intellectuals and academics is not something new at all. A role model for Thai intellectuals and academics is Pridi Phanomyong, one of the leading figures of the Peoples' Party which overthrew the absolute monarchy in 1932.[107] During that crisis intellectuals and academics also influenced the course of political change. For instance, a coalition of intellectuals, academics and students was able to force General Praphat to resign in 1973. The democratic period of 1973-1976 saw the rise of the democratic spheres in Thailand, which encouraged a further politicisation of intellectuals and academics.

During the 1980s the intellectuals continued to be critical of the Prem government. When the Prem regime granted an amnesty to those students and intellectuals who fled to the jungle after the October 1976 uprising, some of them returned to the universities and engaged in political activities. Many of them have become prominent and respected academics. In the aftermath of the military coup in 1991, 90 academics signed a petition opposing the coup. Also many intellectuals and academics joined political coalitions such as the Confederation for Democracy as well as Poll Watch.[108]

Trade and Labour Unions

The origins of the union movement in Thailand date back to the beginning of the 20th century when Thailand began to integrate into the world economy. The union movement has never been well organised and this has made it easy for authoritarian governments to repress it.[109] During the brief democratic period of 1973-1976, the unions and their representative organisations such as the Thai Trade Union Congress (TTUC) and the Labour Congress of Thailand (LCT) became more politicised. Also during this period, the number of strikes was certainly high compared to any other period in Thailand's modern history.[110] The Prem period in the 1980s saw a different approach to controlling the power of the union movement in Thailand. In order to maintain the economic reforms and political stability, the Prem regime, big business groups and unions came to a tripartite agreement, which gradually established basic conditions for workers including minimum wages, and a mechanism for dispute settlement.[111] However, the freedom of unions to organise was suppressed again after the military coup of 1991. Despite this, the union movement did not collapse, indeed it participated in resistance against the military in 1991-1992, with some union leaders participating in the leadership of the Confederation for Democracy.[112] The involvement of unions in organising anti-military protests in the streets of Bangkok during the May 1992 uprising indicated that the union movement in Thailand was still relatively strong.

Independent Think Tanks

After Thailand began to enjoy the rapid economic growth of the 1980s and the 1990s, many independent think tanks emerged to participate in public debate. These bodies predominantly belong to the private sector and some of them are funded by overseas organisations. The Thailand Development Research Institute (TDRI) is probably the most influential one. It was formed in 1984 and initially headed by Dr. Ammar Siamwalla, a well-known economist. Later on, it was run by Dr. Chalongphop Sussangkarn, who is also an economist.[113] Since it came into existence, the TDRI has played an important role in influencing government policies through its publications and academic meetings. For instance, in 1996, TDRI launched 'Thailand Vision 2020', a public campaign aimed at encouraging political leaders and policy makers to prepare development strategies for the next millennium.[114]

Some of the other think tanks are the Institute of Public Policy Studies, the Political Economy Center of the Chulalongkorn University, the Thai Farmers' Bank Research (owned by the Thai Farmers' Bank), Phatra Research Institute (owned by Phatra Thanakit Public Company), and Bangkok Bank's Research Department (owned by the Bangkok Bank, the largest private bank in Thailand). These think tanks regularly produce their own publications and research findings with the aim of influencing government policy. As the Thai economy has became more globalised and interdependent with the world economy in the 1990s, the role of these independent think tanks is important and will remain so in the future.[115]

Conclusion

This chapter has examined the political economy of Thailand's boom in the 1980s and 1990s. The integration of Thailand into the world economy early in the twentieth century brought about political, social and economic changes that shaped modern Thailand. In the ensuing decades Thailand experienced a variety of political systems, from absolutist monarchy, authoritarianism, to parliamentary democracy. Dramatic changes occurred during the Sarit period in the 1960s. At that point Thai politics transformed into what was known as a "bureaucratic polity" meaning that power was solely in the hands of a small group of the military elites and the bureaucracy. In this political climate, Thailand's economy also underwent dramatic change. General Sarit Thanarat launched the first capitalist-led economic development in the early 1960s. As a result, Thailand's economy was integrated more deeply into the world economy, and has been in that state ever since. Foreign investors (especially those from the US and Japan) helped the existing domestic big businesses (many of which were owned by Chinese immigrants in Thailand) to transform the Thai economy during the 1970s and the 1980s. The technocrats, who controlled many of the important economic policy-making institutions such as the Ministry of Finance and Bank of Thailand also helped. It was during the Sarit period also that the US intensified its strategic role through providing financial and technical assistance (particularly from the International Monetary Fund and the World Bank) for economic development programmes in Thailand.

However, after student-led protests brought about the collapse of the authoritarian regime in 1973, Thailand experienced a brief democratic period, which lasted until 1976. During this period, the power of the Thai military was reduced. From 1976 until 1980 Thailand experienced a resurgence of authoritarian politics, which was marked by constant power struggles among the political and economic actors. This led to the arrival of General Prem Tinsulanonda who gradually changed the political and economic situation in Thailand during the 1980s. The Prem period was marked by the rise of the elected politicians and of business groups and their representative organisations in national politics. Thai political life was much more open in the sense that the military and the bureaucracy were no longer the dominant political players. General Prem implemented economic reform policies aimed at moving the economy away from protectionism and domestic orientation to a more export-driven economy. This reform process did not go entirely smoothly, but a broad-based coalition among political and economic actors was formed on the basis that economic reform was needed. With this, Thailand experienced rapid economic growth from the mid 1980s and eventually attained the status of a "second generation" newly industrialising country (NIC) in the Southeast Asian region.

After Chatichai Choonhavan won the general election of 1988 the domination of the military and the bureaucracy was dismantled by transferring the policy-making process to the hands of elected politicians. More importantly, the Chatichai government also liberalised Thai politics by allowing non-bureaucratic forces to exercise their rights freely. However, Thailand's road to democracy was interrupted when the military launched a coup in 1991. From 1991 until 1992 an intense power struggle between pro-democracy and pro-military camps brought regime changes, political protests, and two general elections. This political struggle was finally won by the pro-democracy camp, which then contributed to the consolidation of parliamentary democracy, which has taken place in Thailand since 1992. Thailand's political and economic progress had positive and negative outcomes. The return of parliamentary democracy widened the gap between Bangkok-based and province-based elected politicians, and increased corruption activities and vote buying. As the power of elected politicians increased, the Thai military, bureaucracy and technocrats were gradually sidelined. The 1990s saw the birth of a civil society in which independent organisations encompassing business, NGOs, unions, the media, environment groups and others began to influence policy-making. It is in this sense that Thai political life has become increasingly "pluralist". Without doubt, Thailand in the 1990s became more open and sophisticated both politically and economically. But this created a situation in which the country was more vulnerable to the changes in the global economy. The following chapter will examine in greater detail how globalisation took place in Thailand and its implications for the domestic economy and politics.

Notes

[1] On the Bowring Treaty, see Suehiro Akira, *Capital Accumulation on Thailand, 1885-1985* (Tokyo: The Centre of East Asian Cultural Studies, 1989), chapter two.

[2] Pasuk Phongpaichit and Chris Baker, *Thailand, Economy and Politics* (Singapore: Oxford University Press, 1997), p. 99; also Kevin Hewison, "The Development of Industrial Capital and Its Situation in the 1980s", in Kevin Hewison (ed.) *Power and Politics in Thailand: Essays in Political Economy* (Manila: Journal of Contemporary Asia Publishers, 1989), p. 145.

[3] On the origins of the Sakdina society in Thailand, see Kevin Hewison, *Bankers and Bureaucrats, Capital and the Role of the State in Thailand* (New Heaven: Yale University Southeast Asian Studies, 1989), especially chapter two; Chattip Nartsupha, Suthy Prasartset, and Montri Chenvidyakarn, *The Political Economy of Siam 1910-1932* (Bangkok: The Social Science Association of Thailand, 1981); and also Benjamin A. Batson, *The End of Absolute Monarchy in Siam* (Singapore: Oxford University Press, 1984).

[4] John Girling, *Thailand, Society and Politics* (Ithaca and London: Cornell University Press, 1981), pp. 62-63.

[5] During this time, the Privy Purse Bureau (PPB) managed the economic activities of the Royal family as had been the case since the early Nineteenth century. Pasuk and Baker, *op.cit*, pp. 104-105.

[6] Batson, pp. 8-9.

[7] The first British economic adviser to be appointed by King Chulalongkorn in 1896 was Mr. Mitchel Innes. The tradition of appointing British economic advisers continued until the Second World War and in many ways influenced the establishment of monetary conservatism in the government's financial institutions. See T. H. Silcock, "Money and Banking" in T. H. Silcock (ed.) *Thailand, Social and Economic Studies in Development* (Canberra: Australian National University Press, 1967), p. 171. On the origins of Thailand's economic policies, see Ian Brown, *The Elite and the Economy in Siam, c. 1890-1920* (Singapore: Oxford University Press, 1988).

[8] For a good study of the evolution of Thai financial institutions, see James C. Ingram, *Economic Change in Thailand 1850-1970* (Stanford: Stanford University Press, 1971).

[9] Richard Doner and Daniel Unger, "The Politics of Finance in Thai Economic Development" in Stephan Haggard, Chung H. Lee and Sylvia Maxfield (eds.) *The Politics of Finance in Developing Countries* (Ithaca and London: Cornell University Press, 1993), p. 96.

[10] Doner and Unger, ibid, p. 96; and Pasuk and Baker, *Thailand, Economy and Politics*, p. 105.

[11] Pasuk and Baker, pp. 250-251.

[12] On the origins of the 1932 coup in Thailand, can be found in Batson, *The End of Absolute Monarchy in Siam*, especially chapter seven.

[13] On the Phibun period and his economic policies, see Kobkua Suwannathat-Pian, *Thailand's Durable Premier, Phibun through Three Decades 1932-1957* (Kuala Lumpur: Oxford University Press, 1995).

[14] Kewin Hewison, *Bankers and Bureaucrats*, pp. 72-73.

[15] Doner and Unger, " The Politics of Finance", p. 100.

[16] Girling, *Thailand, Society and Politics*, pp. 111-112.

[17] On US-Thailand relations, see Robert J. Muscat, *Thailand and the United States, Development, Security, and Foreign Aid* (New York: Columbia University, 1990), especially chapter two.

[18] Pasuk and Baker, *Thailand, Economy and Politics*, p. 125.

[19] Ibid, p. 137.

[20] For further discussion about the "bureaucratic polity" in Thailand, see Fred W. Riggs, *Thailand, The Modernization of a Bureaucratic Polity* (Honolulu: East-West Center Press, 1966), especially chapter ten.

[21] Hewison, "The Industrial Capital", p. 149.

[22] As quoted in Pasuk and Baker, *Thailand, Economy and Politics*, p. 129.

[23] Hewison, *op.cit*, pp. 149-150.

[24] Pasuk and Baker, *op.cit*, p. 131.

[25] Kesorn Chantarapootirat, *Thai Export-Oriented Growth Performace and Industrial Development*, unpublished Ph.D thesis (Fordham University, 1991), pp. 128-131.

[26] Pasuk and Baker, *Thailand, Economy and Politics*, pp. 144-145.

[27] Ibid, pp. 192-193.

[28] On the nature of the democratic period in Thailand (1973-1976), see David Morell and Chai-anan Samudavanija, *Political Conflict in Thailand, Reform, Reaction, Revolution* (Cambridge: Oelgeschlager, Gunn and Hain Publishers Inc., 1981).

[29] Anek Laothamatas, *Business Associations and the New Political Economy of Thailand, From Bureaucratic Polity to Liberal Corporatism* (Boulder and Singapore: Westview Press and Institute of Southeast Asian Studies, 1992), pp. 34-35.

[30] James S. Ockey, *Business Leaders, Gangsters, and the Middle Class: Societal Groups and Civilian Rule in Thailand*, unpublished Ph.D thesis (Ithaca: Cornell University, 1992), pp. 204-205.

[31] Anek, pp. 36-37.

[32] Pasuk and Baker, *Thailand, Economy and Politics*, p. 147.

[33] Ansil Ramsay, "Thailand 1979: A Government in Trouble", *Asian Survey*, vol. xx, no. 2 (February 1980), p. 114.

[34] Girling, *Thailand, Society and Politics*, p. 225.

[35] On military factionalism in Thailand during the 1980s, see Chai-anan Samudavanija, *The Thai Young Turks* (Singapore: Institute of Southeast Asian Studies, 1982).

[36] In 1981 the baht was devalued by 1.07 per cent (in April) and again by 8.7 per cent (in July), by 14.7 per cent in November 1984 and then over by 20 per cent in 1985 and 1987. See Pasuk Phongpaicit, "Technocrats, Businessmen, and Generals: Democracy and Economic Policy-Making in Thailand" in Andrew MacIntyre and Kanishka Jayasuriya (eds.) *The Dynamics of Economic Policy Reform in South-east and the South-west Pacific* (Singapore: Oxford University Press, 1992), p. 21.

[37] Pasuk and Baker, *Thailand, Economy and Politics*, p. 153.

[38] Ibid, p. 156.

[39] Clark D. Neher, "Thailand in 1987, Semi-Successful, Semi-Democracy", *Asian Survey*, vol. xxviii, no. 2 (February 1988), p. 200.

[40] Anek Laothamtas, "From Clientelism to Partnership: Business-Government Relations in Thailand", in Andrew MacIntyre (ed.) *Business and Government in Industrialising Asia* (Sydney: Allen and Unwin, 1994), pp. 204-205.

[41] Patcharee Siroros and Sylvia Maxfield, "The Politics of Central Bank in Thailand", a paper presented for *the Annual Meeting of the Association for Asian Studies*, Washington D.C., 2-5 April 1992, pp. 16-17.

[42] Silcock, "Money and Banking", p. 174; also see G. A. Marzouk, *Economic Development and Policies, Case Study of Thailand* (Rotterdam: Rotterdam University Press, 1972), pp. 375-376.

[43] Patcharee and Maxfield, pp. 22-25.

[44] Yoshihara Kunio, *The Nation and Economic Growth, The Philippines and Thailand* (Singapore: Oxford University Press, 1994), pp. 75-76; also Patchare and Maxfield, pp. 25-26.

[45] Doner and Unger, "The Politics of Finance", pp. 108-109; and Patcharee and Maxfield, "The Politics of Central Bank", pp. 30-31.

[46] On the role of Thai technocrats in Thailand, see Robert S. Muscat, *The Fifth Tiger, A Study of Thai Development Policy* (New York: United Nations University Press, 1994), especially chapter six.

[47] Johannes Drasgbaek Schmidt, "Paternalism and Planning in Thailand: Facilitating Growth without Social Benefits", in Michael J. G. Parnwell (ed.) *Uneven Development in Thailand* (Aldershot: Avebury Publishing Ltd., 1996), p. 72.

[48] Chai-anan Samudavanija, Thailand, "Economic Policy-Making in a Liberal Technocratic Polity" in John W. Langford and K. Lorne Brownsey (eds.) *Economic Policy-Making in the Asia-Pacific Region* (Halifax: The Institute for Research on Public Policy, 1990), p. 197.

[49] Anek Laothamatas, "The Politics of Structural Adjustment in Thailand: A Political Explanation of Economic Success" in Andrew MacIntyre and Kanishka Jayasuriya (eds.) *The Dynamics of Economic Policy Reform in South-east Asia and the South-west Pacific* (Singapore: Oxford University Press, 1992), pp. 32-49.

[50] Tienhcai Wongchaisuwan, *The Political Economy of Thailand: The Thai Peripheral State, 1958-1988*, unpublished Ph.D thesis (Binghamton: State University of New York, 1993), pp. 333-335.

[51] Pasuk, "Technocrats, Businessman, and Generals", pp. 13-14.

[52] According to Riggs there were at least three factions within the Thai military elite: the Phin-Phao faction, the Sarit faction, and the Phibun faction. Further dicussion on factional politics in Thailand during the 1950s, can be found in Fred Riggs, *Thailand, The Modernization of a Bureaucratic Polity* (Honolulu: University of Hawaii Press, 1966), especially chapter eight.

[53] Maxfield and Patcharee, "The Politics of Central Bank in Thailand", pp. 27-28.

[54] Akira Suehiro, "Capitalist Development in Postwar Thailand: Commercial Bankers, Industrial Elite, and Agribusiness Groups", in Ruth McVey (ed.) *Southeast Asian Capitalists* (Ithaca: Southeast Asia Program, 1992), pp. 45-47; and also in David L. Elliott, *Thailand: Origins of Military Rule* (London: Zed Press Ltd., 1978), p. 121.

[55] Kunio Yoshihara, *The Rise of Ersatz Capitalism in Southeast Asia* (Singapore: Oxford University Press, 1987).

[56] Daniel Unger, "Government and Business in Thailand" in Young C. Kim (ed.) *The Southeast Asian Economic Miracle* (New Brunswick and London: Transaction Publishers, 1995), pp. 149-150.

[57] Kevin Hewison, "National Interests and Economic Downturn: Thailand", in Richard Robison, Kevin Hewison, and Richard Higgott (eds.) *Southeast Asia in the 1980s: The Politics of Economic Crisis* (Sydney: Allen and Unwin, 1987), pp. 71-75.

[58] Anek, *Business Associations and the New Political Economy of Thailand*, especially chapter four; and also Chai-anan Samudavanija and Sukhumband Paribatra, "Thailand: Liberalization without Democracy" in James W. Morley (ed.) *Driven by Growth, Political Change in the Asia-Pacific Region* (London and New York: M.E. Sharpe, 1993), pp. 138-139.

[59] Jamie Mackie, "Changing Patterns of Chinese Big Business in Southeast Asia" in Ruth McVey (ed.) *Southeast Asian Capitalists* (Ithaca: Southeast Asia Program, Cornell University, 1992), pp. 176-178.

[60] Pasuk and Baker, *Thailand, Economy and Politics, p. 126*; and also Muscat, *Thailand and the United States*, p. 37.

[61] Pasuk and Baker, p. 128; also on the origins of the NEDB, see Robert J. Muscat, *Development Strategy in Thailand, A Study of Economic Growth* (New York: Frederick A. Praeger, Publishers, 1966), pp. 282-283.

[62] Hewison, *Bankers and Bureaucrats*, especially chapter six.

[63] The writer visited Thailand in mid-July 1988, and in November-December 1989, and finally lived there from 1990-1991, and experienced the political and economic dynamics in Thailand during the Chatichai government. Also see Surin Maisrikrod, "The Making of Thai Democracy, A Study of Political

Alliances Among the State, the Capitalists, and the Middle Class" in Anek Laothamatas (ed.) *Democratization in Southeast and East Asia* (Singapore: Institute of Southeast Asian Studies, 1997), pp. 159-163.

[64] Chatichai himself held two positions, Prime Minister and Minister of Defence. Praman, Chatichai's brother-in-law was appointed Minister of Interior, Pramuan Sabhavasu Minister of Finance, and Montree Pongpanich Minister of Transport and Communications. See Pasuk and Baker, *Thailand, Economy and Politics*, p. 349.

[65] These leaders are General Sunthorn Kongsompong, General Suchinda Kaprayoon, Admiral Praphat Krisanachan, Air Chief Marshal Kaset Rojananil and General Issarapong Noonpakdi. For further discussion on the military coup in 1991, see Kevin Hewison, "Of Regimes, State and Pluralities: Thai Politics enters the 1990s" in Kevin Hewison, Richard Robison and Garry Rodan (eds.) *Southeast Asia in the 1990s, Authoritarianism, Democracy and Capitalism* (Sydney: Allen and Unwin, 1993), pp. 61-189.

[66] The military also accused many politicians in the Chatichai cabinet of involvment in corruption activities and of being linked to various the so-called "dark influences". See Suchit Bunbongkarn, "Thailand in 1991, Coping with the Military Guardianship", *Asian Survey*, vol. xxxii, no. 2 (February 1992), p. 132.

[67] Pasuk and Baker, *Thailand, Economy and Politics*, p. 356.

[68] Ananya Bhuchongkul, "Thailand in 1991, The Return of the Military" in *Southeast Asian Affairs 1992* (Singapore: Institute of Southeast Asian Studies, 1992), pp. 327-329.

[69] See David Murray, *Angels and Devils, Thai Politics from February 1991 to September 1992 – A Struggle for Democracy* (Bangkok: White Orchid Press, 1996), pp. 68-84.

[70] Suchit Bunbongkarn, "Thailand in 1992, In Search of a Democratic Order", *Asian Survey*, vol. xxxiii, no. 2 (February 1993), p. 219.

[71] For details of the political developments in Thailand during the May 1992 uprising, see Murray, especially chapter six; and for a Left perspective, see Ji Ungpakorn, *The Struggle for Democracy and Social Justice in Thailand* (Bangkok: Arom Pongpangan Foundation, 1997).

[72] Murray, p. 166.

[73] Surin Maisrikrod, *Thailand's Two General Elections in 1992, Democracy Sustained* (Singapore: Institute of Southeast Asian Studies, 1992), pp. 44-45.

[74] Interview with Ji Ungpakorn, Bangkok, 11 November 1997.

[75] On the dynamics of the Thai electoral process in the 1980s and the 1990, see, Suchit Bunbongkarn, "Elections and Democratization in Thailand" in Robert H. Taylor (ed.) *The Politics of Elections in Southeast Asia* (New York and Melbourne: The Woodrow Wilson Centre Press and Cambridge University Press, 1996), pp. 184-200.

[76] Clark D. Neher, "The Transition to Democracy in Thailand, *Asian Perspective*, vol. 20, no. 2 (Fall-Winter 1996), pp. 316-317.

[77] Interview with Dr. Anek Laothamatas, Bangkok, 28 October 1997.

[78] Pasuk Phongpaichit and Sungsidh Piriyarangsan, *Corruption and Democracy in Thailand* (Bangkok: Silkworm Books, 1994), pp. 44-45.

[79] Ibid, p. 54; and for the origins of corruption in Thai politics, see James Ockey, "Political Parties, Factions, and Corruption in Thailand", *Modern Asian Studies*, vol. 28, no. 2 (1994), pp. 251-277.

[80] Daniel E. King, "Thailand in 1996, Economic Slowdown Clouds Year", *Asian Survey*, vol. xxxvii, no.2 (February 1997), p. 161.

[81] Scott R. Christensen, *Coalitions and Collective Choice: The Politics of Institutional Change in Thai Agriculture*, unpublished Ph.D thesis, The University of Wisconsin-Madison, 1993, pp. 95-96.

[82] Interview with Ji Ungpakorn, Bangkok, 11 November 1997.

[83] Pasuk and Baker, *Thailand, Economy and Politics*, p. 351.

[84] For further discussion on the role of the Thai military in the 1990s, see Chai-Anan Samudavanija, "Old Soldiers Never Die, They are just Bypassed: The Military, Bureaucracy and Globalisation" in Kevin Hewison (ed.) *Political Change in Thailand, Democracy and Participation* (London and New York: Routledge, 1997), pp. 42-57.

[85] Neher, "The Transition to Democracy in Thailand", pp. 319.

[86] Pasuk and Baker, *Thailand, Economy and Politics*, especially chapter eleven.

[87] According to an official source there are many business/trade associations in various industries established in Thailand, but only three of them are actively involved in the Parliament's joint standing committee on banking, commerce and industry.   These are the Thai Bankers' Association, the Board of Trade of Thailand, and the Federation of Thai Industries.   *Thailand Government Office* (Bangkok: Alpha Research Co. Ltd., 1996).

[88] Murray, *Angels and Devils*, pp. 141.

[89] According to Paul Handley, a journalist with the *Far Eastern Economic Review*, several groups dominate the business activities in the Bangkok Stock Exchange; these are the Business Management Services (BMS) group comprising a small group of foreign-trained economists, bankers, academics and senior bureaucrats; the Pairoj group (led by Pairoj Piempongsam), a small group of business figures mostly involved in real estate and the property sector; the Shinawatra group (led by telecommunications tycoon Thaksin Shinawatra); and the Song Vatcharasriroj and Group 16 led by Newin Chidchob and Suchart Tancharoen, who are both close to the Chart Pattana Party. See, Paul Handley, "More of the Same?, Politics and Business, 1987-96", in Kevin Hewison (ed.) *Political Change in Thailand, Democracy and Participation* (London and New York: Routledge, 1997), pp. 94-113.

[90] Interview with Anek Laothamatas, Bangkok, 28 October 1997; and also see Surin, *Thailand's Two General Elections in 1992*, pp. 38-39.

[91] Thitinan Pongsudhirak, "Thailand's Media, Whose Watchdog?" in Kevin Hewison (ed.) *Political Change in Thailand, Democracy and Participation* (London and New York: Routledge, 1997), pp. 217-232.

[92] Murray, *Angels and Devils*, pp. 60-61.

[93] Pasuk and Baker, *Thailand, Economy and Politics*, pp. 372-373.

[94] Murray, pp. 143-145.

[95] Thitinan Pongsudhirak, *op.cit*, p. 224.

[96] Ibid, pp. 224-226.

[97] Pasuk and Baker, *Thailand, Economy and Politics*, pp. 384-385.

[98] Prudhisan Jumbala and Maneerat Mitprasat, "Non-Governmental Development Organizations: Empowerment and Environment" in Kevin Hewison (ed.) *Political Change in Thailand, Democracy and Participation* (London and New York: Routledge, 1997), pp. 198-199; and also see Benedict Anderson, "Murder and Progress in Modern Siam" in Benedict Anderson, *The Spectre of Comparisons, Nationalism, Southeast Asia and the World* (London and New York: Verso, 1998), 185-186.

[99] Pasuk and Baker, pp. 313-314.

[100] On the origins of the NGO movement in Thailand, see Suthy Prasartset, "The Rise of NGOs as Critical Social Movement in Thailand", in *Thai NGOs: The Continuing Struggle for Democracy* (Bangkok: Thai NGO Support Project, 1995), pp. 97-134.

[101] On the downfall of General Suchinda, see Murray, *Angels and Devils*, 1996, especially chapter six.

[102] Prudhisan and Maneerat, *op.cit*, p. 207.

[103] "Assembly of the Poor: Down to the finer details", *Thai Development Newsletter*, No. 32, January-June 1997, pp. 2-3.

[104] Prudhisan and Maneerat, "Non-Governmental Development Organizations", p. 202.

[105] Phillip Hirch, "The Politics of Environment, Opposition and Legitimacy" in Kevin Hewison (ed.) *Political Change in Thailand, Democracy and Participation* (London and New York: Routledge, 1997), pp. 182-183; and for the origins of the environmental movement in Thailand, see Philip Hirch, *Political Economy of Environment in Thailand* (Manila: Journal of Contemporary Asia Publishers, 1993).

[106] Pasuk and Baker, *Thailand, Economy and Politics*, pp. 390-391.

[107] Kevin Hewison, "Political Oppositions and Regime Change in Thailand" in Garry Rodan (ed.) *Political Oppositions in Industrialising Asia* (London and New York: Routledge 1996) pp. 76-77; and on the origins of the Confederation for Democracy, see Duncan McCargo, *Chamlong Srimuang and the New Thai Politics* (London: Hurst and Company, 1997), pp. 255-257.

[108] Kevin Hewison, "Of Regimes, State and Pluralities: Thai Politics Enters the 1990s" in Kevin Hewison, Richard Robison and Garry Rodan (eds.) *Southeast*

Asia in the 1990s, Authoritarianism, Democracy and Capitalism (Sydney: Allen and Unwin), 1993, p. 177.

[109] Pasuk and Baker, *Thailand, Economy and Politics*, pp. 187-188.

[110] According to an official source, there were 501 strikes with more than 100,000 workers involved in 1973, while the numbers decreased to 357 strikes in 1974, 241 in 1975, and 133 in 1976. Pasuk and Baker, p. 193.

[111] Ibid, p. 203.

[112] Somsak Kosaisuk, the leader of the Railway Workers Union was one of the executive members of the Confederation for Democracy. See Ji Ungpakorn, *The Struggle for Democracy and Social Justice in Thailand*, p. 111.

[113] Pasuk Phongpaichit, "Among Dragons, Geese and Tigers: the Thai Economy in Global and Local Perspective", a paper presented to *the 6th International Conference on Thai Studies*, Chiang Mai, Thailand, 14-17 October 1996.

[114] This is similar to Malaysia's Vision 2020 advocated by Prime Minister Mahathir Mohammad. Ibid.

[115] Ibid.

Chapter Four

Thailand's Crisis

This chapter examines the interplay between globalisation and domestic politics in Thailand during the 1990s, in particular the causes and consequences of the economic crisis that occurred in 1997. It begins by looking closely at recent efforts by Thai policy makers to liberalise the Thai financial sector and their contribution to the performance of the Thai economy. Then it examines the failure of these economic policy makers under previous coalition governments to come up with credible policies in responding to the early signs of deterioration in the Thai economy. Finally it analyses the power struggles which occurred among political players before and after the decision to implement the free-float exchange rate policy on 2 July 1997 and the impact of the economic crisis on the collapse of the Chaovalit coalition government in November 1997.

Causes of the Crisis

Financial Liberalisation and its Impact

Historically Thailand's financial sector was highly regulated and protected from foreign competition.[1] There are only eight major financial institutions established in Thailand: banks; finance, securities and credit companies; specialised banks; development finance corporations; the stock exchange; insurance companies; saving cooperatives and mortgage institutions.[2] In 1990 just 29 commercial banks controlled about 71 per cent of the total financial assets in Thailand, and only the "big four" banks (Bangkok Bank, the Siam Commercial Bank, the Thai Farmers' Bank, and the Krung Thai Bank) dominated the interbank loan market and other financial transactions in the financial sector.[3]

The first effort to liberalise this sector was made after the financial crisis in 1983 when about 24 financial institutions were forced to close their operations.[4] As Thailand's financial sector opened up to foreign investors, the demand for foreign capital also increased. In the early 1990s the Ministry of Finance (MOF) and the Bank of Thailand (BOT) came up with a three-year plan for financial liberalisation. Among other things, it liberalised the ceilings on interest rates, signed Article VIII of the International Monetary Agreement which eased restrictions on capital inflows and international payments with respect to current-account transactions, promoted new financial institutions and services, adopted the guidelines from the Bank for International Settlements (BIS) on capital adequacy ratio (CAR), signed the ASEAN Free Trade Agreement (AFTA) and General Agreement on Tariffs and Trade (GATT) agreements, and improved supervision and regulatory measures in the financial sector.[5]

Under the Anand caretaker government in 1991, the BOT liberalised foreign-exchange transactions such as repatriation of investment funds, dividends and profits without prior authorisation.[6] Under the Chuan Leekpai coalition government, Thailand's financial sector was liberalised further. In 1992 the Securities and Exchange Act was enacted and was followed by the establishment of the Stock Exchange of Thailand (SET). In order to invite more foreign capital into Thailand, the BOT established an offshore banking institution, the Bangkok International Banking Facilities (BIBF), in 1993. This latter policy was very important because it contributed to the increase of capital outflows, which was needed to fuel economic growth in Thailand. The idea of establishing the BIBF came up in 1990, the aim being to make Thailand a financial market centre that could facilitate the flow of capital into neighbouring countries such as Vietnam, Cambodia, Laos and Burma.[7] In the early stages, the BOT granted BIBF licences to 47 commercial banks, comprising 15 domestic banks, 12 foreign bank branches already based in Thailand and 20 new foreign banks. With these licences, the banks were given many privileges, such as tax exemption, and they were allowed to take deposits in foreign currencies, to lend in foreign currencies to both residents and non-residents, and, more importantly, to engage in cross-currency foreign-exchange trading.[8] Then in 1995 the BOT granted another 37 licences to the Provincial International Banking Facilities (PIBF) to increase the flow of foreign capital into the provincial areas of Thailand.

The impact of the establishment of the BIBF and the PIBF facilities upon the Thai economy was enormous. First of all, there was a rapid increase in capital inflow into Thailand. According to a Bank of Thailand study, from 1990 until 1995 the average growth of capital inflow was about 10 per cent of the gross of domestic products (GDP).[9] During the early 1990s Thailand was an emerging market, which attracted foreign banks or financial institutions to lend their money. The BIBF facilitated the flow of foreign capital into Thailand.[10] More importantly, borrowing money through the BIBF was very popular among Thai companies because through the BIBF they could obtain loans at low rates of interest (about four to six per cent below interest rates offered by domestic banks).[11]

The rapid increase of foreign capital also resulted in an increase in the current account deficit from 5.1 per cent in 1993 to 8.1 per cent of the GDP in 1995.[12] The current account is calculated from the trade in goods and services. The current account deficit showed that Thailand was importing more goods and services than it was exporting. Therefore, the gap would need to be filled by borrowing foreign capital.[13] In theory, there is nothing wrong with a current account deficit if foreign capital is invested in an export-driven sector. But this is not always the case. In Thailand, foreign capital (much of it channelled through the BIBF) was generally invested in the property sector, which from 1994 enjoyed a boom period. The property boom in Thailand encouraged huge amounts of investment, but two years later it became clear that this sector was oversupplied.

In other words, too much money had been spent on the construction of office buildings, apartments, condominiums, and shopping malls, only a few of which were actually sold.[14] Consequently, many property companies in Thailand could not repay their loans (which were mostly in US dollars), or were forced to stop or delay their investments in the property sector.[15] Evidence of the collapse of the property sector was seen clearly in 1997. Numerous high-rise buildings scattered around the business districts such as Silom, Siam Square, and Sukhumvit were vacant.[16]

Table 4.1 Thailand's Economic Fundamentals (annual percentage growth)

	1991	1992	1993	1994	1995	1996
GDP	8.5	8.1	8.3	8.8	8.6	5.5
Exports	23.5	13.1	13	21.3	23.6	-1.3
Inflation	5.7	4.1	3.3	5	5.8	5.8
Investment (% GDP)	42.7	40	40.4	41.2	42.9	41.7
Saving (% GDP)	34.4	34.4	34.5	35.6	34.8	33.7
Fiscal surplus (% GDP)	4.9	3	2.2	1.8	2.7	2.3
Current account (% GDP)	-7.7	-5.7	-5.1	-5.6	-8.1	-14.4
Exchange rate (baht/US$)	25.5	25.4	25.3	25.1	24.9	25.3
Official reserves (US$ bn)	18.4	21.2	25.4	30.3	36.9	38.7

Sources: Bank of Thailand, *Annual Economic Report 1996* (Bangkok: Bank of Thailand, 1997) and Asia Pacific Economies Group, *Asia Pacific Profiles 1998, Overview* (Singapore: Financial Times, 1998).

Nonetheless, in 1995 the current account deficit had not reached a point that could erode confidence in the Thai economy. The policy makers believed that Thailand's economic fundamentals were performing very well and that concern about the current account deficit could be minimised by looking at positive indicators such as low inflation, high investment and reasonably good domestic saving (Table 4.1).[17]   But this optimism was short-lived as, by 1996 Thai exports began to drop dramatically as they lost their competitiveness in the international market (Table 4.2).[18]

Table 4.2 Commodity Structure of Thailand's Export Slow-down

	1994	*1995*	*1996*
Total exports (million baht)	1,137,602	1,406,310	1,401,392
Growth rate (%)	20.9	23.6	-0.35
Computers and parts	44.9	38.7	31.3
Garments	12.4	1.3	-21.9
Rubber	43.3	46.5	1.4
Integrated circuits	27.5	28.4	3.4
Gems and jewellery	8.3	11.5	8.4
Rice	18.9	24.1	8.4
Sugar	41.2	67.2	11.7
Frozen shrimps	29.9	2.3	-17.8
Televisions and parts	26.2	12.7	14.1
Shoes and parts	40.5	37	-40.9
Canned seafood	24.7	4.1	-0.3
Air conditioners and parts	62.1	49.6	33.6
Plastic products	-29.1	102.2	51.4
Tapioca products	-13.6	-2.8	16.7
Textiles	4.5	22.1	-4.4

Source: As quoted from *Bangkok Post Year-end Economic Review*, December 1996 in Peter G. Warr, "The Thai Economy: From Boom to Gloom?", *Southeast Asian Affairs 1997* (Singapore: Institute of Southeast Asian Studies, 1997), p. 320.

The sharp rise in capital inflow also increased the external debt of Thailand. By the end of 1996, the total external debt was about US$ 79.1 billion. About 78.9 per cent of this was in US dollars and 17.8 per cent in Japanese yen.[19] Private debt amounted to US$62.3 billion, half of which was the BIBF's short-term debt (US$31.2 billion).[20] It must be noted here that short-term debt usually has a maturity of one year or less. Therefore in that year the BIBF's short-term debt actually reached about 44 per cent of the total external debt of Thailand. Despite the fact that the BOT did not regard this situation as critical, observers were concerned that the high level of short-term debt could cause serious problems in the financial market and potentially make Thailand more vulnerable to external shock and sudden capital outflow (Figure 4.1 and Figure 4.2).[21]

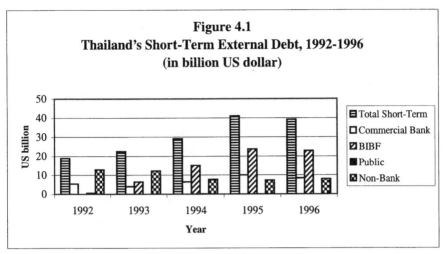

Figure 4.1
Thailand's Short-Term External Debt, 1992-1996
(in billion US dollar)

Source: Bank of Thailand, *Annual Economic Report 1996* (Bangkok: Bank of Thailand, 1997).

Source: Bank of Thailand, *Annual Economic Report 1996* (Bangkok: Bank of Thailand, 1997).

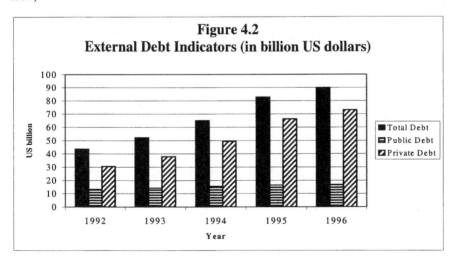

Figure 4.2
External Debt Indicators (in billion US dollars)

The Decline of the Thai Technocracy

It was becoming clear that with the increase in capital inflow into Thailand, the BOT was under pressure to review its own exchange-rate management. For decades the BOT had been known to preserve monetary conservatism and uphold its autonomy, by avoiding the use of the exchange rate as an instrument of discretionary macroeconomic management.[22] From the 1950s until the early 1980s the baht was fixed to the US dollar at the level of 20 baht/US dollar. But when Thailand experienced a balance of payments crisis in the 1980s, the BOT was forced to devalue the baht several times. And in 1984 the BOT adopted the managed float and the baht was fixed to the US dollar.[23] With this type of exchange rate management (at levels between 24-27 baht/US dollar) the BOT was effectively able to monitor the movement of foreign capital entering Thailand and was therefore also able to control the domestic money supply.

With the increase in capital inflow, however, the BOT began to lose its capacity to manage the domestic money supply, especially with the fixed exchange rate policy. When the baht was overvalued, the BOT had two options: one was to float the currency, and the other was to impose restrictions on the flow of foreign capital coming into Thailand.[24] It seems the BOT preferred the latter option. In 1996, the BOT imposed new measures on Thailand's financial institutions. They were required to deposit 7 per cent of reserve requirement on new short-term foreign liabilities and non-resident deposits with maturity of less than one year, and to increase the capital adequacy ratio (CAR) requirements for both domestic banks (from 8% to 8.5%) and foreign banks (from 6.75% to 7.5%).[25] However, these measures did not help at all. The decision not to float the baht as early as 1996 created problems domestically and Ammar Siamwalla, a well-known Thai economist, has subsequently argued that this was the biggest policy error ever made by the BOT.[26]

The question, then, is why the BOT failed to come up with better policy in respect to exchange rate management? To answer this we must look at the factors that contributed to the decline of the Thai technocracy and the independence of the BOT in the economic policy-making process in the 1990s. As already discussed in the previous chapter, from the Sarit period in the 1960s until the Prem period in the 1980s, the technocrats played an important role in overseeing economic policy in Thailand. When Thailand experienced an economic boom at the end of the 1980s, many talented and respected technocrats who had worked in these institutions moved into the private sector.[27] This left the government with a lack of capable technocrats and the Thai technocrats lost its influence, although did not necessarily disappear from political scenes. The rise of parliamentary democracy also contributed to the decline of the Thai technocracy, particularly during the Chatichai period from 1988 until 1991.

Soon after Chatichai Choonhavan gained the premiership, he appointed elected politicians to all ministerial portfolios. Chatichai also downgraded the NESDB (National Economic, Social and Development Board) position from an overseeing and formulating economic policy-making institution to an advisory body and he shifted the policy-making processes away from the technocrats.[28] Other important institutions like the BOT, and the Finance Department's Fiscal Policy Office (FPO) became less powerful and were replaced by Chatichai's own policy think-tank known as Phitsanulok House (*Ban Phitsanulok*) led by Phansak Vinyaratna, a veteran journalist, and Kraisak Choonhavan, Chatichai's son and an academic.[29]

When the Chatichai coalition government was overthrown by a military coup in 1991, the power of the Thai technocrats was briefly restored under the caretaker Prime Minister Anand Panyarachun. Some prominent technocrats were given important economic portfolios in the cabinet. For instance, Dr. Snoh Unakul, a former head of the NESDB and governor of the BOT, was appointed Deputy Prime Minister, Dr. Amaret Sila-on, a former executive president of Siam Cement, was appointed Minister of Commerce, and Dr. Virabongsa Ramangkura, was appointed Deputy Finance Minister. The Anand government was built on a coalition of military, technocrats and businesspeople, which in some ways reflected the type of coalition that was in power in the Prem government.

Nonetheless, the influence of the Thai technocracy was gradually eroded after Chuan Leekpai was elected Prime Minister in the September 1992 general election. As elected politicians regained power, they occupied all ministerial positions again, and the technocrats were pushed aside again from the economic policy-making process. Since then the technocrats have only exercised influence by joining the government or by setting up their own political parties. Evidence of the decline of the Thai technocracy can also be found in the erosion of the independence of the BOT from political interference.[30] In the past, the independence of the BOT was strong, but as elected politicians gained more power throughout the 1990s, the BOT was less insulated and their policies became subject to political interference from various government leaders. For instance, the independence of the BOT suffered under the leadership of Governor Vijit Supinit (1988-1995), who was known to be close to several leaders of the Chart Thai Party.[31] It was during Vijit's governorship that the BOT failed to change the exchange-rate policy to favour flexibility with the rapid change in capital inflow into the Thai economy in the 1990s.[32]

All of those factors, in various ways, created a crisis of confidence in the Thai economy. It was revealed in 1996 that several key sectors, such as property and heavy industries, were in trouble because of over-investment.[33] The crisis of confidence deepened with the fact that the Thai baht was becoming overvalued as a result of the strengthening of the US dollar against other currencies after 1992. The weakening of the baht made it hard for Thai companies to repay their loans in US dollars or other international currencies. However, since the baht remained fixed to the US dollar, many Thai borrowers felt that they were still safe. But this was a false sense of security, based on a belief that the fixed exchange-rate policy would remain in place. As the baht was overvalued, rumours of devaluation began to spread, deepening the existing crisis of confidence.[34] Clear indications of this were evident throughout 1996 when the stock market index and the baht plummeted several times. In August 1996, the baht was under attack from money speculators and the BOT responded by widening the band of the baht-US$ exchange rates and by launching a direct intervention in the money market aiming to preserve the value of the baht at roughly 25 baht/US$.[35] In its initial response the BOT did not hesitate to use the international reserves which according to an official source were worth about 38.7 billion US$ at the end of 1996, to intervene in the money market when the baht lost value against other international currencies.[36] But this action proved too expensive because of the potential to dry up Thailand's international reserves.

In sum, the efforts by Thai policy makers to liberalise the financial sector in Thailand in the early 1990s changed the Thai economy. More and more foreign capital entered the country. This capital inflow helped Thailand to sustain its economic growth. However, this also increased Thailand's current account deficit and external debt, including its short-term debt. At the same time, the capacity of the Thai policy makers, particularly the technocrats, to respond to the new economic reality was under question. It seems that the failure of the BOT to come up with good policy in the area of the exchange rate and, and more specifically, their refusal to float the baht in 1996, contributed to the crisis of confidence among domestic and foreign investors.

Bad Politics under the Banharn Coalition Government

Politics under the Banharn coalition government in 1996 also worsened the economic situation, arguably contributing to the deepening crisis of confidence in Thailand. From July 1995 until November 1996, Thailand was governed by Prime Minister Banharn Silapa-archa, who was also the leader of the Chart Thai Party (CTP), one of the main political parties in

Thailand with a strong power base in the provincial areas. Banharn himself was formerly a successful businessperson in Supan Buri province. He became a politician in 1976 and was elected as the leader of the Chart Thai Party in 1994. From the beginning, the Banharn coalition government had image and legitimacy problems. This government consisted predominantly of elected politicians from provincial areas, many of whom were known to be involved in vote buying and "money politics" practices. Some elected politicians belonged to the so-called "dark influences" (*chao pho* or *itthipon muet*) meaning they were involved in legal and illegal business activities such as night clubs, gambling, drug trafficking, and alcohol in their respective provinces.[37] Banharn himself was known as "Mr ATM" (automatic teller machine) because of his wealth and his propensity to spend huge amounts of money during election campaigns.[38]

However, it must be pointed out that the Banharn coalition government was a product of the recent changes in Thai politics which had brought r·ore provincial politicians into power. As has already been explained at length in the previous chapter, provincial politicians started to enter the national parliament during the Prem period in the 1980s. They began to occupy ministerial positions after the return to parliamentary democracy, particularly with the arrival of the Chatichai coalition government in 1988. This continued into the early 1990s. In the view of Anek Laothamatas, Thai politics in the 1990s was "a tale of two democracies". By this he meant that the return of parliamentary democracy in Thailand had divided the Thai politicians and their voters between the Bangkok or urban-based politicians and the provincial politicians.[39] The Bangkok-based politicians and the urban voters usually aligned themselves with the Democrat Party and other small parties with a strong power base in Bangkok (the Palang Dharma, the Prachakorn Thai Party, and the Nam Thai Party, while the province-based politicians and the rural voters mainly belonged to the Chart Thai Party (especially in Central Thailand), the New Aspiration Party (mostly in Northeast Thailand), and the Social Action Party and the Chart Pattana Party.[40] It was in this political context that the domination of the province-based politicians in the Banharn coalition government made this government unpopular among the urban people of Bangkok.

During 1996 the performance of Prime Minister Banharn himself and his cabinet ministers was scrutinised and came under constant criticism from the opposition parties in the parliament, particularly the Democrat Party and the media which in many ways represented the views of the Bangkok middle class.[41] Serious criticism was made of the credibility of Finance Minister Surakiat Sathienthai, a former dean of the Faculty of Law at Chulalongkorn University. Surakiat was known to be close to Prime Minister Banharn and was nominated for the ministerial position by the Chart Thai Party. Although Surakiat promised to continue the implementation of the financial liberalisation policies which were initiated during the Chuan period, he failed to come up with the sound economic policies which were needed to deal with the problems caused by a more open financial sector. He was involved in a series of controversial moves that ruined his reputation as the Finance Minister and also played a part in generating public disillusion with the Banharn coalition government in 1996.[42]

However, the most serious setback for the Banharn coalition government occurred when the Bangkok Bank of Commerce (BBC), the eighth largest of Thailand's 15 commercial banks, collapsed in May 1996. In order to prevent further instability in the financial sector, the BOT quickly intervened and placed the BBC under the supervision of the government owned Krung Thai Bank. During parliamentary sessions after the collapse of the BBC, it was revealed that the BOT had been aware of the problem with the BBC since 1992, and that in 1994 the BBC was basically insolvent with a massive debt of bad loans worth about 80 billion baht ($US3.2 billion).[43] Most of these loans were invested in the real estate sector. It also appeared that the then BOT governor Vijit Supinit had known of the problem and did not try to prevent the collapse of the BBC. Instead, the BOT, through the Financial Institution Development Fund (FIDF), continued to inject funds worth about $US7 billion (based on the exchange rate in 1996) to rescue the BBC.[44]

But the political issues surrounding the collapse of the BBC raised the question of the independence of the BOT. The Thai media reported that it was believed that six members of the Chart Thai Party, including the then deputy Finance Minister, Newin Chidchob, had borrowed about 7 billion baht from the BBC and it was believed that the BOT's governor, Vijit Supinit, was under pressure from the Chart Thai Party and from the Finance Minister, Surakiat, who was a former executive president of the BBC, to bail out the BBC. It was also revealed that Surakiat had ignored warnings from the BOT about the violation of the Commercial Bank Act and unlawful practices of the BBC.[45]

The collapse of the BBC forced Prime Minister Banharn to reshuffle his cabinet at the end of May 1996 and in the reshuffle the Finance Minister Surakiat was replaced by Bodi Chunnananda, the head of the Bureau of Budget (BOB). In early July 1996 Rerngchai Marakanond, who also came from the BOT, replaced the BOT's governor, Vijit Supinit. With the replacement of both of them the independence of the most important economic policy-institutions, the MOF and the BOT suffered badly, particularly from the political interference of the parties in the government.[46] Moreover, the collapse of the BBC eroded the credibility of the Banharn coalition government which from the beginning had been riven with factionalism.[47] The reshuffle opened up the disunity within. The Palang Dharma Party, one of the minor parties in the coalition, left the government and joined the opposition in August 1996. But the most serious issue was the internal rivalry within the Chart Thai Party, between the Banharn faction and the Therd Thai faction led by Snoh Thienthong, the secretary general of the Chart Thai Party. The latter had threatened to withdraw from the Chart Thai Party after Prime Minister Banharn failed to give the Ministry of the Interior portfolio to Snoh following the cabinet reshuffle.[48] Later on, this rivalry caused the downfall of the Banharn coalition government after Snoh's *Therd Thai* faction decided to defect to the New Aspiration Party (NAP). This faction comprised about 40 MPs, mostly from provinces in Northeast Thailand. It was very powerful because it represented half of the Chart Thai Party in the parliament.[49]

The collapse of the BBC raised concerns among domestic and foreign investors. The American credit-rating agency Moody's Service Investor downgraded the rating of Thailand's short-term debt in September 1996 and the International Monetary Fund (IMF) made similar warnings about the Thai economy.[50] In the same month the Stock Exchange of Thailand Index fell significantly which again indicated the declining confidence of investors in Thailand.[51] Under these gloomy circumstances, some business groups, including the Board of Trade, and other leading figures in Thailand urged Prime Minister Banharn to resign immediately.[52] Finally when it was clear that Banharn could not survive politically with the defection of the *Therd Thai* faction and the withdrawal of support from the NAP, he had no other choice except to dissolve the parliament at the end of September 1996 and call for fresh general elections to be held on 17 November 1996.

In sum, it must be underlined that, under the Banharn coalition government, political problems became an obstacle to finding credible policies with which to respond to the side effects of financial liberalisation in Thailand. It has already been suggested that Prime Minister Banharn himself and his government failed to provide the political stability and credible economic policies which were needed in 1996 when the signs of trouble in the Thai economy began to emerge. The collapse of the BBC and its political and economic ramifications gradually deepened the crisis of confidence among domestic and foreign investors. The new government would have to deal with these political and economic legacies of the Banharn coalition government.

Responses to the Crisis

Internal Rivalries and Policy Inconsistencies under the Chaovalit Coalition Government

Two issues dominated the November 1996 general election in Thailand and every political party tried very hard to promote their views on these issues: good economic policy and political stability. In the lead-up to the polls, there was a tight contest between the Democrat Party (led by Chuan Leekpai) and the New Aspiration Party (led by Chaovalit Yongchaiyuth) to win the election. Both attempted to convince voters of their ability to solve the economic and political problems Thailand was experiencing. The Democrat Party offered capable and respected politicians who were well equipped to handle the economic issues, Dr. Supachai Panickpakdee and Dr. Tarrin Nimmanhaeminda. Both of them were former ministers in the Chuan cabinet of 1992-1995. Meanwhile, the NAP promised to form a so-called "dream team" that would oversee economic policy if the party won and proposed Dr. Amnuay Virawan, a respected economist and a former deputy prime minister of the Banharn government, to lead this team.[53]

Soon after the counting of votes began, it appeared that the New Aspiration Party (NAP), led by Chaovalit Yongchaiyuth, had won 125 seats in the parliament. The NAP had increased its number of seats nationally after the *Therd Thai* faction of Banharn's Chart Thai Party defected to the NAP. With these numbers the NAP was in a position to form a new government. The success of the NAP cannot be separated from Chaovalit himself. Unlike other civilian politicians, he was a former military general and also a former Commander-in-Chief of the Army in the late 1980s. With the support of ex-military officers and senior bureaucrats, he set up the NAP in October 1990.[54] Under the leadership of Chaovalit, the NAP grew rapidly to become one of the main political parties in Thailand. The NAP claimed to have about a half million members and 60 branches, but, as mentioned earlier, its supporters were concentrated in Northeast Thailand.[55] The result of the election was received with little joy among the Bangkok voters who believed that the Democrat Party led by Chuan Leekpai would win the election. Instead, the Democrat Party won only 123 seats, which ranked it second behind the NAP.

Similar to the Chart Thai party, which led the Banharn coalition government until the last days before the election, the NAP was also dominated by provincial politicians who mainly came from Northeast Thailand. It was reported that the NAP and other political parties with strong support in the provincial areas had been involved in vote buying, and according to the Thai Farmers' Bank Research, it was estimated that these parties spent more than US$1 billion during the election campaign period.[56] Given the fact that these provincial politicians dominated the party, it seemed likely that the NAP-led coalition government would not differ greatly from its predecessor. Moreover, the process of forming a new government after the 1996 elections was not a smooth one. Two factors contributed to this situation: the leadership style of Chaovalit Yongchaiyuth, the NAP leader, and conflict over the decisions about which parties would control the economic portfolios in the cabinet. As the NAP won the election, that party's leader, Chaovalit Yongchaoyuth, automatically became the new Prime Minister.

There is no doubt that Chaovalit was regarded as one of the most prominent political leaders in Thailand at that time, but the quality of his leadership was questioned. He was Deputy Prime Minister in the Chatichai government, the Minister of Interior in the Chuan coalition government and later the Minister of Defence under Banharn. Despite this, he was not known as a strong leader, but instead as a leader who promised a lot but did very little and because of this he was also known as a weak and indecisive leader when it came to making tough decisions. A Thai analyst described Chaovalit as "the master of disguises and the master of compromise".[57] His background as a general gave rise to suspicion about his democratic credentials, and his role in the downfall of both the Chuan and the Banharn governments even caused his political morality to be questioned because it appeared to demonstrate that he did not hesitate to do anything to serve his long-held ambition to be the Prime Minister of Thailand.[58] There was widespread scepticism among the Thais after the elections in 1996 as to whether he would be able to restore confidence in Thailand and bring Thailand out of the economic crisis and the political instability left by the previous government.[59] Grounds for this sentiment were shown in the following months of 1997 as Thailand entered more deeply into financial crisis.

From the beginning, there was conflict over which parties were going to oversee the economy. The conflict centred on Chaovalit's decision to appoint two non-elected politicians, Dr. Amnuay Viravan and Dr. Narongchai Akrasanee, a former head of a securities company and a respected economist from the Thailand Development Research Institute (TDRI), as the Minister of Finance and Minister of Commerce respectively. These appointments were made under the NAP's quota of seats in the cabinet and were aimed at depoliticising the economic policy-making institutions, which had lost some autonomy and independence in the previous years.[60] Chaovalit believed that by appointing these two prominent economists, he could deliver his vision of a "dream team" which would be able to solve Thailand's economic malaise.

These appointments caused disappointment among the political leaders in the Chart Pattana Party (CPP, the National Development Party) who were led by former Prime Minister Chatichai Choonhavan. The CPP was formed in 1992 by Chatichai himself and Korn Dabbaransi, Chatichai's cousin and also a former member of the Chart Thai Party.[61] CPP members were drawn from a variety of backgrounds, including the Chart Thai Party, the Social Action Party, the Democrat Party and the defunct Samakkhitham Party. The Chart Pattana Party was strong financially and attracted many supporters both in the provinces and in the cities. Under the leadership of Chatichai, the CPP was regarded as one of the political parties, which had strengths and knowledge in both economic and foreign policy areas. As the second largest political party (with 53 seats in the parliament) in the Chaovalit coalition government, the Chart Pattana Party demanded full control of the formulation of the economic policy and that of important economic portfolios. The CPP believed that Dr. Amnuay and Dr. Narongchai were not entitled to the positions of finance and commerce ministers because they were unelected politicians and therefore they would have little control over the economic policy-making process.[62] After a series of closed-door negotiations, Chatichai finally accepted the position of senior economic adviser and two senior leaders of the Chart Pattana Party, Korn Dabbaransi and Prachuab Chaiyasarn, were given the industry and foreign affairs portfolios.

However, this acceptance by the CPP was more symbolic than genuine. Conflict over control of economic policy between the Amnuay-Narongchai camp and the Chart Pattana Party camp remained unreconciled during 1997.[63] Although both camps were genuinely trying to solve the economic problems, they had different approaches. The first camp advocated the implementation of tough economic measures such as budget cutbacks and reform of the financial sector, while the latter proposed an expansion of economic activities through an increase in budget and investment funding, an acceleration in the inflow of foreign capital, and the creation of new markets in the neighbouring countries of Indochina in order to stimulate Thai exports.[64] As was seen in the months leading up to the financial crisis of July 1997, this conflict, and the rivalry among the political parties in the coalition, ruined the performance of the Chaovalit coalition government, causing a loss of confidence in the government. The following section explains how the Chaovalit coalition government and the economic policy makers tried to restore confidence and respond to concerted attacks on the baht, during the first six months of 1997.

From Defending to Floating the Baht

In the initial effort to ease the deterioration of the Thai economy and to restore confidence in March 1997, Dr. Amnuay Viravan, the Minister of Finance, and the Bank of Thailand announced measures such as cutting government spending (including military spending) and reforming the financial sector.[65] The reduction of military spending by between 40-50 billion baht (US$1.5-2 billion) caused disappointment among the military elites which potentially could have been a destabilising factor, but since Chaovalit himself took the defence portfolio, he was able to calm the military leaders and reduce the tension.[66]

Reforming the financial sector was problematic and difficult. The magnitude of the problems surrounding the collapse of the Bangkok Bank of Commerce, which was widely debated in the parliament and reported in the Thai media, indicated that the BOT had failed to monitor the soundness of Thailand's financial institutions.[67] And the collapse of Finance One (one of the largest financial institutions) in February 1997 and the confirmation by the MOF and the BOT of the debt crisis of 91 finance and securities institutions finally forced the Chaovalit government to take urgent steps to reform the financial sector.[68] As a result, in early March 1997, the BOT announced the establishment of a Property Loan Management Organisation (PLMO), which aimed to provide a 100 billion baht rescue fund to help those troubled financial institutions within a five-year framework. As those troubled financial institutions had bad loans estimated at about 800 billion baht (US$31 billion), there were serious doubts as to whether the Chaovalit government could solve the problems in this way.[69] In addition, the Chaovalit government did not hesitate to use rescue funds from the Financial Institution Development Fund (FIDF) to bail out the ailing financial institutions. The question is why did the Chaovalit government opt to rescue these institutions rather than let them all close down? The answer lay in politics. It was revealed that the BOT was under pressure to rescue those financial institutions because of political interference from the political parties within the coalition, and also because some of Chaovalit's cabinet members were shareholders or investors in these financial institutions.[70]

Consequently, the decision of the government to rescue the troubled financial institutions and the subsequent political muddling gave cause for concern to domestic and foreign investors because the Chaovalit government had not come up with sound policy for reforming the financial sector in Thailand.[71] The pessimistic assessment of the soundness of several financial institutions in Thailand from international credit monitoring institution Standard and Poor brought the credibility of the Chaovalit government into question.[72] Thus Thailand continued to become an easy target for a concerted attack on its currency, the baht.

In the first week of April 1997, the baht plunged to an eight-year low of 26.1/US$ as a result of the strength of the dollar after an increase in interest rates in the US. This was followed by attacks from money speculators who gambled on the decision of the BOT to defend the baht by intervening directly in` the market. In the middle of May 1997, the baht dived further after a concerted attack by money speculators who saw that there was no sign of economic recovery or political stability in Thailand.[73] It is believed that the George Soros-owned Soros Fund Management and other hedge fund managers spent about US$6 billion speculating on a baht devaluation.[74] In response, the BOT decided to intervene by imposing restrictions on foreign currency trading and by widening the baht-US$ band.[75] And in order to avoid contagion in the Southeast Asian region, the BOT and the Monetary Authority of Singapore (MAS) acted together to defend the baht.[76]

The attacks on the baht had political consequences. The local media reported that Prime Minister Chaovalit was not satisfied with the performance of Finance Minister Amnuay Viravan, and the Chart Pattana Party, the second biggest party in the coalition, wanted him replaced.[77] It seemed that after about six months in power, the "dream team" led by Amnuay had failed to ease the economic crisis. Chatichai Choonhavan, the leader of the Chart Pattana Party, lobbied Prime Minister Chaovalit to give the Chart Pattana Party total control over economic policy.[78] As mentioned earlier, after the Chaovalit coalition government was formed in December 1996, Finance Minister Amnuay and the Chart Pattana Party were in conflict over control of economic policy. Both sides had their economic teams. Chatichai was then the head of his own economic team known as the Baan Manangkasila group, which was supported by some prominent figures including Surakiat Sathirathai, a former finance minister in the Banharn government and Vijit Supinit, a former governor of the BOT. Meanwhile, Finance Minister Amnuay was the head of Baan Phitsanulok's economic team, which was supported by some respected economists, including Surasak Nanukul and Veerachai Techavichit.[79]

The inability of Chaovalit to demonstrate leadership in reconciling these two camps, presented the public with the idea that Thailand was run by "two economic ministers".[80] The Thai media reported that some companies and exporters had moved their money offshore in the form of other currencies as a precautionary measure.[81] This situation worsened with opposition leaders in the parliament calling on the Chaovalit government to step down over its failure to successfully tackle the problems in the Thai economy, while Dr. Virabongsa Ramangkura, a former minister of finance in the Prem period in the 1980s, suggested the Chaovalit government take urgent steps to end the economic crisis by implementing microeconomic reforms particularly in the area of foreign exchange and financial reforms.[82] In response to this, the French bank Credit Lyonnais predicted that Thailand's GDP forecast for 1997 would be one per cent negative, which was the first negative growth in more than thirty years.[83]

Furthermore, prominent figures such as Prachai Leophairatna (the chief executive of Thai Petrochemical Industry Group), Viroj Nualkhair (executive chairman of Phatra Thanakit), one of the top financial institutions, and Chatri Sophonpanich (the head of the Bangkok Bank, the largest private bank), also criticised the manner in which the Chaovalit government handled the economic situation in Thailand.[84] The unpopularity of the Chaovalit government was also revealed in a survey conducted by the Thai Farmers' Bank Research Centre in the middle of June 1997, which showed that about 60.5 per cent of a total of 2,369 respondents in Bangkok said that government performance was very poor and that they wanted a change of economic team.[85]

As the economic and political uncertainties continued, on 19 June 1997, Dr. Amnuay Viravan, the Finance Minister and Dr. Narongchai Akrasanee together resigned from the cabinet. The Stock Exchange of Thailand (SET) index dropped to the lowest point in nearly 10 years in response to the news, and the baht was again under attack, indicating that investors had lost confidence in the Chaovalit government.[86] The Thai media reported that Amnuay had decided to resign after the Chart Pattana Party rejected his proposal to increase the excise tax on two-stroke motorcycles, car batteries and marble and granite products.[87] Besides that, Amnuay was also frustrated that his efforts to float the baht and to implement far-reaching reform in the financial sector had not received much support from the parties in the coalition.[88] Porchanok Watunyuta, economist at Phatra Research Institute, described the difficulties faced by Amnuay in the cabinet:

> At that time Dr. Amnuay said "this is the Finance Minister's decision to impose tariff and taxes on particular items". It was passed by the cabinet. But then the next day, the Chart Pattana and the big corporations doing the business in these areas came out and said "we oppose the decision"...That was a big struggle. I think Dr. Amnuay has been trying very hard to, you know, restructure the financial system and he sees this kind of nonsense. There is nothing more he can do.[89]

Dr. Thanong Bidaya, a Japanese-educated economist and the President of the Thai Military Bank, was chosen by Chaovalit to be the successor of Amnuay. However, the public and the investors did not react positively to the appointment of Dr. Thanong, who was also a non-elected person and thus was weak politically.[90] Urgent issues, such as dealing with the troubled financial institutions and defending the value of the baht, were among those that Dr. Thanong (as the new Finance Minister) had to tackle. With the support of the Cabinet, on 27 June 1997, he announced the suspension of operation of 16 troubled financial institutions and forced them to merge into five institutions.[91] At the same time, the Bank of Thailand Governor Rerngchai Marakanonda announced the establishment of a private-public sector committee to oversee the rehabilitation of those institutions and to implement measures to guarantee their depositors.[92] Indeed, these announcements were intended to demonstrate the seriousness of the resolve of the financial authorities to restore confidence in the Thai economy.

However, on the issue of what to do with the baht, there was no agreement either among the parties within the Cabinet or the public. Some agreed with the devaluation of the currency and others disagreed, while a few had in fact advocated the floating of the baht. For instance, Prime Minister Chaovalit, Korn Dabbaransi, the Minister of Industry and also the secretary general of the Chart Pattana Party, and Chumpol Na Lamlieng, the president of Siam Cement, were publicly opposed to the devaluation of the baht on the grounds that it might worsen the economic situation in

Thailand.[93] Big industries with overseas loans were concerned about the potential increase in their debt burdens. The devaluation also meant that the government was still required to use international reserves in order to defend the baht at a certain level after it was devalued. Meanwhile, Dr. Nipon Puapongsathorn, the vice-chairman of the Thailand Development Research Institute (TDRI), urged the government to devalue the baht by 15 per cent and was strongly against the government policy of using billions of baht to rescue the troubled financial institutions.[94]

At the same time, it was reported that the Finance Minister Thanong, the Governor of BOT Rerngchai Marakanond, former Prime Minister Prem Tinsulanonda and former Finance Minister Virabongsa Ramangkura had lobbied Prime Minister Chaovalit to press ahead with the flotation of the baht.[95] The compelling reason for this was that Thailand could not continue to defend the currency by using its international reserves. According to an official source, the international reserve was US$33 billion in May 1997, down from US$38 billion in the previous month. This is evidence that between April and May 1997 the BOT spent between US$4-6 billion to defend the baht.[96] However, independent economists and foreign bankers believe that the BOT had probably used about US$20 billion of the international reserve during the early part of 1997.[97] Meanwhile, Dr. Chalongphob Sussangkarn, the head of the Thailand Development Research Institute (TDRI), in a paper published in May 1998, points out that the BOT used almost US$30 billion in forward contracts to defend the baht.[98]

Although the real figures remain debatable, it is suggested that by the end of June 1997, Prime Minister Chaovalit was convinced by the fact that Thailand could no longer afford to use its international reserves to defend the baht and therefore realised that the baht had to be floated.[99] Under these circumstances and after months of hesitation, the BOT finally announced the "free float" of the baht on 2 July 1997. This meant that the value of the currency would be determined by market forces to reflect Thailand's economic fundamentals. The announcement ended 13 years of the fixed exchange rate system which had been adopted by the BOT.[100]

The announcement also caused the value of the baht to drop from 24.45/US$ to a record low of 28.80/US$, before it settled at 27.50/US$, but the Stock Exchange of Thailand index soared by 7.8 per cent increasing from 415.1 points to 568.69 as foreign investors bought blue chip shares at prices that were suddenly lowered following the floating of the currency.[101] To avoid further speculation, the BOT raised the bank rate from 10.5 per cent to 12.5 per cent, while the commercial banks raised the interbank rate to 30 per cent.[102] To justify this decision, the BOT governor Rerngchai Marakanond and Finance Minister Thanong Bidaya made a special appearance on national television to convince the public that the currency would fluctuate for a while before it stabilised at a certain point.[103]   Indeed, this was the case, as the value of the baht settled at 29.50/US$ in April 1998, ten months after it was floated (Figure 4.3).

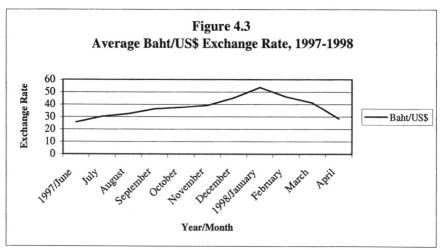

Figure 4.3
Average Baht/US$ Exchange Rate, 1997-1998

Source: Chalongphob Sussangkarn, "Thailand's Debt Crisis and Economic Outlook", Thailand Development Research Institute's Website <http://www.info.tdri.or.th>

Was the BOT policy of defending the currency appropriate?   A prominent figure in the banking sector suggests that the BOT should not be blamed for defending it for too long because the policy makers in the BOT had not experienced attacks from currency speculators before. As Somchai Sakulsurarat, President of the Bank of Ayudhya states:

> Very easy to say now...that it [the decision to defend the currency] was wrong. But, personally, I think, at that time nobody really knew. Many people praised the BOT at that time because Thailand had successfully defeated the speculators. Even foreign governments. Difficult, I think, to make adjustment. But one thing, I think, they [BOT] made a mistake in not realising they could not fight [against the currency speculators], what they should have done was just to make outright devaluation...They were betting too high. They should have tested the water. And once you realised you cannot go on, you just have to leave [float] it...They should have set up a limit.[104]

This view was also supported by Desmond Holmes, a representative of a foreign-based bank in Bangkok, who said:

> I think the government of the day simply did not have an understanding of how the currency and everything else is linked together. They thought they could fight and hold the currency in its place.[105]

Was the decision to float the baht taken too late? According to an official in the Bank of Thailand, the delay was mainly caused by BOT's concerns about the ability of Thai companies to pay back their debt. As a BOT insider argued:

> When we look back, we think that it [the decision of floating the baht] was a bit too late...I think we should have been floating [the baht] two or three years ago. But our concern was that the private sector has too much external debt. So every time you float the currency, there is a tendency that the currency will be depreciated. With the amount of the external debt being high...debt burden in terms of domestic currency [in Thai baht] will be increasing very much. If they [the private sector] cannot service their private debt, they have to go bankrupt. Or, at least, their profit will reduce by a certain amount. This is our concern.[106]

However, inside Thailand, the floating of the currency received mixed reactions from business groups. It was arguable that the managed float would benefit Thailand in the long-term although not in the short-term, particularly in the case of small and medium-sized companies, which were very dependent on imported goods in their business activities.[107] The fluctuation in exchange rate between the baht and the US dollar created a greater burden for those companies because they were forced to restructure their financial plans. Meanwhile, those domestic firms and exporters who earned mainly in US dollars or other international currencies were clear winners. The cheaper baht had the potential to increase the international competitiveness of Thai exports. More importantly, the floating of the baht would change the macroeconomic outlook and therefore Thailand would enter a period of slowdown in economic growth, with a consequent decline in per capita income and the possibility of rising inflation and unemployment rates in the ensuing years.[108]

Regionally, the floating of the baht caused great concern among the financial authorities and governments of the other Southeast Asian countries.[109] This contagion effect triggered a currency crisis in neighbouring countries with the Philippines being affected first, followed by Malaysia, Indonesia, Singapore, and, to some degree, Hong Kong.

Collectively, the central banks in these countries intervened in the market by buying currency or by widening their currency trading bands.[110] Indeed, the currency crisis that originated in Thailand extended to the Southeast Asian region as a whole. It also reached South Korea in November 1998 and later on Japan as well. South Korea and Japan are among the main economic partners of Thailand and are also the most important of Thailand's export destinations.

Consequences of the Crisis

Enter the IMF

Despite the floating of the baht, there was still no sign that the Thai economy was improving. Capital flight continued and domestic and foreign investors were still in doubt over the ability of the Chaovalit government to lead the economic recovery.[111] Even the idea of forming a so-called "national front" government comprising both the ruling and opposition parties was being considered as a bi-partisan effort to tackle the economic crisis.[112] An announcement on 21 July 1997 by the Japanese trading conglomerate Marubeni regarding the delaying of an investment worth US$500 million further worsened the investment climate.[113] Then the sudden resignation of the BOT Governor Rerngchai Marakanond on 28 July 1997 damaged the credibility of the Chaovalit coalition government. Immediately, Dr. Chaiyawat Wibulswasdi, a BOT insider, was appointed to this important job. Indeed, the level of international reserves had been reduced, and, combined with the fluctuation of the baht, which had reached 30-33/US$ by the end of July 1997, Prime Minister Chaovalit and his economic ministers came under increasing pressure to look for outside assistance.

In the wake of Rerngchai's resignation, and after a series of debates in the Cabinet, on 28 July 1997, Finance Minister Thanong called for financial assistance from the IMF and he also announced other measures to reform the financial sector in Thailand.[114] Prime Minister Chaovalit quickly sent Finance Minister Thanong to Tokyo to seek financial assistance, but the Japanese government refused to act unilaterally.[115] Meanwhile, the opposition leaders, respected economists and business leaders called on the Chaovalit government to seek financial assistance from the IMF.[116] On 5 August 1997 the Cabinet approved the conditions set by the IMF in providing an economic reform package and other measures aimed at slashing the government budget, reducing the current account deficit, imposing new taxes, and importantly, suspending the operation of a further 42 troubled financial institutions.[117] In order to boost the credibility of the government, Prime Minister Chaovalit appointed Dr. Virabongsa Ramangkura, a well-known economist, as Deputy Prime Minister with responsibility to negotiate with the IMF.[118]

On 11 August 1997 the IMF agreed to provide US$16 billion in loans to Thailand.[119] Japan was the biggest contributor, giving US$4 billion, followed by the IMF, the World Bank, the Asian Development Bank and other countries in the region, Singapore, Australia, Hong Kong, South Korea, China, Malaysia, Indonesia, and Brunei being the contributor of this package. At the same time, Thailand sought an additional US$3.3 billion loan from the Bank for International Settlements (BIS) to support the existing IMF loans.[120] Indeed, the involvement of these neighbouring countries was evidence of the fear that the scale of the financial crisis in Thailand potentially could have a devastating impact on the whole Asian region.

Under the conditions set by the IMF, Chaovalit had no choice but to accept the economically tough measures.[121] These measures were as follows: economic growth rate should be maintained at 3-4 per cent in 1997 and 6-7 per cent in the following years and the budget deficit must be reduced. Second, monetary policy should be kept tight by controlling inflation and by stopping the BOT from printing more money with the aim of rescuing the troubled financial institutions. Third, raising the value-added tax rate from seven per cent to ten per cent and gradually abolishing the subsidies on certain commodities. Fourth, the reduction of the current account deficit to five per cent in 1997 and to three per cent in 1998. Fifth, maintaining the international reserve at the level of US$23 billion in 1997 and US$25 billion in 1998. For the Chaovalit coalition government, the implementation of the IMF reform package not only changed the economic outlook, it also eroded its legitimacy. The following section will look closely at this aspect, placing particular emphasis on the constitutional reform process and the political events which surrounded the downfall of Chaovalit in November 1997.

Constitutional Reforms

As mentioned earlier, the financial crisis of 1997 created political tensions both within and outside the government, and therefore the pressure for political reform increased. Soon after Prime Minister Chaovalit

Yongchaiyuth assumed his premiership, he promised to reform Thai politics and one of the important items on his agenda was the drafting of a new constitution. The experience of political instability under the Banharn government convinced the Thais that in order to overcome the negative aspects of the recent changes in the Thai political climate, constitutional reform was inevitable.

As already explained, since the absolute monarchy was overthrown in 1932, Thailand had had 14 constitutions, but there were high expectations in early 1997 that the 15th constitution would be a more democratic one.[122] In March 1997, the Chaovalit coalition government paved the way for the formation of the Constitutional Drafting Assembly (CDA), which comprised 76 elected representatives from all the provinces in Thailand and 23 constitutional experts appointed by the parliament.[123] Former Prime Minister Anand Panyarachun was appointed as the president of the CDA, with the primary task of leading the drafting process of the new constitution and submitting it to the parliament in the middle of August 1997.

The drafting process, which lasted from April until its approval in the parliament in September 1997, was not a smooth one and it involved political struggles between reformists and conservatives. In the reformist camp were those who wanted to change the old constitution, which they believed had failed to prevent the spread of money politics and vote buying in Thailand. This camp believed that Thailand should have a new constitution, which would foster a more accountable and transparent political system and would guarantee the basic rights of the Thai people.[124] Among those who were in this camp were the pro-democracy groups, the liberal newspapers (*Matichon, Bangkok Post, The Nation*), the progressive elected politicians, both in the government and the opposition, and other prominent figures such as former Prime Minister Prem Tinsulanonda and Anand Panyarachun. The conservative camp, on the other hand, comprised those who wanted to retain the old constitution and the existing current political system. Many of these came from the existing political establishment, the province-based politicians, the appointed senators, a few monarchists, and those village leaders who were closely associated with the Ministry of Interior. Prominent figures in this camp were Snoh Thienthong, the Minister of Interior and also the secretary-general of the leading party in the coalition, the New Aspiration Party (NAP), which rejected the new constitution on the grounds that it would abolish the symbolism of monarchy in Thailand.[125]

Nonetheless, it is certainly true that the drafting of the new constitution received the attention of Thai people throughout the country.[126] During the drafting process there were, among other things, two important issues which invited much heated public debate. One was the clause which required all MPs to give up their parliamentary seats if they were chosen for the cabinet, and the other was the proposal to replace the appointment system for senators with a direct system of elections.[127] The first change was intended to prevent the abuse of power and corruption among elected politicians, while the second was aimed at allowing the Thai public to elect their own representatives for a more democratic and transparent senate.[128]

After weeks of debate and deliberation, the CDA approved a draft constitution in mid-August and it was expected to be approved by the parliament in September 1997. The draft consisted of 336 articles and it was the most comprehensive and democratic constitution in Thailand's history. It was a major achievement and there was hope that it could open the way to a fully democratic political system in Thailand. Some of the important features of the new draft constitution can be seen in the following page (Box 4.1). However, the real political battles appeared in the weeks leading up to the parliamentary sessions in September 1997. There were strong indications that the Thai public was divided over whether the draft constitution should be approved by parliament. The middle class and urban dwellers publicly called upon the parliament to approve the new constitution, while the Minister of Interior Snoh Theinthong's faction and rural leaders organised a series of public demonstrations to put pressure on Prime Minister Chaovalit not to approve it.[129]

During the parliamentary sessions the situation developed to the point where it seemed there could be political confrontations in the streets of Bangkok. The military then led the way to a political compromise. Despite the reservations of some military leaders about the clause in the new constitution which would restrict the military's role in politics, for the sake of political stability the army commander General Chetta Thanajaro and other military leaders supported the new constitution. The Thai military believed that by supporting the new constitution, the public would feel that the military was on their side and, more importantly, it maintained the political stability needed to deal with the economic situation. The support of the military changed the political atmosphere in the country. For instance, the Chart Pattana Party, the second biggest party in the coalition, along with opposition parties like the Democrat Party and the

Chart Thai Party, followed the political line of the military. The reformist camp was able to convince a broader political constituency that support for a new constitution was the best option. Politically, all of this placed Prime Minister Chaovalit in a difficult position, particularly as there was division within his own party between those MPs (led by Minister of Interior Snoh, who opposed the new constitution), and those (led by the House speaker Wan Mohammad Noer, who supported it).[130]

Box 4.1 The Old and New Constitutions[131] (main features only)

Old	New
393 MPs from multi-member constituencies	House of Representatives to consist of 400 MPs from single-member constituencies plus another 100 from party list
Cabinet ministers can serve as MPs	Cabinet ministers must relinquish their seats in Parliament
No minimum education standards for MPs	MPs must have at least a university degree
Senators appointed by the prime minister	Directly elected 200-member Senate
Elections controlled by the Interior Ministry	Elections controlled by Election Commission
Courts can order closure of media	Press freedom guaranteed
Vote-counting at polling stations	Vote-counting centralised

At this point, Chaovalit had only two options: he could either dissolve the parliament and call fresh general elections with the consequence of losing his democratic credibility in the eyes of the Thai public, or he could convince his opponents in the conservative camp to accept the new constitution and have this achievement written into Thai history. Chaovalit chose the second option and successfully persuaded the conservative camp to change their position. The result was that on 27 September 1997 the parliament passed the draft constitution overwhelmingly with 578 MPs voting in approval, 16 against, and 17 in abstention.[132]

However, it must be noted that this successful vote was a result of the desire of the Chaovalit coalition government to send a clear message that it was able to undertake political reform although it had failed in the economic arena. Through the new constitution, Chaovalit and his coalition parties hoped to gain the necessary political momentum to implement the IMF economic reform package and also to restore confidence in the economy. For the middle class in Bangkok the economic crisis opened a window of opportunity for political change.[133] Anek Laothamatas says:

> Actually that we have a severe economic crisis is a bargain in the hands of urban middle class to force the government to accept political reform. Otherwise, the politicians never want to accept a new constitution…In my view, I think, we got political progress from our economic problems.[134]

The Downfall of Prime Minister Chaovalit Yongchaiyuth

Having survived politically through the approval of the new constitution, on 14 October 1997 the Chaovalit government, with the assistance of the IMF and the World Bank, launched a reform package aimed at rebuilding the Thai economy. Budget savings and the policies to restructure the financial sector were the major components in the package.[135] To create a budget surplus of one per cent of GDP, the target set by the IMF, the government needed to increase the tax on luxury goods, alcohol, tobacco and oil. Meanwhile, to restructure the financial sector, the government had set up two agencies, the Financial Restructuring Agency (FRA), whose main task would be to supervise the rehabilitation or liquidation of the 58 suspended financial institutions, and the Asset Management Corporation (AMC) whose main task would be to buy the assets of those suspended firms and possibly restructure and sell them in the future under the approval of the FRA. The package also contained measures for dealing with bad loans and unrestricted access for foreigners to own majority shares in financial institutions in Thailand.

Unfortunately, the market did not receive this announcement positively.[136] In addition, the popularity of the Chaovalit coalition government was eroded further by widespread rumours of a cabinet reshuffle and the insistence of the Chart Pattana Party on having control over economic policy. But one of the heaviest blows fell when Finance Minister Thanong Bidaya tendered his resignation on 19 October 1997, two days after the cabinet, under considerable pressure from the Chart Pattana Party, had reversed the decision to raise taxes on petrol and gasoline as part of the budget cut exercises.[137] In response, the market reacted negatively, with investors selling the baht, which fell to the level of US$/37-38, with the stock market losing three per cent in value. For those in the government, the correlation between domestic politics and the fluctuation of the baht was found after the float of currency since July 1997. Michael Vatikiotis, a *Far Eastern Economic Review* correspondent based in Bangkok, wrote:

> When the baht was pegged to the dollar, Thailand's turbulent record of political change had little impact on the currency. Now that the baht is free of the dollar peg, local discontent with the government is directly reflected [in] speculation.[138]

So at this point, there was a strong consensus among the middle class and the political elites in Bangkok that Prime Minister Chaovalit and his government had to be replaced. This sentiment was found in the growing protests in the streets of Bangkok at the end of October 1997. For instance, on 20 October 1997 mass protests led by businesspeople were held in Silom Road, Bangkok's financial centre, and these were later joined by students and workers.[139] The following day, the protesters marched toward Government House and called upon Prime Minister Chaovalit to resign immediately.

In response, the Prime Minister planned to declare a state of emergency but he did not get support from the military leaders, the army commander General Chettha Thanajaro and the Supreme Commander Mongkol Ampornpisit. These leaders were aware that the public would not accept another direct intervention from the military, which could potentially lead to bloody confrontations with protesters in the streets of Bangkok similar to those of May 1992.[140] To ease the political tension, on 24 October 1997 Prime Minister Chaovalit announced a cabinet reshuffle and promised to call a general election at the end of 1997. Chaovalit invited ten outsiders into the new cabinet. Some of them were respected economists and professional bankers such as Kosit Panpiemras, a senior executive of the Bangkok Bank, who was appointed as the Finance Minister; Som Jatusripitak, a former president of the Siam City Bank, who was appointed Commerce Minister; and Maruey Padungsit, a former manager of the Stock Exchange of Thailand.[141] However, the cabinet reshuffle did not get much public support and the business community was disappointed because it did not believe the reshuffle could bring about change in the Thai economy.[142] Although some new ministers were believed to be capable persons for the jobs, others were unpopular ministers such as Snoh Theinthong (the Minister of Interior), Chucheep Harnsawat (the Minister of Agriculture), Sukhavich Rangsitpol (the Deputy Prime Minister), and Chalerm Yubamrung (the Deputy Minister of the Interior), who retained their positions despite strong public criticism.

Ironically, the cabinet reshuffle did not ease the internal tensions within the Chaovalit coalition government. Some of the NAP MPs disagreed with the new cabinet line-up, while, at the same time, there were widespread rumours that the Chart Pattana Party had threatened to leave the coalition.[143]

Standard and Poor downgraded Thailand's long-term foreign currency rating on the grounds that the political uncertainty and Chaovalit's weak leadership had contributed to the delay of financial reforms in Thailand.[144] And in response to those rumours and the discouraging political news, the baht fell from US$/39.45 to the lowest level of US$/40.02 (despite the intervention of the BOT which spent US$30 million to defend the currency) and the Stock Exchange of Thailand index dropped 2.64 per cent on 31 October 1997.[145] At this point, the pressure for Prime Minister Chaovalit to resign had intensified and it was only a matter of time before he had to do so. On 3 November 1997 he announced his resignation. In his announcement, Chaovalit said that no one had forced him to resign but the Thai media reported that the army commander, General Chetta Thanajaro, had persuaded Chaovalit to resign in order to ease the political uncertainty in Thailand.[146] On the night of his resignation, Chaovalit went to see Chatichai Choonhavan, the leader of the Chart Pattana Party, and offered him the premiership position. Surprisingly, Chatichai refused to take the position but suggested it be offered to former prime minister Prem Tinsulanonda, or to Chuan Leekpai, the leader of the opposition Democrat Party, if Prem refused to accept the offer.[147]

As the biggest opposition political party in the parliament, the Democrat Party could get the numbers to form a government but this possibility was blocked by the fact that the Chart Pattana Party, with the support of Chaovalit's New Aspiration Party, was also interested in leading the new coalition government. Political lobbying to form a new coalition government was intense. Between 5 and 7 November 1997 the Thai media reported that there were two contenders for power: a Democrat Party-led coalition government and a Chart Pattana Party-led coalition government.[148] Both sides declared that they had the numbers to form a government with the Democrat Party receiving the support of 196 MPs and the Chart Pattana Party having 197 MPs behind it.[149] On 8 November 1997 the political stalemate ended after 14 MPs from the Prachakorn Thai Party decided to support the Democrat Party and therefore made it possible for Chuan Leekpai (with the support of 210 out of 393 MPs in the parliament) to form a coalition government.[150] On the following day, the Democrat

Party claimed that they had the numbers and the nomination of the Democrat Party leader Chuan Leekpai as the new Prime Minister was approved by King Bhumipol Adulyadey. The Thai people, the media and the markets responded positively to the appointment of Chuan Leekpai because they believed the Democrat Party, which had a capable economic team led by respected economists such as Dr. Supachai Panitchpakdee and Dr. Tarrin Nimmanhaeminda, was the best option available.[151]

As has already been explained, the failure of Chaovalit and his economic ministers to come up with sound economic policy to respond to the financial crisis, particularly after the baht was floated on 2 July 1997, contributed to his own downfall and that of his coalition government. Indeed, the arrival of the Democrat Party-led coalition government ended the political uncertainty left by Chaovalit's resignation but it would not necessarily end the financial crisis in Thailand.[152] The new Prime Minister Chuan Leekpai and his coalition government had just begun to face the unpredictable and difficult tasks ahead.

Conclusion

This chapter makes several points regarding the interplay between globalisation and domestic politics in Thailand in the 1990s. First of all, financial liberalisation in Thailand in the early 1990s changed the outlook of the Thai economy. The establishment of the Bangkok International Bank Facility (BIBF) in 1993 increased the capital inflow into Thailand at the rate of 10 per cent of GDP per year between 1990 and 1995. Although this rapid increase helped to sustain Thailand's economic growth over several years, it also increased the current account deficit and the external debt, including the country's short-term debt. Early signs of the economic crisis appeared when Thailand's exports began to lose competitiveness in the international market in 1996. The failure of the Thai economic policy makers to come up with credible policies, particularly in exchange-rate management, worsened the economic situation. The refusal of the Bank of Thailand (BOT) to devalue, or to float, the baht as early as 1996 contributed to the deepening crisis of confidence among domestic and foreign investors.

Second, Thai politics under the Banharn coalition government, which lasted from July 1995 until September 1996, became an obstacle to the possibility of formulating sound economic policy, which was needed to respond to the side effects of financial liberalisation. The collapse of the

Bangkok Bank of Commerce (BBC) in 1996 and its economic and political ramifications brought the confidence of the markets to their lowest level. It was the economic and political legacy of the Banharn coalition government which was, ultimately, the source of the financial crisis of 1997. The Chaovalit coalition government, which came to power in November 1996, was committed to handling two important tasks: providing sound economic policy and political stability. Under this government, internal rivalry from earlier days caused political instablity. The most harmful rivalry was the conflict over control of economic policy between Finance Minister Amnuay Viravan and the Chart Pattana Party, the second biggest coalition party, which contributed to the inability of the Chaovalit government to deal with the financial crisis in 1997. This conflict, together with the resignation of Finance Minister Amnuay in June 1997, sent a strong message to domestic and foreign investors that the Chaovalit coalition government lacked unity. The financial crisis in Thailand deepened with the suspension of 58 troubled financial institutions and the floating of the baht on 2 July 1997. After spending billions of US dollars to defend the Thai currency, the government had no other option than to ask for external assistance from the International Monetary Fund (IMF). Nonetheless, the implementation of the IMF economic reform package was not an easy process either economically or politically. This worsened the conflict between the then Finance Minister Thanong Bidaya and the Chart Pattana Party over the control of economic policy.

Finally, in the political arena, the financial crisis in Thailand increased the pressure on the Chaovalit government to proceed with constitutional reform. The new constitution, which was passed by the parliament in September 1997, was an important step towards dealing with the issues of money politics and vote buying. The new constitution also reflected the desire of the Thai people to make the government in particular, and Thai politics in general, more democratic and accountable.[153] Nonetheless, the inability of Prime Minister Chaovalit to gain political support from his own coalition parties and of his economic ministers to come up with economic policies that could restore confidence in the Thai economy, eventually brought about the downfall of Chaovalit and his coalition government.

Notes

[1] Pakorn Vichyanond, *Thailand's Financial System: Structure and Liberalization* (Bangkok: Thailand Development Research Institute, 1994), p. 71.

[2] Peter G. Warr and Bhanupong Nidhiprabha, *Thailand's Macroeconomic Miracle, Stable Adjustment and Sustained Growth* (Washington D.C.,: The World Bank, 1996), p. 39.

[3] Ibid, p. 40.

[4] David Robison, Yango Byeon and Ranjit Teja, *Thailand: Adjusting to Success, Current Policy Issues* (Washington D.C.: International Monetary Fund, 1991), p. 22.

[5] Pakorn, pp. 72-77.

[6] Naris Chaiyasoot, "Industrialization, Financial Reform and Monetary Policy" in Medhi Krongkaew (ed.) *Thailand's Industrialization and Its Consequences* (London: St. Martin's Press, 1995), pp. 170-171.

[7] Ibid, p. 172.

[8] Pakorn, *Thailand's Financial System*, p. 78.

[9] Bank of Thailand, "Analysing Thailand's Short-Term Debt", *Bank of Thailand Economic Focus*, vol. 1, no. 3 (July-September 1996), p. 1.

[10] International Monetary Bank, *World Economic Outlook, Interim Assessement* (Washington D.C.: International Monetary Fund, 1997), pp. 4-5.

[11] Interview with Nitaya Pibulratagit, Bangkok, 26 November 1997.

[12] Bank of Thailand, *Annual Economic Report 1996* (Bangkok: Bank of Thailand, 1997), p. 94; and Bank of Thailand, "Analysing Thailand's Short-Term Debt", p. 3.

[13] Gordon Fairclough, "Tempest in a Teacup?", *Far Eastern Economic Review* (28 March 1996).

[14] Sirilaksana Khoman, "The Asian Financial Crisis and Prospects for Trade and Business with Thailand", *Thammasat Review*, vol. 3, no. 1 (June 1998), p. 71.

[15] Danny Unger, *Building Social Capital in Thailand, Fibers, Finance, and Infrastructure* (Cambridge University Press, 1998), pp. 101-102.

[16] Michael Vatikiotis and Gary Silvernan, "State of Denial", *Far Eastern Economic Review*, 6 March 1997.

[17] Bank of Thailand, "Analysing Thailand's Current Account Decifit", *Bank of Thailand Economic Focus*, vol. 1, no. 1 (January-March 1996), p. 6.

[18] For a critical view on this issue, see Ammar Siamwalla, "Trying to figure out how Thailand got into such a mess", *Nation*, 12 November 1997; and Peter G. Warr, "The Thai Economy: From Boom to Gloom?", *Southeast Asian Affairs* (Singapore: Institute of Southeast Asian Studies, 1997).

[19] Bank of Thailand, *Annual Economic Report 1996*, 1997, p. 101.

[20] Ibid, p. 102.

[21] Bank of Thailand, "Analysing Thailand's Short-Term Debt", 1996, p. 2; Sirilaksana, "The Asian Financial Crisis", p. 73; and a critical view on this issue can be found in Phatra Research Institute, "The Impact of Liberalization on

Thailand's Financial Market", a paper presented to *The 5th Convention of the East Asian Economic Association* organised by the East Asian Economic Association (EAEA) and the Faculty of Economics, Thammasat University, Bangkok, 25-26 October 1996.

[22] Warr and Bhanupong, *Thailand's Macroeconomic Miracle*, especially chapter nine.

[23] Ibid, p. 205.

[24] Peter G. Warr, "The Thai Economy", p. 324.

[25] Bank of Thailand, *Annual Economic Report 1996*, p. 105; and The Economist Intelligence Unit, *Thailand, Country Report*, 1st quarter, 1996.

[26] Ammar, "Trying to figure out how Thailand got into such a mess", *Nation*, 12 November 1997.

[27] For instance, Dr. Kosit Panpiemrat, a prominent economist at the National Economic and Social Development Board (NESDB), took up the chairmanship at the Padaeng group, a mining conglomerate and later of the Bangkok Bank, the biggest private bank in Thailand. Anand Panyarachum, a respected diplomat, joined the Saha Union, a textile conglomerate, as the chairman. A few other prominent economists from the Ministry of Finance and the Bank of Thailand such as Dr. Supachai Panickpadee and Dr. Tarrin Nimmanahaeminda also moved into the banking sector and later joined the Democrat Party as politicians. See Pasuk Phongpaicit and Chris Baker, *Thailand ,Economy and Politics* (Singapore: Oxford University Press, 1997), p. 169.

[28] Larry A. Niksch, "Thailand in 1988, The Economic Surge", *Asian Survey*, vol. xxix, no. 2 (February 1989), p. 168.

[29] Pasuk and Baker, *op.cit*, p. 352.

[30] Interview with Professor Krirkkiat Phipatseritham, Bangkok, 22 November 1997.

[31] Interview with Dr. Patcharee Siroros, Bangkok, 13 November 1997; and also interview with Professor Krirkkiat Phipatseritham, Bangkok, 22 November 1997.

[32] Ammar Siamwalla, "What a Little Negligence can do", *Nation*, 14 November 1997.

[33] Jennifer Gampell, "Is This Estate Real?", *Far Eastern Economic Review*, 15 August 1996; and see, Chalongphob Sussangkarn, "Thailand's Debt Crisis and Economic Outlook", a paper published at *Thailand Development Research Institute's Homepage* (hhtp://www.info.tdri.or.th), 1998.

[34] Interview with a banker from the National Australia Bank, Bangkok (7 November 1997).

[35] Daniel E. King, "Thailand in 1996, Economic Slowdown Clouds Year", *Asian Survey*, vol. xxxvii, no. 2 (February 1997), p. 163.

[36] Bank of Thailand, *Annual Economic Report 1996*, p. 101.

[37] See more in Pasuk Phongpaichit and Sungsidh Piriyarangsan, *Corruption and Democracy in Thailand* (Bangkok: Silkworm Books, 1994), pp. 44-45.

[38] The Economist Intelligence Unit, *Thailand, Country Report*, 3rd quarter, 1995, p. 9.

[39] See Anek Laothamatas, "A Tale of Two Democracies: Conflicting Perceptions of Elections and Democracy in Thailand" in Robert H. Taylor (ed.) *The Politics of Elections in Southeast Asia* (New York and Melbourne: The Woodrow Wilson Center Press and Cambridge University Press, 1996), pp. 201-223.

[40] Surin Maisrikrod, "Thailand 1992: Repression and Return of Democracy", *Southeast Asian Affairs 1993* (Singapore: Institute of Southeast Asian Studies, 1993), pp. 337-338.

[41] Rodney Tasker, "Let This Be a Warning", *Far Eastern Economic Review*, 9 May 1996.

[42] For example, in December 1995, Surakiat intervened personally by sacking the chief of the Stock Exchange of Thailand (SET) on the grounds that prominent Chart Thai Party politicians were involved in insider trading activities. Before that, he also persuaded the Secretary General of the Securities and Exchange Commission (SEC), Ekamol Khiriwat, to resign. The Economist Intelligence Unit, *Thailand, A Country Report*, 1st quarter, 1996, p. 11; James Ockey, "Thailand, The Crafting of Democracy", *Southeast Asian Affairs 1997* (Singapore: Institute of Southeast Asian Studies, 1997), p. 305; and Michael Vatikiotis, "Ministry Minder", *Far Eastern Economic Review* (18 January 1996).

[43] The Economist Intelligence Unit, *Thailand, a Country Report*, 2nd quarter, 1996, p. 26.

[44] Ammar, "Trying to figure out how Thailand got into such a mess", *Nation*, 12 November 1997.

[45] The Economist Intelligence Unit, *op.cit*, p. 27; also see, Michael Vatikiotis, "Collapse of Confidence", *Far Eastern Economic Review*, 14 November 1996.

[46] Interview with Dr. Patcharee Siroros, Bangkok, 13 November 1997; also see Ammar, "Trying to figure out", 1997.

[47] Gordon Fairclough, "Crisis of Confidence", *Far Eastern Economic Review*, 22 August 1996.

[48] The Economist Intelligence Unit, *Thailand, a Country Report*, 3rd quarter, 1996, pp. 10-11.

[49] The Economist Intelligence Unit, *Thailand, a Country Report*, 4th quarter, 1996, pp. 12-13; also see Michael Vatikiotis and Rodney Tasker, "Banharn's Cliff-Hanger", *Far Eastern Economic Review*, 3 October 1996.

[50] The Economist Intelligence Unit, *op.cit*, p.27; also see, Michael Vatikiotis, "Downwardly Mobile", *Far Eastern Economic Review*, 12 September 1996.

[51] Gordon Fairclough, "Mayday", *Far Eastern Economic Review*, 19 September 1996.

[52] Gordon Fairclough, "Critical Mass", *Far Eastern Economic Review*, 26 September 1996; and Michael Vatikiotis and Rodney Tasker, "Banharn's Cliff-Hanger", *Far Eastern Economic Review*, 3 October 1996.

[53] During the campaign period, the NAP promised to give tax incentives and saving schemes to importers and to reduce public spending. See The Economist Intelligence Unit, *Thailand*, 4th quarter, 1996, p. 16; also Michael Vatikiotis and Gordon Fairclough, "Brave Talk", *Far Eastern Economic Review*, 7 November 1996.

[54] Further discussions on the role of the NAP in Thai politics can be found in Duncan McCargo, "Thailand's Political Parties: Real, Authentic and Actual", in Kevin Hewison (ed.) *Political Change in Thailand, Democracy and Participation* (London and New York, 1997), pp. 127-130; Surin Maisrikrod, *Thailand's Two General Elections in 1992, Democracy Sustained* (Singapore: Institute of Southeast Asian Studies, 1992), pp. 8-11; and David Murray, *Angels and Devils, Thai Politics from February 1991 to September 1992* (Bangkok: White Orchid Press, 1996), pp. 35-39.

[55] Murray, p. 36.

[56] Michael Vatikiotis and Gordon Fairclough, "Mission Impossible", *Far Eastern Economic Review*, 28 November 1996.

[57] Rodney Tasker, "Show Time", *Far Eastern Economic Review*, 12 December 1996.

[58] McCargo, p. 129.

[59] For an assessment of Chaovalit's political ambition, see Michael Vatikiotis, "Confidence Man", *Far Eastern Economic Review*, 28 November 1996.

[60] The Economist Intelligence Unit, *Thailand, a Country Report*, 2nd quarter, 1997, p. 7.

[61] Surin, *Thailand's Two General Elections in 1992*, pp. 7-8.

[62] Rodney Tasker, "Show Time", *Far Eastern Economic Review*, 12 December 1996.

[63] Interview with Pornchanok Watunyuta, Bangkok, 21 November 1997.

[64] Michael Vatikiotis, "Tough Medicine", *Far Eastern Economic Review*, 23 January 1997; and for the Chart Pattana Party's economic policies, see Institute of Public Policy Studies, *Policies of Thai Political Parties in the 1995 General Election* (Bangkok: Institute of Public Policy Studies, 1995).

[65] The Economist Intelligence Unit, 2nd quarter, 1997, pp. 16-17.

[66] "Officers and Gentlemen", Editorial, *Far Eastern Economic Review*, 30 January 1997; and Michael Vatikiotis, "Exercises in Control", *Far Eastern Economic Review*, 6 February 1997.

[67] Michael Vatikiotis, "Timed Out", *Far Eastern Economic Review*, 27 February 1997.

[68] Later on, Finance One agreed to merge with the Thai Danu Bank but this merger collapsed in May 1997. See Henry Sender and Michael Vatikiotis,

"Towards the Brink", *Far Eastern Economic Review*, 13 March 1997; and The Economist Intelligence Unit, 2nd quarter, p. 18.

[69] Rodney Tasker, "Surface Measures", *Far Eastern Economic Review*, 10 April 1997.

[70] The Economist Intelligence Unit, 2nd quarter, p. 29.

[71] Interview with a banker from the National Australia Bank, Bangkok, 7 November 1997.

[72] Michael Vatikiotis, "Deeper Down", *Far Eastern Economic Review*, 1 May 1997.

[73] Interview with James Roe, Bangkok, 13 November 1997.

[74] "Pickings may be slim for speculators, Soros", *Nation*, 3 July 1997.

[75] The Economist Intelligence Unit, *Thailand, a Country Report*, 3rd quarter, 1997, p. 16.

[76] Murray Hiebert and Michael Vatikiotis, "Collateral Damage", *Far Eastern Economic Review*, 29 May 1997.

[77] Michael Vatikiotis, "Rudderless", *Far Eastern Economic Review,* 29 May 1997; also "Decisive action amy stop recession", *Nation*, 9 June 1997.

[78] "Chatichai to take reins of economy", *Nation*, 10 June 1997.

[79] "Chatihcai takes control of all economic advice", *Nation*, 13 June 1997.

[80] Sopon Onkgara, "A tale of one country, two economic ministers", *Nation*, 15 June 1997.

[81] "Damned if it did, and damned if it didn't", *Nation*, 3 July 1997.

[82] "Ex-financial heads call for urgent action", *Nation*, 11 June 1997; and "Govt urged to quit for failure to fix economy", *Nation*, 11 June 1997.

[83] "Credit Lyonnais cuts '97 GDP forecast to -1 per cent", *Nation*, 10 June 1997.

[84] "Top industrialists warn of economic crisis", *Nation*, 18 June 1997; and "Time waits for no man", *Nation*, 18 June 1997.

[85] "Poll reveals majority want change", *Bangkok Post*, 20 June 1997.

[86] Kowit Sanandang, "No time for the weak of heart", *Bangkok Post*, 20 June 1997.

[87] "Painting a bleak economic picture", *Nation*, 20 June 1997; and Michael Vatikiotis, "Crisis of Confidence", *Far Eastern Economic Review*, 3 July 1997.

[88] The Economist Intelligence Unit, 3rd quarter, 1997, p. 17.

[89] Interview with Pornchanok Watunyuta, Bangkok, 21 November 1997.

[90] Interview with Desmond Holmes, Bangkok, 6 November 1997; and "New finance chief gets weak rating", *Bangkok Post*, 22 June 1997.

[91] The five financial institutions known to have strong financial backing are Krung Thai Thanakit, Phatra Thanakit, Dhana Siam, National Finance and Securities, and Nava Finance and Securities. See, "16 firms frozen as Thanong sets 'rescue' deadline", *The Nation* (28 June 1997); and "The Situation in June and Trends for July", *Bangkok Bank Monthly Review*, vol. 38, no. 7 (July 1997), p. 6.

[92] The committee comprised Governor Rerngchai as chairman, a representative from the Ministry of Finance; Olarn Chaipravat, president of the Thai Bankers' Association; Banterng Tantivit, president of the Association of Finance Companies; Pakorn Malakul, president of the Securities and Exchange Commission; and Singha Tanhatsawad, president of the Stock Exchange of Thailand. See, "BOT finally acts to bolster finance sector", *Nation*, 28 June 1997.

[93] Prime Minister Chaovalit appeared in the national television and guaranteed that they won't be the devaluation of the baht. See, "Financial authorities must spell out clear policies", *Bangkok Post*, 27 June 1997; and "Chaovalit sees an end to economic troubles", *Nation*, 1 July 1997.

[94] "Call for 15% baht devaluation", *Bangkok Post*, 30 June 1997.

[95] The Economist Intelligent Unit, 3rd quarter, 1997, p. 18.

[96] "Baht safe despite drop in BOT reserves", *Nation*, 30 June 1997.

[97] Henry Sender and Rodney Tasker, "The Plot Sickens", *Far Eastern Economic Review*, 17 July 1997.

[98] Chalongphob Sussangkarn, "Thailand's Debt Crisis and Economic Outlook", a paper published at the *Thailand Development Research Institute's Homepage (http://www.info.tdri.or.th)*, 1998, p. 3.

[99] "It's time to get real and let the baht float", *Bangkok Post*, 3 July 1997; and Michael Vatikiotis, "Free at Last", *Far Eastern Economic Review*, 10 July 1997.

[100] "The baht cut loose", *Nation*, 3 July 1997; "Bank of Thailand statement on currency crisis", *Nation*, 3 July 1997; and "Bubble bursts as market rules", *Bangkok Post*, 3 July 1997.

[101] "Floating the baht, pain to herald gain", *Bangkok Post*, 3 July 1997.

[102] "Baht flotation announced by Bank of Thailand", *Bangkok Bank Monthly Review*, vol. 38, no. 8 (August 1997), pp. 2-3.

[103] "Bank's governor believes baht will soon stabilise", *Bangkok Post*, 3 July 1997.

[104] Interview with Somchai Sakulsurarat, Bangkok, 18 November 1997.

[105] Interview with Desmond Holmes, Bangkok, 6 November 1997.

[106] Interview with Nitaya Pibulratagit, Bangkok, 26 November 1997.

[107] "Mixed reaction greets Government move", *Nation*, 3 July 1997.

[108] "Chief economist warns of negative growth", *Bangkok Post*, 7 July 1997; "Central bank back to drawing board", *Bangkok Post*, 11 July 1997; and also "6% inflation likely this year, says bank", *Bangkok Post*, 14 July 1997.

[109] For further discussion on this issue, see, L. R. Rosenberger, "Southeast Asia's Currency Crisis: A Diagnosis and Prescription", *Contemporary Southeast Asia*, vol. 19, no. 3 (December 1997), pp. 223-251.

[110] "Regional rush to defend currencies", *Bangkok Post*, 3 July 1997.

[111] Interview with Dr. Chareonchai Lengsiriwat, Bangkok, 11 November 1997.

[112] Originally the idea was suggested by Korn Dabbaransi, the Minister of Industry and deputy leader of the Chart Pattana Party and the opposition leaders of Democrat Party. However, the idea did not get much support because there were disagreements over who should be leader of the "national front" government. See "Meeting with Prem 'political'", *Bangkok Post*, 26 July 1997.

[113] Henny Sender, "Bad to Worse", *Far Eastern Economic Review*, 31 July 1997.

[114] "Thanong to ask for standby credits to defend baht value", *Bangkok Post*, 29 July 1997.

[115] "Rerngchai makes no pleas for funds", *Nation*, 18 July 1997.

[116] "Assistance from IMF urged as fast remedy", *Nation*, 25 July 1997; "Tarrin sees foreign aid as essential", *Nation*, 25 July 1997; "Big business wants Prem to lend a hand", *Bangkok Post*, 26 July 1997; "'Credibility' calls for fast aid from IMF", *Nation*, 26 July 1997; and "IMF aid needed, says Virabongsa", *Nation*, 27 July 1997.

[117] Assif Shameen, "Worse than you think", *Asiaweek*, 15 August 1997; Rodney Tasker, "The First Step", *Far Eastern Economic Review*, 14 August 1997; and "IMF conditions accepted", *Bangkok Bank Monthly Review*, vol. 38, no. 9 (September 1997), pp. 2-3.

[118] It was reported that this appointment was the result of lobbying by, among others, former prime minister Prem Tinsulanonda and the army commander General Chettha Tanajaro. Indeed, this suggests that the Thai military still had the ability to manoeuvre behind the scenes in this appointment. See, Michael Vatikiotis, "Indirect Intervention", *Far Eastern Economic Review*, 4 September 1997.

[119] Rodney Tasker, "The Bright Side", *Far Eastern Economic Review*, 21 August 1997.

[120] "US$ 3.3 billion sought to increase bail out funds to US$ 20 billion", *Bangkok Bank Monthly Review*, 1997, pp. 5-6.

[121] A summary of the conditions of the IMF rescue package for Thailand can be found in Pimjai Siripotiprapan, "The IMF and Thailand's Economic Rehabilitation", *Bangkok Bank Monthly Review*, vol. 38, no. 10 (October 1997), pp. 7-10; and also The Economist Intelligence Unit, 3rd quarter, 1997, pp. 18-19.

[122] See Richard Doner and Ansil Ramsay, "Thailand: From Economic Miracle to Economic Crisis" in Karl D. Jackson (ed.) *Asian Contagion, The Causes and Consequences of a Financial Crisis* (Singapore: Institute of Southeast Asian Studies, 1999), pp. 188-189.

[123] Michael Vatikiotis, "Tilting at Windmills", *Far Eastern Economic Review*, 3 April 1997.

[124] For a critical assessment on this issue, see John Laird, *Proposal for Constitutional Reform* (Bangkok: Craftsman Press Co., Ltd., 1997).

[125] The Economist Intelligence Unit, 3rd quarter, 1997, p. 11.

[126] The major newspapers and magazines and television reported the events relating to the drafting of the new constitution during the months of April-September 1997. Some international media such as *Far Eastern Economic Review* and *Asiaweek* also gave special attention on this issue, as they did to the financial crisis.

[127] Rodney Tasker, "Hard Times Roll", *Far Eastern Economic Review*, 7 August 1997.

[128] Doner and Ramsay, "Thailand: From Economic Miracle to Economic Crisis", p. 196.

[129] Michael Vatikiotis and Rodney Tasker, "Danger Ahead", *Far Eastern Economic Review*, 11 September 1997.

[130] The Economist Intelligence Unit, 3rd quarter, 1997, p. 13.

[131] Drawn from an article written by Michael Vatikiotis, "People's Putsch", *Far Eastern Economic Review*, 18 September 1997.

[132] Michael Vatikiotis, "Trial by Fire", *Far Eastern Economic Review*, 9 October 1997.

[133] Doner and Ramsay, "Thailand: From Economic Miracle to Economic Crisis", p. 197.

[134] Interview with Dr. Anek Laothamatas, Bangkok, 28 October 1997.

[135] The details of this package can be found in The Economist Intelligence Unit, *Thailand, Country Report*, 4th quarter, 1997, pp. 15-16.

[136] Michael Vatikiotis and Rodney Tasker, "Confidence Trick", *Far Eastern Economic Review*, 23 October 1997.

[137] The Economist Intelligence Unit, *op.cit*, p. 13.

[138] Michael Vatikiotis, "Home Truths", *Far Eastern Economic Review*, 30 October 1997.

[139] Thana Poopat, "Thailand's own escape artist", *Nation*, 26 October 1997.

[140] The Economist Intelligence Unit, *Thailand, Country Report*, 4th quarter, 1997, p. 15

[141] "Unpopular ministers stay", *Bangkok Post*, 25 October 1997; "Snap poll will follow reshuffle", *Nation*, 25 October 1997; and "Kosit accepts offer to take post of Finance Minister", *Business Day*, 24-25 October 1997.

[142] "Changes disappoint business community", *Nation*, 25 October 1997.

[143] "Chatichai accuses PM of delaying investment", *Bangkok Post*, 31 October 1997.

[144] "S&P cites downgrade on 'weak leadership'", *Bangkok Post*, 25 October 1997.

[145] "Baht dives to 40, its lowest-ever level", *Bangkok Post*, 31 October 1997.

[146] "Premier has few options after quitting", *Nation*, 4 November 1997.

[147] "Prem to be offer post", *Bangkok Post*, 4 November 1997; and "Prem urged to take charge", *Nation*, 4 November 1997.

[148] "Chartichai battles to stay in the running", *Bangkok Post*, 6 November 1997; "Coalition plums for Chatichai", *Nation*, 6 November 1997; "Political Stalemate", *Bangkok Post*, 7 November 1997; "Race to be photo-finish", *Nation*, 7 November 1997; "Wan Noor holds key to power", *Nation*, 8 November 1997; "Chuan set to be new PM", *Bangkok Post*, 8 November 1997; and "Chuan, Chatichai Race too close to call", *Business Day*, 7-8 November 1997.

[149] "Two sides claim victory in unison", *Nation*, 7 November 1997.

[150] "Wan Noor picks Chuan", *Bangkok Post*, 9 November 1997; and "Democrats move ahead on Cabinet", *Nation*, 9 November 1997.

[151] "Partners give Chuan a free hand", *Bangkok Post*, 10 November 1997; and "Tension-filled climax to tightest race", *Nation*, 10 November 1997; and "Markets seen strongly welcoming Chuan's victory", *Business Day*, 10 November 1997.

[152] Interview with Ji Ungpakorn, Bangkok (11 November 1997); Thana Poopat, "Antidote to cynicism", *Nation*, 16 November 1997: and also Michael Vatikiotis, "No quick fix", *Far Eastern Economic Review*, 13 November 1997.

[153] Doner and Ramsay, "Thailand: From Economic Miracle to Economic Crisis", p. 198.

Chapter Five

Indonesia's Boom

Under the New Order government, which lasted from 1966-1998, Indonesia enjoyed relative political stability and economic progress. There is a consensus among scholars that Indonesia is a case where economic success did not automatically lead to political liberalisation.[1] Economic success in Indonesia was built on the strong personal power of President Suharto who dominated Indonesian politics for three decades and who became a stumbling block to the establishment of a democratic political system in Indonesia. The economic boom of the 1980s and 1990s gradually changed the political landscape, leading to limited political openness and increasing pressure for political change. This chapter examines the historical, social, political, institutional and external factors that contributed to the economic boom in Indonesia during the 1980s and 1990s and their political implications.

Historical Setting

Indonesia is a multi-ethnic country with a population of more than 200 million. It is rich in natural resources and is strategically located on the trading route between the Indian and Pacific Oceans. Three important factors influenced political and economic life in Indonesia in the early twentieth century. First, Indonesia was still under the rule of the Dutch colonial government. When Indonesia declared Independence in 1945, it had been colonialised by the Dutch for about three hundred years, one of the longest colonial periods in the Southeast Asian region. This experience of colonisation created a strong sense of nationalism among the Indonesian people.[2] It also shaped political and economic developments in Indonesia in the post-independence period. A second factor was that colonisation also integrated Indonesia into the world economy. The Dutch colonial government achieved this by monopolising the trade in products such as cloves, nutmeg, rattan, sugar, coffee, tea, teak, rice and other primary products. The colonial government used the Dutch East India Company

(VOC), which in fact had for more than two hundred years monopolised and controlled the trading routes across the islands of Indonesia, as a vehicle for domestic and international business. It was in this way that the colonial government dominated the economic sector in Indonesia. Despite this, small groups of people such as indigenous Muslim traders, Arab immigrants, and Chinese traders were also involved in economic activities. But as Richard Robison argues, the legacy of colonisation left Indonesia without a strong domestic capitalist class.[3] A third factor which influenced economic and political life early this century was the fact that the Dutch colonial government also created a fragmented society in which only a few elites – the Dutch and Indonesian aristocrats – occupied the bureaucracy, the Chinese and a small Indian minority controlled business activities, and the majority of Indonesians lived from, and depended very much on, agricultural activities. This was also the experience of other colonised countries in the Southeast Asian region. These political and economic structures were not only criticised domestically, also drew criticism from outsiders.[4] They also led to the strengthening of the nationalist movement in Indonesia.

Only around the 1920s and the 1930s, when the Dutch colonial government was criticised by progressive elements in the Netherlands, did it begin to introduce social reforms. Gradually, the Indonesian people were given a limited taste of democracy through participating in public meetings and political gatherings. From here the nationalist movement blossomed and stimulated the idea of establishing the Indonesian state.[5] When the Japanese defeated the Dutch colonial government in the early 1940s, the Indonesian nationalist leaders began to think seriously about the future of Indonesian independence.[6] It was at this point that the issue of what kind of political system Indonesia should adopt emerged. Some early leaders preferred an authoritarian political system with a strong leader who could unify the country. The supporters of this idea found Japan's political system a good model.[7] Therefore, a few Indonesian nationalist leaders collaborated with the Japanese occupation administration in order to liberate Indonesia. In addition, the Japanese occupation army also provided training in military skills for many young Indonesians and the chauvinist and militarist thinking among the Japanese army officers influenced some of them. With these skills, the Indonesians started to build what would become the Indonesian army and then prepared for civil war against the Dutch at the end of the 1940s.

Meanwhile, other Indonesian nationalist leaders (many of them educated in Europe) chose other ways. They admired the idea of western liberal democracy and believed the future Indonesia should be built along these lines. In achieving independence from the Dutch, they preferred diplomacy over military solutions. Despite their differences, both sides contributed to the struggle for independence and therefore a combination of these two aspirations featured in political life during the revolutionary period at the end of the 1940s.[8] Indeed, Indonesia finally gained its Independence in August 1945, but the struggle against the Dutch did not end at this point. When the Dutch colonial government finally left Indonesia at the end of the 1940s, Indonesia entered a new period of western parliamentary democracy. During the 1950s, civilian governments rose and fell in quick succession, creating a climate of uncertainty despite the fact that the degree of political participation of the Indonesian people was very high.[9] Feith documented the political dynamics of this period and argues that this was the most democratic period in modern Indonesian history.[10] As Adnan Buyung Nasution argued, the desire of the Indonesian people to create a constitutional government was widespread despite the fact that Indonesia experienced economic and political uncertainty.[11]

During the democratic period, the Indonesian government implemented economic strategies which had a strong nationalist flavour. Sentiment against foreigners (especially the Dutch) and foreign capital was very marked during the 1950s. In response to this mood, various coalition governments implemented a series of economic policies aimed at creating a domestic capitalist class in Indonesia. For instance, in 1951, Dr. Sumitro, then the Minister of Economic Planning, implemented the Urgency Economic Programme, aimed at empowering indigenously-owned business groups by giving subsidies and other government financial assistance so that they could be strong economically.[12] However, many of them failed simply because the policies were politically motivated and produced "rent seeker" types of business groups who relied on political patronage in expanding their business activities, rather than concentrating on broader commercial principles. Also, the rise of anti-foreign sentiment encouraged Sukarno to nationalise the Dutch-owned and other foreign-owned companies operating in Indonesia. At the same time, he also declared a state of emergency as local rebellions flared in various places. In doing this, Sukarno gave the Indonesian military the mandate to take over these foreign companies and to impose martial law in troubled regions throughout the country.[13]

From 1957 until 1965, Sukarno governed using a new style of political system which he called Guided Democracy (*Demokrasi Terpimpin*).[14] This period was marked by the heavy involvement of state enterprises in economic activities. Sukarno pursued a strongly nationalist economic policy that was based on the principle of self-sufficiency. He also promoted an aggressive foreign policy, with a focus on strengthening the bargaining position of Third World countries.[15] As a result, anti-western sentiment in Indonesia (especially towards the US and Britain) grew very rapidly and caused the withdrawal of many foreign companies from Indonesia. By the mid 1960s, the Indonesian economy was on the point of collapse, with basic commodity prices rising rapidly and inflation rates reaching about 600 per cent.[16] Politically, Sukarno governed Indonesia in a dictatorial style and his political survival was based on the support of major political actors such as the Indonesian National Party (*Partai Nasional Indonesia*, PNI), the *Nahdathul Ulama* (Islam-based political party), the Indonesian Communist Party (*Partai Komunis Indonesia*, PKI) and, lastly, the military. This kind of support, however, eventually crumbled because of the tension and rivalry among the component groups, particularly between the communists and the military. Later on, this tension led Indonesia into the political crisis of 1965, which brought Major General Suharto to power.[17] The clear winner in this crisis was the military and it would soon be shown that the biggest losers were Sukarno himself, the Indonesian Communist Party and other left-wing organisations.[18]

Suharto's Power and the New Order Regime

The collapse of the Communist party and the departure of President Sukarno marked the end of the Guided Democracy period and led to the emergence of the New Order government. The longevity of the latter cannot be separated from the role of General Suharto. Unlike the Sarit and Prem regimes in Thailand, Suharto held power for more than three decades.[19]   The question is why did Suharto and the New Order government survive for more than thirty years and what sort of political system was built in Indonesia? Many studies have been carried out on the origins and the nature of the New Order government. It has been described variously as a "military regime", a "bureaucratic state", a "patrimonial state", a "bureaucratic authoritarian state", a "corporatist authoritarian state", a "bureaucratic pluralist" state, and also a "restricted pluralism regime".[20]   However, it seems that scholars agree that there are three important factors that can be described as the foundations of the New Order government: President Suharto, the military and the bureaucracy.[21]

The Stabilisation Period

Restoring political stability and economic rehabilitation were the two main issues that Suharto and the New Order government were determined to address. To do this, Suharto needed the support of the military (particularly the Army) and the bureaucracy. To achieve political stability Suharto set out, with the support of the military, to repress members of the Communist Party and left wing organisations and also the supporters of former President Sukarno. Over the next two years, an estimated 500,000 people were killed, mainly in Java and Bali, and further hundred of thousands were imprisoned, some until the present day.[22] After his political opposition was eliminated, Suharto held general elections in 1971. In the lead-up to those elections, Suharto and the military officers created a new political organisation called *Golongan Karya* (Golkar) meaning Functional Groups, as the government's front runner. Golkar won the 1971 general elections, although not overwhelmingly.[23] This win was achieved by enforcing political pressure and intimidation on public servants and the general population. In the ensuing decades, the New Order government imposed an authoritarian political system on the country through which it maintained the domination of Golkar in national politics.

For the task of rehabilitating the Indonesian economy, Suharto relied very much on the support of a team of prominent economists led by Professor Widjojo Nitisastro, from the Faculty of Economics at the University of Indonesia.[24] These economists were known as the "Berkeley Mafia" because many of them had graduated from the University of California at Berkeley in the US in the early 1960s. They advocated a free market and export-oriented policies and implemented new laws favouring the return of foreign investors to Indonesia. Suharto also asked the International Monetary Fund (IMF) and the World Bank to provide financial and technical assistance during the stabilisation period. With this support, the technocrats implemented tight fiscal and monetary policies aimed at controlling inflation. By the end of the 1960s, the New Order had lowered the inflation rate, imposed disciplined monetary and fiscal policies, rehabilitated the national infrastructure and, more importantly, created economic growth of between six to ten per cent annually.[25] This was quite a significant achievement given the economic legacy of the Sukarno period, helping thereby in strengthening the legitimacy of President Suharto and the New Order government.

The Oil Boom and the Economic Nationalism Period

The rise of the international oil price in the 1970s contributed significantly to the Indonesian economy and its economic growth. In the mid-1970s, the total export earning from oil was about 70 per cent, while non-oil domestic earning was about 25 per cent, and foreign aid was about 12 per cent. With the oil money, an increasing number of state-owned enterprises (SOEs) and big private companies became involved in financing and investing in a variety of costly industrial projects. This period was also the early phase of the import-substitution industrialisation (ISI) period. The government implemented policies to nurture the growth of domestic industries so that they could be protected against foreign companies. The government also initiated many expensive and prestigious projects such as aircraft building, shipbuilding industries, petrochemical plants, cement, steel, fertiliser, and other heavy industries, which could not have been funded in any earlier period.[26]

This stage marked the early growth of ethnic Chinese-owned business and also of a few Indonesian *pribumi* (native) businesspersons. Their business activities expanded rapidly because the government gave monopoly rights in a number of areas and preferential credit and loans to such as Liem Sioe Liong, Bob Hassan, Prajoga Pangestu and others, who had close political connections with many powerful figures including President Suharto.[27] This situation in many respects mirrored relationships between the ethnic Chinese business leaders and political figures in Thailand during the Sarit period in the 1960s. Such relationships soon strengthened with the involvement of the Suharto family in a number of business groups owned by ethnic Chinese.[28] The oil boom period also saw the resurgence of nationalist and protectionist attitudes to the direction of economic policy in Indonesia. The nationalist and protectionist camp began to expand their influence by the end of the 1970s and, consequently, they minimised the role of the technocrat camp.[29] The proponents of the nationalist and protectionist camp in the 1970s included Ibnu Sutowo, the head of the government-owned Indonesian oil company Pertamina, Soehoed and later Hartarto, Ministers of Industry, and B.J. Habibie, the Minister of Research and Technology.[30]

This oil boom period was also marked by political and economic crises. The first of these occurred in Jakarta in January 1974, when students from various universities protested against the government's economic policies, which favoured foreign investors (particularly those from Japan).[31] The students also attacked the widespread corruption among high level officers. The protests soon developed into riots, which took place during an official visit by the Japanese Prime Minister, Kakuei Tanaka. During the same period a financial crisis occurred, caused by the excessive debt of the government-owned oil company Pertamina which reportedly reached as high as US$10.5 billion.[32] Much of this money came from overseas banks and financial syndicates. Both the anti-Japanese protest and the collapse of Pertamina had serious consequences for President Suharto and the New Order government. The government suppressed opposition groups within the Parliament itself and at universities across the country. The government also began to change economic policy, paying more attention to strengthening the domestic economic players and to the issue of equity for the poor. Suharto survived politically, as did his regime, but from that point the direction of Indonesian politics and the economy continued to change.

The Economic Deregulation Period

The collapse of the oil price and the global economic recession which occurred in the early 1980s, caused serious problems for the Indonesian economy. The New Order government responded by seeking sources of revenue from the non-oil sector and, more importantly, by making the Indonesian economy more efficient and open to outsiders.[33] Between 1983 and 1989 the government gradually introduced policies to deregulate the financial sector, taxation, customs, exports and imports, tariffs, foreign investment and state-owned enterprises.[34] The government also devalued the rupiah in 1983 and 1986 in order to help exports and to stabilise the balance of payments. The deregulation policies were generally aimed at reorientating the structure of Indonesia's economy more toward export-oriented industrialisation (EOI) and increasing the competitiveness of the Indonesian exports and commodities in the international market.

The 1980s were thus known as the deregulation period. The technocrat camp, also known as the pro-market camp was the main force behind the formulation of the deregulation policies. At that time the technocrat camp was represented by prominent figures such as Ali Wardana, Radius Prawiro and Sumarlin, who were also members of the "Berkeley Mafia". It was the deteriorating situation of the Indonesian economy in the 1980s that brought the technocrat camp back into a position of influence in the economic policy-making process. But the technocrat camp did not regain this influence without the support of Suharto himself. This support was certainly needed in order to give political weight to the implementation of the deregulation policies. This was similar to the early period of the New Order at the end of the 1960s, when Suharto became directly involved in discussion with the technocrat camp (led by Professor Widjojo Nitisastro) about the details of the economic stabilisation policies.[35] However, the implementation of the deregulation policies in the 1980s was not a smooth process.[36] During the 1980s the technocrats, through the Ministry of Finance, discovered that many of the state-owned enterprises (SOEs) were facing severe debt problems and were insufficiently funded. Like in Burma, the SOEs also became the centres of corruption, favouring former military officers and the elite bureaucracy. Since the existence of SOEs was guaranteed by the 1945 Constitution, the government had a responsibility to protect them. Therefore, deregulation slowly eroded the economic interests of SOEs and thus developed a political battle line between the technocrat camp and the bureaucrats in SOEs, whose interests were threatened.[37]

Not everyone was satisfied with the deregulation of the 1980s. The technocrats were criticised because of the widening gap between the rich and the poor in Indonesia. Generally speaking, those who benefited the most from deregulation were the ethnic Chinese-owned conglomerates and the business groups belonging to the children of President Suharto and others who had close connections with the political elites.[38] There is plenty of evidence that their business activities expanded during this period. Indeed, there were not many competitors and therefore since they were already major economic players in Indonesia, these politically connected business groups were the ones who were ready to engage with the new rules of "market forces" set up by the technocrats.[39] Despite the disputes about the success of deregulation in the 1980s, the Indonesian economy now became more open and modern than before. This change expanded the growth of various non-agricultural sectors, such as manufacturing, finance, and construction (Table 5.1). This economic boom at the end of the 1980s and the 1990s in many ways strengthened the legitimacy of Suharto and the New Order government, but, at the same time, it also created new social and political conditions which Suharto himself was no longer able to ignore.

Table 5.1   Sectoral Contributions to GDP Growth, 1967-1992 (per cent)

Sector	1967-73	1973-81	1982-86	1987-92
Agriculture	28.2	16.4	23.2	10.4
Mining	12.8	4.9	-5.0	7.4
Manufacturing	10.0	22.9	28.9	29.2
Utilities	0.6	1.1	2.5	1.2
Construction	7.3	8.8	2.0	9.3
Trade	25.4	17.2	12.5	18.3
Transport	4.2	8.0	10.2	7.3
Finance	4.3	2.8	4.7	7.1
Housing	1.6	4.3	3.2	1.6
Public administration	3.8	12.6	15.5	5.4
Other services	1.6	1.1	2.2	2.8
Annual GDP growth	7.90	7.51	4.01	6.73

Source: Hal Hill, *The Indonesian Economy since 1966* (Melbourne: Cambridge University Press, 1996), p. 21.

Economic Policy-Making Institutions

The oil boom period of the 1970s and early 1980s gave the government more power in directing economic policy and also in shaping the society. During this period, several institutions played an important role in this respect. These were the Presidential Office and Cabinet Secretariat, the National Development Planning Board (*Badan Perencana Pembangunan Nasional*, Bappenas), the Ministry of Finance (MOF), and Bank Indonesia (BI), Indonesia's central bank.

The role of the Presidential Office and Cabinet Secretariat, and in particular of President Suharto himself, was crucial in the process of formulation and implementation of economic policy in Indonesia.[40] In 1968, for instance, the Economic Stabilisation Council was set up to oversee the stabilisation policies and Suharto appointed himself Chairman with members including the governor of Bank Indonesia, the Coordinating Minister of State for Economic, Financial and Industrial Affairs, the head of the National Development and Planning Agency, and other key ministers.[41] When the stabilisation period ended in the 1960s, the Council's role was downgraded to ministerial level, with a new name being given to it, the Economic Coordinating Ministry. Within the Cabinet, there was also the Monetary Board (*Dewan Moneter*), headed by the Minister of Finance (MOF), which played an important role in overseeing monetary and financial policy. The governor of Bank Indonesia together with other key ministers were members of the Board. The Board met frequently to discuss macroeconomic issues and then reported directly to the Presidential Office and Cabinet Secretariat for further consultation or, if needed, for approval.[42]

The National Development Planning Board (Bappenas) which was also formed by a group of technocrats led by Professor Widjojo Nitisastro, played a crucial role in preparing policy proposals, including those dealing with the budget, financial allocations, and annual economic forecasts. Bappenas worked closely with the Ministry of Finance and Bank Indonesia to ensure that the government implemented the policies of macroeconomic stability and a balanced budget principle.[43] By holding to the tradition of fiscal and monetary discipline, Bappenas was regarded as an institution that was committed to pro-market policies. This was supported by the fact that Bappenas had strong links with external institutions such as the IMF, the World Bank, and also the Harvard Institute of International Development (HIID).[44] Apart from these, there were also other policy institutions or think tanks which played a minor role in the policy-making processes. These were, for instance, the Centre of Strategic and International Studies (CSIS), the Centre of Policy and Implementation Studies and the Institute of Indonesian Sciences *(Lembaga Ilmu Pengetahuan Indonesia*, LIPI). Their roles were often limited to providing commentary and suggestions on particular issues to the policy makers in the government.

However, the domination of the technocrat camp was not to last long. It was challenged by the technologist camp led by the then powerful Minister for Research and Technology, B. J. Habibie. Habibie believed that by embarking on high technology projects such as aircraft, construction shipbuilding, military industry, telecommunications. Indonesia could increase its comparative advantage, similar to countries of Europe and North America.[45] To implement his ideas, Habibie established institutions such as the Agency for Assessment and Application of Technology *(Badan Penelitian dan Penerapan Tehnologi*, BPPT), the Agency for the Management of Strategic Industries *(Badan Pengelola Industri-Industri Strategis*, BPIS), the National Research Council *(Dewan Riset National,* DRN), and the state-owned aircraft company IPTN *(Industri Pesawat Terbang Nusantara).*[46] As Robison argues, through these institutions, the role of Habibie in influencing the policy-making process intensified to the point where his power was unmatched by any other political leader, except Suharto.[47]

It must be mentioned that Habibie arose from his own political constituency and his political skills improved subsequently. In the early

1990s, for instance, Habibie and his supporters set up a think tank called the Centre for Information and Development Studies (CIDES). Through CIDES, Habibie disseminated his ideas and engaged in public debate on issues as diverse as the economy, politics, culture, and human rights.[48] Habibie's position was further strengthened when he was appointed as the head of the influential Indonesian Muslim scholars' organisation ICMI (*Ikatan Cendekiawan Muslim Indonesia*) and of the ruling party Golkar.[49] He had the support of several important figures in the government, including the Minister of Industry Hartarto and Ginandjar Kartasasmita who was the head of Bappenas from 1993-1997. Habibie demonstrated his power by appointing his supporters (many of whom came from ICMI) to ministerial positions in Suharto's new cabinet in 1993. As a proponent of high technology policies, Habibie was always at odds with the technocrat camp, or those who advocated free-market policies such as the IMF and the World Bank. The technocrat camp held the opinion that Habibie's high technology projects needed a great deal of capital and, at the same time, were unprofitable and therefore created financial burdens for the government. One of Habibie's many high technology projects was the first Indonesian-made jet aircraft project, which cost the government about US$2 billion.[50] But since many of the high-cost projects carried out by Habibie's institutions received approval from Suharto, it was difficult for the technocrat camp to win their case.

Later on, the rivalry between the technocrat and the technologist camps over the policy-making process became more pronounced, especially during Suharto's Sixth Cabinet period (1993-1997). This also exposed the lack of unity among the policy makers in Indonesia. Evidence of this rivalry can be found in the events that led to Indonesia's economic crisis in 1997, which will be explored in detail in Chapter Six. It can be argued that the economic policy-making process under the New Order government was very much insulated from social pressure. MacIntyre describes correctly the nature of the policy-making process in Indonesia, when he writes:

> In this environment, policy-making has very largely been in the hands of the bureaucrats, who have been able to operate with relative immunity from collective societal demands. With the important exception of particular patrimonial links between individual officials and business people, the prevailing picture is that the economic-policy making is mainly a story of bargaining and alliance building within the state elite.[51]

Indeed, the insulated and "elitist" nature of the economic policy-making process in Indonesia remained unchanged during the 1980s and 1990s.

Domestic Coalition

Indonesia's economic boom also resulted from an informal domestic coalition among groups such as the predominantly ethnic Chinese business leaders, the bureaucrats, and the military. This coalition was formed soon after Suharto assumed power and he needed to encourage its role in order to ensure that his economic policies would foster economic growth in Indonesia. In addition, Suharto developed the ideology of "development", or *pembangunan*, a state ideology that engineered the Indonesian people to participate in a variety of economic activities throughout the country.[52] In practice, however, Suharto and the coalition relied very much on the skills of the ethnic Chinese businesspeople in encouraging economic activity in Indonesia. Since only a few native Indonesians were involved in business and since the ethnic Chinese already controlled the business sector and the distribution of goods throughout Indonesia, the economic area became more than ever the place where the ethnic Chinese concentrated (Table 5.2).[53]

The success of this domestic coalition in creating the conditions for economic boom was evidenced during the 1980s and the 1990s. This period saw the expansion of the ethnic Chinese-owned businesses into conglomerates. Apart from the ethnic Chinese, the business groups owned by the Suharto family were also among those which benefited from the economic boom. The Suharto family members in business included Sudwikatmono (Suharto's cousin), Probosutedjo (Suharto's foster brother), Siti Harjati Rukmana or "Tutut" (Suharto's eldest daughter), Sigit (Suharto's oldest son), Bambang Trihatmodjo (Suharto's second son), and Hutomo "Tommy" Mandala Putra (Suharto's youngest son). Much has already been written about the family wealth of President Suharto.[54]

However, it must be pointed out that at the beginning the Suharto family members were helped by ethnic Chinese business leaders in developing their business companies. This type of cosy relationship became common practice in the Indonesian business world. The Chinese-owned companies appointed members of Suharto's family to the boards of their companies and gave them minor shareholdings in them. For instance, Sigit and Tutut were given shares in Liem Sioe Liong's Bank Central Asia, and Tommy held shares in Bob Hasan's companies.[55]

Table 5.2 Major Business Conglomerates in Indonesia

Company name	Principal owner	Principal activities	No. of companies (1993)	Ranking (1993)
Salim	Liem Sioe Liong	Cement, finance, autos, agro-industry	450	1
Astra	Prasetia Mulya group and public	Autos, estates	205	2
Lippo	Mochtar Riady	Finance	78	3
Sinar Mas	Eka Tjipta Widjaja	Agro-industry, pulp and paper, finance	150	4
Gudang Garam	Rachman Halim	Kretek cigarettes	6	5
Bob Hassan	Bob Hassan, Sigit Hardjojudanto (Suharto's eldest son)	Timber, estates	92	6
Barito Pacific	Prajogo Pangestu	Timber	92	7
Bimantara	Bambang Trihatmodjo	Trade, real estate, chemicals	134	8
Argo Manunggal	The Ning King	Textiles	54	9
Dharmala	Soehargo Gondokusumo	Agro-industry, real estate	151	10
Djarum	Budi and Michael Hartono	Kretek cigarettes	25	11
Ongko	Kaharudin Ongko	Real estate, finance	59	12
Panin	Mu'min Ali Gunawan	Finance	43	13
Rodamas	Tan Siong Kie	Chemicals	41	14
Surya Raya	Soerjadjaja	Property, estates, trade	242	15
Jan Darmadi	Jan Darmadi	Real estate	60	16
CCM/Berca	Murdaya Widyawimarta Poo	Electronics, electricity	32	17
Humpuss	Hutomo "Tommy" Mandala Putera	Oil, trade, chemicals	11	18
Gadjah Tunggal	Sjamsul Nursalim	Tyres, finance, real estate	49	19
Raja Garuda Mas	Sukanto Tanoto	Pulp and rayon, finance	66	20
Gemala	Sofjan Wanandi	Chemicals, autos	78	21
Pembangunan Jaya	Tjiputra ad others	Real estate	57	22
Metropolitan	several	Real estate	57	23
Soedarpo	Soedarpo Sastrosatomo	Shipping, trade, pharmaceuticals	35	23
Tahija	Julius Tahija	Finance	39	23

Source: Hal Hill, *The Indonesian Economy since 1966* (Melbourne: Cambridge University Press, 1996), p. 111.

With economic deregulation, new business opportunities emerged and conglomerates were able to do business in a wide range of areas, including cement, flour, automotive industries, banking, electric industries, manufacturing, textiles, pharmaceutical, retail, transportation, telecommunications, and property. The ethnic Chinese-owned conglomerates became major players in banking, agribusiness, manufacturing, and other sectors, while Bambang Trihatmodjo (Suharto's second son), through his conglomerate Bimantara, became the first to establish a private television channel in Indonesia. There were a number of other successful Indonesian or *pribumi* business figures such as Aburizal Bakrie (the Bakrie Group), Fadel Muhammad (Bukaka Group), Fahmi Idris (Kodel Group), Imam Taufik (Gunanusa Utama Group), Ponco Sutowo (Nugra Santana Group), Agus Kartasasmita (Catur Yasa Group), Bambang Wiyoga (Wiyoga Group), and Siswono Yudohusodo. These figures emerged as new economic players in Indonesia.[56] Many of their business activities flourished because of political connections with the then State Secretary Soedharmono and the Junior Minister for Domestic Industry Ginandjar Kartasasmita.[57]

However, among the problems which emerged during the boom period were the issues of equality and ethnicity. Not everyone could enjoy, let alone benefit from, the economic boom in Indonesia. The economic boom widened the gap between the rich and the poor in Indonesia. It also divided the country into two arenas: city and countryside, the former being associated with modernity and economic growth, the latter with decline and stagnation.[58] Indeed, the boom enjoyed by those who had resources and those who had political links with the elite and the bureaucracy. Those who had been excluded from it were the ordinary urban and rural people, and those who had been critical of the economic and political policies of the New Order government.

Sentiment against the ethnic Chinese increased during the boom period. Although the government attempted to encourage *pribumi* businesspeople, it failed to create business groups that could match the strength of the ethnic Chinese in the economy. Shobirin Nadj, senior researcher at the Centre for the Study of Democracy, puts this in the following way:

> One policy to balance out the economic growth among the ethnic Chinese businesspeople has been support for the development of *pribumi* businesspeople among the children of the elites...However it can be said now that for the large part, those *pribumi* businesspeople have lacked professional skills and many have failed. And indeed, they have not

engaged in pure business. They have relied on facilities. I think I can say that the Chinese have also advanced because of facilities, but they have carried out their business in a proper, businesslike manner, with the result that they have been able to advance, to develop.[59]

The ethnic Chinese are believed to control more than fifty per cent of the private sector of the economy in Indonesia in the 1990s.[60] As in Thailand, the success of the ethnic Chinese in the economy arose not only from their business skills but also from their connections with the political elites, including Suharto. This type of relationship was not new and parallels can be drawn on this point with the other countries in the Southeast Asian region.[61] Indeed, the success of the Chinese in the economic arena had long been the subject of suspicion and jealousy from ordinary Indonesians.

External Factors

Foreign aid from Western countries, especially the US and Japan, also contributed to economic growth in Indonesia. In 1967 the Western countries formed a consortium known as the Inter-Governmental Group on Indonesia (IGGI).[62] The involvement of the IGGI in Indonesia cannot be underestimated especially since this consortium helped Indonesia to deal with the balance of payments crisis at the end of the 1960s. Although Indonesia was not entirely dependent on foreign aid to finance its economic activities, the IGGI (later renamed the Consortium on Government of Indonesia, CGI) continued to provide financial aid throughout the New Order period.

As with Thailand, from the 1980s Japan replaced the US as Indonesia's major trading partner. This resulted from the strength of the Japanese economy and the yen, which encouraged Japanese companies to relocate their business activities to the Southeast Asian region, including Indonesia. The expansion of Japanese investment indeed assisted economic growth in Indonesia, which had begun to implement economic deregulation (Table 5.3). Many of Indonesia's natural products, such as oil, gas and minerals were exported to Japan. Other East Asian countries such as South Korea, Taiwan, and Hong Kong were also destinations for some of Indonesian's exports. However, Japanese investors in Indonesia prevailed in the manufacturing sector. For instance, the Astra Group, a joint venture between the Suryadjaya family and Honda, dominated the automotive sector in Indonesia over three decades.[63]

Table 5.3 Major Foreign Investors in Indonesia, 1980 and 1992 (per cent of total)

Countries	1980	1992
Japan	44.4	31.8
Hong Kong	11.5	13.0
Taiwan	1.3	9.9
Korea	0.9	7.2
Singapore	2.5	5.1
Australia	3.1	3.1
Western Pacific	6.9	1.5
Netherlands	3.7	5.6
United Kingdom	5.6	5.5
Germany	2.9	4.7
Other European countries	4.9	5.9
USA	10.5	4.8
Other	1.8	1.8
Total	100	100

Source: Hal Hill, *The Indonesian Economy since 1966* (Melbourne: Cambridge University Press, 1996), p. 90.

Limited Political Openness and Pressure for Political Change

It was suggested earlier that the implementation of economic deregulation in the 1980s changed the dynamics of Indonesian politics. To understand the political developments in Indonesia during this period, we must look closely at the factors that influenced the dynamics of political change in the 1990s. These were political openness, the political succession issue, the domination of the Indonesian military, the role of parliament, and the emergence of non-state actors in national politics.

Political Openness (Keterbukaan Politik)

The first signs of the growing pressure for political change in Indonesia emerged at the end of the 1980s when Indonesians participated in a series of public debates on political openness, or *keterbukaan politik*. The phrase "political openness" itself originated from Paul Wolfowitz, then US ambassador to Indonesia, in his farewell speech in 1989. Political openness quickly became a "buzzword" in Indonesia.[64] The government was unable to ignore this. Even among the members of the Indonesian elite, including Suharto, there was acknowledgment that political openness was needed, as Indonesia became more open economically, and there was acknowledgment that this could only be done by allowing individuals to speak freely on national issues.[65] Other high profile figures like the late General Sumitro and the Petition of 50 (*Petisi 50*) Group (a group of retired generals and politicians who had been critical of Suharto) suggested that there was a need for reform of the existing political system, and that this would require allowing more political parties to contest general elections, creating a new electoral system, and strengthening the Parliament.[66] The non-state actors such as NGOs, students, and academics used the debates on political openness as a starting point from which to argue the need for fully democratising the Indonesian political system.[67]

For a short period between 1990 and 1994, which was known as the period of political openness (*jaman keterbukaan politik*), urban Indonesians experienced relative freedom of speech and expression. This is not to say that a genuine democratic space was established in Indonesia. During this period, in fact, the government continued to carry out political crackdowns, such as banning theatre performances and repressing student protests, workers' disputes, and NGO activities in a number of cities.[68] The most serious crackdown that ended the period of political openness, occurred on 21 June 1994, when Minister of Information Harmoko banned two respected weekly news magazines *Tempo* and *Editor*, and the tabloid *Detik*.[69]

We can reach some conclusions here. It can be argued that there are several factors that might have influenced the government officials to clamp down on the public debate about political openness. First, the meaning of political openness had been interpreted in different ways, and it seemed many government officials at both upper and lower levels had no clear idea about what was and what was not "allowed" during the brief period of political openness. The safest way was to use security-minded approaches in responding to the growing public demands for political openness. Second, it is suggested that President Suharto himself was the one who decided to end the period of political openness, when it appeared that the debate had reached a level which could have threatened his power. At that time, and especially between 1992-1993, he was securing his presidential re-election and, consequently, he and his supporters wanted to ensure that he would be nominated again and his political future secured.[70]

Furthermore, there was no consensus among the political elites about the scope and nature of political openness. This made it hard for either side, both the pro-status quo and the pro-reform camps, to come to a consensus about what sort of political openness suited Indonesia. An idea put forward by Arief Budiman deserves mention here. In a paper published in 1992, he argued a point about *limited democracy*:

> This democracy exists when there is a conflict among the state elites. This conflict also creates some kind of democratic space. People can criticise one faction of the 'powers that be', and be protected by the opposition faction...However, when the conflict within the elites is over, this democratic space will probably disappear also.[71]

The conflict in question here was the disagreement of top military leaders (led by Chief of the Armed Forces General Benny Murdani) over Suharto's decision to appoint Sudharmono as Vice-President in 1988.[72] This conflict was not resolved until Suharto was re-elected as President at the Peoples' Consultative Assembly (*Majelis Permusyawaratan Rakyat*) meeting in 1993. The price for the appointment of Sudharmono was that General Benny Murdani and his supporters lost their positions in the government, as Suharto moved quickly to eliminate his opponents and critics in 1993.

The other factor that made the period of political openness short-lived can be found in the nature of the civil society in Indonesia. There had been much debate on this issue and the general consensus was that the creation of a democratic political system in Indonesia would only be achieved when the civil society was strong.[73] As Arief Budiman has pointed out, civil society in Indonesia was weak and divided along religious, racial and class lines.[74] More importantly, there was not a solid and united opposition force that could challenge Suharto. In other words, there was no coalition of opposition groups that could replace the New Order government. The result was that Suharto and his government found it relatively easy to defeat the opposition forces.

The Political Succession Debacle

Another important factor in Indonesian politics in the 1990s was the uncertainty surrounding the political succession of President Suharto, who had dominated Indonesian politics since the 1960s. The authoritarian political system ensured Suharto's supremacy over other contenders for power. His political survival was based on his capacity to create and manipulate a situation where every political group and leader looked for his support, and thus he easily exercised his power whenever and however he chose. In the same way, Suharto was able to eliminate potential contenders for his power, whether they were students, civilian politicians, or former generals.[75] In describing Suharto's personal power, Loekman Soetrisno says:

...one issue that is problematic in Indonesia is that decision-making is in the hands of a single person, that is Suharto...because he is skilled at playing the cards as the Commander in Chief. And further, perhaps, he is skilled at bringing his adjutants into powerful positions. This makes them dependent on him. Whether that will be so in the time ahead, we don't know. But what concerns me is that if he dies, nothing is really ready. The system does not yet really function. This could be a big problem for Indonesia.[76]

During the period of political openness, the political succession issue became an important discussion topic in Indonesia. Questions arose both domestically and internationally: Who would replace Suharto? Would he handle the political succession smoothly? When would it take place and would the nature of Indonesian politics change when he was finally gone? No one knew the answers, of course. Given the extent of Suharto's power, it was impossible to sustain political openness in Indonesia without including him in the process. Until Suharto was forced to resign in May 1998, any effort towards establishing a democratic political system in Indonesia was fraught with difficulty.[77]

A number of historical and political factors made the political succession in Indonesia a compelling issue. First, Indonesia had no experience of a peaceful and smooth transition from one political regime to another. The Dutch colonial government left Indonesia and was replaced by the Japanese through a war, and it was again through war that Indonesia gained its Independence. The transition from Sukarno to Suharto in the mid-1960s was accompanied by economic, political and social crises, which traumatised a whole generation of Indonesians. Most Indonesian political leaders had no experience in, or understanding of, proper institutional mechanisms for political succession. Second, related to the above point is the fact that it was a failure of the existing political system that it did not address the political succession issue. In the absence of any system of "checks and balances" a situation was created in which Suharto could act as a dictator, and Suharto would become a victim of the political system he created. Third, the issue of Suharto's children also complicated the political succession issue in Indonesia. With the involvement of his children in a wide range of businesses with monopoly rights and other special privileges, Suharto held concerns for their safety in the future when he would be no longer in power.[78]

Indeed, the short period of political openness that ended in 1994 failed to change the political system which already had provided Suharto with too much power. Although a democratic space emerged during this period, there was no development of political initiatives that could have led to the establishment of a more representative political system in Indonesia. This happened partly because the civil society in Indonesia was weak and also because there was no organised opposition group to challenge the New Order government. In addition, the absence of a structure through which the question of the political succession could be addressed made it difficult for the government to change the course of Indonesian politics.

The Political Role of the Indonesian Military

During the period of political openness in the 1990s, more and more Indonesians, even former military leaders, began to openly question the role of the Indonesian military (*Angkatan Bersenjata Republik Indonesia* or ABRI) in politics.[79] Criticism of the Indonesian military focused on three things.[80] First, the need to abolish the appointment system for representatives of the Indonesian military in the House of Representatives (*Dewan Perwakilan Rakyat*, DPR). Until the 1990s the military had always been allocated 100 seats in the House of Representatives. The public demanded that the allocation of seats for the military be reduced gradually, or even abolished, in order to make the House of Representatives more democratic and more accountable to the people. Second, there was pressure for the Indonesian military to withdraw from its political role and to allow civilian leaders to take charge of political and social affairs, on the grounds that as Indonesia approached the challenges and complexities of the new millennium, there was a need for the Indonesian military to be more professional in its own field, that is military affairs. Thirdly, there was a call for the military to take a stand for the interests of the nation.[81]

The difficulty of removing the Indonesian military from politics is primarily centred on its insistence on what is known in Indonesia as its dual function (*dwi fungsi*) role. The roots of *dwi fungsi* are found in the Independence period of the 1940s. It was developed into a concept by General Nasution in the 1950s with the aim of increasing military involvement in non-military affairs.[82] After Suharto gained power in 1966, he used the concept to institutionalise the role of the military in politics, with the result that it soon dominated the political and economic life of the nation. In contrast to Thailand, where the involvement of the Thai military in politics gradually decreased during the 1990s, the Indonesian military maintained its dominant position. Many military officers, both active and retired, occupied top positions in the bureaucracy, Parliament, state-owned enterprises (SOEs), and in the Cabinet. The Indonesian military had since the 1960s controlled the social and political life of the nation by using a security network system that provided a chain of command from the cities down to the smallest village units throughout Indonesia.[83] This domination caused resentment not only among civilian politicians, but also among more radical groups such as students and activists who believed that the military's *dwi fungsi* role was a major stumbling block on the path to the establishment of a democratic political system in Indonesia.[84]

The Weak Parliament

The New Order government put in place a political system that put an emphasis on "harmony" over "conflict" in solving political differences. In Indonesia this principle is known as *musyawarah untuk mufakat* (decision based on a mutual agreement). This political system did not recognise the government-opposition type of political culture which operates in most Western democratic countries. To implement it, the New Order government allowed only three political parties to compete in the general elections and to be represented in the House of Representatives. These political parties were the ruling Golkar party (*Golongan Karya*), the Indonesian Democratic Party (*Partai Demokrasi Indonesia*, PDI, which was an alliance of the nationalist and Christian-based political parties) and the Development Unity Party (*Partai Persatuan Pembangunan*, PPP, or an alliance of Islam-based political parties).

From the 1971 general election until the most recent in 1997, the Golkar Party won overwhelmingly (Figure 5.1). Consequently, six general elections in Indonesia did not change the government or the head of state, President Suharto. Rather they formalised and justified the dominance of the New Order government. In addition, Golkar occupied more than fifty per cent of 400 seats for elected members in the House of Representatives (*Dewan Perwakilan Rakyat*, DPR), and with the support of the appointed members from the Indonesian military, the bargaining position of Golkar easily overwhelmed that of the other two parties. Furthermore, as a legislative branch of the government, the House of Representatives was weak. It never scrutinised or used its legislative rights. Hadimulyo, a member of parliament from the Development Unity Party observed:

> As a legislative body, parliament indeed formulates laws. But the 1945 Constitution states that this should be done with the President. The President cannot pass laws except with the agreement of parliament. Parliament actually has the right of initiative, but from 1971 until now [1997], there has not been a single law initiated by the parliament.[85]

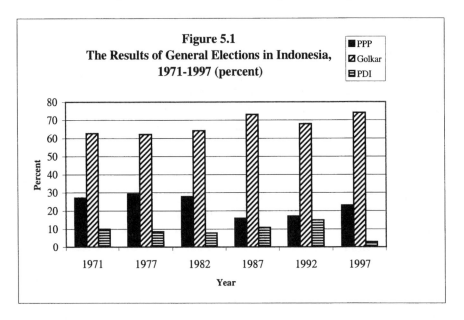

Figure 5.1
The Results of General Elections in Indonesia, 1971-1997 (percent)

Source: Priyambudi Sulistiyanto, "The May 1997 General Election in Indonesia, What Went Wrong?", *Current Affairs Bulletin*, vol. 74, no. 2 (August-September, 1997).

In other words, during the New Order period, the House of Representatives operated only as a rubber stamp for government policies. During the 1990s the demands for reform of the existing political system and the House of Representatives became stronger and louder. The rapid economic changes that had resulted in the expansion of the educated and middle class had also gradually changed political expectations in Indonesia. This, of course, put pressure on the House of Representatives to perform well in representing the people as well as in constructively criticising government policies. But with political parties under tight control and with appointed military representatives, the House of Representatives was simply not able to represent the interests and aspirations of the Indonesian people whose demands were more sophisticated than two or three decades ago.

Arbi Sanit argued in 1997 that the political system was basically unsustainable and therefore had to be changed.[86] He proposed a wide range of reforms including reforming the political parties' regulations and the electoral law, establishing political parties, making political parties more independent financially, abolishing the appointment system for military representatives, and strengthening the bargaining position of the House of

Representatives as a legislative body.[87] In the lead-up to the resignation of Suharto in 1998, there were no attempts to reform the political system in Indonesia. It could be concluded, therefore, that the establishment of a more democratic political system in Indonesia would only be possible when Suharto was no longer in power.

The Non-State Actors and Pressure for Political Change

Although the existing political system and the formal political institutions had not changed much in over three decades, the rapid economic growth that Indonesia enjoyed during the 1980s and into the 1990s had influenced the emergence of non-state actors in national politics. In contrast to Thailand, the emergence of these non-state actors in Indonesia did not lead to the growth of a civil society to the point that it could act as a counter-balance to the New Order government.[88] MacIntyre points out that business groups were beginning to influence the policy-making process too, but it is suggested that the political system under Suharto did not allow non-bureaucratic groups to participate to any significant extent.[89] Nonetheless, the emergence of these non-state actors was important, particularly as they became advocates for political change in Indonesia.

The Elites and Moderate Groups

The elite conflict that occurred during the 1980s resulted in the opening of a democratic space in Indonesia. It was during this time that a number of small groupings consistently called for political change in Indonesia. These were, for instance, the Petition of 50 (*Petisi 50*) group, the Forum for the Restoration of Public Sovereignty (*Forum untuk Pemulihan Kedaulatan Rakyat*, FPKR), the Indonesian League for the Restoration of Democracy, and the Democracy Forum (*Forum Demokrasi*, Fordem). The political orientation of these groups was basically moderate and therefore they accommodated people from a variety of backgrounds, including retired generals, politicians, former bureaucrats, intellectuals, academics, prominent lawyers, senior journalists, businesspeople and also religious leaders. Two of them, the FPKR and the Forum Demokrasi, will be described here.

The FPKR was formed in May 1991 in Jakarta and was led by three prominent figures, namely retired Lt. Gen. Dharsono, Abdul Madjid, and Professor Deliar Noer.[90] This political group was an interesting one because it represented a broad political coalition of progressive elements of the military, nationalists, and modernist Islam leaders. This coalition called for the restoration of the people's rights, and they believed this could be achieved by strengthening the bargaining position of the parliament against the government. The Forum Demokrasi was formed in April 1991 and was led by Abdurrachman Wahid, the leader of *Nahdlatul Ulama* (the largest Islamic organisation in Indonesia) with the support of 45 prominent figures such as the well-known Catholic priest Y.B. Mangunwijaya, the human rights lawyer T. Mulya Lubis, the outspoken academic Arief Budiman, and the journalist Gunawan Muhammad.[91] The Forum Demokrasi was not a political party, but a forum where Indonesians could engage freely in debate and discussion about the importance of democracy in Indonesia. Its focus, therefore, was on public education and influencing government policy rather than on organising a popular or mass movement with the aim of replacing President Suharto and the New Order government.

The Middle Class-based Groups

In the debate about the emergence of the Indonesian middle class during the 1980s and the 1990s, it was generally accepted that its political role was a weak one and that therefore it had not become a driving force for democratisation in Indonesia.[92] Moore argued in his seminal work, *Social Origins of Dictatorship and Democracy* that this was certainly different from the experiences of many Western democratic countries, where the middle class played an important role in strengthening democratic institutions such as parliament, and the rule of law, and the promotion of human rights.[93] However, there were signs of emergence of opposition activities organised by middle class-based groups from the early 1990s. Those who joined these groups were mainly educated and urban people, students, non-government organisation (NGO) activists, academics, artists, and journalists. These groups became involved in different types of activities in the areas of human rights, the environment, consumerism, the media, public policy, women's and gender issues, and others. Two of these groups, the Alliance of Independent Journalists (*Aliansi Jurnalis Indonesia*, AJI) and the Women's Solidarity for Human Rights (*Solidaritas Perempuan*, SP), are worth looking at in some detail.

The *Aliansi Jurnalis Indonesia* (AJI) was established in August 1994 in response to the government's decision to close down the *Tempo* and *Editor* news magazines and the *Detik* tabloid.[94] It was established by a group of young journalists, many of whom had previously worked for these three banned publications. The AJI became a rival to the government-backed journalist union *Persatuan Wartawan Indonesia* (PWI), which had refused to protest the government closure of *Tempo, Editor* and *Detik*. The significance of the AJI was that it was the first organisation of this sort which advocated strongly the importance of freedom of the press in Indonesia. This freedom was certainly denied by the New Order government, which used methods such as censoring and banning to repress the freedom of the press in Indonesia.[95] The presence of the AJI was important, because it showed that some elements of the middle class were becoming interested in pressuring the government on this issue. The *Solidaritas Perempuan* (SP) was established in December 1990 in Jakarta, with the aim of promoting women's rights particularly among workers and Indonesian migrant workers.[96] SP was not the first women's organisation, it was one of many already established in Indonesia, its work was significant because SP was the first women's organisation to raise awareness about the poor working conditions of Indonesian women working outside Indonesia. SP both promoted and advocated women's rights through public education campaigns and public demonstrations. This was quite an achievement, given that many NGOs in Indonesia avoided using public demonstrations or protests because of government restrictions on these.

The Popular and Grassroots Groups

The 1990s also saw the rise of popular movements in Indonesia's major cities. It is true that popular movements had strong historical roots in Indonesia, but under the New Order government any popular-based activities had been suppressed because the government regarded them as supporting the ideology of communism. The collective trauma caused by government elimination of left wing activities and ideas remained strong, making it difficult for the spread of popular and grassroots movements under the New Order.

However, there were several NGOs and political groups in the 1990s which advocated the need to uphold the rights of the people, especially those who were losers from the economic boom such as workers and peasants.[97] They used more radical approaches in advocating their opinions and views. They, too, often held mass protests and demonstrations, which frequently led to confrontation with the government. The presence of these groups was significant in bringing about change in that they helped to strengthen the bargaining position of the people who mostly lived at the bottom end of the social scale of

Indonesian society. The Solidarity Free Trade Union (*Serikat Buruh Merdeka Setia Kawan*), the Indonesian Welfare Trade Union (*Serikat Buruh Sejahtera Indonesia*, SBSI), the new People's Democratic Party (*Partai Rakyat Demokrat*) and Megawati Sukarnoputri's Indonesian Democratic Party (*Partai Demokrasi Indonesia-Perjuangan*) are just a few of them.

With the support mostly of factory workers in the major cities, the Solidarity Free Trade Union was formed in 1990, led by Saut Aritonang, and, in 1993, a union lawyer Dr. Mochtar Pakpahan formed the Indonesian Welfare Trade Union (SBSI).[98] The formation of these labour unions was significant politically because the latter challenged the domination of the government-backed All Indonesian Workers' Union (*Serikat Pekerja Seluruh Indonesia*, SPSI), which was the only labour union that had been allowed to exist in Indonesia in the previous three decades.[99] Although the SPSI had always claimed to represent the interests of Indonesian workers, in reality it failed to protect the welfare of Indonesian workers and to guarantee workers' rights. In almost every labour dispute the SPSI took the side of the government and employer rather than that of the workers. The new labour unions were established to increase the bargaining power of workers in Indonesia.

A new political party, the Peoples' Democratic Party (*Partai Rakyat Demokrat*, PRD), was formed in July 1996, and was led by Budiman Sujatmiko, a prominent student activist. With the support of students and NGO activists throughout Indonesia, the PRD openly challenged the government law which allowed only three political parties to exist in Indonesia. It called for popular democracy in Indonesia. The PRD's profile and popularity rose after it was scapegoated for the riots that occurred in Jakarta following the government's decision to topple Megawati Sukarnoputri as the leader of the Indonesian Democratic Party on 27 July 1996.[100] The political significance of the PRD was that it represented the views and aspirations of the young generation that did not believe that the existing political system could bring about the political change Indonesia needed.

Meanwhile, the rise of Megawati's Indonesian Democratic Party, known as *PDI-Perjuangan*, was also an important phenomenon in Indonesian politics in the 1990s. There is no doubt that the popularity of *PDI-Perjuangan* lay in the charisma of its leader, Megawati Sukarnoputri, one of the daughters of Indonesia's first President, Sukarno. Although Megawati herself was part of the political establishment in Indonesia, her party gained much support from the young generation and from poor people in cities throughout Indonesia. It also represented those who wanted to see the return of a democratic political system in Indonesia.

Conclusion

This chapter has examined the political and economic issues surrounding Indonesia's economic boom in the 1980s and the 1990s. It is suggested that anti-colonial feeling and a strong sense of nationalism among the Indonesian people shaped political and economic life during the post-independence period. The colonial experience was deeply rooted in the political leaders in Indonesia and influenced the way they formulated and implemented their policies. This was particularly true during the 1950s when the political leaders inherited a colonial economic structure which was dominated by Dutch-owned companies and the ethnic Chinese business groups. This legacy led the political leaders to implement state-led and nationalist economic strategies to dismantle that colonial structure. Indonesia and its leaders faced a difficult choice between establishing a democratic or authoritarian political system during the 1950s and the 1960s. As became clear during the Guided Democracy period, Sukarno ultimately chose authoritarianism over democracy as the political system for Indonesia.

The economic and political crises brought about by Sukarno prompted Suharto to implement political and economic policies aimed at creating political stability and economic growth. The support of the military and technocrats helped Suharto to implement these policies and to firmly establish his grip on power in the early days of the New Order government. Political stability was needed in order to create economic development. However, political stability was achieved at the expense of civil society. An authoritarian political system was established which allowed only three parties to exist and to contest elections. That political system enabled the maintenance over three decades of Suharto's dominant position above all other contenders in Indonesian politics.

But the economic growth did not last and Indonesia experienced the collapse of oil and commodity prices and the world recession in the early 1980s. After this Indonesia faced an economic crisis, which forced the government to implement economic deregulation policies aimed at making the economy more open and export-oriented. Between the 1980s and the mid-1990s Indonesia embarked on a period of economic deregulation. As a result, Indonesia experienced an economic boom during this period. The boom created opportunities for the private sector to become involved in economic activities in areas which previously were restricted to the government. However, those who benefited from this boom were mainly those domestic business groups, which had connections with the political elites and many of these belonged to the ethnic Chinese.

The economic boom of the 1980s and 1990s did not change Indonesian political life, in the sense that the New Order government remained in power. But pressure for political change began to emerge at the end of the 1980s and continued through the 1990s, triggered by elite conflict which resulted in a limited opening of democratic space. It was during this limited political openness that competing groups began to put pressure on the government to replace the existing political system with a more democratic one. The uncertainty surrounding the political succession of President Suharto combined with the dominant political role of the Indonesian military and the weak parliament became a stumbling block on the path to further political change. The pressure for political change continued with the emergence of non-state actors in the 1990s, who steadily called for the establishment of a democratic political system in Indonesia. It is in this context that the causes and consequences of the economic crisis which occurred in Indonesia in 1997 and 1998 which will be explored in the following chapter, are situated.

Notes

[1] This view can be found in Harold Crouch and Hal Hill (eds.) *Indonesia Assessment 1992, Political Perspectives on the 1990s* (Canberra: Department of Political and Social Change, Research School of Pacific Studies, Australian National University P, 1992); also see Richard Robison, "Indonesia: Tensions in State and Regime" in Kevin Hewison, Richard Robison and Garry Rodan (eds.) *Southeast Asia in the 1990s, Authoritarianism, Democracy and Capitalism* (Sydney: Allen and Unwin, 1993), pp. 41-74.

[2] Benedict Anderson, *Imagined Communities, Reflections on the Origin and Spread of Nationalism*, revised edition (London and New York, 1991), pp. 116-118.

[3] Richard Robison, *Indonesia: The Rise of Capital* (Sydney: Allen and Unwin, 1986), p. 29.

[4] John S. Furnival, *Colonial Policy and Practice: A Comparative Study of Burma and Netherlands India* (New York: New York University Press, 1947).

[5] M. C. Ricklefs, *A History of Modern Indonesia Since c. 1300*, Second Edition (London: Macmillan Press Ltd., 1993), especially chapter fourteen.

[6] Anton Lucas, *One Soul One Struggle, Region and Revolution in Indonesia* (Sydney: Allen and Unwin, 1991), especially chapter four.

[7] Ricklefs, *op.cit*, p. 204.

[8] The best study of the Independence period in Indonesia can be found in George McT. Kahin, *Nationalism and Revolution in Indonesia* (Ithaca: Cornell University Press, 1952).

[9] Ricklefs, *A History of Modern Indonesia*, p. 237.

[10] Herbert Feith, *The Decline of Constitutional Democracy in Indonesia* (Ithaca: Cornell University Press, 1962).

[11] Adnan Buyung Nasution, *The Aspiration for Constitutional Government in Indonesia: A Socio-legal Study of the Indonesian Konstituante 1956-1959* (Den Haag: CIP-Gegevens Koninklijke Biblioteek, 1992).

[12] Robison, *Indonesia: The Rise of Capital*, p. 41.

[13] Ricklefs, *A History of Modern Indonesia*, pp. 259-262.

[14] Daniel S. Lev, *The Transition to Guided Democracy: Indonesian Politics, 1957-1959* (Ithaca: Southeast Asia Program, Cornell University, 1966).

[15] Ricklefs, p. 273.

[16] Iwan J. Azis, "Indonesia" in John Williamson (ed.) *The Political Economy of Policy Reform* (Washington D.C.: Institute for International Economics, 1994), pp. 385-386.

[17] On the role of the Indonesian military in the attempted coup in 1965, see Harold Crouch, *The Army and Politics in Indonesia* (Ithaca: Cornell University Press, 1978).

[18] Ricklefs, *A History of Modern Indonesia*, pp. 280-281; and also see Benedict Anderson and Ruth McVey, *A Preliminary Analysis of the October 1, 1965 Coup in Indonesia* (Ithaca: Cornell Modern Indonesia Project, Cornell University, 1971).

[19] He was forced to resign on 21 May 1998. By then he was one of the world's longest serving political leaders, second only to Fidel Castro in Cuba. On the circumstances of his resignation, see the following chapter.

[20] On the debate about the theoretical approaches of the New Order government, see Andrew MacIntyre, *Business and Politics in Indonesia* (Sydney: Allen and Unwin, 1990), especially chapter two; and also see Indria Samego, "Politik Pembangunan Orde Baru: Beberapa Interpretasi Teoritik Mengenai Peran Negara dalam Mengembangkan Pengusaha Nasional" [The Politics of New Order's Development: Some Theoretical Interpretation on the Role of State in the Development of National Entrepreneur] in Syamsuddin and Riza Sihbudi (eds.) *Menelaah Kembali Format Politik Orde Baru* [Rethinking the Political Format of New Order] (Jakarta: LIPI and Gramedia, 1995), pp. 115-141.

[21] Jamie Mackie and Andrew MacIntyre, "Politics" in Hal Hill (ed.) *Indonesia's New Order, The Dynamics of Socio-economic Transformation* (Sydney: Allen and Unwin, 1994), pp. 1-53.

[22] Robert Cribb (ed.) *The Indonesian Killings of 1965-1966: Studies from Java and Bali* (Clayton: Monash University Centre of Southeast Asian Studies, 1990).

[23] Ricklefs, *A History of Modern Indonesia*, p. 299; and also see Ken Ward, *The 1971 Election in Indonesia: An East Java Case Study* (Clayton: Monash University Centre of Southeast Asian Studies, 1974).

[24] Azis, "Indonesia", p. 398.

[25] Hal Hill, *The Indonesian Economy since 1966* (Melbourne: Cambridge University Press, 1996).

[26] Ibid, p. 172.

[27] Adam Schwarz, *A Nation in Waiting, Indonesia in the 1990s* (Sydney: Allen and Unwin, 1994), pp. 107-108.

[28] Jamie Mackie, "Changing Patterns of Chinese Big Business in Southeast Asia" in Ruth MacVey (ed.) *Southeast Asian Capitalists* (Ithaca: Southeast Asia Program, Cornell University, 1992), p. 180.

[29] Ian Chalmers, "Introduction" in Ian Chalmers and Vedi R. Hadiz, *The Politics of Economic Development in Indonesia, Contending Perspectives* (London and New York: Routledge, 1997), pp. 22-23.

[30] Azis, "Indonesia", pp. 411-412; and also Robison, pp. 169-170.

[31] Robison, pp. 164-165.

[32] On the Pertamina affair, see John Bresnan, *Managing Indonesia, The Modern Political Economy* (New York: Columbia University Press, 1993), pp. 166-167.

[33] Jamie Mackie, "Indonesia: Economic Growth and Depoliticization" in James Morley (ed.) *Driven by Growth, Political Change in the Asia-Pacific Region* (London: East Gate, 1993), p. 87.

[34] Sjahrir, "The Indonesian Deregulation Process: Problems, Constraints and Prospects" in John W. Langford and K. Lorne Brownsey (eds.) *Economic Policy-Making in the Asia-Pacific Region* (Halifax: The Institute for Research on Public Policy, 1990), pp. 321-339.

[35] Azis, "Indonesia", p. 414.

[36] Sjahrir, p. 333.

[37] Richard Robison, "Politics and Markets in Indonesia's Post-oil Era" in Garry Rodan, Kevin Hewison and Richard Robison (eds.) *The Political Economy of South-East Asia* (Melbourne: Oxford University Press, 1997), pp. 48-49.

[38] Jamie, "Changing Patterns of Chinese Big Business in Southeast Asia", p. 182.

[39] Robison, pp. 40-41.

[40] Azis, "Indonesia", p. 398.

[41] Amar Bhattacharya and Mari Pangestu, *Indonesia, Development Transformation and Public Policy* (Washington D.C.: The World Bank, 1993).

[42] Mari Pangestu, "Managing Economic Policy Reforms in Indonesia" in Mari Pangestu (ed.) *Economic Reform, Deregulation and Privatization, The*

Indonesian Experience (Jakarta: Centre for Strategic and International Studies, 1996), p. 7.

[43] Ibid, pp. 8-9.

[44] Bhattacharya and Pangestu, *op.cit*, p. 39; and also Robison, "Politics and Markets in Indonesia's Post-oil Era", p. 55.

[45] For further discussion on Habibie and his intellectual background, see B. J. Habibie, *Ilmu Pengetahuan, Tehnologi dan Pembangunan Bangsa, Menuju Dimensi Baru Pembangunan Indonesia* (Jakarta: Center for Information and Development Studies, 1995). For foreign observers' comments, see Robert C. Rice, "The Habibie Approach to Science, Technology and National Development" in Hal Hill and Thee Kian Wie (eds.) *Indonesia's Technological Challenge* (Singapore and Canberra: Institute of Southeast Asian Studies and Research School of Pacific and Asian Studies, Australian National University, 1998), pp. 185-198.

[46] Takashi Shiraishi, "Rewiring the Indonesian State" in Daniel S. Lev and Ruth McVey (eds.) *Making Indonesia* (Ithaca: Southeast Asia Program, Cornell University, 1996), pp. 171-174.

[47] Robison, p. 52.

[48] For more information about CIDES, see <http://www.cides.org.id>

[49] Robert W. Hefner, "Islam, State, and Civil Society: ICMI and the Struggle for the Indonesian Middle Class", *Indonesia*, no. 56 (1993), pp. 1-35.

[50] Ross H. McLeod, "Some Comments on 'The Funding of PT DSTP: A High-Technology Project'" in Hal Hill and Thee Kian Wie (eds.) *Indonesia's Technological Challenge* (Singapore and Canberra: Institute of Southeast Asian Studies and Research School of Pacific and Asian Studies, Australian National University, 1998), pp. 234-237.

[51] Andrew MacIntyre, "The Politics of Finance in Indonesia: Command, Confusion, and Competition" in Stephan Haggard, Chung H. Lee and Sylvia Maxfield (eds.) *The Politics of Finance in Developing Countries* (Ithaca and London: Cornell University Press, 1993), p. 154

[52] On the ideology of *pembangunan*, see Chalmers, "Introduction" in *The Politics of Economic Development in Indonesia, Contending Perspectives*, pp. 4-5.

[53] Interview with Dr. Alex Irwan, Jakarta, 23 September 1997.

[54] Schwarz, *A Nation in Waiting*, pp. 139-144.

[55] For more discussion on the Bank Central Asia, see Robison, *Indonesia: The Rise of Capital*, pp. 306-308.

[56] Schwarz, p. 128.

[57] On the roles of Sudharmono and Ginanjar in expanding the role of Indonesian pribumi business figures, see Jeffrey Winters, *Power in Motion: Capital Mobility and the Indonesian State* (Ithaca: Cornell University Press, 1996)

[58] Schwarz, *A Nation in Waiting*, p. 58.

[59] Interview with E. Shobirin Nadj, Jakarta (19 September 1997).

[60] Schwarz, *op.cit*, p. 99.

[61] Ruth McVey, "The Materialization of the Southeast Asian Entrepreneur" in *Southeast Asian Capitalists* (Ithaca: Southeast Asian Program, Cornell University, 1992), pp. 7-33.

[62] Hal Hill, *The Indonesian Economy since 1966*, pp. 65-66.

[63] Yuri Sato, "The Astra Group: A Pioneer of Management Modernization in Indonesia", *The Developing Economies*, vol. xxxiv, no. (September 1996), pp. 247-280.

[64] On the debate about political openness at the end of the 1980s, see Max Lane, *'Openness', Political Discontent and Succession in Indonesia: Political Developments in Indonesia, 1989-91* (Brisbane: Centre for the Study of Australia-Asia Relations, Griffith University, 1991).

[65] Suharto mentioned the need for political openness in Indonesia during his speech to celebrate Independence Day in August 1990. See Schwarz, *A Nation in Waiting*, p. 231.

[66] Lane, p. 35.

[67] On the opposition movement in the 1990s, see Edward Aspinall, "The Broadening Base of Political Opposition in Indonesia" in Garry Rodan (ed.) *Political Oppositions in Industrialising Asia* (London and New York: Routledge, 1996), pp. 215-240.

[68] Theatre performances of *Suksesi* and *Opera Kecoa* organised by Nano Riantiarno were banned by the authorities. See Schwarz, *A Nation in Waiting*, pp. 232-233.

[69] For further discussion on this issue, see Ariel Heryanto, "Indonesian Middle-Class Opposition in the 1990s" in Garry Rodan (ed.) *Political Oppositions in Industrialising Asia* (London and New York: Routledge, 1996), pp. 241-271.

[70] In fact, Suharto was re-elected without opposition for the 1993-1998 term and former Chief of Armed Forces, General Try Sutrisno was elected as Vice-President.

[71] Arief Budiman, "Indonesian Politics in the 1990s" in Harold Crouch and Hal Hill (eds.) *Indonesia Assessment 1992, Political Perspectives on the 1990s* (Canberra: Department of Political and Social Change, Research School of Pacific Studies, Australian National University, 1992), p. 132.

[72] Michael Vatikiotis, *Indonesian Politics under Suharto, Order, Development and Pressure for Change* (London and New York: Routledge, 1993), p. 145.

[73] For a discussion on civil society in Indonesia, see Arief Budiman, "Introduction: From A Conference to a Book", in Arief Budiman (ed.), *State and Civil Society in Indonesia* (Clayton: Centre of Southeast Asian Studies, Monash University, 1990), pp. 1-14; and also, see Muhammad AS Hikam, *Demokrasi dan Civil Society* (Jakarta: LP3ES, 1996).

[74] Budiman, "Indonesian Politics in the 1990s", pp. 133-134.

[75] On oppositional politics within the Indonesian Armed Forces during the 1980s, see David Jenkins, *Soeharto and his Generals: Indonesian Military Politics 1975-1983* (Ithaca: Cornell Modern Indonesia Project, Cornell University, 1984).

[76] Interview with Professor Loekman Soetrisno, Yogyakarta (15 August 1997).

[77] Vatikiotis, *Indonesian Politics under Suharto*, pp. 139-164; and also Schwarz, *A Nation in Waiting*, pp. 276-281.

[78] Suharto's concern can be seen to have been well-founded on the basis that one of his children, Hutomo "Tommy" Mandala Putera, is currently on trial for corruption.

[79] For instance, see Hasnan Habib, "The Role of the Armed Forces in Indonesia's Future Political Development", in Harold Crouch and Hal Hill (eds.) *Indonesia Assessment 1992, Political Perspectives on the 1990s* (Canberra: Department of Political and Social Change, Research School of Pacific Studies, Australian National University, 1992), pp. 83-94; and also Soemitro, "Tempat and Peran Abri dalam Politik" [Place and the Role of Armed Forces in Politics] in Rustam Ibrahim (ed.) *Mempertimbangkan Kembali Format Politik Orde Baru* [Rethinking the Political Format of the New Order] (Jakarta: Centre for the Study of Democracy, 1997), pp. 113-121.

[80] For instance, in 1996, the Institute of Indonesian Sciences (*Lembaga Ilmu Pengetahuan Indonesia*, LIPI), outlined a proposal calling for a gradual reduction in the number of military seats in the House of Representatives. See LIPI, "Menuju Reformasi Politik Orde Baru: Beberapa Usulan Perbaikan" [Towards Political Reform of the New Order: Some Suggestions for Improvement] in Syamsudin Haris and Riza Sihbudi (eds.) *Menelaah Kembali Format Politik Orde Baru* [Rethinking the Political Format of the New Order] (Jakarta: Gramedia Pustaka Utama, 1996), pp. 182-191.

[81] Harold Crouch, "Masalah Dwifungsi ABRI" [On the Dual Function of the Indonesian Armed Forces] in Syamsuddin Haris and Riza Sihbudi (eds.) *Menelaah Kembali Format Politik Orde Baru* [Rethinking about the Political Format of the New Order] (Jakarta:Gramedia Pustaka Utama, 1996), pp. 97-114.

[82] On the origins of the dual function role, see Salim Said, *Genesis of Power: General Sudirman and the Indonesian Military in Politics, 1945-1949* (Jakarta: Pustaka Sinar Harapan, 1992).

[83] Ricklefs, *A History of Modern Indonesia*, pp. 267-268.

[84] LIPI, "Menuju Reformasi Politik Orde Baru: Beberapa Usulan Perbaikan" [Towards Political Reform of the New Order: Some Suggestions for Improvement], p. 184.

[85] Interview with Hadimulyo, Jakarta (16 September 1997).

[86] Arbi Sanit, "Transformasi Partai dan Reformasi Sistem Kepartaian Indonesia" in Rustam Ibrahim (ed.) *Mempertimbangkan Kembali Format Orde Baru* (Jakarta: Centre for the Study of Democracy, 1997), pp. 83-95.

[87] Ibid, p. 93.

[88] Hikam, *Demokrasi dan Civil Society*, pp. 7-8.

[89] Andrew MacIntyre, "State-Society Relations in New Order Indonesia: The Case of Business" in Arief Budiman (ed.) *State and Civil Society in Indonesia* (Clayton: Centre of Southeast Asian Studies, Monash University, 1990), pp. 369-394.

[90] Lane, *'Openness', Political Discontent and Succession in Indonesia*, pp. 69-70.

[91] It must be noted that according to Abdurrahman Wahid the establishment of the Forum Demokrasi was prompted by the rise of sectarianism in Indonesian politics especially after President Suharto openly gave his support to the formation of the Indonesian Muslim scholars organization ICMI. See Colin Brown, "Political Developments, 1990-91" in Hal Hill (ed.) *Indonesia Assessment 1991* (Canberra: Department of Political and Social Change, Research School of Pacific Studies, the Australian National University, 1991), pp. 47-48; Harold Crouch, "An Ageing President, An Ageing Regime" in Harold Crouch and Hal Hill (eds.) *Indonesia Assessment 1992, Political Perspectives on the 1990s* (Canberra: Department of Political and Social Change: Research School of Pacific Studies, Australian National University, 1992), p. 58; Lane, *'Openness', Political Discontent and Succession in Indonesia*, pp. 66-67; and also Schwarz, *A Nation in Waiting*, pp. 190-191.

[92] Kenneth Young and Richard Tanter (eds.) *The Politics of Middle Class Indonesia* (Clayton: Centre of Southeast Asian Studies, Monash University, 1990); and for a recent assessment, see Richard Robison, "The Middle Class and the Bourgeoisie in Indonesia" in Richard Robison and David S. G. Goodman (eds.) *The New Rich in Asia, Mobile Phones, McDonalds and Middle-Class Revolution* (London and New York: Routledge, 1996), pp. 77-101.

[93] On the historical roots of democracy, see Barrington Moore, *Social Origins of Dictatorship and Democracy: Lord and Peasant in the Making of the Modern World* (Boston: Beacon Press, 1966).

[94] Heryanto, "Indonesian Middle-Class Opposition in the 1990s", pp. 250-251.

[95] For further discussion on this issue, see David Hill, *The Press in New Order Indonesia* (Perth: Asia Research Centre, Murdoch University, 1994).

[96] For a profile of the *Solidaritas Perempuan* (SP), see their own homepage <http://www.angelfire.com/or/soliper>

[97] See Philip Eldridge, "Non-government Organizations, the State, and Democratization in Indonesia" in Jim Schiller and Barbara Martin-Schiller (eds.) *Imagining Indonesia, Cultural Politics and Political Culture* (Athens: Ohio University Center for International Studies, 1997), 198-228.

[98] Schwarz, *A Nation in Waiting*, pp. 260-261.

[99] Vedy R. Hadiz, "Workers and Working Class Politics in the 1990s" in Chris Manning and Joan Hardjono (eds.) *Indonesia Assessment 1993, Labour:*

Sharing in the Benefits of Growth? (Canberra: Department of Political and Social Change, Research School of Pacific and Asian Studies, 1993), pp. 186-200.

[100] On the implications of the 27 July 1996 affair, see Geoff Forester, "Towards March 1998, With Determination" in Hal Hill and Thee Kian Wie (eds.) *Indonesia's Technological Challenge* (Singapore and Canberra: Institute of Southeast Asian Studies and Research School of Pacific and Asian Studies, the Australian National University, 1998), pp. 55-56.

Chapter Six

Indonesia's Crisis

This chapter examines the impact of the globalisation of the Indonesian economy during the 1990s especially looking at the causes and consequences of the economic crisis in Indonesia in 1997-1998. It is important to note that Indonesia was one of the victims of contagion from Thailand's economic crisis. However, domestic factors deepened the economic crisis in Indonesia. This chapter begins with an examination of efforts by Indonesian policy makers to liberalise the financial sector in Indonesia and the impact this had upon the performance of the Indonesian economy in the 1990s. It follows a discussion of the changes in domestic politics during the last months of Suharto's Sixth Cabinet, which contributed to the erosion of confidence among domestic and foreign investors. It concludes by focusing on the economic and political consequences of the economic crisis, which led to the downfall of President Suharto in May 1998.

Causes of the Crisis

Financial Liberalisation and its Impact

Until the early 1980s, the Indonesian financial sector was generally heavily regulated and protected from foreign competition. The first effort to liberalise the financial sector came in 1983 and affected only a few areas in it. It included measures such as abolishing the ceiling on interest rates and abandoning the monopoly on credit allocation held by the government-owned banks. And to encourage competition among banks and financial institutions, Bank Indonesia (BI), the Indonesian central bank, introduced new bank certificates such as Bank Indonesia Certificates (*Sertifikat Bank Indonesia*, SBI) and Bank Indonesia Money Market Securities (*Surat Berharga Pasar Uang*, SBSU).[1] The pace of financial liberalisation increased after the then Finance Minister Sumarlin introduced a reform package in October 1988. This package, which was known as the "Sumarlin Shock", or the October Package (*Paket October*, Pakto), was the first more serious effort to open up the Indonesian financial sector by removing the financial restrictions applied to domestic and foreign banks.[2] From 1988 until 1996, the Ministry of Finance (MOF) and Bank Indonesia implemented a variety of financial reform packages, making the Indonesian financial sector more competitive and open internationally. For instance, the financial authorities persuaded Indonesian banks to adopt the capital adequacy ratio as suggested by the Bank for International Settlements (BIS); they reduced the reserve requirements so that more banks could be established, permitted banks to engage in exchange rate risk exposure activities; privatised the stock exchange; allowed foreign investors to buy up to 49 per cent of issues of securities of companies listed on the stock exchange; and improved the central bank's supervision and prudential roles.[3] As a result of the "Sumarlin shock" there were over 200 domestic and foreign banks and financial institutions operating in Indonesia. Supported by the improvement in information technology and the increase in capitalisation, these banks were able to provide a variety of new financial products and services. But the expansion of the Indonesian financial sector also increased liquidity and credit allocations in this sector. This had already caused over-heating of the economy in the early 1990s. In response, the government imposed a tight monetary policy aimed at slowing economic activity and Bank Indonesia also increased domestic interest rates and reduced the expansion of bank lending.[4]

Financial liberalisation in Indonesia had its consequences. First, much of the money circulation and loans were accumulated in the government-owned banks and the big private banks.[5] Among these were Bank Nasional Indonesia (BNI), Bank Dagang Negara (BDN), and Bank Rakyat Indonesia (BRI), while the main private banks were Bank Central Asia (BCA), Bank Lippo, Bank Danamon, and Bank International Indonesia (BII). These banks lent their money mainly to state-owned companies and to the politically connected big conglomerates, which had been enjoying protection from the government for decades.[6] Second, many banks were faced with the problem of non-performing loans and bad loans. This happened because many of these loans had gone into property and non-productive projects such as building condominiums, shopping centres, malls, luxury offices, and golf courses.[7] It was estimated that between 1993 and 1996 non-performing loans accounted for between 10-14 per cent, while bad loans accounted for between 3 and 4 per cent of the total loans which had been allocated by the government-owned banks and private banks.[8] Third, the Ministry of Finance and Bank Indonesia had failed to improve banking supervision and provide prudential regulations, leading to the collapse and closure of several banks like Bank Duta in 1990, Bank Summa in 1992, and the government-owned Bank Pembangunan Indonesia (Bapindo) in 1994 and Bank Perniagaan and Bank Pacific in 1997.[9]

Despite all of this, the financial liberalisation policies helped to sustain an economic boom during the 1990s (Table 6.1). It appears that a combination of the government's ability to maintain macroeconomic policies and political stability contributed to this growth. Indonesia's success in this area was recognised in a 1997 World Bank publication, in which it was suggested that up to early 1997 the Indonesian economy was generally performing reasonably well.[10] Nonetheless, the report also pointed out that there were several issues that needed attention. First, it was observed that the financial liberalisation carried out during the 1990s had serious implications for economic policy-making in Indonesia. The capacity of the Ministry of Finance and Bank Indonesia to manage the monetary policies was questioned, particularly in the area of exchange-rate management. From the 1980s Indonesia had adopted a fixed exchange rate system but the rapid increase in capital inflow had gradually weakened the rupiah against the US dollar. To defend it, Bank Indonesia frequently intervened in the market by using band intervention to widen the rupiah-US dollar band. In 1996 the band was widened twice and again in mid-June 1997.[11] However, this strategy was under criticism because of its potential to dry up the international reserve. This put pressure on Bank Indonesia to adopt a more flexible exchange rate system.[12] The delay in making this decision meant that later on, in 1997, Indonesia was more vulnerable to sudden external shock and, more importantly, it invited attacks from currency speculators.

Table 6.1   Indonesia's Economic Fundamentals (annual percentage growth)

	1991	1992	1993	1994	1995	1996
GDP growth	8.9	7.2	7.2	7.5	8.1	8.0
Exports	19.9	15.2	3.3	9.0	4.3	5.9
Inflation	9.0	8.3	9.3	8.5	9.3	6.5
Investment (% GDP)	27.0	25.8	27.6	28.3	28.4	31.1
Saving (% GDP)	24.1	24.2	24.6	25.3	25.4	24.3
Fiscal surplus (% GDP)	-0.6	-0.4	-0.6	0.2	0.3	-
Current account (% GDP)	-3.3	-2.0	-1.3	-1.6	-3.5	-3.4
Exchange rate (rupiah/US$)	1842.8	1950.3	2029.9	2087.1	2248.6	2342.3
Official reserves (US$ bn)	12.6	16.8	18.7	17.2	18.6	2

Source: Asia Pacific Economics Groups, *Asia Pacific Profiles 1998, Overview* (Singapore: Financial Times, 1998), pp. 214-215.

A second issue that was raised by the World Bank was that as the capital inflow increased, so did the current account deficit, from 1.8 per cent of GDP in 1992-1993 to 3.5 per cent of GDP in 1996-1997. This increase was brought about largely through the increase in foreign direct investment (FDI), which had risen by about US$17 billion in the previous few years.[13] The high demand for foreign capital and the rapid growth of the private sector since the early 1990s contributed to the flow of FDI in Indonesia. A third concern was that at the same time as the current account widened, external debt also increased from US$96.5 billion in 1994 to US$107.8 billion by the end of 1995, before peaking at US$139.9 billion at the end of 1997 (Figure 6.1).[14]

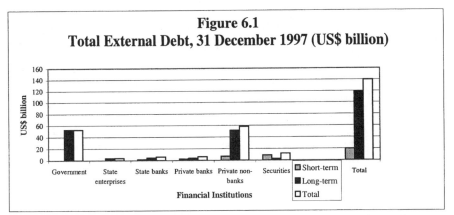

Figure 6.1
Total External Debt, 31 December 1997 (US$ billion)

Source: Bank Indonesia as quoted in Hadi Soesastro and M. Chatib Basri, "Survey Recents Developments", *Bulletin of Indonesian Economic Studies*, vol. 34, no. 1 (April 1998), p. 38.

Given the high interest rates offered by the domestic banks, many companies in Indonesia were eager to borrow from overseas, generally in US dollars and Japanese yen.[15] As with Thailand's case, private debt made up about half of the total of Indonesia's external debt. A fourth concern was the slowdown in exports after 1994, particularly in oil and gas products (Table 6.2). For decades the oil and gas sector was the backbone of Indonesia's exports, but the weaker prices of commodities, and the relocation of regional industries in the 1990s caused Indonesia's exports to lose their international competitiveness. According to the Institute for Management Development (IMD) and the World Economic Forum in their reports published in 1995 and 1996 Indonesia's competitiveness rate was still behind neighbouring countries like Singapore, Thailand and the Philippines.[16]

Table 6.2 Export Growth in Indonesia, 1994-1996 (percentage)

Sector/Commodity	1994	1995	1996
Oil and Gas exports	-0.5	8.0	9.7
Non-Oil and Gas	12.1	15.1	9.0
Mining	23.6	48.8	11.6
Copper	23.5	79.3	13.7
Coal	27.6	26.1	8.5
Agriculture	22.7	2.5	0.9
Seafood	8.3	6.0	-1.0
Manufacturing	10.3	14.1	9.5
Plywood	-12.0	-6.9	3.9
Pulp and wood products	16.0	27.9	0.1
Gold and mineral products	53.5	6.3	5.1
Chemicals	27.1	50.2	-0.6
Plastic and plastic products	8.7	85.6	27.7
Paper and paper products	34.7	22.0	-5.6
Rubber products	30.9	57.5	1.6
Vegetable oil	60.3	-7.4	32.5
Processed food	10.1	0.7	17.5
Garments	-8.1	5.0	5.5
Other textiles	-3.7	9.0	5.5
Footwear	13.7	8.8	6.8
Furniture	17.0	10.2	10.0
Electrical goods and computers	40.6	19.1	28.4
Other manufacturing	7.4	14.1	29.0

Source: Biro Pusat Statistik as quoted in World Bank, *Indonesia, Sustaining High Growth with Equity* (Washington D.C.: World Bank, 1997), p. 13.

Struggle over Economic Policy and "Deregulation Fatigue"

Although rhetorically the Indonesian government embraced the spirit of free trade and participated in multilateral agreements such as the Asean Free Trade Agreement (AFTA), the Asia Pacific Economic Cooperation (APEC) and the World Trade Organisation (WTO), Indonesia experienced "deregulation fatigue" during the 1990s.[17] Consequently the speed of the economic deregulation slowed and in some respects moved backward. Regulations and restrictions were being applied in the economy, causing price distortions and the increasing the cost of doing business in Indonesia.

There are two common explanations for this. First, as explained in the previous chapter, the implementation of deregulation policies in the 1980s had been overshadowed by constant rivalry between the technocrat camp and the technologist camp (the latter led by B. J. Habibie).[18] The technocrat camp was represented then by the Coordinating Minister for the Economy Saleh Affif, Finance Minister Mar'ie Muhammad and Bank Indonesia Governor Soedradjat Djiwandono who had tirelessly pushed for the implementation of the deregulation policies. The technocrat camp did not always get its way. It had to fight hard to get support from President Suharto and to convince him of the benefits of deregulation for Indonesia.[19] By the 1990s, the influence of the technocrat camp in the economic policy-making process had gradually diminished and been replaced by the technologist camp. The then Minister of Research and Technology B. J. Habibie and his supporters initiated much policy formulation. This camp also received support from other leading policy makers such as Ginandjar Kartasasmita, who was the Head of the Economic Planning Board (*Badan Perencanaan Pembangunan Nasional*, Bapennas), and Hartarto, who was then the Coordinating Minister for Industry. With the personal support of Suharto, Habibie and his supporters gained more power in overseeing economic policy and, more importantly, in persuading the government to finance high-cost strategic industries such as aircraft, shipbuilding and military equipment.[20] Because of this, on many occasions, the technocrat camp was involved in, as economist Umar Juoro put it, a "tug of war" with the technologist camp.[21]

The other common explanation for Indonesia's apparent "deregulation fatigue" was that the implementation of deregulation policies was often resisted by the state-owned enterprises such as the Indonesian Petroleum Company (Pertamina) or the State Logistical Agency (*Badan Usaha Logistik*, Bulog) and the politically-connected conglomerates, many of them owned by the Indonesian ethnic Chinese and Suharto's family. These were important economic actors who had monopolised and controlled the Indonesian economy for decades. Their business interests encompassed sectors ranging from food distribution, the retail industry, manufacturing, and food, to banking, infrastructure and the telecommunications sector (Boxes 6.1 and 6.2).[22] Because of their privileges, they resisted deregulation, because it threatened their business interests. The inability of the technocrat camp to dismantle the monopolies of these conglomerates sent a negative signal to domestic and foreign investors about the future direction of deregulation in Indonesia, as it was clear that the pace of deregulation had been stalled by the monopolistic structure of the Indonesian economy.[23]

Box 6.1 Monopolies of State-owned Enterprises

Ministry	Name of Company	Commodity
Agriculture	Perum Perkebunan Kapas Indonesia	Cotton
	JSPU	na
	Aneka Jasa	na
	Kantor Pemasaran Bersama	Marketing
	Kantor Administrasi Hasil	same as above
	Kantor Pemasaran Bersama Jatim	same as above
	Pertani	Distributor
	PT Bina Mulia Tehnik	Supplying
	Perikani Airtembaga	Fishery
	Perum Perikanan Maluku	same as above
	Usaha Mina	same as above
	Karya Mina	same as above
	Perikanan Samudra	same as above
	Tirta Raya Mina	same as above
	Perum Sang Hyang Seri	Rice seeds
Forestry	Inhutani I-III	Wood products
	Perhutani	same as above
Transportation	Perum Kereta Api	Railway services
	Pelni	Water services
	ASDF	Ferry services
	Varuna Tirtaprakarsa	Storage facilities
	Angkasa Pura	Airport
	Garuda Indonesia	Air services
	Merpati Nusantara	same as above
Post and Telecommunication	Perum Pos dan Giro	Postal services
	Perumtel	Telephone services
	Indosat	International links
Finance	Peruri	Printing
	Perum Taspen	Insurance
	Jasa Raharja	Insurance
	Askrindo	Insurance
	Perum Pegadaian	Pawn services
	PT PANN	Transportation
Industry	PT Kertas Leces	Paper
	Semen (Gresik, Padang)	Cement
	Pupuk (Sriwijaya, Kujang)	Fertiliser
	Perum Garam	Salt
	Industri Soda	Soda
	Perum Pengeringan Tembakau	Tobacco
Mining and Energy	Tambah Timah	Tin
	Tambang Batu Bara	Coal
	Aneka Tambang	same as above
	Pertamina	Oil and Gas
	PLN	Electricity
	PN Gas	Gas
Trade	Dharma Niaga	Trading
	Satya Niaga	same as above
	Dirga Niaga	same as above

	Panca Niaga	same as above
	Kerta Niaga	same as above
	Aduma Niaga	same as above
	Cipta Niaga	same as above
	Aneka Niaga	same as above
	Mega Eltra	Supplier engines
	Pembangunan Niaga	same as above
Public Works	Perusahaan Aspal Negara	Asphalt
Research and Technology	PT PAL	Shipbuilding
	PT Pindad	Engineering equipment
	PT IPTN	Aircraft
	PT Bharata Indonesia	Machine/Metal
	PT Inka	Train
	PT INTI	Telecommunications
	PT Boma Bisma Indra	Turbines, engines
	PT Krakatau Steel	Steel
	PT LEN	Electronics
	PT Dahana	Ammunition
Health	Kimia Farma	Pharmaceutical
	Bulog	Basic commodities

Source: *Kompas*, 23 August 1997.

Box 6.2 Monopolies of Privately-owned Conglomerates

Conglomerate Group	Name of Company	Commodity
Humpuss (Tommy Suharto)	PT Kembang Cengkih Nasional	Clove
Sinar Mas, Salim, Bakrie,		
Bimantara, Astra		Palm oil
Dharmala Group		Dried cassava
PENGKO		Copra
Nusamba (Bob Hasan)	ASMINDO	Rattan/Wood
Salim (Liem Sioe Liong)	PT Bakti Bersama Sejahtera	Soy bean flour and Soy bean oil
Salim	PT Indomilk	Condensed milk
Salim	PT Oceanis Timber	Blackwood
Salim	PT Usaha Manggar	Coconut oil
Salim	PT Filma	Margarine
Astra (Surjadjaya family)	PT Bina Pertiwi	Agriculture tools
Astra	PT Huma Dharma Loka	Tapioca
--	ETKIFC	Sandalwood, Eaglewood
Mercu Buana (Probosutedjo)	Cipendawa	Poultry
Dharmala	PT AC. TOEFFER	Bird nests
Astra		Aluminium Chloride
Salim	PT Abravana Utama	Ethylalchohol
Astra	PT United Tractors	Heavy machinery
Salim	PT Indo Mfg. Int.	Automobile spare parts
Astra		Brake systems
Humpuss	PT Humpuss Mitsubishi	Methanol

Salim	PT Roda Megah and Tiga Roda Prasetya	Cement
Salim	PT Digicon Mega Pratama	Gas exploration
Humpuss	PT Humpuss Petrokimia	Purified Terephthalic Acid
--	PT Sembada Kriya Prima	Plastic bottles
Salim	PT Kaolin Indah Utama	Kaolin
Salim	PT First Polyester Prima	Polyester film
Salim	PT Argha Karya Prima	Propylene film
Salim	PT Stainless Steel Indo	Stainless steel
Salim	PT Branta Mulya	Tyres
Bimantara (Bambang T.)	PT Permindo	Crude oil
Heineken	PT Multi Bintang Indonesia	Beer
Salim	PT Bogasari	Wheat flour
Bimantara	PT Kapsulindo	Medicine capsule
Nusamba	PT McDermott	Offshore oil exploration
Nusamba	PT Kertas Kraft Aceh	Cement paper
Humpuss	PT Sempati Air	Air services
21 Group	PT Subentra and Subtan Film	Film importers and Cinema networks
Bimantara/Salim	PT Istana Mutiara Mas dan Trikora	Gas transportation
--	PT Sari Arcadia Food	Food catering
Surya Paloh	PT Indo Cater	Food catering
Bimantara and Subentra	RCTI and SCTV	Television
Citra Lamtoro (Tutut)	PT Telivisi Pendidikan Ind.	Television
Napan Group	PT Mekatama Raya	Television fees
Salim	PT Indofood Sukses Makmur	Instant noodles

Source: *Kompas*, 23 August 1997

The "KKN" Factor

One of the important factors that contributed to the crisis of confidence in the Indonesian economy was the weakness of the rule of law and the lack of transparency, which means that all transactions must be published and be accountable for scrutiny. Under the existent political networks, which had nurtured a patronage system, corruption, collusion and nepotistic practices, (known in Indonesia as "KKN" (*korupsi, kolusi,* and *nepotisme*)) were widespread. Under this corrupt patronage system, it was those who had access to the political elites that were given government projects and contracts.[24] Those who had this access were mainly the big business groups or conglomerates owned by the ethnic Chinese and Suharto's family. There are many examples, but the most clear manifestation of this could be found in the Chandra Asri and National Car cases.

In the former case, a decision was made by the government to give preferential treatment to PT Chandra Asri, a new petrochemical company owned by Bambang Trihatmodjo (Suharto's second son) and three business partners, Peter F. Gontha, Henry Pribadi, and timber tycoon and Suharto family friend Prajogo Pangestu.[25] Chandra Asri was established in 1991, and in 1994 asked for tariff protection of up to 40 per cent against imports on the grounds that as an infant industry it deserved this protection against international competitors. As the Indonesian economy expanded rapidly in the 1990s, the need for petrochemical products increased as well. In the past this need had been met by importing from overseas. Therefore, the decision to give protection contradicted the commitment of the government to gradually reduce tariffs, which was in the spirit of free trade. Thus from the beginning there was disagreement among the government ministers on how to respond to Chandra Asri's demand for protection. Minister of Finance Mari'e was against it, while others, such as the Minister of Trade and Commerce Tunky Aribowo and Minister of Investment Sanyoto, were for it. Opposition to the idea of giving special treatment to Chandra Asri also came from industry associations such as the Association of the Plastic Industry of Indonesia, the Formalin and Thermosetting Association and some public figures. As a response, in 1994 Suharto formed a committee known as the Tariff Team, made up of government ministers and headed by the Coordinating Minister for Industry and Commerce Hartarto, to review the existing import tariff in various manufacturing and trade sectors. However, it soon became apparent that the Tariff Team was not able to resist the political pressure from the owners of Chandra Asri with their strong political connection to President Suharto. Consequently, in 1996, the government, through the Tariff Team, gave Chandra Asri tariff protection of up to 25 per cent to import olefines.[26]

The second case refers to President Suharto's launch of the national car policy in 1996.[27] This was intended to encourage Indonesian car makers to produce a "national car", with 60 per cent domestic components. But instead of allowing all car manufacturers and automobile companies to compete equally in an open and transparent tendering process, President Suharto granted the contract to PT Timor Putra Nasional, a new car manufacturing company owned by Hutomo "Tommy" Mandala Putra (Suharto's youngest son), despite the fact that this company had not yet produced any cars at all. Nonetheless, PT Timor was given a three year tax exemption by the government until it could produce its own cars. In order to compete in the domestic market in Indonesia, which had been dominated by Japanese cars for two decades, PT Timor Putra Nasional entered a joint venture with South Korea's KIA Motors. Through this joint venture, PT Timor simply imported a sedan-type car directly from South Korea, and renamed it "Timor" once it arrived in Indonesia. Indeed, the "national car" policy showed the power of the interest groups in intervening the policy-making process in Indonesia. Indria Samego said of this:

> The "national car" case is an example of inconsistency in the law. It shows that there is still strength in the interventionist elements of certain powers. So we must not assume that deregulation in Indonesia is a process that has resulted from mature thinking...deregulation has also been carried out due to pressure from the interests of certain groups...Although on the macro level it is paraded as protecting the national interest, on the micro level there are certain interests, certain business groups benefiting.[28]

This special treatment brought protests both domestically and internationally. Other domestic car makers such as PT Bimantara (owned by Tommy's older brother, Bambang Trihatmodjo) and PT Bakrie Motor (owned by the Bakrie family) were angry over the decision. Meanwhile, Japan and the US argued that the Indonesian government had violated the principle of non-discrimination and they expressed their disappointment to the World Trade Organisation (WTO).

Political Unrest

Political developments from the middle of 1996 until early 1997 had a significant impact on the rise in the political temperature in Indonesia. The political legitimacy of Suharto's New Order government was damaged when government officials were involved in masterminding a plan to depose Megawati Sukarnoputri from the leadership of the Indonesian Democratic Party (*Partai Demokrasi Indonesia*, PDI). This happened on 27 July 1996, when the headquarters of the PDI, which was then occupied by Megawati supporters, was taken over by the government-backed faction led by Suryadi. As a result, the supporters of Megawati launched mass protests, which led to riots in the business districts of Jakarta.[29] The government saw that the rise in popularity of Megawati could potentially challenge the ruling party Golkar in the general election, which would be held in May 1997 and could also threaten the re-election of President Suharto in March 1998. By eliminating her from the political race, the government felt more secure. Ironically, the government's act was doomed to failure. Megawati became increasingly popular beyond the boundaries of her own political party, attracting a wider community of followers from among the middle class, students, NGOs, and even ex-military officers.[30]

The significance of this event in Indonesian politics cannot be underestimated. First, the riots shook the economic and political stability in Indonesia, and contributed to the erosion of confidence among domestic and foreign investors.[31] This was evidenced by the fall of the rupiah from Rp 2338/US$ to Rp 2357/US$ and the index of the Jakarta Stock Exchange, which dropped 20.57 points on 28 July 1996.[32] Second, the riots showed that the ordinary people mistrusted the government and the Indonesian Chinese community, particularly those who benefited from and grew obviously wealthier under Suharto's New Order government. Evidence of this was in the fact that the mob attacks targeted government offices and big banks (many of them owned by Chinese Indonesians).[33] After the riots in Jakarta in July 1996, further riots and unrest broke out in other parts of Indonesia.[34] In October 1996 riots erupted in the city of Situbondo in East Java province and in December riots occurred in Dili, East Timor, and in the city of Tasikmalaya in West Java province. This continued into January 1997, when ethnic conflict between the local Dayak and the immigrant Madurans broke out in the Pontianak region of West Kalimantan province. In April 1997, there were more riots in Java, in Rengasdengklok near Jakarta and in Pekalongan, Central Java.

Most Indonesians believed that the riots and unrest occurred because the economic development of the previous few decades had widened the gap between the rich and the poor, and only benefited a relatively few people in the urban areas.[35] The majority of people in the provinces did not share in the new wealth. Given the authoritarian political system, which did not allow for criticism of the government, and the unwillingness of the political institutions and their leaders to be responsive to public dissatisfaction, it is understandable that some people decided to take matters into their own hands. In these circumstances the general election was held on 29 May 1997. This was the sixth election under Suharto's New Order government and was contested by the three permitted parties, the Development Unity Party (*Partai Persatuan Pembangunan*, PPP), the ruling party Golkar (*Golongan Karya*), and the Indonesian Democratic Party (*Partai Demokrasi Indonesia*, PDI). Golkar won the election, as was expected, however the election was overshadowed by fraud committed by government officials and political upheaval throughout the country, which undermined the legitimacy of Suharto's New Order government.[36]

Indeed, the events surrounding the May 1997 general election posed serious questions about the ongoing ability of the political system to maintain political stability in Indonesia. It was also clear that the "three-party" system, which was created in the early 1970s, no longer embodied the political aspirations of the Indonesian people.[37] It was against this backdrop that the economic crisis occurred in Indonesia.

Responses to the Crisis

The Floating of the Rupiah

The contagion effect of the floating of the baht on 2 July 1997 spread to the Philippines and Malaysia before reaching Indonesia. The fall of the rupiah took the government by surprise, and created panic among domestic and foreign investors. Those who had praised Indonesia's economic growth over the previous few years struggled to understand the magnitude of this contagion effect. One of them was the World Bank representative in Jakarta, who in September 1997 said:

> I have to be honest that the currency [crisis] situation has taken the World Bank, me personally, a bit by surprise. It was not that we did not think there would be some spill-over effects to Thailand and the regional problems. But the degree of the spill-over effects has been much greater than I would [have] predict [ed] ahead of time.[38]

From July until early August 1997, the value of the rupiah depreciated by between 2-10 per cent under heavy attack from currency speculators. In response, Bank Indonesia (BI) intervened in the market by widening the rupiah-US dollar band from 8 per cent to 12 per cent on 11 July 1997. Later on, Bank Indonesia also made a repurchase agreement with several central banks such as the Bank of Japan (US$1 billion), the Monetary Authority of Singapore (US$1 billion) and Australia's Reserve Bank (US$ 500 million).[39] According to the Bank Indonesia Governor, Soedradjat Djiwandono, the decision to widen the rupiah-US dollar band at this stage had its own rationale.[40] First, it was aimed at defending the rupiah from further attack from currency speculators. This was not a new strategy and, as mentioned earlier, Bank Indonesia had used it before. In principle, by widening the band, the speculators would not know the "correct" level of the rupiah maintained by Bank Indonesia. Second, with only about US$21 billion (equivalent of imports expense for five and a half months) in its international reserve, Bank Indonesia was not interested in defending the rupiah for a longer time. The number of foreign exchange transactions in Indonesia had grown very quickly over the previous years. For example, in 1991 and 1992 foreign exchange transactions amounted to less than US$2 billion per day, in 1995 to about US$5 billion per day, and in 1996 and 1997 to somewhere between US$9-10 billion per day.[41] With this magnitude, Bank Indonesia certainly was incapable of defending the rupiah any longer. Nonetheless, this initial response was short-lived. On 21 July 1997 the rupiah and other currencies in the region depreciated further. In Indonesia, according to the market analyst Theo F. Toemion, both domestic and foreign speculators played a crucial part in this attack by selling the rupiah heavily on the market.[42] Bank Indonesia responded by implementing a tight monetary policy through increasing the interest rates on Bank Indonesia Certificates (*Sertifikat Bank Indonesia*, SBI) and stopping the flow of Bank Indonesia Money Market Certificates (*Surat Berharga Pasar Uang*, SBSU). Principally, this decision was taken because Bank Indonesia wanted to make sure that the speculators would not be able to get more access to the rupiah in order to buy the US dollar.[43]

However, Bank Indonesia's tight monetary policy caused a side effect. The interbank interest rates increased, with the consequence that small banks faced liquidity problems and this worsened with the fact that only 20 top banks controlled about 50 to 60 per cent of money circulation.[44] This also caused serious trouble in the capital market, where the composite index at the Jakarta Stock Exchange (JSE) dropped sharply to the record low of below the 700 point in 4 August 1997.[45] In the long-term, the tight monetary policy could bring about the slowing down of economic activity because many companies would have trouble financing their business.[46] When the market players and speculators saw that the government was no longer able to defend the rupiah, they launched another attack on the rupiah on 12 and 13 August 1997 and consequently the value of the rupiah dropped to Rp 2685:US$, or three points above Bank Indonesia's preferred level. This situation caused panic among the policy makers and it gave both Finance Minister Mar'ie Mohammad and Bank Indonesia Governor Soedradjat Djiwandono no other option but to float the rupiah on the 14 August 1997.[47] It was acknowledged that using band intervention as an initial strategy to defend the rupiah was costly and unproductive. It was reported widely in the media that between 21 July and 14 August 1997 Bank Indonesia had spent about US$2 billion from its international reserves in propping up the currency.[48]

This announcement was followed by the fall of the rupiah to a new record low of Rp 2770:US dollar and the composite index dropped to 643.01 points.[49] The float of the rupiah, however, was not widely supported among the business leaders, most of whom were content with the pegged exchange rate system. For most Indonesian companies and those who were trading on the stock exchange, the free floating exchange rate system was a new thing and it would take a while for them to adapt to this system.[50] Many of these companies had debt denominated in US dollars and not hedged, which worsened the situation. But the exporters and those who did not use many imported components in their businesses were very pleased with the new exchange rate system because, in theory, it would make their products more competitive internationally. Nonetheless, the shift to a free floating exchange rate system was welcomed by domestic and foreign investors. Stanley Fisher, managing director of the International Monetary Fund, believed that the floating of the rupiah would make the implementation of macroeconomic policies more effective.[51] Unfortunately, the floating of the currency did not stop the depreciation process. When the rupiah reached the level of Rp 3000:US$ in the middle of August 1997, a sense of nervousness among government officials and the business community emerged. This developed into panic, which again generated heavy selling of the rupiah in the market. On 16 August 1997, in his speech to celebrate the 52nd anniversary of Indonesian independence, President Suharto reminded the business community of the uncertainty and difficult times ahead. He said:

> I appeal to our business community to seriously understand these new realities. They shall all discover that foreign loans are no longer easily and cheaply obtained [as they were] before the storm. All parties concerned are reminded by the recent events to act prudently in borrowing...and to seek safer and steadier ways of funding.[52]

In an act of desperation, Bank Indonesia raised the interest rates of Bank Indonesia Certificates by 30 per cent and forced government-owned enterprises (*Badan Usaha Milik Negara* [BUMN]) to transfer their savings and deposits back to the central bank. Finance Minister Mar'ie Muhammad and Bank Indonesia Governor Soedradjat Djiwandono also urged the public and the private sector to reassess their business activities.[53]

To avoid a further economic downturn, President Suharto set up a special crisis-management committee known as the Monetary Council, comprised of Coordinating Minister for Economic, Financial and Industrial Affairs and Development Supervision, Saleh Afiff, Minister of Finance Mar'ie Muhammad, Bank Indonesia Governor Soedradjat Djiwandono, State Secretary Moerdiono and the special presidential advisers Professor Widjojo Nitisastro and Ali Wardhana. Professor Widjojo was Suharto's former and long-time economic minister and also an architect of the Indonesian economic strategy since the early days of the New Order government. He was known both nationally and internationally and his inclusion in this council was intended to reassure domestic and international investors.[54] Both the Presidential address and the establishment of the monetary council opened the debate about the soundness of the Indonesian economy. The currency crisis demonstrated that the Indonesian economy in fact was not as strong as many people had thought. The technocrat camp used the crisis as an opportunity to reassert their influence in economic policy making and urged the government to implement deregulation policies. The media speculated that the crisis had increased the leverage of the technocrat camp.[55]

Coordinating Minister Saleh Afiff, who was part of the technocrat camp, called for the abolition of the monopolies that had distorted economic activities and were inefficient because they benefited only a few rather than the whole population.[56] Afiff specifically mentioned the need to abolish the monopolies of the State Logistical Agency (*Bulog*) and the big conglomerates, but he also urged the government to review the funding of Habibie's control of strategic industries and other government-funded infrastructure projects.[57] Afiff's statement fed the public debate on the merits of monopoly. Generally the public agreed with Afiff's idea except, of course, those who had enjoyed and benefited from monopoly rights and other privileges for decades. One of them was the then Minister of Research and Technology B. J. Habibie, who strongly argued that the funding for strategic industries was very important for Indonesia and therefore he urged the government not to reschedule despite the fact that these industries were not profitable.[58] Indeed, the conflicting views between Afiff and Habibie indicated that the move to abolish the monopolies and the other privileges that had distorted the Indonesian economy could be potentially explosive, especially approaching the presidential election in 1998. *The Jakarta Post* described the situation in the following way:

> ...Market distortions such as monopolistic practices should be abolished...There are obviously many vested-interest groups who prefer the retention of the monopolies as these exclusive trading rights, funded by huge sums of subsidised credits from the central bank, have so far served as cash cows for rent-seeking businesspeople and officials. True, the monopolies have so far helped maintain price stability but at a great cost to the economy. It is to be expected that the commodities market will be jolted and become wildly volatile temporarily after the removal of the monopolies...The question now is whether the government has the political will to swallow the bitter pill – a temporary market jolt after the removal of monopolies – in view of the upcoming presidential election in March [1998].[59]

It seemed that the technocrat camp faced a long and hard battle.

Mar'ie Muhammad's "Shock"

The rupiah depreciated further, reaching the level of Rp 3000:US dollar at the end of August 1997. This showed that the existing government measures to defend the rupiah had failed, including Bank Indonesia's move on 31 August 1997 to restrict forward transactions of foreign exchange against the rupiah by domestic banks to foreign or non-resident investors.[60] This led to a more comprehensive response by the government. On 3 September 1997, Finance Minister Mar'ie announced 10 measures intended to restore the confidence of the market. These were: reducing the interest rates step by step, synchronising economic activity, revising Budget targets, strengthening export-driven activities, rescheduling the government-funded infrastructure projects, reorganising the financial sector through mergers and liquidations, urging the private sector to review its activities, abolishing the ceiling of 49 per cent for foreign investors in companies listed in the stock exchange, and maintaining the flow and distribution of basic commodities and price stability.[61] These measures, which became known as the "Mar'ie shock", were welcomed both domestically and internationally, and appeared to indicate that the government had made a strong commitment to undertake economic reform. At a special meeting with the members of the Peoples' Representative Council (*Dewan Perwakilan Rakyat*, DPR) held on 16 September 1997, Finance Minister Mar'ie took the opportunity to tell the public that the rupiah would remain unstable and urged everyone to be prepared for this.[62] Mar'ie acknowledged that the depreciation of the rupiah had already created economic crisis, but he argued that there was something good to come out of it. He explained:

> Although the negative impact [from the crisis] had been felt heavy enough, this momentum must be used as an opportunity to consolidate the national economy by undertaking various structural adjustments. This structural adjustment [was] needed so that all components of the national economy would be ready to face the economic globalisation which already became the reality.[63]

However, not everyone was satisfied with the "Mar'ie shock". There were some who doubted whether these measures would achieve their targets. McLeod argued that the measure of revising the budget had implications such as slowing down economic activity, which consequently would lessen economic growth.[64] This could create fiscal contraction and other social and political problems due to increased unemployment. This would worsen when combined with Bank Indonesia's high interest rate policy.

Meanwhile, Sjahrir strongly criticised this policy and urged Bank Indonesia to immediately reduce the interest rates so that companies and traders in money and capital markets could continue their activities.[65] The decision to reschedule government-funded projects was also likely to create problems. The central point here was whether the government had the courage to implement some of the measures in the face of strong resistance from within. Many projects, such as the National Car, the Jakarta Tower, the Malaka Strait Bridge, the Belitung Indah Resort, and other infrastructure projects, belonged to the Suharto family members and other powerful conglomerates.[66]

As we will see later, the inability of the government and President Suharto to make a decision about this, contributed to worsening economic crisis. The measure of abolishing restrictions for foreign investors in stock exchange trading also raised concerns among observers and local investors.[67] It is true that this measure was announced in an atmosphere of panic among the policy makers and it was taken hurriedly to slow capital outflow from Indonesia.[68] The government was criticised for not consulting about this decision which consequently could led to the increase of domination of foreign investors in stock exchange trading in Indonesia and, therefore, in the long-term this had the potential to attract resentment and a nationalist backlash.[69]

It appeared the "Mar'ie shock" measures did not reassure the domestic and international investors. At the end of September 1997 the rupiah reached the level of between Rp 3000-3500:US dollar and the index price at the Jakarta Stock Exchange fluctuated between 500 and 550 points. The fall of currencies in other Southeast Asian countries made it impossible for the rupiah to recover. These currencies continued to depreciate after Malaysian Prime Minister Mahathir Mohammad strongly criticised the fund managers, particularly George Soros (with his company Quantum Funds), who contributed to the collapse of these currencies through their speculation activities. In addition, the "Mahathir-Soros" issue overshadowed the World Bank meeting held in Hong Kong at the end of September 1997 and contributed to a further weakening of the rupiah.[70] Moreover, any prospect of the rupiah's recovery was damned by several domestic events which took place in September such as the forest fires, whose smoke covered almost half of the region, the Garuda aeroplane crash in Medan, the banking crisis, and the issue of political succession in Indonesia.

Enter the IMF, the Closure of 16 Banks, and the "Panic" Factor

With the government having failed to stop the fall of the rupiah, on 8 October 1997 Finance Minister Mar'ie announced a plan to look for external assistance from the International Monetary Fund (IMF) and the World Bank.[71] The government appointed Professor Widjojo Nitisastro as the head of the Indonesian negotiating team. Widjojo was a respected figure and known widely in international financial institutions. The aim of this appointment was to send a clear message to the international financial community that the Indonesian government was serious in trying to end the crisis and to restore confidence in the economy. To show the determination of the government to end the crisis, Mar'ie and other top government officials met with a wide range of representatives of the banking sector, corporations, and also foreign fund managers. A few important issues emerged from this meeting, such as exactly how much debt the private sector had in US dollars and would the government accept the conditions attached to the IMF loans?

On the private debt issue, until then the government knew little about it, though it was estimated that private debt stood somewhere between US$55-80 billion.[72] This information was needed to help the government to gauge the seriousness of the crisis and therefore to know how much external assistance they had to ask of the IMF. On the issue of the conditions attached to the IMF loan, not everyone believed that the involvement of the IMF would help Indonesia out of the crisis.[73] Often the conditions attached to IMF programmes were too tough both economically and politically and these were, for instance, budget cuts and structural reforms by abolishing government and private monopolies.[74] Sjahrir argued then that he was not sure that the government itself would have the capacity to implement the IMF programmes, considering that private monopolies, for instance, were controlled by the powerful politically connected elites.[75] Any attempt to disturb these practices would create opposition from those business groups and therefore could jeopardise the IMF programmes.

It must be pointed out that at first the government sought technical assistance rather than loans from the IMF. But once the Indonesian negotiating team realised the seriousness of the crisis, the government quickly came to the conclusion that IMF loans were needed.[76] After a series of closed-door meetings between the Indonesian negotiating team and IMF officials, held both in Jakarta and Washington D.C., on 31 October 1997 the IMF agreed to provide a three-year rescue loan worth US$23 billion, comprising US$10 billion from the IMF, US$4.5 billion from the World

Bank, US$3.5 billion from the Asian Development Bank (ADB) and US$5 billion from Indonesia's own external assets.[77] Indonesia also received a stand-by loan worth US$15 billion, which was provided by Japan (US$5 billion), Singapore (US$5 billion), the United States (US$3 billion), Malaysia (US$1 billion), and Australia (US$1 billion).[78] Brunei Darrusalam also provided US$1.5 billion, as did as China and Hong Kong. The total of the IMF rescue package thus reached US$43 billion, which was composed of US$38 billion from external sources and US$5 billion from Indonesia's own funds.[79] This became the second largest rescue loan that the IMF had ever made. The largest was the US$50 billion Mexican rescue loan in 1995.

Unlike other IMF rescue packages, the package for Indonesia appeared ambitious and outside the usual IMF style. The package contained a wide range of economic reform programmes, with three important issues being highlighted: tightening monetary and fiscal policies, restructuring the financial sector and implementing further economic deregulation and trade reforms.[80] One might wonder whether the IMF itself drafted this package or whether it came from the Indonesian government. The public perception was that it was the Indonesian side, particularly the technocrat camp, which proposed that the IMF include more than just the "usual" IMF prescriptions, with the result that structural reform measures, such as abolishing the monopolies of the government-owned enterprises and the conglomerates, were included.[81] The logic behind this was that by widening the scope of the IMF reform package, the confidence of the market might improve and, more importantly, the package would win public support.

There was also criticism of the IMF rescue package. Some argued that the package could create "moral hazard", in that it gave the impression to other countries, particularly developing countries, that whatever economic situation might occur as the result of implementing bad policies, the IMF would be ready to rescue or bail out.[82] But the most vocal critique of the IMF rescue package for Indonesia came from Professor Jeffrey Sachs, an economist and Director of the Harvard Institute of International Development (HIID).[83] Sachs believed that the IMF had formulated wrong policy prescriptions, based on the "standard" IMF prescriptions for the conditions of the 1970s and the 1980s, rather than those of the 1990s.[84] At the centre of the economic crisis in Indonesia was high private, rather than government, debt. He believed that the IMF rescue package would not lead to recovery but rather could create financial panic. Sachs' experience in advising the Russian government in implementing economic reforms in the early 1990s influenced his criticism of the IMF involvement in Indonesia.

As part of the IMF reform package requirements, on 1 November 1997 Finance Minister Mar'ie announced the closure of 16 private banks, some of them owned by prominent business persons and others by President Suharto's children and relatives (Box 6.3). According to an official source, these banks were closed because they were categorised as "unhealthy" and had not operated according to prudential rules such as the capital adequacy ratio (CAR) and good management as required by the Banking Law No. 7 of 1992.[85] This announcement justified rumours that had been circulating about Bank Indonesia's plan to liquidate the financially troubled banks.

Box 6.3 Profiles of 16 Troubled Banks

Name	Assets (Million Rupiah)*	Principal Owner
Bank Pinaesaan	425.697	Fritz H. Eman
Bank Industri	543.901	Hasyim/Titiek Prabowo
Bank Anrico	122.720	Anwar Syukur
Bank Astria	715.767	PT Pendawa Intisurya
Bank Andromeda	1.383.377	Bambang Trihatmodjo
Bank Harapan Santosa	4.291.625	Hendra Rahardja
Bank Guna International	449.886	Hendra Rahardja
Bank SBU	2.220.045	PT Abad Andal Asri
Bank Majapahit	176.000	Effendy Ongko
Bank Jakarta	296.822	H. Probosutedjo
Bank Kosa	201.323	Setiawan Chandra
Bank Mataram	305.262	Hamengku Buwono X
Bank SEAB	458.117	Handi Sunardjo
Bank Pacific	2.276.050	Ibnu Sutowo family
Bank Dwipa	159.305	Bambang Samijono
Bank Citra	163.506	Soeyono Soekarno

* Value before the rupiah was floated in August 1997.
Source: *Gatra*, 8 November 1997.

As mentioned earlier, the banking sector was stricken with non-performing loans as a consequence of excessive lending in the property sector and other non-productive areas of the economy. The closure of these banks received a mixed reaction. Some point out that this decision created panic in Jakarta and other cities.[86] Despite the government promise to guarantee the safety of depositors by allowing them to withdraw up to Rp 20 million, thousands of depositors rushed into these banks to withdraw their money. This gave a strong impression that the decision was too far-reaching and suggested that Sachs and others who were concerned about whether the government and the IMF had made a wrong move towards ending the crisis, might have been right.[87]

The political temperature increased when the media reported that Suharto's son, Bambang Trihatmojo (who owned Bank Andromeda) and Suharto's stepbrother, Probosutedjo (who owned Bank Jakarta), had challenged the legality of the liquidation of these banks in Jakarta's administrative court.[88] They argued that the Finance Minister's decision to liquidate their respective banks was politically motivated, aimed at destroying the image of Suharto and his family. They later withdrew their legal suit after a "compromise" was reached in which Bambang was given the rights to another bank, Bank Alfa.[89]

The Suharto Factor

The credibility of the government was further eroded by the decision taken by President Suharto on 1 November 1997 to allow 15 government-funded projects to proceed after having been rescheduled six weeks earlier.[90] These projects included electricity power plants, building a new airport, property and others (Box 6.4). This announcement sent a conflicting signal to the market about the seriousness of the governments' determination to abolish collusion and cronyism in the Indonesian business sector. It also contradicted the government's own commitment to the IMF reform package, which had been signed at the end of October. This was seen by some as a retreat from the economic reform agenda.[91] All of this contributed to the continuing fall of the rupiah, which hit between Rp 4000-5000:US$ at the end of November 1997. But by this time the "Suharto factor" was contributing as well. In December 1997, the rupiah depreciated further because of the news and rumours concerning Suharto's failing health and the cancellation of his trip to Kuala Lumpur for the ASEAN meeting.[92] This happened the day after State Secretary Moerdiono informed the media that Suharto had decided to take a ten-day rest at the suggestion of the presidential medical team. The fact that this affected the stability of the rupiah was evidence that the life and health of this aging president had begun to directly affect the health of the economy.

Box 6.4 15 Mega Projects Allowed to Proceed in November 1997

Name of Project	Company	Location	Value (US$)
Polonia Airport	PT Citra Lamtoro	Medan	600 million
Waru-Tanjungperak Freeway	PT Citra Marga Nusaphala	Surabaya	247 million
PLTGU Palembang Timur	PT Astra and Coastral Corp.	Palembang	168.5 million
PLTP Karaha	Kahara Bodas Co. LLG	West Java	380 million
PLTP Sarulla	Nusamba and Unocal Corp.	North Sumatera	330 million
PLTP Darajat Unit I and Unit II	PT Prasarana Nusantara	West Java	475 million
Meteorology and Geophysics Equipments	Ministry of Transport	Jakarta	2.6 billion
Semarang Freeway	PT Adhi Karya	Central Java	65 million
Aren-Serpong Freeway	PT Cipta Marga Nusaphala	West Java	93 million
Ujung Pandang Freeway	PT Bosowa Marga Nusantara	South Sulawesi	51 million
PLTP Patuha Unit I	Patuha Power Ltd.	West Java	95 million
PLTA Asahan I	PT Tridaya Esta and PT Bajradaya	North Sumatera	180 million
PLTU Tanjung Jati A	Bakrie Power Corp and PT Maharani Paramita	Central Java	1.66 billion
PLTU Tanjung Jati C	PT CEPA Indonesia	Central Java	1.77 billion
Jamsostek Tower	PT Jamsostek	Jakarta	148 million

Source: Detektif dan Romantika, 15 November 1997.

Many investors and also the opposition leaders believed that Suharto was too old to handle the economic crisis and the pressure for him to resign increased.[93] There was a perception that Suharto was becoming a problem rather than a solution and therefore a new leader was required; one who could act as a circuit breaker. A new leader could help to restore investor confidence in Indonesia. In this situation, speculation on the political succession grew. In December 1997, *Gatra*, an influential weekly, ran a special report on the succession issue and suggested replacements for Suharto, such as the then vice-president Try Sutrisno, B. J. Habibie, Harmoko, Ginanjar Kartasasmita, General Hartono, and, on the opposition side, Megawati Sukarnoputri and Amien Rais.[94] Indeed, the issue of the political succession came into the centre of the crisis.

Why did this happen? Until the end of December 1997 there was no sign of the rupiah stabilising. Some observers suggest that the "panic" factor caused a massive capital outflow (particularly the exodus of the capital owned by the ethnic Chinese and withdrawal of foreign capital) from

Indonesia.[95] According to this view, the panic weakened Indonesia's economic fundamentals and this caused the rupiah to depreciate. As we will see, the issues surrounding the economic crisis do not end at this point.

Consequences of the Crisis

The IMF-Suharto Stand Off

In January 1998 the rupiah fell further and reached the critical level of Rp 10,000:US$, after Suharto delivered the 1998-1999 budget which contained unrealistic targets. The market reacted with heavy selling of the rupiah. Panic broke out among members of the Jakartan middle class, who immediately rushed into the shopping centres to stock up on daily goods in reaction to rumours of rising prices.[96] News and the television footage of the panic, which was broadcast worldwide, had the potential to create regional political instability. This prompted the international community to put pressure on Suharto to revise the budget and to renegotiate with the IMF. Among those who telephoned Suharto directly were the US President, Bill Clinton, the Japanese Prime Minister, Hashimoto, the German Chancellor, Helmut Kohl, and also the Australian Prime Minister, John Howard. The US government also sent a special envoy to convince Suharto of the urgency of sticking with the implementation of the IMF reform package.[97]

As a result, a second IMF agreement was signed in Jakarta on 15 January 1998. It was signed by President Suharto in the presence of the IMF Managing Director Michel Camdessus.[98] This agreement contained 50 points of economic reform, which were divided into seven main programmes: (1) to adjust and improve macroeconomic performance through measures such as maintaining the inflation rate at no higher than 20 per cent and bringing the current account into surplus; (2) to revise the 1998-1999 budget target by making a deficit of 1 per cent of GDP to be achieved by increasing petrol and electricity prices, but not those of kerosene; (3) to increase fiscal transparency and make the activity of the government more accountable, for instance, by allocating the Reforestation and Investment Funds onto the 1998-1999 budget; (4) to cancel 12 government-funded infrastructure projects which were allowed to proceed in November 1997, including scrapping the funding and tax incentives for Habibie's aeroplanes project (IPTN) and the national car project; (5) to strengthen the independence of Bank Indonesia in managing monetary policy, including maintaining the stability of the rupiah and reducing interest rates gradually; (6) to prepare a series of measures to restructure the banking sector; and (7) to set a time-table for implementing structural reforms, including abolishing all restrictions that had been applied in the economy, including the monopolies of the State Logistical Agency (*Bulog*) and others.[99]

Suharto had no choice but to agree with the IMF although many of the measures required the dismantling of privileges granted to his own family members. To monitor the implementation of the IMF reform package effectively, the government established the Council for Economic and Financial Stabilisation (*Dewan Pemantapan Ketahanan Economi dan Keuangan*), headed by President Suharto himself, with former senior economic minister Professor Widjojo Nitisastro as the Secretary General. To restore confidence in the banking sector, the government formed the Indonesian Bank Restructuring Agency (IBRA) on 27 January 1998. This was accompanied by the merging of four government-owned banks such as Bank Bumi Daya, Bank Ekspor-Impor Indonesia, Bank Pembangunan Indonesia, and Bank Dagang Negara and several private banks.[100] In addition, the revised 1998-1999 budget was also announced on 23 January 1998. The signing of the second IMF agreement did not stop the depreciation of the rupiah. The rupiah fell to just above Rp 15,000:US$ with the news about the nomination of Suharto's protege, B. J. Habibie, as a future vice-president. Habibie's record of being a strong advocate of high-cost and inefficient industries made him an unpopular figure in some circles, and therefore the market was in doubt as to whether he had the ability to end the crisis should Suharto be replaced or step down.[101]

At this point, Suharto was contemplating using a currency board system (CBS) to replace the free float policy (which primarily was blamed for the collapse of the rupiah). Suharto was attracted to the CBS after his daughter Tutut introduced him to Professor Steve Hanke, an American economist.[102] Without consulting the Governor of Bank Indonesia, Soedradjat Djiwandono, or the Finance Minister, Mar'ie Muhammad, Suharto proposed the idea of "IMF Plus", meaning the addition of the CBS to the existing IMF reform package. Suharto believed this could stabilise the rupiah.[103] This move caused serious concern among Suharto's own economic advisers, investors, and of course, the IMF itself. In a show of defiance and protest against the implementation of the CBS, Soedradjat resigned from his position as Governor of Bank Indonesia and was replaced by Dr. Sjahril Sabirin.[104] Suharto's plan to adopt the IMF-Plus idea was arguably a delaying tactic in the lead up to the Presidential election in March 1998. In attempting to delay the implementation of the IMF reform package Suharto hoped to maintain the loyalty of his supporters, who would suffer the economic consequences of the IMF reforms.

This stand-off reached its peak with the decision of the IMF on 6 March 1998 to postpone its second US$3 billion tranche. The situation was exacerbated by the inability of the IMF to review the programme because some ministers were busy preparing for the meeting of the People's Consultative Assembly, which would vote in the Presidential election in March 1998. In this political uncertainty the rupiah continued to fall.

The Political Reform Movement

Another significant impact of the currency crisis was the erosion of the legitimacy of the Suharto government and this resulted in deepening political crisis in Indonesia. From January until early March 1998 two political developments resulted from the crisis. First, the political reform movement (known in Indonesia as *gerakan reformasi politik*) gained momentum. Evidence of this was found in the emergence of a broad-based anti-Suharto coalition comprised of students, non-government organisations (NGOs), academics, journalists, religious leaders, ex-government officials, and leading opposition figures like Megawati, Amien Rais and a former Minister Emil Salim. This coalition regarded the deepening crisis as an opportunity to increase the pressure on the People's Consultative Assembly not to re-elect Suharto in March 1998 and also to call upon the government to implement political reform alongside the economic reforms.[105]

The political reform movement exposed the social and political problems which were contributing factors to the deepening of the economic crisis. Some of these problems have already been discussed earlier. With the momentum provided by the economic crisis, the political reform movement in Indonesia was able to transform them into a series of clear political demands. These included the demand to hold a special session of the People's Consultative Assembly to replace Suharto, to draft new and more democratic political bills, to restore the rights of free speech and assembly and uphold human rights, to release political prisoners, to hold free and fair general elections, and to abolish corruption, collusion and nepotism in business and government.[106]

The economic crisis also triggered widespread unorganised protests by ordinary Indonesians, which turned into riots in Java and some other islands. The main issue here was abolishing the subsidies on basic commodities such as oil, rice, and sugar, known in Indonesia as *Sembako* (an acronym for *sembilan bahan pokok* [nine basic commodities]). It is hard to know whether these riots were spontaneous or orchestrated by groups aiming to destabilise the government.[107] But what was clear was that the ethnic Chinese were the victims of the riots.[108] Anti-Chinese sentiment gained support among the elites at this time because some ethnic Chinese business leaders had refused to support the so-called "love the rupiah movement" led by Tutut, Suharto's eldest daughter.[109] In order to mobilise support for this movement from the wider population, the supporters of Suharto and his children launched a public campaign, which utilised nationalist symbols, anti-American sentiment, and also opposition to the IMF reform package.[110] Even Suharto himself began to state that some of the IMF reform measures were not consistent with the constitution and therefore must not be implemented.[111] All of this meant the government and Suharto personally lost popular support, which made it difficult for the government to implement the IMF reform package. Indeed, many of the measures had the potential to increase political tension in Indonesia.

The Downfall of Suharto

With the potential of further political upheaval, Suharto decided to consolidate his power by appointing several of his loyalists to top military positions. These were General Wiranto (as the Chief of the Indonesian Armed Forces), General Subagio (as the Chief of the Army), and Lieutenant-General Prabowo Subianto (as the Chief of the powerful Strategic Command of the Army).[112] Both Wiranto and Subagio had been Suharto's personal adjutants in the past, while Prabowo was Suharto's son-in-law. This military reshuffle suggested that Suharto wanted to prevent the possibility of division among the military leaders, which could jeopardise his re-election in March 1998.

When Suharto was indeed re-elected as President, with B. J. Habibie as the new Vice-President, the market and the public reacted cautiously.[113] But public disappointment was clear when the new cabinet was announced. It was described by many as a "crony cabinet" because it included less capable people, including Suharto's daughter Tutut, his golfing partner (and business tycoon) Bob Hasan and other Suharto loyalists.[114] This again eroded the credibility of the government in undertaking the IMF reform package, which had been put on hold during the presidential election period. The international community lobbied the IMF and donor countries to find a more appropriate economic reform programme that would suit the domestic situation in Indonesia.[115] The result was that in mid-March 1998, the "new" government renegotiated with the IMF and signed a third agreement, which contained small revisions of the previous agreements. In this agreement, the IMF and the government agreed to rehabilitate those private companies who had debt problem and to draft for the first time a new bankruptcy law in Indonesia.[116]

Nonetheless, the re-election of Suharto did not ease the political tension. When the prices of basic commodities such as petrol, cooking oil and flour increased in early May 1998, the poor were angered and their feelings of desperation spilled over into unorganised protests. At the same time, students and other pro-democracy groups urged the government to reverse the decision to abolish the subsidies and demanded the resignation of Suharto. Mass demonstrations led by the students occurred in the major cities of Jakarta, Bandung, Yogyakarta, Solo, Surabaya, Medan and Ujung Pandang. The death of five students from the prestigious Trisakti University on 12 May 1998, while Suharto was on a state visit in Cairo, triggered anti-Chinese mass demonstrations and riots in Jakarta and other big cities, which lasted for three days and caused the death of about five hundred people.[117] When Suharto returned to Jakarta, he discovered the capital city still smouldering, with some sections ruined, and his political future uncertain.

These appeared to be conflict in the elites, particularly between those who wanted to replace Suharto by staging a military coup, led by Lieutenant General Prabowo Subianto, and those who believed Suharto could be replaced constitutionally (the latter group represented by General Wiranto).[118] As the pressure on Suharto grew, he lost supporters in the military, the ruling party Golkar, and also among his own cabinet ministers. Eventually this loss of support forced Suharto's resignation on 21 May 1998, with B. J. Habibie replacing him as President. The change in leadership marked the end of the Suharto era, but not of the economic and political crises.

Conclusion

This chapter has examined the causes and the implications of Indonesia's economic crisis of 1997 and 1998. It discussed the ability of Indonesian economic policy makers to respond to the financial crisis and its impact on domestic politics in Indonesia. It argued that the economic crisis was exacerbated by the "panic" factor, which led to the withdrawal of foreign capital and a major crisis of confidence among domestic and foreign investors. The financial liberalisation undertaken during the 1980s and 1990s integrated the Indonesian economy into the global economy. This increased capital inflow into Indonesia, which helped to sustain economic growth.

The expansion in capital inflow, however, also increased the current account deficit and external debt, particularly private and short-term debts. In part this happened because many foreign loans were invested in the property sector or other non-productive sectors. The other issue was the fact that there had been a decline in export growth in Indonesia in the previous years. Indonesian exports had became less competitive in the international market, as a result of the decline in commodity prices globally and also of the relocation of manufacturing companies to neighbouring countries in the region. In addition, weaknesses in banking supervision and regulatory measures made Indonesia vulnerable to external shock.

The early signs of economic downturn in Indonesia did not send a clear signal to political leaders and policy makers. In the US economic growth had increased rapidly since the mid-1990s, making the US dollar stronger than the Japanese yen and other currencies, including the rupiah. As the rupiah had been fixed to the US dollar since the mid-1980s, its value was inflating and therefore pressure was put on policy makers to adjust the exchange-rate policy. The adjustment happened after the rupiah depreciated as a result of contagion from the float of the baht in Thailand on 2 July 1997. The experience of Thailand demonstrated to Indonesian policy makers that defending the rupiah in the globalised economy would be costly and unproductive. Moreover, domestic factors such as "deregulation fatigue", internal rivalry between the technocrat and the Habibie camps, the uncertainty of the political succession, widespread corruption, collusion and nepotism and mass protests and riots all contributed to the deepening crisis. Thus, domestic politics played an important role in the economic crisis in Indonesia.

What, then, were the responses to the currency crisis in Indonesia? Similarly to Thailand, Indonesia had to call for external assistance from the IMF and several donor countries. The economic crisis caused the contraction of economic activity, but the introduction and implementation of an IMF reform package did not end the crisis. Indeed, the implementation of the IMF reform package, the closure of 16 banks in November 1997, and the inconsistencies of the reform policies, created a situation in which panic led to an increase in capital outflow. Meanwhile, the currency crisis also had political consequences. In Indonesia, the economic crisis opened up public debate about the need to implement political reforms alongside economic reforms. The crisis also catalysed the political opposition, which led to the downfall of President Suharto in May 1998.

Notes

[1] On the dynamics of the financial liberalisation policies in Indonesia, see Mari Pangestu, "Financial Markets and Policies" in Mari Pangestu (ed.) *Economic Reform, Deregulation and Privatization, The Indonesian Experience* (Jakarta: Centre for Strategic and International Studies, 1996), pp. 133-149; David D. Cole and Betty F. Slade, *Building a Modern Financial System, The Indonesian Experience* (Cambridge: Cambridge University Press, 1996); Miranda S. Goeltom, *The Financial Liberalisation in Indonesia* (Singapore: Institute of Southeast Asian Studies, 1994); Ross H. McLeod (ed.) *Indonesia Assessment 1994, Finance as a Key Sector in Indonesia's Development* (Singapore and Canberra: Institute of Southeast Asian Studies and Research School of Pacific Studies, Australian National U·:versity, 1994).

[2] Anwar Nasution, "Banking Sector Reforms in Indonesia, 1983-93" in Ross H. McLeod (ed.) *Indonesia Assessment 1994, Finance as a Key Sector in Indonesia's Development* (Singapore and Canberra: Institute of Southeast Asian Studies and Research School of Pacific and Asian Studies, ANU, 1994), pp. 130-157.

[3] Miranda S. Goeltom, "Perubahan Struktural Sektor Keuangan di Indonesia: Visi dan Tantangan" [Structural Changes in Indonesia's Financial Sector: Vision and Challenges] in Mari Pangestu and Ira Setiawati (eds.) *Mencari Paradigma Baru Pembangunan Indonesia* [Searching for a Paradigm of Indonesia's Development] (Jakarta: Centre for Strategic and International Studies), pp. 51-91.

[4] Ibid, p. 68.

[5] Interview with Dr. Didik Rachbini, Jakarta, 24 September 1997.

[6] Nasution, p. 152.

[7] Ross McLeod, "Indonesia's Crisis and Future Prospects" in Karl D. Jackson (ed.) *Asian Contagion, The Causes and Consequences of a Financial Crisis* (Singapore: Institute of Southeast Asian Studies, 1999), pp. 209-210.

[8] Goeltom, "Perubahan Struktural Sektor Keuangan di Indonesia", pp. 76-77.

[9] Nasution, "Banking Sector Reforms in Indonesia", pp. 149-150; on the collapse of Bapindo (government-owned the Indonesian Development Bank) see Nasyith Majidi, *Mega Skandal, Drama Pembobolan dan Kolusi Bapindo* [Mega Scandal, the Drama of the Closure and Collusion of Bapindo] (Bandung: Mizan, 1994); *Info Bank*, August 1997; and *Panji Masyarakat*, 30 June 1997.

[10] World Bank, *Indonesia, Sustaining High Growth with Equity* (Washington D.C.: World Bank, 1997).

[11] Ibid, p.16.

[12] World Bank, *Indonesia, Sustaining High Growth with Equity*, p. 19.

[13] Ibid, p.14.

[14] Ibid, p. 9-13; and for a critical assessment, see Econit, *Kinerja Kabinet Pembangunan VII: Dibawah Bayang-Bayang Keraguan* [The Performance of the 7th Development Cabinet: Under the Shadow of Doubt], a Public Policy Review, 1997, (<http://www.indoexchange.com/econit/>).

[15] World Bank, *Indonesia, Sustaining High Growth with Equity*, p. 14.

[16] As quoted by Jasso Winarto (ed.) *Pasar Modal Indonesia, Retrospeksi Lima Tahun Swastanisasi BEJ* [Indonesia's Capital Market, Restrospection of Five Years' Privatization of Jakarta Stock Exchange] (Jakarta: Pustaka Sinar Harapan dan Jakarta Stock Exchange, 1997), pp. 208-209.

[17] Ibid, p. 116.

[18] For more discussion on this issue, see John Bresnan, *Managing Indonesia, The Modern Political Economy* (New York: Columbia University Press, 1993); Adam Schwarz, *A Nation in Waiting, Indonesia in the 1990s* (Sydney: Allen and Unwin, 1994); and Mari Pangestu, *Economic Reform, Deregulation and Privatization, The Indonesian Experience* (Jakarta: Centre for Strategic and International Studies, 1996).

[19] Schwarz, pp. 84-85.

[20] Takashi Shiraisi, "Rewiring the Indonesian State" in Daniel S. Lev and Ruth McVey (eds.) *Making Indonesia* (Ithaca: Southeast Asia Program, Cornell University, 1996), p. 175.

[21] Interview with Umar Juoro, Jakarta, 2 September 1997.

[22] Import items on which Bulog had held a monopoly for years were, among others, rice and rice flour, wheat and wheat flour, sugar, soybeans, onions, garlic, shallots.

[23] Interview with Dr. Dennis de Tray, Jakarta, 24 September 1997.

[24] Richard Robison, "Politics and Markets in Indonesia's Post-oil Era" in Garry Rodan, Kevin Hewison and Richard Robison (eds.) *The Political Economy of South-East Asia* (Melbourne: Oxford University Press, 1997), pp. 29-63.

[25] "Kontroversi Akhir Tahun: Polemik Proteksi" [Controversy at the End of the Year: Polemic on Protection], *Warta Ekonomi*, 19 December 1994.

[26] "Dibalik Permohonan Proteksi" [Behind the Demand for Protection], *Gatra*, 24 Desember 1994.

[27] Anggito Abimanyu, "Recent Economic Events in Indonesia: From Rapid Economic Growth to National Car Policy", in Gavin W. Jones and Terence H. Hull (eds.) *Indonesia Assessment, Population and Human Resources* (Singapore and Canberra: Institute of Southeast Asian Studies and Research School of Pacific and Asian Studies, Australian National University, 1997), pp. 51-53; and World Bank, *Indonesia, Sustaining High Growth with Equity*, p. 116.

[28] Interview with Dr. Indria Samego, Jakarta, 4 September 1997.

[29] Priyambudi Sulistiyanto, "The Urban Riots that Rocked Jakarta", *Current Affairs Bulletin*, vol. 73, no. 1 (June-July, 1996), pp. 26-28.

[30] On the causes and consequences of the the 27 July 1996 Uprising, see Lukas Luwarso (ed.) *Jakarta Crackdown* (Jakarta: Alliance of Independence Journalists, 1997).

[31] William Liddle and Rizal Mallarangeng, "Indonesia in 1996, Pressures from Above and Below", *Asian Survey*, vol. xxxvii, no. 2 (February 1997), pp. 167-174.

[32] Abimanyu, *Recent Economic Events in Indonesia*, pp. 55-56.

[33] Kuntowijoyo, "Sebab-Musabab" [Causes], *Gatra*, 8 February 1997.

[34] Liddle and Mallarangeng, *op.cit*, pp. 171-172; and also "Kerusuhan Sepanjang Tahun 1995-1996" [Riots throughout 1995-1996], *Gatra*, 8 February 1997.

[35] Rizal Mallarangeng, "Teori dam Kerusuhan di Dua Kota" [Theory and Riots in Two Cities], *Gatra*, 8 February 1997.

[36] Priyambudi Sulistiyanto, "The May 1997 General Election in Indonesia, What went wrong?", *Current Affairs Bulletin*, vol. 74, no. 2 (August-September 1997), pp. 13-19: and also see Muhammad Asfar, "Kekerasan Politik dan Demokrasi di Seputar Pemilu 1997", *Prisma*, no. 1 (1998), 17-31.

[37] Interview with Shobirin Nadj, Jakarta,19 September 1997.

[38] Interview with Dr. Dennis de Tray, Jakarta, 24 September 1997.

[39] "Meredam Gempuran Spekulan" [To ease the speculators attacks], *Gatra*, 26 July 1997; and J. Thomas Lindblad, "Survey of Recent Developments", *Bulletin of Indonesian Economic Studies*, vol. 33, no. 3 (December 1997), pp. 4-5.

[40] "Otoritas Moneter Harus Bersatu" [Monetary Authority must unite], an interview with Soedradjat Djiwandono published in *Gatra*, 26 July 1997.

[41] Ibid.

[42] "Theo F. Toemion: 'Apapun Namanya, Sudah Terjadi Devaluasi...'"[Whatever the name, devaluation has already happened], *Detektif dan Romantika*, 23 August 1997.

[43] "Untuk Sementara Masih Ketat" [Still tight for the time being], *Gatra*, 16 August 1997.

[44] "Bank-Bank Kecil Bisa Kelabakan" [Small banks will be in trouble], *Gatra*, 16 August 1997.

[45] Hadi Soesastro and M. Chatib Basri, "Survey of Recent Developments", *Bulletin of Indonesian Economic Studies*, vol. 34, no. 1 (April 1998), p. 14.

[46] "Sjahrir: Ada Peluang Lebarkan Spread" [Sjahrir: There is a chance of widening spread], *Bisnis Indonesia*, 11 August 1997; "Tight money hits stock", *The Jakarta Post*, 12 August 1997; and "Uang Ketat" [Tight money], *Gatra*, 16 August 1997.

[47] "Duet Mar'ie dan Soedradjat Pilih Fleksibel" [Mar'ie and Soedradjat duo choose flexibility], *Prospek* 25 August 1997; and "Rupiah Terpuruk atau Devaluasi

Terselubung" [Falling Rupiah or covered devaluation], *Detektif dan Romantika*, 23 August 1997.

[48] "Indonesia Floats Rupiah", *Jakarta Post*, 15 August 1997; "Pita Pembatas itu Akhirnya Dipangkas" [The band finally is no longer needed], *Prospek*, 25 Ausgust 1997; and for an observer's view, see Judith Bird, "Indonesia in 1997, The Tinderbox Year", *Asian Survey*, vol. 38, no. 2 (February 1998), p. 173.

[49] The Economist Intelligence Unit, *A Country Report, Indonesia*, 3rd quarter, 1997, p. 20.

[50] "Mereka bicara putusnya Pita" [They talk about the end of the band], *Prospek*, 25 August 1997.

[51] "Nasib Rupiah Setelah Mengambang" [The fate of the rupiah after float], *Gatra*, 23 August 1997.

[52] Quoted in Lindblad, "Survey of Recent Developments" 1997, p. 6, from the Presidential address on 16 August 1997, as translated by *Jakarta Post*, 18 August 1997.

[53] "Yang Tak Perlu Nanti Dulu" [What is not urgent can wait], *Gatra*, 23 August 1997.

[54] The Economist Intelligence Unit, *A Country Report, Indonesia*, 4th quarter, 1997, p. 18.

[55] "Teka-teki Politik di Balik Gejolak Rupiah" [The political speculation behind the collapse of the rupiah], *Adil*, 27 August-2 September 1997.

[56] "Saleh Afiff: Hapuskan Monopoli" [Saleh Afiff: Abolish Monopoly], *Kompas*, 21 August 1997; and "Praktek Monopoli tidak Menyejahterakan Rakyat" [Monopoly practices do not create the welfare of the people], *Kompas*, 23 August 1997.

[57] "Govt's plan on Bulog hailed", *Jakarta Post*, 27 August 1997.

[58] "BJ Habibie: Industri Strategis takkan Dijadwal Ulang" [BJ Habibie: Strategic industries will not be rescheduled], *Kompas*, 21 August 1997.

[59] "Slashing Monopolies", editorial, *Jakarta Post*, 22 August 1997.

[60] The Economist Intelligence Unit, *A Country Report, Indonesia*, 4th quarter, 1997, p. 19.

[61] John McBeth, "Action Faction", *Far Eastern Economic Review*, 4 September 1997; "Sepuluh Langkah Pulihkan Ekonomi" [Ten steps to rebuild the economy], *Republika*, 4 September 1997; and "10 Kiat Penyelamatan dari Bina Graha" [Ten rescue steps from Bina Graha], *Prospek*, 15 September 1997.

[62] *Keterangan Pemerintah Mengenai Gejolak Rupiah dan Upaya untuk Mengatasinya* [Government Explanation about the Fluctuation of the Rupiah and Efforts to overcome with it], Finance Minister Mar'ie Muhammad's speech at the House of Representatives, Jakarta, 16 September 1997.

[63] Ibid.

[64] This can be found in Ross H. McLeod, "Postscript to the Survey of Recent Developments: On Causes and Cures for the Rupiah Crisis", *Bulletin of Indonesian Economic Studies*, vol. 33, no. 3 (December 1997), pp. 45-46.

[65] Sjahrir, "Stabilitas Yang Bagaimana?" [What kind of stability?], *Warta Ekonomi*, 22 September 1997.

[66] "Untung Ada Krisis..." [Thank Goodness, there is a crisis...], *Warta Ekonomi*, 15 September 1997.

[67] Keputusan Menteri Keuangan Republik Indonesia Nomor 455/ KMK 01/1997 tentang *Pembelian Saham oleh Pemodal Asing Melalui Pasar Modal* [The Finance Ministerial Decree Number 455/KMK 01/1997 about Purchasing Stock by Foreign Investors through Capital Market].

[68] "Investor Asing, Belanjalah Sepuasnya...!" [Foreign investors, Shop till you drop...!], *Kompas*, 9 September 1997; "Obat Generik dari Mar'ie Muhammad" [Generic medicine from Mar'ie Muhammad], *Prospek*, 22 September 1997; and "Bursa Indonesia makin liberal" [Indonesian stock exchange increasingly liberal], *Bisnis Indonesia*, 8 September 1997.

[69] This sentiment was observed when the writer participated in a closed-door discussion organised by *The Republika* daily involving prominent observers such as Dr. Mochtar Mas'oed, Dr. Indria Samego, Umar Juoro, Zalim Saidi, and Nasyith Madjidi. A summary of this discussion was published with headline "Menakar Dimensi Politik Krisis Rupiah" [To predict the political dimension of the rupiah crisis], *Republika*, 8 September 1997; and "Pencabutan ini Bukannya Tanpa Risiko" [The float of the rupiah is not without risk], *Prospek*, 22 September 1997.

[70] "Mahathir, Soros dan Pertumbuhan Ekonomi" [Mahathir, Soros and economic growth], *Republika*, 29 September 1997; and "Dari Efek Domino, Korporasi, Hingga Kritik PM Mahathir" [From the domino and corporate effect to the critics of P M Mahathir's criticism], *Kompas*, 3 October 1997.

[71] The Economist Intelligence Unit, 4th quarter, 1997, p. 23.

[72] Henry Sender and John McBeth, "Default Options", *Far Eastern Economic Review*, 23 October 1997.

[73] "Syarat IMF, Apa Pemerintah Mau" [IMF conditionality, Does the government want it?], *Detektif dan Romantika*, 25 October 1997.

[74] Soesastro and Basri, "Survey of Recent Developments", pp. 22-23.

[75] See Sjahrir, "Bantuan IMF dan Implikasinya" [IMF rescue package and its implications], *Detektif dan Romantika*, 25 October 1997.

[76] Soesastro and Basri, p. 10.

[77] The Economist Intelligent Unit, 4th quarter, 1997, pp. 23-24.

[78] "Akhirnya Ada Kesepakatan" [Finally there is an agreement], *Gatra*, 8 November 1997.

[79] Soesastro and Basri, p. 11.

[80] Ibid.

[81] This view can be found in Faisal H. Basri, "Logika Kedatangan IMF" [Logic of the arrival of the IMF], *Detektif dan Romantika*, 25 October 1997; also see Soesastro and Basri, "Survey of Recent Developments", p. 16.

[82] The Economist Intelligence Unit, 4th quarter, 1997, pp. 24-25.

[83] On Sachs' central argument, see Soesastro and Basri, "Survey of Recent Developments", p. 17.

[84] Ibid, p. 18.

[85] "Belasan Bank itu Akhirnya kena Gulung" [Finally more than a dozen banks forced to close down], *Forum Keadilan*, 17 November 1997.

[86] John McBeth, "Suharto's Test", *Far Eastern Economic Review*, 20 November 1997.

[87] This view can be found in an interview with Thomas Suyatno, head of the Association of the National Private Bank (*Perhimpunan Bank-Bank Swasta National* [Perbanas]), "Likuidasi Tindakan Paling Akhir" [Liquidation is the last resort], *Gatra*, 15 November 1997.

[88] "In Indonesia, Mar'ie Faces Intense Pressure", *The Asian Wall Street Journal*, 12 November 1997; "Likuidasi, Rekayasa Politik?" [Liquidation, political engineering?], *Detektif dan Romantika*, 15 November 1997; and "Setelah Likuidasi Berbagai Masalah Menanti", [After liquidation more problems waiting], *Gatra*, 15 November 1997.

[89] The Economist Intelligence Unit, *A Country Report, Indonesia*, 4th quarter, 1997, p. 27.

[90] "Lima Belas Proyek Boleh Terus, Apa Kata IMF" [Fifteen projects can go ahead, What will the IMF say?] , *Detektif dan Romantika*, 15 November 1997.

[91] An interview with Stanley Fisher, IMF Vice-Managing Director, "Tak Ada Orang Sehat Memanggil Dokter" [No healthy person would call a doctor], *Detektif dan Romantika*, 15 November 1997.

[92] "Dihempas Kabar Angin" [Swept away by rumours], *Gatra*, 20 December 1997.

[93] The view of foreign investors as reported in the editorial of the *Economist*, 17 January 1998.

[94] *Gatra*, 20 December 1997.

[95] Ross McLeod, "Postcript to the Survey of Recent Developments", pp. 51-52; and also Steven Radelet and Jeffrey Sachs, *The East Asian Financial Crisis: Diagnosis, Remedies*, Prospects, a paper presented to the Brooking Panel, Washington D.C., March 26-27 1998.

[96] Patrick Walters, "Suharto's fighting rhetoric falls on deaf market ears", *The Australian*, 8 January 1998; and "Suharto stands firm as rumour mill churns", *The Weekend Australian*, 10-11 January 1998.

[97] Patrick Walters and Michael McGuire, "Clinton bid to calm Asia crisis", *The Weekend Australian*, 10-11 January 1998.

[98] Patrick Walters, "Suharto bites the bullet on reform", *The Australian*, 16 January 1998; Louise Williams, "Suharto surrenders to IMF", *The Age*, 16 January 1998; and Greg Earl, "Soeharto yields to IMF", *The Australian Financial Review*, 16 January 1998.

[99] "Kesepakatan Reformasi Ekonomi Indonesia-IMF" [Indonesia-IMF Agreement on economic reform], *Republika*, 16 January 1998; and also Soesastro and Basri, "Survey of Recent Development", pp. 22-23.

[100] Colin Johnson, "Survey of Recent Developments", *Bulletin of Indonesian Economic Studies*, vol 34, no. 2 (August 1998), p. 47; and also "Ramai-ramai Merger" [Everyone is merging], *Gatra*, 31 January 1998.

[101] It must be noted here that domestically the nomination of B.J. Habibie was not fully supported. Some elements within the armed forces and within the ruling party Golkar were not happy with this nomination. However, since Habibie received the personal support of Suharto, the nomination went ahead.

[102] "Jurus Menghajar Spekulan" [Ways to punish speculators], *Gatra*, 14 February 1998.

[103] Johnson, "Survey of Recent Developments", p. 28.

[104] "Gubernur BI Sjahril Sabirin: Perlu Kurs Rupiah yang Terjangkau" [BI Governor Sjahril Sabirin: We need an attainable exchange rate], *Kompas*, 20 February 1998.

[105] Jose Manuel Tesoro, "Forging a Shaky Alliance", *Asiaweek*, 6 February 1998.

[106] For further discussion on the political reform movement prior to the downfall of Suharto see John Sidel, "Macet Total: Logics of Circulation and Accumulation in the Demise of Indonesia's New Order", *Indonesia*, no. 66 (October 1998), pp. 159-194.

[107] John McBeth, "Playing with Ire, The Puzzling Origins of anti-Chinese Riots in Java", *Far Eastern Economic Review*, 2 March 1998.

[108] Soesastro and Basri, "Survey of Recent Developments", p. 36.

[109] Bob Catley and Priyambudi Sulistiyanto, "The 1998 Indonesian Crisis and Australia's Strategic Interests", *Current Affairs Bulletin*, vol. 75, no. 1 (June-July 1998), pp. 16-17.

[110] Soesastro and Basri, *op.cit*, p. 52.

[111] "Kita tak Menuju Liberalisme" [We do not want liberalism], *Republika Homepage*, 5 March 1998.

[112] "Presiden Lantik Pangab dan KASAD" [President appoints the Chief of Staff and the Chief of Army], *Kompas Homepage*, 17 February 1998.

[113] Patrick Walters, "Suharto wins five more years", *The Australian*, 11 March 1998; and Greg Earl, "Soeharto set to name factional, smaller Cabinet", *The Australian Financial Review*, 11 March 1998.

[114] The Economist Intelligence Unit, *A Country Report, Indonesia*, 2nd quarter, 1998, p. 15.

[115] On the role of Australian diplomacy, see Catley and Sulistiyanto, "The 1998 Indonesian Crisis and Australia's Strategic Interests", pp. 18-19.

[116] For more detail about the IMF III can be found in Johnson, "Survey of Recent Developments", p. 32.

[117] Patrick Walters, Don Greenlees, and Robert Garran, "Rioters rule Jakarta streets", *The Australian*, 15 May 1998.

[118] Sidel, "*Macet Total*: Logics of Circulation and Accumulation in the Demise of Indonesia's New Order", *Indonesia*, no. 66 (October 1998), pp. 185-191.

Chapter Seven

Burma's Unreal Boom

Burma, like Indonesia, is a multi-ethnic country, with a population of 47.3 million in the 1990s. In 1988 the military government of the State Law and Order Restoration Council (SLORC) announced economic reforms and opened Burma to foreign investors. However, not much was achieved during the 1990s. Burma is a case where the failure of economic reform has been accompanied by increasingly authoritarian politics. This chapter examines the history that shaped contemporary Burma's economic and political situations. It then analyses the politics of the SLORC economic reforms and the domestic and external factors which contributed to the failure of the reform process. This is followed by a discussion of the increasing political authoritarianism and popular opposition in Burma during the 1990s.

Historical Setting

Burma is a country rich in natural resources and historically was the focus of international rivalry. It was one of the most prosperous countries in the region after it gained independence from Britain, but has experienced economic stagnation and political crisis in the past three decades.[1] Three important factors shaped political and economic life in Burma in the course of the twentieth century. First, before annexation by the British colonial government at the end of the nineteenth century, strong central leaders such as King Anurawtha of Pagan, King Bayyinaung of Taungoo, and King Alaungpaya of the Konbaung monarchy ruled Burma.[2] The collapse of the Burmese monarchies humiliated the Burmese people.[3] Under colonial power, Burma became a province of British India. The power of the British colonial government rested on the bureaucracy and on using repressive means to maintain power.[4] The transition to colonial power under the British was not a peaceful process and it was accompanied by resistance and rebellions throughout Burma.

Second, as in Indonesia, the experience of colonisation gave rise to a strong sense of nationalism. Under British rule, Burmese society was divided into three categories: the British expatriates and the Burmese upper class, who occupied important positions in the bureaucracy; the Indians and local traders (many of the latter being Chinese) who controlled economic activities; and the ordinary people.[5] The British divided the country into two territories: Burma proper, which was occupied by the majority ethnic Burmans and the frontier areas, where the ethnic minorities lived. Silverstein has pointed out that this division was particularly important in influencing political developments in Burma in the post-colonial period.[6]

Third, the British colonial government also introduced a laissez-faire system, which allowed the private sector to run the economy and, indeed, helped to increase international trading activities.[7] The expansion of international trading became an important source of revenue. As noted by Adas, Burma was then integrated into the world economy and became a major exporter of rice to the international market.[8] But economic development early in the twentieth century also had its cost. Increasing numbers of Indian immigrants arrived in Burma to work there, forcing the Burmese off their land.[9] Those who benefited most from the economic growth were the British, a small Burmese elite, the Indians, and the Chinese.[10] This social and economic gap contributed to the emergence of the nationalist movement in Burma and it continued to affect political and economic developments in Burma in the post-independence period.

The idea of creating a modern state of Burma grew rapidly during the 1920s and the 1930s.[11] As in Indonesia, during the Japanese occupation period the Burmese nationalist leaders were divided into two camps. In the first camp were those who wanted to collaborate with the Japanese, including some prominent nationalist leaders trained by the Japanese Army to prepare for war against the British colonial government. In the second were those who wanted to create a democratic political system along the lines of the British tradition. This created political division, especially at the time when the Japanese occupation government was about to leave Burma in the 1940s.[12] The future of the ethnic minorities was uncertain. Some groups demanded their own states while others were happy to be part of Burma. As a result, Aung San, a prominent nationalist leader, signed a peace agreement with the ethnic leaders, which guaranteed the right of the ethnic minorities to gain independence ten years after the independence of Burma was declared.[13]

The U Nu Period

On 19 July 1947, Aung San, along with six members of the new parliament was assassinated. This was a blow for the country. As Silverstein points out, Aung San was seen by many as the leader who could unify the people of Burma.[14] U Nu, another prominent nationalist, took up the leadership of the Independence movement and, in 1948, he proclaimed the independence of Burma and introduced parliamentary democracy as the system of government. The immediate issues that U Nu and his government had to face were to unite and to develop the country. Unfortunately, from the start U Nu had to contend with civil war in Burma.[15] Several armed groups, including the communists, several ethnic minorities, and the *Kuomintang* (KMT) armies on the Burma-China border, joined forces to undermine the U Nu government.[16] Despite the fact that this political system was not successful in establishing political stability, the U Nu government gave the Burmese people a taste of democracy.[17] Under the U Nu government, Burma held several general elections in the 1950s, all with a very high level of public participation. During the U Nu period, Burma also began to implement industrialisation policies and invited foreign investors into the country. Burma was experiencing economic growth at a level that was admired by other countries in the region.[18] The development of international trade was one of the main achievements of the U Nu government.

However, a political crisis in the 1950s was seized upon by the Burmese military as justification for it to enter the political arena. The Burmese military leaders felt that they had a mandate to defend the country from disintegration and thus never concealed their intention to replace the U Nu government.[19] In 1958, as Burma was in political crisis, General Ne Win, the Chief of the Army, was asked by U Nu to establish a caretaker government, with the tasks of ending the civil war, rebuilding the economy, and preparing for general elections. General Ne Win used this opportunity to expand the involvement of military officers (through the Defence Services Institute) in a wide range of activities, including business.[20] The caretaker role of the Burmese military ended in 1960, but by this time they had acquired a taste for running the country. Although U Nu and his Union Party won the 1960 general election, General Ne Win and other high ranking military officers were waiting for an opportunity to enter politics once again. When U Nu and his Union Party government failed to reach a political settlement with the ethnic minorities in 1962, General Ne Win launched a military coup and overthrew the government in March 1962.[21] This marked the end of a period of parliamentary democracy in Burma.

The Ne Win Period

Soon after General Ne Win took power, he established a Revolutionary Council, headed by himself, along with seventeen high-ranking military officers. He produced a political manifesto known as the "Burmese Way to Socialism", which explained the reasons for the military seizure of power and also contained explanations of the economic and political programmes through which the creation of a socialist society in Burma would be achieved.[22] General Ne Win strengthened the role of the state to aid the implementation of radical socialist economic policies. Over the next three decades, General Ne Win ruled as a dictator and the military became Burma's major national decision-making institution.[23] In the 1960s Ne Win's socialist state nationalised all private companies and held a monopoly on the management of economic activity throughout the country. The Burmese economy became highly centralised and regulated.[24] By 1963 about 15,000 companies in various sectors and 24 foreign and domestic banks were nationalised in Burma.[25] As a side effect of this nationalisation policy, many middle class Burmese and local traders, especially those of Indian and Pakistani origin, left Burma.[26]

The nationalisation programme also forced a few foreign-based institutions such as the Ford Foundation, the Asia Foundation and the British Council to leave the country.[27] The inflow of foreign aid declined (see Table 7.1) and Burma depended very much on domestic resources for financing its economic and development programmes. However, a few Western countries continued to grant special loans for particular development projects and between 1962 and 1972, in that period Burma received about US$ 28 million per year in foreign aid.[28] In the first two decades of socialist rule, there was no real progress in the Burmese economy. According to Steinberg, although the Ne Win government increased the financial allocation to the industrial sector from about 3.6 per cent in 1961 to 37 per cent in 1971, its overall share of Burma's gross domestic product (GDP) was only 10 per cent.[29] The agricultural sector showed a similar outlook, particularly with respect to the level of rice production. Rice had always been a significant source of revenue for Burma. Although many incentive programmes were provided for farmers soon after the socialist government was in place, rice production increased only slowly, from 6.726 million tons in the 1960s to 7.261 million tons in the 1970s.[30] This was not enough to supply the needs of the Burmese population, which in fact had increased by about 25 per cent over these same two decades.[31]

Table 7.1 Foreign Capital Assistance, 1978 (million)

Country/Bank	Loans	Grants
World Bank	US$ 40.0	-
Asian Development Bank	US$ 65.5	US$ 0.237
Australia	-	US$ 9.21
Canada	US$ 7.2	US$ 3.8
Denmark	Kroner 30.0	-
India	-	US$ 2.5
Germany (FRG)	DM 85.0	DM 10.0
Japan	US$ 81.5	US$ 25.5
Netherlands	-	US$ 15.0
United Kingdom	-	Pounds 2.67
China	-	US$ 15.0
United Nations	-	US 18.4

Source: David I. Steinberg, *Burma's Road Toward Development: Growth and Ideology under Military Rule* (Boulder: Westview Press, 1981), p. 60.

Under the socialist economic structure, state-owned enterprises (SOEs) dominated economic activity, while the private sector was not allowed to operate in the market.[32] But due to the inefficiency and lack of managerial skill of the SOEs, in combination with widespread corruption, the black market economy increased in size. This caused the economy to deteriorate and the government failed to provide goods and services to the Burmese people.[33] Official figures show that the growth of the Burmese economy from the 1960s until the end of the 1980s was not impressive (Table 7.2).

Table 7.2 Growth, Investment and Savings in Burma, 1962-1988 (per cent of GDP)

Years	Growth	Investment	Savings	Resource Gap
1962-1965	4.9	13.5	15.4	-1.9
1966-1969	2.2	10.9	8.7	2.2
1970-1973	1.3	11.2	10.5	0.7
1974-1977	4.7	10.9	10	0.9
1978-1981	6.5	20.9	16.5	4.4
1982-1985	4.7	17.7	12.5	5.2
1986-1988	1.7	12.5	9.7	2.8

Source: U Tun Wai, "The Myanmar Economy at the Crossroads, Options and Constraints", in Mya Than and Joseph L. H. Tan (eds.) *The Myanmar Economy at The Crossroads: Options and Constraints* (Singapore: Institute of Southeast Asian Studies, 1990), p. 24.

General Ne Win also instituted a single party system, with the Burmese Socialist Programme Party (BSPP) becoming the only legal party in Burma. To achieve mass support, the BSPP formed mass organisations throughout Burma, with assistance from the military apparatus.[34] This type of political system was intended to create the political stability that could help in the creation of a socialist society in Burma. Instead, from the 1960s until the 1980s, General Ne Win and his government faced increasing opposition both in Burma proper and in the ethnic minority areas. Students, civilian politicians, Buddhist monks, and armed groups such as the communists and ethnic minorities were the main opposition groups which challenged the leadership of General Ne Win.[35] Signs that Burma was entering economic and political crisis were acknowledged by General Ne Win and other military leaders during the BSPP Congress held in August 1987.[36] In response, the government announced the demonetisation of several denominations of Burmese currency, the kyat.[37] This was intended to eliminate the black markets and smuggling activity along the border areas. The government also lifted restrictions on private companies trading in rice and other basic commodities. However, these changes did not improve the economic situation. It was ordinary people who suffered most from the demonetisation.

In December 1987 the United Nations conferred Least Developed Country (LDC) status on Burma, ranking it among the ten poorest countries in the world.[38] This humiliated and angered the Burmese people. Their frustration culminated in what became known as the 1988 Uprising. This occurred between March and September that year, with a series of nationwide popular protests against General Ne Win and his military government, and their failure to foster economic progress. The single party system was denounced and demands were made for it to be replaced by a multi-party political system.

The SLORC and the Politics of Economic Reform

The 1988 Uprising forced the resignation of General Ne Win and other military leaders from various government positions, but it did not oust the military from power.[39] After Ne Win's resignation, two caretaker governments were formed by proteges of Ne Win, General Sein Lwin and a civilian Maung Maung, but each lasted only a short time. On 18 September 1988, General Saw Maung, Minister of Defence, launched a military coup. He immediately announced the establishment of a military junta known as the State Law and Order Restoration Council (SLORC), comprised of senior military generals.[40] On the same day, he also imposed a state of emergency, which banned all political activity and abolished important institutions such as the parliament and the judiciary.[41]

The military coup was opposed by opposition figures such as retired General Tin Oo, Aung San Suu Kyi, and the former Prime Minister U Nu, who believed that the coup was a setback for the return to democracy in Burma.[42] The military junta reacted to the protests by sending anti-riot troops into the streets, where clashes between protesters and the government troops occurred. It is believed about three thousand protesters were killed during these clashes.[43] Thousands of the protesters fled Burma proper to look for sanctuary in the ethnic minority-controlled areas along the borders with the neighbouring countries of Thailand, India, and China.[44] The sudden exodus of refugees from Burma attracted the attention of the international media and this put pressure on the military leaders to seek a political solution to the crisis.[45]

The SLORC made a political concession and announced multi-party general elections to be held in May 1990. The SLORC was confident of the success of the military-backed National Unity Party (NUP), formerly the BSPP. However, it quickly became clear that the National League for Democracy (NLD), led by former Minister of Defence, Tin Oo, and Aung San Suu Kyi (daughter of the assassinated nationalist leader Aung San), was the most popular political party in Burma. The NLD won more than 80 per cent of the votes, gaining 392 of 485 seats in the national parliament (*Pyithu Hluttaw*). The remaining seats were distributed among 30 other political parties including the NUP, which received only about 2.1 per cent, or 10 seats (Table 7.3).[46]

Although in the lead-up to the election day, some military leaders had promised to transfer power to whoever won, when they discovered that the NLD had won, the military leaders refused to accept defeat and delayed making arrangements for the transfer of power.[47] Consequently the SLORC and the NLD were caught in a political deadlock over who had the right to run the country. Indeed, the power of the Burmese military had increased with the abolition of the parliament or the People's Assembly (*Pyithu Hluttaw*) as a legislative branch in 1988. Although in the May 1990 general elections, the NLD won a clear majority of the votes, the military refused to allow the newly elected politicians to assemble and therefore the military retained control over legislation. In addition, martial law was imposed, creating a situation in which due and fair legal process was eliminated.

Table 7.3 The Results of the 27 May 1990 General Election

Parties	Seats	Per cent
National League for Democracy (NLD)	392	80.8
Shan Nationalities League for Democracy	23	4.7
Rakhine Democracy League	11	2.3
National Unity Party (NUP)	10	2.1
Independent	6	1.2
Mon National Democratic Front	5	1.0
National Democratic Party for Human Rights	4	0.8
Chin National League for Democracy	3	0.6
Kachin State National Congress for Democracy	3	0.6
Party for National Democracy	3	0.6
Union Paoh National Organisation	3	0.6
Democratic Organisation for Kayan National Unity	2	0.4
Kayah State Nationalities League for Democracy	2	0.4
Naga Hills Regional Development Party	2	0.4
Ta-ang (Palaung) National League for Democracy	2	0.4
Union Danu League for Democracy Party	2	0.4
Zomi National Congress	2	0.4
Democracy Party	1	0.2
Graduates and Old Students Democratic Association	1	0.2
Kamans National League for Democracy	1	0.2
Karen State National Organisation	1	0.2
Lahu National Development Party	1	0.2
Khami National Solidarity Organisation	1	0.2
Mara People Party	1	0.2
Patriotic Old Comrades League	1	0.2
Shan State Kokang Democratic Party	1	0.2
Union National Democracy Party	1	0.2
United Nationalities League for Democracy	1	0.2
Total	485	100

Sources: James Guyot, "Myanmar in 1990, The Unconsummated Election", *Asian Survey*, xxxi, no. 2 (February 1991), p. 210; and Mark Weller (ed.) *Democracy and Politics in Burma* (Manerplaw: The National Coalition Government of the Union of Burma, 1993), pp. 187-188.

One of the reasons for the collapse of the Ne Win government was the failure of the "Burmese Way to Socialism" to bring prosperity and economic progress to Burma. After the coup in September 1988, the military began to implement economic reforms, aiming to change the nature of the Burmese economy away from a socialist economy to be more like a free-market economy.[48] Between late 1988 and 1995, the SLORC introduced a wide-range of economic reforms, such as new foreign investment laws, trade regulations, financial regulations and privatisation programmes. The reforms were implemented in a gradual way. This response to the economic stagnation left by the Ne Win government was seen by some as simply a survival strategy.[49] But later on, the reform

policies broadened into measures such as reforming the Central Bank of
Myanmar, permitting private banks to operate, and allowing domestic and
foreign investors to invest in Burma, among others (Box 7.1).

Box 7.1 Economic Reform Policies in Burma, 1988-1995

Years	Policies
1987	-Removal of restrictions on private sector involvement in domestic and foreign trade
1988	-Introduction of new Foreign Investment Law -Restitution of small and medium-sized business establishments
1989	-Decontrol of prices -Revoking of the 1985 Law of Establishment of Socialist Economic System -Legalisation of border trade -Privatising State-owned Enterprises (SOEs) -Abolishing the restrictions on private investment -Enacting the Central Bank of Myanmar Law
1990	-Introduction of Myanmar Tourism Law -Introduction of hundred per cent retention of export earnings law -Enacting of the Financial Institutions of Myanmar Law -Enacting of the Myanmar Agricultural and Rural Development Law -Enacting of the Commercial Tax Law
1991	-Announcement of the Central Bank of Myanmar Rules and Regulations -Reestablishment of Myanmar Chamber of Commerce and Industry
1992	-Leasing the inefficient state-owned factories -Denationalisation of nationalised sawmills -Selling the government-owned palm oil firms -Establishment of four private banks
1993	-Introduction of foreign exchange certificate (FEC) -Establishment of another four private banks
1994	-Enacting of the domestic investment law -Establishment of three more private banks -Licensing of representatives offices of eleven foreign banks
1995	-Amendment of the Central Bank of Myanmar Law

Sources: Myat Thein and Mya Than, "Transitional Economy of Myanmar: Performance, Issues, and Problems" in Seiji F. Naya and Joseph L. H. Tan (eds.) *Asian Transitional Economies, Challenges and Prospects for Reform and Transformation* (Singapore: Institute of Southeast Asian Studies, 1995), p. 217; and U Myat Thein, "An Assessment of the Measures taken for the Proper Evolution of the Market-oriented Economic System" in Office of Strategic Studies, *Symposium on Socio-Economic Factors Contributing to National Consolidation* (Rangoon: Office of Strategic Studies, Ministry of Defence, 1997), pp. 3-14.

Nonetheless, the economic reform policies brought immediate responses from neighbouring countries. For instance, Thailand responded by sending a military and trade delegation led by the then Chief of the Army, General Chaovalit Yongchaiyuth, just two months after the military coup. This visit resulted in the signing of many trade agreements. Overall there was a dramatic increase in foreign investment, from just about US$10 million in September 1988 to US$28 million in March 1989 and US$150 million in June 1989.[50] Companies from China, Japan, South Korea, Singapore, Malaysia, and Australia also entered Burma. However, the level of foreign investment in Burma was still low compared with other countries in the region. This was a result of the high competition for capital in those years, particularly with industrial relocation to the new markets in Vietnam, Bangladesh, and Southern China. According to an official source, in the first three years after the economic reforms were implemented, foreign investment coming to Burma reached about US$3 billion with much of this being invested in oil and gas, hotels and tourism, fisheries, mining, property and manufacturing.[51]

Despite the fact that the SLORC kept the economy open to foreign investors the overall economic situation in Burma did not change greatly and the ideal of a free-market economy being established in Burma was still far from reality. Dapice points out that the slow economic progress in Burma happened because the government implemented reform in "a half-hearted way", rather than in a comprehensive fashion.[52] It can be argued that the inability of the military government to implement economic reform comprehensively was caused by both domestic and external constraints.[53] These included the lack of credible economic policy-making institutions, lack of domestic business groups who could generate economic activity, and limited external support.

Lack of Credible Policy-Making Institutions

The lack of capable economic policy-making institutions was part of the legacy of the Ne Win period.[54] However, there were ministries such as the Prime Minister's Office, the Ministry of National Planning, the Ministry of Finance, the Ministry of Trade, and the Ministry of Industry. The most prominent minister involved in formulating economic policies was the Minister of National Planning, Major General David O. Abel. It is still not clear whether there were technocrats or prominent economists who worked on and advised Abel on economic matters. But it is quite clear that the SLORC's human resources lacked the expertise which was needed to establish sound and credible policy-making institutions.[55] There were not many professional and academic research institutions that could encourage policy debates and the dissemination of economic, political and strategic ideas.[56]

This all led to a situation where important institutions such as the Ministry of Finance and Revenue and the Central Bank of Myanmar lacked expertise and independence in formulating economic policy. Often these institutions suffered from political intervention particularly in the context of the need to implement a balanced budget policy and to implement comprehensive economic policies in Burma. Without credible policy-making institutions, the military government was not able to come up with a strategic vision and long-term economic policies for Burma.

State-owned Enterprises and "Rent Seekers"

Economic reform did not succeed in altering the fact that the Burmese economy was entirely dominated by the government through the state-owned enterprises (SOEs). Legacies of socialism in the economy were not easily abolished. As mentioned earlier, the military government was unwilling to comprehensively reform the state-owned enterprise economy because this had the potential to erode their economic interests and their grip on power. The magnitude of the government domination of the economy can be found in the monopoly rights given to the state-owned enterprises (Table 7.4).

In addition, this economic reform did not foster the establishment of domestic business groups that could increase the level of economic activity, which was also needed in Burma. Instead, it only created "rent seekers", because the economic reforms generally only benefited those who were involved in business with the military government. One of these groups was the military-owned holding company, the Union of Myanmar Economic Holdings (UMEH). This was the biggest company in Burma, established in 1990 and owned by the Directorate of Procurement of the Defence Department (about 40 per cent) and the rest by retired military officer shareholders.[57] The UMEH became the main domestic partner for foreign investors who wanted to establish joint venture agreements for business activities in Burma. There was also the Myan Goen Myint Company, a private company owned by the government-backed Union Solidarity and Development Association (USDA), which controlled the property investment and transport sector in Rangoon.[58] In addition, a small number of private business groups also benefited from the economic reforms. One of them was the Asian World Group, a new conglomerate owned by Steven Law, who had a huge investment in hotel and tourism and property and who in 1996 also made a joint venture agreement with the prominent Malaysian business figure Robert Kuok.[59]

Table 7.4 State-owned Enterprises and their Business Activities

Ministry	Name of SOEs	Business Activities
Ministry of Information	Printing and Publishing Enterprise	Printing
	News and Periodical Enterprise	Publication
	Motion Picture Enterprise	Cinema
Ministry of Labor	Social Security Board	-
Ministry of Forest	Myanmar Timber Enterprise	Logging
Ministry of Agriculture	Myanmar Agriculture Enterprise	Agricultural products
	Myanmar Farms Enterprise	Agricultural products
	Myanmar Jute Industries	Jute
	Myanmar Cotton and Sericulture Enterprise	Cotton
	Myanmar Sugar Cane Enterprise	Sugar cane
	Myanmar Plantation Crops Enterprise	Agriculture products
Ministry of Livestock Breeding and Fisheries	Livestock Food and Milk Product Enterprise	Dairy products
Ministry of Mines	No. (1) Mining Enterprise	Mining
	No. (2) Mining Enterprise	Mining
	No. (3) Mining Enterprise	Mining
	Myanmar Gems Enterprise	Gems
	Myanmar Salt and Marine Chemical Enterprise	Sea products
	Myanmar Pearl Enterprise	Pearls
Ministry of Industry (1)	Myanmar Textile Industries	Textiles
	Myanmar Foodstuff Industries	Food processing
	Myanmar Pharmaceutical Industries	Pharmaceutical product
	Myanmar Ceramic Industries	Ceramics
	Myanmar Paper and Chemical Industries	Paper
	Myanmar General and Maintenance Industries	Manufacturing
Ministry of Industry (2)	Technical Services	-
	Myanmar Heavy Industries	Machinery
Ministry of Energy	Myanmar Oil and Gas Enterprise	Oil and gas
	Myanmar Petrochemical Enterprise	Petrochemical
	Myanmar Petroleum Products Enterprise	Oil
	Myanmar Electric Power Enterprise	Electricity
Ministry of Construction	Public Works	-
Ministry of Transport	Inland Water Transport	Water transportation
	Myanmar Five Star Line	Transportation
	Myanmar Ports Authority	Ports management
	Myanmar Shipyards	Ship-building
	Myanmar Airways	Airline
Ministry of Railways	Myanmar Railways	Train transportation
	Road Transport	Road transportation
Ministry of Communications	Myanmar Posts and Telecommunications	Postal and Post and Telegraphs
Ministry of Trade	Myanmar Agricultural Produce Trading	Agricultural products
	General Merchandise Trading	Trading
	Myanmar Department Stores	Trading
	Stationary, Printing and Photographic Store	Trading
	Medicines and Medical Equipment Trading	Medical products

	Vehicles, Machinery and Equipment Trading	Spare parts
	Construction and Electrical Stores Trading	Property
	Inspection and Agency Services	-
	Myanmar Export and Import Services	Export-import
Ministry of Hotel and Tourism	Myanmar Hotel and Tourism Services	Tourism
	Restaurant and Beverage Enterprise	Restaurants
Ministry of Co-operatives	Co-operative Export Import Enterprise	Export-import
Ministry of Planning and Finance	Central Bank of Myanmar	Printing currency
	Myanmar Economic Bank	Banking
	Myanmar Investment and Commercial Bank	Banking
	Myanmar Foreign Trade Bank	Banking
	Myanmar Agricultural and Rural Development Bank	Banking
	Myanmar Small Loan	Credit loan
	Myanmar Insurance	Insurance
	Security Printing Works	-

Source: World Bank, *Myanmar, Policies for Sustaining Economic Reform* (Washington D.C.: World Bank, 1995), pp. 91-92.

Limited External Support

Lack of external support was also a factor in the slow pace of reform in Burma. The international community responded in various ways to the military coup in 1988. The western countries advocated tough pressure through economic and military sanctions. The members of the Association of South-East Asian Nations (ASEAN) pursued diplomatic pressure through a "constructive engagement" approach. This difference affected Burma's relationship with the international community in the years that followed.[60] As a result, foreign investors (particularly those from the Western countries) hesitated in investing in large-scale and long-term investment projects because of their belief that the future of the SLORC remained uncertain.[61] Other considerations such as the poor infrastructure, bad exchange rate policy, and the continuing economic sanctions imposed by the US, contributed to the hesitancy to invest heavily in Burma.[62] The SLORC was not accepted in the international community and this caused difficulties for Burma in gaining access to international financial institutions.[63] Consequently, it was impossible for the SLORC to attract a consortium of donor countries which could help Burma to rebuild its economy.

Political Authoritarianism and the Opposition Groups

Having explained the various factors that influenced the failure of the economic reforms, the following section will examine the political developments in Burma during the 1990s. It is clear that the implementation of economic reforms in Burma was not followed by political liberalisation. Instead, the military government maintained authoritarian politics in Burma.[64] At the same time, however, there is clear evidence that political resistance against the military government could not be entirely suppressed, even with harsh political restrictions in place.

Maintaining Authoritarian Politics

How did the Burmese military maintain its authoritarian political style despite the fact that criticism towards it was so widespread? It can be argued that authoritarianism in Burma was the result of the excessive involvement of the Burmese military in social and political affairs.[65] As mentioned earlier, the experiences of the Burmese military during the War of Independence in the 1940s, the civil war in the 1950s and in government since the 1960s, had led to a perception of themselves as the true protectors of the nation. The Burmese military also claims to be the only institution that has united Burma and that therefore it is in the national interest that the Burmese military should maintain its role in social and political affairs.[66] Historically, the Burmese military and its leaders were always suspicious of the integrity of civilian politicians. This attitude was based on their assessment of the failure of the civilian politicians to maintain political stability in the 1950s.[67] The Burmese military had no experience in running the country democratically either and this became an obstacle to them accepting the fact that authoritarianism in Burma was no longer acceptable to the Burmese people or the international community.[68] Therefore, it was difficult for the military leaders to contemplate a future in which the civilian NLD leaders would be in power and running the country. Instead, the Burmese military continued their authoritarian rule based on their control of important national institutions and of political process in Burma.

Government and Military Intelligence Networks

As mentioned earlier, a new military regime took power in Burma through a military coup in 1988. The military government was run by active and retired high-ranking military officers. From 1988 until 1992, General Saw Maung was the Head of State (as Prime Minister) as well as the Chief of the Armed Forces or the *Tatmadaw*, and this continued with General Than Shwe, who held both positions from 1992. Many members of the SLORC also held positions in the cabinet. Similar institutional arrangements applied throughout Burmese society. For instance, Burma was divided into 7 divisions (Yangon, Bago, Ayeyarwady, Mandalay, Magway, Tanintharyi, and Sagaing) and 7 states (Chin State, Kachin State, Kayin State, Kayah State, Mon State, Rakhine State, and Shan State). Local military officers governed all of these places.

The military government used its own military and intelligence apparatus for surveillance and also for repression of the population. Through the 1990s it expanded in size and technological capacity. The acquisition of military equipment from China and other countries increased the combat capability of the Burmese military.[69] It is believed that in the 1990s the Burmese military numbered almost 500,000 personnel, making it one of the largest military forces in the region.[70] However, it is difficult to explain this expansion, given that Burma was not in a civil war situation and had no external enemies or threats. Logically the aim of this expansion was to be ready to respond to opposition activities inside Burma that might threaten military power.

On top of this, the Burmese military had one of the best intelligence networks in the region. The national intelligence network was under the control of the National Intelligence Bureau (NIB) headed by Lieutenant General Khin Nyunt, who was also the First Secretary of SLORC.[71] Other intelligence organisations existed also, such as the Directorate of the Defence Service Intelligence (DDSI) and the Office of Strategic Studies (OSS). Lieutenant General Khin Nyunt was able to establish himself as a powerful figure in Burma mainly through his capacity to expand the DDSI intelligence operations. After the 1988 Uprising, the DDSI intelligence officers operated extensively, spying on the activities of opposition leaders, student activists, and also military officers.[72] The intelligence apparatus could be found anywhere in Burma, from cities to villages, creating a "culture of fear" where everyone was suspicious of one another. With the support of strong military personnel and intelligence networks, the military government was able to divide and rule and to intimidate the population.[73]

Constitutional Arrangements

In 1993, the Burmese military established a National Convention to oversee the drafting of a new constitution. The National Convention failed to win popular support and became the subject of criticism from domestic opposition groups and the international community. However, a new constitution was drafted.[74] The proposed new constitution upheld the supremacy of the military in national politics. Under the new constitution the military would pursue a political system of its own, which it named "disciplined democracy".[75] In this political system, power would be centred on the President (who had to be a military person) and the parliament made less powerful.[76] The Burmese military also established a mass organisation of functional groups called the Union Solidarity and Development Association (USDA) in 1993. The membership of USDA was comprised of farmers, workers, public servants, professionals, artists and social organisations. According to some observers, the USDA was modelled on the political system in Indonesia at that time, where the Indonesian military used the ruling *Golkar* party to contest general elections.[77] Although the USDA appeared to be a non-political organisation, it was believed that the Burmese military intended to use it as a political vehicle in future general elections.

Having put in place constitutional and institutional arrangements that guaranteed the place of the Burmese military in national politics, the military leaders continued to destroy the opposition groups, notably the NLD, and the ethnic minorities who were still fighting against the military government.[78] After refusing to transfer power to the NLD, who had a landslide victory in the May 1990 general elections, the Burmese military continually refused the demands of the opposition and the international community to transfer power to the NLD. Although the NLD leaders, including Aung San Suu Kyi, were officially released from house arrest in 1995, their personal and political freedoms continued to be curtailed, and the prospect of a political settlement with the military remained remote.[79]

The Media

The military also controlled the media by not allowing freedom of the press in Burma. The government media such as Myanmar Television, Radio Myanmar, and the New Light of Myanmar daily newspaper (formerly the Working People's Daily) was used to advance and to disseminate the government's version of news and events, and to portray the military as upholding the national good. The media were often used by military leaders to attack the opposition groups and their leaders and to respond to criticism from the international community. Burma observer Steinberg points out that:

> Because information is power, the SLORC vigorously controls the media. Images presented both internally and to the outside world sift and winnow

only those data that SLORC wishes to present, and colours such information to attempt to shape public opinion.[80]

Nonetheless, the arrival of advanced information technology in the 1990s (in the forms of internet and satellite antennae) provided a means for the spread of alternative news in Burma, including news from opposition groups inside and abroad.[81] This presented a serious threat to the military government. In response, in 1996, the military government imposed two regulations, the Television and Video Law and the Computer Science Development Law, aiming to restrict the flow of information to the public in Burma.[82]

The Opposition Groups

The opposition in Burma has over the decades, and particularly since 1988, presented a challenge to the military rulers.[83] Throughout the 1990s the opposition groups remained strong and visible despite the many risks attached to their work. In terms of geographical location, there were two main types of opposition group: those that operated inside Burma, and those that operated along the borders and abroad.

The National League for Democracy (NLD)

The NLD was the most vocal opposition group in Burma.[84] The supporters of the NLD mainly came from inside Burma, with a few drawn from the ethnic controlled areas along the border. The leaders of the NLD held that the results of the May 1990 general elections showed that the vast majority of the Burmese people had given them a mandate to govern the country. The NLD did not relax its demand that the military honour the 1990 election results. In response to the refusal by the Burmese military to do this, as well as to the ongoing political repression of the NLD MPs and its members throughout the country, the leaders of the NLD continued to bring political pressure to bear against the military. They did it by sending protest letters to the military leaders demanding the transfer of power to the NLD. This was intended to show the public and the international community that the NLD was a legitimate political entity. After Aung San Suu Kyi was released from house arrest in 1995, she held weekend meetings in order to talk with her supporters and to improve the political education of the general public, although the military later restricted her public activities.[85] The NLD also attempted to take a more active role in bringing about political change in Burma by inviting the elected MPs from the 1990 elections to reconvene the parliament. The NLD also drafted its own version of a new constitution, differing from that drafted by the military government.

Students

Students played a central role in the 1988 Uprising.[86] After the military closed all universities in 1990, student activists still continued their political activities. Many students left for the border areas or abroad. This left only a few student activists still working in Burma, without an umbrella organisation. However, this did not mean that those who remained inside Burma did not engage in political activity. A few continued to coordinate underground activities that linked Burmese students within the country with those in the border areas or abroad. Others were also secretly in alliance with the NLD and Aung San Suu Kyi.

Evidence of student activism was to be found in the demonstrations in Rangoon in early December 1996.[87] During the protests, the students demanded the re-establishment of the All-Burma Students Union (ABSU), which had been banned by the military government. But the military did not give in to student demands. Instead, many of them were arrested and a plan to re-open universities throughout the country suspended. The universities were reopened briefly in 1996. The students demonstrated again between August and September 1998, protesting against the restrictions applied to them at major universities, such as Rangoon University and the Rangoon Institute of Technology by the military government.[88] Students were forced underground again because they were not able to meet, or to organise political activities openly on their campuses. The DDSI's intelligence officers also arrested many underground student activists.[89]

Prominent Politicians and Buddhist Monks

There were a number of politicians who were still critical of the Burmese military and these came from a variety of backgrounds. Some of them belonged to the independence period generation such as U Nu, Mahn Win Maung, and Thakin Bo Khin Maung, others were from the 1960s, or the 1970s generations.[90] A few of them were also former military officers (Aung Shwe and Saw Myint) who had once served under the Ne Win government. Their motivation in criticising the military government was a desire to end the political stalemate in Burma. In August 1997, a group of Burmese politicians known as the Thirty Comrades, led by Bohmu Aung, a veteran independence hero, urged the military leaders to enter into political dialogue with the NLD.[91]

Similar actions were taken by a number of Buddhist monks in Burma. Acts of moral opposition by the Buddhist monks drew the attention of Burmese society, which respected and regarded them as a source of wisdom.[92] Although the institution of Buddhism was mainly dedicated to religious affairs, a growing number of Buddhist monks were becoming politicised.[93] In Mandalay in 1990, as a symbol of civil disobedience against the military, the Buddhist monks openly refused to perform religious ceremonies for the military personnel and their families for months.[94] This event led to the establishment of the All Burma Young Monks Union, who consistently advocated non-violent resistance in Burma.[95]

The Ethnic Minorities

Armed conflict between the central government and the ethnic minorities remained a critical political issue in Burma. Between 1989 and the mid-1990s, the military government claimed to have persuaded more than half of the armed ethnic groups to sign ceasefire agreements.[96] Among these were the Kachin Independent Army (KIA), the United Wa State Army, and the Shan State Army. However, a few ethnic minority groups continued to fight against the Burmese military. Prominent among these was the Karen National Union (KNU), which had been fighting against the central government since 1948.[97] This armed group operated along the Thai-Burma border. Other smaller groups were the Arakan Liberation Army (ALA), the Rohingya Solidarity Organisation, the Chin National Army, and the National Socialist Council of Nagaland, which operated on the western border.[98]

The continuing opposition of a few armed ethnic groups was due mainly to their resistance to the domination of the majority ethnic Burmans. They were disappointed over the contents of ceasefire agreements that had already been signed by other ethnic groups, which did not address the real needs of the ethnic minorities.[99] A peace settlement with these groups would only be possible when the military could accommodate the ethnic minorities' right to autonomy or self-determination. The aspirations of the ethnic minorities were strong, as was the continuing anti-Burmese military feeling among those minority people who live along the Thai-Burmese borders. It was apparent that even if change came about in their political relationship with Burma proper, the depth of their mistrust and sense of injustice suffered at the hands of the Burmese military would take another generation to overcome.[100] A long-time standing Burma observer Silverstein wrote of the Burmese military and its relationship with the minority areas:

> The record of the civil war until 1992 indicated that the Burma army was not winning on the ground. In the areas it controlled, it behaved like a foreign occupation force rather than an army of the people. Without popular support anywhere in Burma, especially in the minority areas, and with its own rank and file suffering from ever declining morale, the army was slowly losing the military struggle...The politics of the border areas were becoming ever more important and influential in determining Burma's future.[101]

The Coalition of Opposition Groups in Border Areas

There were political groups which opposed the Burmese military operating along the Thai-Burma border.[102] Among them were the Democratic Alliance of Burma (DAB), a coalition of several ethnic minority groups and Burman opposition groups (established during the 1988 Uprising), the National Coalition Government of the Union of Burma (NCGUB), a political group set up by NLD MPs who left for the border areas after the 1990 general elections, and also the All Burma Students' Democratic Front (ABSDF), a student organisation formed by Burmese students who left Burma after the 1988 Uprising.[103]

The ability of these groups to continue to challenge the dominance of the military in national politics was remarkable considering they were themselves from diverse backgrounds. Despite the fact that their bases along the border were targeted for continuous military attack, these coalition groups were able to survive and, more importantly, to attract international attention to Burma. For instance, the role that was played by the NCGUB in bringing Burma's case to international forums, particularly the United Nations, was crucial.[104] Furthermore, the achievement of unity between members of both Burman and ethnic minority backgrounds posed a serious threat to the military government, especially as these resistance groups were able to link up with the NLD and other opposition groups inside Burma.

Conclusion

This chapter has examined the political economy of Burma's unreal economic boom. As was explained, since gaining independence from the

British, Burma has never experienced durable political stability. The transition from one power to another has not been through peaceful means and often was brought about through war and military coups. In 1962, the Burmese military, led by General Ne Win, launched a coup, which changed the direction of Burmese politics in the following decades. Since then militarism and authoritarianism have been central features of Burmese politics. The Burmese military emerged as the most powerful force in modern Burma and still dominates Burmese society. During the Ne Win period, Burma embarked on economic socialism and isolationism. The government controlled the economy and did not allow the private sector to engage in economic activity. The result was that Burma experienced economic stagnation and did not share the economic growth that its neighbouring countries enjoyed during the 1980s. The economic stagnation led to a political crisis in 1988, which brought various political groups to demand the establishment of a democratic political system in Burma.

The 1988 Uprising ended with a military coup, through which the power of the military was reasserted. As the economy worsened, the new military government (SLORC) opened up the economy to foreign investors and implemented economic reforms. From 1988 until the mid-1990s the Burmese economy began to change, but the military government remained against the implementation of far reaching economic reforms that could draw the economy away from state-owned and controlled enterprises. The economic reforms failed to dismantle the interests of the government, which still dominated economic activity in Burma. With little external support, and without capable economic institutions and sound policies, the reforms also failed to foster the establishment of domestic business groups which could revitalise economic activity in Burma.

Although the opposition groups were involved in an ongoing challenge of military power, at great personal risk, the military remained in control of power and other institutions in Burma. The refusal of the military government to honour the results of the May 1990 general elections by handing over power to the National League for Democracy (NLD) became a stumbling block to political reform in Burma. Despite changes in military leadership in September 1988 and later in April 1992 (from General Saw Maung to General Than Shwe) the military failed to accommodate the democratic aspirations of the Burmese people. The proposed new constitution, drafted by the military-backed National Convention, did not receive much support. The NLD refused to accept the constitution on the grounds that it guaranteed the dominance of the military in national politics and was therefore against democratic principles. As a result, the political stalemate continued as the military government refused to enter into political dialogue with the NLD leader Aung San Suu Kyi, although they released her from house arrest in mid 1995. In this authoritarian political climate, political opposition inside Burma and on the border areas has survived. With a variety of views and strategies, these resistance groups continue to bring pressure to bear on the military government to find a political settlement that could open the way to the establishment of a democratic political system in Burma. It is in this context that the economic crisis of 1997 and 1998 occurred in Burma and this will be explored in the following chapter.

Notes

[1] David Steinberg (ed.) *In Search of Southeast Asia, A Modern History*, revised edition (Sydney and Wellington: Allen and Unwin, 1987), p. 404.

[2] On the political history of Burma prior to the annexation of the British colonial government, see Michael Aung-Thwin, *Pagan: The Origins of Modern Burma* (Honolulu: University of Hawaii Press, 1985); Victor Lieberman, *Burmese Administrative Cycles: Anarchy and Conquest, c.1580-1760* (Princeton: Princeton University Press, 1984); and Willam J. Koenig, *The Burmese Polity, 1752-1819: Politics, Administration and Social Organisation in the Early Kon-baung Period* (Michigan: Centre for South and Southeast Asian Studies, The University of Michigan, 1990); and Myo Myint, *The Politics of Survival Burma: Diplomacy and Statecraft in the Reign of King Mindon, 1853-1878*, unpublished Ph.D thesis, Cornell University, 1987.

[3] On various interpretations on the last days of the Burmese monarchy, see Ernest C. T. Chew, "The Fall of the Burmese Kingdom in 1885: Review and Reconsideration", *Journal of Southeast Asian Studies*, vol. x, no. 2 (September 1979), pp. 372-380.

[4] See Michael Aung-Thwin, "The British 'Pacification' of Burma: Order Without Meaning", *Journal of Southeast Asian Studies*, vol. xvi, no.2 (September 1985), pp. 250-251.

[5] John S. Furnivall, *Colonial Policy and Practice: A Comparative Study of Burma and Netherlands India* (New York: New York University Press, 1947), pp. 116-118.

[6] Josef Silverstein, *Burma, Military Rule and the Politics of Stagnation* (Ithaca: Cornell University Press, 1977), p. 3.

[7] Furnivall, *op.cit*, p. 23.

[8] Further discussion on this can be found in Michael Adas, *The Burma Delta: Economic Development and Social Change in An Asian Rice Frontier, 1852-1941* (Madison: University of Wisconsin Press, 1974).

[9] Robert Taylor, *The State of Burma* (Honolulu: The University of Hawaii Press, 1987), p. 126.

[10] Furnivall, *Colonial Policy and Practice*, p. 157.

[11] On the origins of the nationalist movement in Burma, see Khin Yi, *The Dobama Movement in Burma, 1930-1938* (Ithaca: Southeast Asia Program, Cornell University, 1988); and also Furnivall, *op.cit*, pp. 142-143.

[12] Silverstein, *Burma, Military Rule and the Politics of Stagnation*, p. 17.

[13] On the role of Aung San during the independence period, see Josef Silverstein, *The Political Legacy of Aung San*, revised edition (Ithaca: Southeast Asian Program, Cornell University, 1993).

[14] Silverstein, pp. 20-21.

[15] Ibid, p. 26.

[16] On the origins of the armed insurgency in modern Burma, see Martin Smith, *Burma, Insurgency and the Politics of Ethnicity* (London and New Jersey: Zed Books, 1991), especially chapters six and seven; Bertil Lintner, *Burma in Revolt, Opium and Insurgency Since 1948* (Boulder: Westview Press, 1994), especially chapters three and four; and also Robert H. Taylor, *The State of Burma* (Honolulu: University of Hawaii Press, 1987), pp. 229-249.

[17] On the economic and political changes during the U Nu period, see John F. Cady, *A History of Modern Burma* (Ithaca: Cornell University Press, 1960), especially chapter twelve.

[18] Hal Hill, "Industrialization in Burma in Historical Perspective", *Journal of Southeast Asian Studies*, vol. xv, no. 1 (March 1984), pp. 134-149.

[19] Smith, pp. 179-180.

[20] Within eighteen months in power as the caretaker government, the Burmese military's involvement in various business activities such as banking, trading, transportation and hotels had increased dramatically. See Silverstein, *Burma, Military Rule and the Politics of Stagnation*, p. 79; and also Taylor, *The State of Burma*, pp. 257-258.

[21] On the fall of the U Nu government, see Smith, *Burma: Insurgency and the Politics of Ethnicity*, pp. 195-196.

[22] David I. Steinberg, *Burma's Road Toward Development, Growth and Ideology under Military Rule* (Boulder: Westview, 1981), pp. 28-29; Silverstein, *op.cit*, pp. 80-81; and Smith, pp. 199-200.

[23] For a critical view on the rise of General Ne Win, see Chao-Tzang Yawnghwe, *Ne Win's Tatmadaw Dictatorship*, unpublished MA thesis, The University of British Columbia, 1990; and also see Lintner, *Burma in Revolt*, especially chapter six.

[24] Josef Silverstein, "First Steps on the Burmese Way to Socialism", *Asian Survey*, vol. iv, no. 2 (February 1964), pp. 716-722.

[25] Steinberg, *Burma's Road Toward Development*, p. 35.

[26] Taylor, *The State of Burma*, p. 341.

[27] Steinberg, p. 39.

[28] Taylor, p. 347.

[29] David Steinberg, *Burma: A Socialist Nation of Southeast Asia* (Boulder: Westview Press, 1982), p. 78.

[30] Ibid, p. 78; and also Steinberg, *Burma's Road Toward Development*, pp. 109.

[31] This was ironic since rice was the most important of Burma's exports. One would suggest that the failure of the Ne Win government in supplying rice to the domestic market indicated that the rice policy had not worked very well under his rule. Steinberg, p. 110.

[32] Hill, "Industrialization in Burma in Historical Perspective", pp. 145-146.

[33] Mya Maung, *The Burma Road to Poverty* (New York: Praeger, 1991).

[34] Silverstein, *Burma, Military Rule and the Politics of Stagnation*, pp. 100-101.

[35] Smith, *Burma, Insurgency and the Politics of Ethnicity*, especially chapter sixteen.

[36] John Haseman, "Burma in 1987", *Asian Survey*, vol. xxviii, no. 2 (February 1988), pp. 223-228.

[37] Bertil Lintner, *Outrage, Burma's Struggle for Democracy*, revised edition (London and Bangkok: White Lotus, 1990), p. 68.

[38] Bertil Lintner, *Outrage, Burma's Struggle for Democracy* (London and Bangkok: White Lotus, 1990), p. 68.

[39] The political events during the 1988 uprising in Burma have become a subject for analysis among scholars and observers of contemporary Burmese politics. Some of their works can be found in Bertil Lintner, *Outrage: Burma's Struggle for Democracy*, revised edition (London and Bangkok: White Lotus, 1990), especially chapter five; Mya Maung, *Burma Road to Poverty* (New York: Praeger, 1991), especially chapter ten; David I. Steinberg, *The Future of Burma: Crisis and Choice in Myanmar* (Lanham: The University Press of America, 1990); Martin Smith, *Burma: Insurgency and the Politics of Ethnicity*, especially chapter seventeen; James J. Guyot, "Burma in 1988: *Perestroika* with a Military Face", *Southeast Asian Affairs 1989* (Singapore: Institute of Southeast Asian Studies, 1989), pp. 107-133; Robert H. Taylor, "Burma's Ambigious Breakthrough", *Journal of Democracy*, 1, 1 (Winter, 1990), pp. 62-72; Josef Silverstein, "Civil War and Rebellion in Burma", *Journal of Southeast Asian Studies*, xxi, 10 (October, 1990), pp. 1007-1019; and also Mya Maung, *Totalitarianism in Burma: Prospects for Economic Development* (New York: Paragon House, 1992), especially chapter two.

[40] The best account of the reasons and circumstances of the military coup in 1998, see Lintner, *Outrage: Burma's Struggle for Democracy*, especially chapter six.

[41] Ibid, p. 131.

[42] Aung San Suu Kyi, *Freedom From Fear and Other Writings* (London: Penguin Books, 1991), pp. 214-216; Bertil Lintner, *Aung San Suu Kyi and Burma's Unfinished Renaissance* (Bangkok: Peacock Press, 1990), pp. 22-23; and also Silverstein, "Civil War and Rebellion in Burma", pp. 126-127.

[43] "Ten Years On", *Asiaweek* (28 August 1998).

[44] It estimated that about 3,000 people were killed and between 7,000 to 10,000 Burmese students left cities for the border areas. On the situation of the Burmese students refugee, see C. Robinson, *The War is Growing Worse and Worse: Refugees and Displaced Persons on the Thai-Burmese Border* (Washington D.C.: United States Committee for Refugees, 1990).

[45] Therese Caouette, "Burmese Refugees in Thailand", a paper presented at *Burma (Myanmar): Challenges and Opportunities for the 1990s*, organised by FCO/Asian Studies Centre Conference, Oxford, England, 13-15 December 1991.

[46] For the official results from the May 1990 general elections in Burma, see *Asia Year Book 1991* (Hong Kong: Far Eastern Economic Review Publisher, 1991), p. 86.

[47] James Guyot, "Myanmar in 1990, The Unconsummated Election", *Asian Survey*, vol. xxxi, no. 2 (February 1991), pp. 209-211.

[48] For an assessment of the transition from the socialist to the free-market economies, see Mya Than and Joseph L. H. Tan (eds.) *The Myanmar Economy at the Crossroads: Options and Constraints* (Singapore: Institute of Southeast Asian Studies, 1990).

[49] This argument can be found in Paul Cook and Martin Minogue, "Economic Reform and Political Change in Myanmar" (Burma), *World Development*, vol. 21, no. 7 (1993), pp. 1151-1161.

[50] Lintner, *Outrage: Burma's Struggle for Democracy*, p. 166.

[51] *The Nation*, 3 December 1994 and *Bangkok Post*, 2 December 1994.

[52] David Dapice, "Development Prospects for Burma, Cycles and Trends" in Robert I. Rotberg (ed.) *Burma, Prospects for Democratic Future* (Washington D.C.: Brookings Institution Press, 1998), pp. 159-160.

[53] Mary Callahan, "Myanmar in 1994, New Dragon or Still Dragging", *Asian Survey*, vol. xxxv, no. 2 (February 1995), pp. 207-208; and also Khin Maung Kyi, "Will Forever Flow the Ayeyarwady?", *Southeast Asian Affairs 1994* (Singapore: Institute of Southeast Asian Studies, 1994), pp. 209-230.

[54] U Tun Wai, "The Myanmar Economy at the Crossroads, Options and Constraints", in Mya Than and Joseph L. H. Tan (eds.) *The Myanmar Economy at the Crossroads: Options and Constraints* (Singapore: Institute of Southeast Asian Studies, 1990), pp.

[55] Only recently did the SLORC set up two important think tanks: the Office of Strategic Studies (OSS) headed by Lt. Gen. Khin Nyunt and the Myanmar Institute of Strategic and International Studies under the auspices of Ministry of Foreign Affairs. These institutions have hosted international seminars held in Rangoon. Anonymous interview, Rangoon (4 December 1997).

[56] Many prominent academics and scholars had left the country in the early 1960s, after General Ne Win took power. These people are now still living abroad and some of them are well known in their fields. Indeed, their expertise could be of great benefit to Burma if and when they decide to return. Some of them are, for instance, Professor Khin Maung Kyi, an economist who lives in Singapore and Professor Mya Maung of Boston College and Professor Ronald Findley in

Columbia University in the US. For Khin Maung Kyi's views on Burma, see Professor Khin Maung Kyi, "In His Own Words", *Burma Debate*, vol. iv, no. 2 (March/June 1997).

[57] David Steinberg, "Democracy, Power and the Economy in Myanmar, Donor Dilemmas", *Asian Survey*, vol. xxxi, no. 8 (August, 1990), pp. 734-735.

[58] The East Asia Analytical Unit, *The New Aseans, Vietnam, Burma, Cambodia and Laos* (Canberra: Department of Foreign Affairs and Trade, 1997), p. 102.

[59] Steven Law is the son of drug tycoon Hlo Hsin Han, and in fact is suspected of using so-called "drug money" in legal business activities. Gordon Fairclough, "Good Connections", *Far Eastern Economic Review*, 15 August 1996.

[60] Josef Silverstein, "Burma in An International Perspective", *Asian Survey*, vol. xxxii, no. 10 (October 1992), pp. 951-963; and also John Bray, "Burma: Resisting the International Community", *The Pacific Review*, vol. 5, no. 3 (1992), pp. 291-296.

[61] For further discussion on this issue, see Mark Mason, "Foreign Direct Investment in Burma, Trends, Determinants, and Prospects" in Robert I. Rotberg (ed.) *Burma, Prospects for a Democratic Future* (Washington D.C.: Brookings Institution Press, 1998), pp. 220-222.

[62] David Steinberg, "Democracy, Power and the Economy in Myanmar, Donor Dilemmas", pp. 738-739.

[63] For instance, the US government reviewed US$7 million worth of development aid, US$ 5 million for anti-narcotic assistance, and US$260,000 for military training; Former West Germany stopped aid worth about DM68 million; the Japanese government suspended about US$300 million for development assistance in Burma; the British government suspended its overseas aid worth about US$1.76 million; and the Australian government also reduced its development aid from US$8 million in 1988 to US$4.7 million in 1989. See Lintner, *Outrage: Burma's Struggle for Democracy*, p. 144.

[64] A recent assessment of this issue can be found in Jalal Alamgir, "Against the Current: The Survival of Authoritarianism in Burma", *Pacific Affairs*, vol. 70, no. 3 (Fall 1997), pp. 333-350.

[65] This has been discussed widely in Chao-Tzang Yawnghwe, "Burma, The Depoliticization of the Political" in Muthiah Alagappa (ed.) *Political Legitimacy in Southeast Asia* (Stanford: Stanford University Press, 1995), pp. 189-192.

[66] In today's language, the Burmese military claims to have a strong commitment to preserving three national goals: non-disintegration of Burma, non-disintegration of national solidarity, and consolidation of national sovereignty. See Tin Maung Maung Than, "Burma's National Security and Defence Posture", *Contemporary Southeast Asia*, vol. 11, no. 1 (June, 1989), pp. 40-59.

[67] Further discussion of this can be found in Tin Maung Maung Than, "Neither Inheritance nor Legacy: Leading the Myanmar State since Independence", *Contemporary Southeast Asia*, vol. 15, no. 1 (June 1993), pp. 24-63.

[68] David Steinberg, "The Road to Political Recovery, The Salience of Politics in Economics" in Robert I. Rotberg (ed.) *Burma, Prospects for a Democratic Future* (Washington D.C.: Brookings Institution Press, 1998), pp. 271-272.

[69] On the role of China in Burma, see Bertil Lintner, "Burma and its Neighbours", *China Report*, vol. 28, no. 3 (1992), pp. 254-255; David Steinberg, "Myanmar as Nexus: Sino-Indian Rivalries on the Frontier", *Terrorism*, vol. 16 (1993), pp. 1-8; J. Mohan Malik, "Sino-Indian Rivalry in Myanmar: Implications for Regional Security", *Contemporary Southeast Asia*, vol. 16, no. 2 (September 1994), pp. 142-143; Andrew Selth, "The Myanmar Army Since 1988: Acquisitions and Adjustments", *Contemporary Southeast Asia*, vol. 17, no. 3 (December 1995), pp. 250-251; Chi-shad Liang, "Burma's Relations with the People's Republic of China: From Delicate Friendship to Genuine Co-operation" in Peter Carey (ed.) *Burma, The Challenge of Change in a Divided Society* (London: Macmillan, 1997), pp. 84-86.

[70] For a recent study of the Burmese military, see Andrew Selth, *Transforming the Tatmadaw: the Burmese Armed Forces Since 1988* (Canberra: Strategic and Defence Studies, Research School of Pacific and Asian Studies, Australian National University, 1996).

[71] For further discussion on this issue, see Andrew Selth, "Burma's Intelligence Apparatus", *Burma Debate*, vol. iv, no. 4 (September/October, 1997), pp. 4-18.

[72] Bertil Lintner, "Burma, Struggle for Power", *Jane's Intelligence Review*, vol. 5, no. 10 (October 1993), pp. 466-471.

[73] Selth, p. 16-17.

[74] Janelle M. Diller, "Constitutional Reform in a Repressive State: The Case of Burma", *Asian Survey*, vol. xxxiii, no. 4 (April 1993), pp. 393-407; and on the current developments, see Janelle M. Diller, "The National Convention: An Impediment to the Restoration of Democracy" in Peter Carey (ed.) *Burma, The Challenge of Change in a Divided Society* (London: Macmillan, 1997), pp. 27-54.

[75] The East Asia Analytical Unit, *The New Aseans, Vietnam, Burma, Cambodia and Laos* (Canberra: Department of Foreign Affairs and Trade, 1997), p. 100.

[76] Ibid, pp. 101-102.

[77] Ulf Sundhaussen, "Indonesia's New Order: A Model for Myanmar?", Asian Survey, vol. xxxvi, no. 8 (1995), pp. 768-780; and see David I. Steinberg, "The Union Solidarity Development Association, Mobilization and Orthodoxy", *Burma Debate*, vol. iv, no. 1 (January/February 1997), pp. 4-11.

[78] Josef Silverstein, "The Civil War, the Minorities and Burma's New Politics" in Peter Carey (ed.) *Burma, The Challenge of Change in a Divided Society* (London: Mamillan, 1997), pp. 149-151.

[79] On the prospects for a political settlement in Burma, see Priyambudi Sulistiyanto, *Burma: The Politics of Uncertain Transition, 1988-1994*, MA thesis

(Adelaide: The Flinders University of South Australia, 1995), especially chapter six.

[80] Steinberg, "The Road to Political Recovery", p. 273.

[81] For instance, Radio Free Asia, the British Broadcasting Corporation (BBC), Voice of America (VOA), and various Burma-related homepages available in internet. See "Return Press Freedom to Burma", *The Irrawaddy*, vol. 7, no. 4 (May 1999).

[82] Tin Maung Maung Than and Mya Than, "Myanmar, Economic Growth in the Shadow of Political Constraints", *Southeast Asian Affairs 1997* (Singapore: Institute of Southeast Asian Studies, 1997), p. 207.

[83] Yawnghwe, "Burma, The Depoliticization of the Political", p. 191.

[84] On the origins of the NLD, see Lintner, *Aung San Suu Kyi and Burma's Unfinished Renaissance*, pp. 4-5; and also Smith, *Burma, Insurgency and the Politics of Ethnicity*, pp. 403-404.

[85] See Aung San Suu Kyi, "Toward a True Refuge", a speech delivered by Dr. Michael Aris at the *Eighth Joyce Pearce Memorial Lecture*, the University of Oxford, England, 19 May 1993; and also Mary P. Callahan, "Burma in 1995, Looking Beyond the Release of Aung San Suu Kyi", *Asian Survey*, vol. xxxvi, no. 2 (February 1996), pp. 158-159.

[86] Lintner, *Outrage, Burma's Struggle for Democracy*, especially chapter one; and also Smith, *Burma, Insurgency and the Politics of Ethnicity*, pp. 406-408.

[87] Peter Carey, *From Burma to Myanmar: Military Rule and the Struggle for Democracy* (London: Research Institute for the Study of Conflict and Terrorism, 1998), p. 21; and also Jose Manuel Tesoro, "The Young and the Restless", *Asiaweek* (13 February 1998).

[88] Bertil Lintner, "Protest and Run", *Far Eastern Economic Review*, 17 September 1998.

[89] Selth, "Burma's Intelligence Apparatus", p. 17.

[90] Smith, *Burma, Insurgency and the Politics of Ethnicity*, p. 403.

[91] Carey, *From Burma to Myanma*, p. 22.

[92] On the role of Buddhism in Burma, see E. Sarkisyanz, *Buddhist Backgrounds of the Burmese Revolution* (The Hague: Martinus Nijhoff, 1965); Michael Mendelson, *Sangha and State in Burma* (Ithaca: Cornell University Press, 1973); Michael Aung-Thwin, "The Role of Sasana Reform in Burmese History: Economic Dimensions of a Religious Purification", *Journal of Asian Studies*, vol. xxxviii, no. 4 (August 1979), pp. 671-688; and also Melford Spiro, *Buddhism and Society: A Great Tradition and Its Burmese Vicissitudes* (Berkeley: University of California Press, 1982).

[93] Smith, p. 418.

[94] Bertil Lintner, *Burma in Revolt, Opium and Insurgency Since 1948*, p. 311; Bruce Matthews, "Buddhism Under a Military Regime, The Iron Hell in Burma", *Asian Survey*, vol. xxxiii, no. 4 (April, 1993), pp. 408-423.

[95] Matthews, p. 421.

[96] Silverstein, "The Civil War, the Minorities and Burma's New Politics", pp. 134-135; and also Carey, *From Burma to Myanmar*, pp. 8-9.

[97] On the origins of the KNU rebellion, see Smith, *Burma, Insurgency and the Politics of Ethnicity*, especially chapter eight.

[98] For more information about the resistance groups on the Western frontier of Burma see Lintner, *Burma in Revolt*, especially Appendix 3, pp. 421-437.

[99] Robert Taylor, "Myanmar, New, but Different?", *Southeast Asian Affairs 1995* (Singapore: Institute of Southeast Asian Studies, 1995), pp. 251-252.

[100] Based on the writer's observation in the Karen National Union base at Manerplaw and on the Thai-Burmese border in January and February 1994. Many of the writer's findings were included in writer's MA thesis, *Burma, The Politics of Uncertain Transition, 1988-1994*, pp. 174-178; and also see Martin Smith, "Burma's Ethnic Minorities: A Central or Peripheral Problem in the Regional Context?" in Peter Carey (ed.) *Burma, The Challenge of Change in a Divided Society* (London: Macmillan, 1997), pp. 119-120.

[101] Silverstein, *The Civil War, the Minorities and Burma's New Politics*, p. 137.

[102] On the origins of the political grouping in the border areas, see Lintner, *Outrage, Burma's Struggle for Democracy*, especially chapter seven; and also Silverstein, "Civil War and Rebellion in Burma", pp. 127-132.

[103] Smith, *Burma, Insurgency and the Politics of Ethnicity*, pp. 418-419; and on the recent developments, see Carey, *From Burma to Myanmar*, pp. 9-10.

[104] Silverstein, pp. 144-145.

Chapter Eight

Burma's Crisis

Burma, like Indonesia, also suffered from the contagion effect of the economic crisis in Thailand. At the time of the crisis Burma was gradually dismantling its socialist policies and trying to move towards a free-market economy. Its economy was not as open those of its neighbours, however this did not mean that Burma was immune to the economic changes which occurred in the region. This chapter examines the responses of the government and its leaders to the economic crisis and to the consequent deepening political crisis. It begins with an overview of recent efforts to reform the Burmese economy. A brief discussion of the problems accompanying the implementation of economic reform will be presented. This chapter will conclude with the examination of the consequences of the crisis for Burma's economy and politics.

Causes of the Crisis

Although there are different interpretations of the results of the economic reforms in Burma, it is argued here that the economic reforms have been far from successful and in terms of growth and size, the Burmese economy is still far behind those of its neighbouring countries.[1] A number of domestic economic and political factors played a part in Burma's economic crisis.[2] These were related to the poor performance of Burma's fundamental economy which featured macroeconomic instability, over-valued exchange rates, lack of progress in the reform of the state-owned enterprises (SOEs), slow inflow of foreign investment, extensive black market economy and drug money, little progress in financial reform, and the political stalemate.

Macroeconomic Instability

Recent independent reports point out that although the Burmese military government implemented economic reform policies, it failed nonetheless to create macroeconomic stability, an important pillar in the reform process.[3] Indeed, the economic reforms carried out from 1988 did not improve the health of the Burmese economy. The average annual growth in gross domestic product (GDP) was not impressive and even this did not reflect the real picture of the Burmese economy because the government used the official exchange rate (which is very overvalued) rather than the market exchange rate to determine the level of GDP.[4]

The poor performance of the Burmese economy can be seen in other indicators such as the high rate of inflation, the high level of current account deficit, the trade imbalance (more imports than exports), a sharp decline in international reserves, and a high debt service ratio (Table 8.1). The failure of the military government to improve the performance of Burma's macroeconomy was caused by the persistence of government in pursuing a budget deficit strategy during this period (Figure 8.1). The deficit was caused by an increase in funding for public infrastructure and social projects and by buying and upgrading military equipment, which accounted for between 2-3 per cent of GDP.[5] According to an official source, the budget deficit for the fiscal year 1996/97 amounted to currency K54.5 billion, equivalent to US$8.72 billion at the official exchange rate of kyat 6.25:US dollar or about US$191 million at the market exchange rate of kyat 285:US dollar.[6]

Table 8.1 Burma's Economic Fundamentals

	1993	1994	1995	1996	1997
GDP growth (%)	6.0	7.5	6.9	5.8	5.0
Inflation (%)	31.8	24.1	25.2	16.3	29.4
Population (m)	43.1	43.9	44.8	45.6	46.5
Exports ($m)	696	917	878	932	972
Imports ($m)	1,302	1,547	1,903	1,997	2,340
Current account ($m)	-194	-147	-513	-515	-814
Reserves ($m)	302.9	422.0	561.1	229.2	180.0
Total external debt ($m)	5,756	6,555	5,771	6,140	6,500
Debt-service ratio (%)	11.8	13.4	20.9	16.3	16.2

Source: The Economist Intelligence Unit, *A Country Report, Myanmar*, 1st quarter, 1998.

To finance the deficit, the authorities had to use monetary measures such as selling Treasury bills to the Central Bank of Myanmar and printing more money (Figure 8.1). Burma's macroeconomy was further hindered by the reluctance of multilateral agencies like the World Bank, the International Monetary Fund (IMF) and the Asian Development Bank

(ADB) and potential donor countries in the West to give financial assistance to Burma.[7]

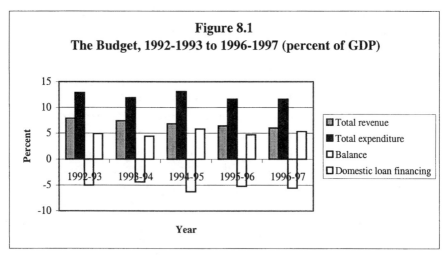

Figure 8.1
The Budget, 1992-1993 to 1996-1997 (percent of GDP)

Source: The East Asia Analytical Unit, *The New Aseans, Vietnam, Burma, Cambodia and Laos* (Canberra: Department of Foreign Affairs and Trade, 1997), p. 125.

The exchange rate policy adopted by the military government also worsened the performance of Burma's macroeconomy. During this period three different exchange rates applied in Burma. First, an official exchange rate (kyat 5-6:US dollar), which was used for every financial transaction related to government and military expenditure, although, it is estimated that about 75 per cent of the Burmese economy operated under the market exchange rate, which was ten times higher than the official one.[8] Second, in 1993, the government introduced Foreign Exchange Certificates (FECs), papers that are equivalent to money and pegged to the US dollar. A similar system was used for some time in China until it was abandoned in 1994. In 1995 the military government legalised the market trading of FECs and as the FECs became popular their rate gradually drew parallel with the market exchange rate. The decision to legalise the trading of FECs also meant that the government had accepted a de facto devaluation. Third, from June 1996, the government used another exchange rate for import purposes, with the slightly higher rate of kyat 100 to the US dollar.

The refusal of the military government to institute a single exchange rate system did not engender investor confidence in the economy. These different exchange rates also created winners and losers.[9]

Those who lost were exporters, since they used the official exchange rate for their business activities and this reduced their earnings from exports. Exporters were also discouraged from expanding their business. Meanwhile, the winners were the importers and the state-owned enterprises (SOEs) who benefited by purchasing imported goods at the official exchange rate. Moreover, the different exchange rates also encouraged corruption and rent-seeking activity among the businesspeople, and with no unified exchange rate system, the general public lost confidence in the kyat.[10]

Inefficiency of the State-owned Enterprises (SOEs)

For decades, the SOEs in Burma had been highly subsidised and unprofitable. During this period there were more than 50 SOEs operating under different ministries and engaged in different economic activities.[11] In 1989 the government announced policies to improve the efficiency and performance of the SOEs in Burma. This was to be done by inviting foreign investors to enter into joint ventures with the SOEs, and also by restructuring and privatising the SOEs. In 1995 the authorities promised to privatise about 69 SOEs, but a year later only a few of them had been sold.[12]

The effort to improve the financial autonomy and the management skills of SOE managers also failed. However, according to prominent Burmese economists Myat Thein and Mya Than the reform of the SOEs could go further and they suggested:

> ...what is needed is not simply legal or regulatory liberalization or decontrol, but actual restructuring of the ownership, management, and operation of these SOEs. Some of the SOEs, set up during the socialist era with the objectives of regional development, employment creation, or whatever, were not economically or financially viable to begin with. Thus, some of them need to be shut down while others need to be rehabilitated...Indeed, along with privatization, financial viability rather than plan fulfilment or increased capacity utilisation ought to be the overriding objective of SOEs in a market-oriented economy.[13]

Similarly, the World Bank report also suggested that there was ambivalence among the political leaders themselves (especially the military elites) about the benefit of reforming the SOEs.[14] There was also strong resistance from influential groups such as government employees, military officers, and those who were engaged in business ventures with

SOEs who believed that the reforming of SOEs could threaten their interests.

Slow Progress in the Inflow of Foreign Investment

After the military government enacted the Foreign Investment Law in 1988, there was an increase in the number of foreign investors entering Burma.[15] They invested in various sectors, ranging from tourism, property development, logging, and mining, to oil and gas exploration. According to an official source, by March 1997 about US$6.05 billion worth of foreign investment had been approved by the Myanmar Investment Commission (Table 8.2). British and Singaporeans were at the top of the list of foreign investors. By country of origin, Asian investors represented more than half of the total foreign investment in Burma.[16]

Table 8.2   Foreign Direct Investment Approvals, by Selected Countries (as of 31 March 1997)

Countries	Number of Approvals	Amount (US$ million)	Percentage of Total Approvals
UK*	27	1,304	21.6
Singapore	55	1,215	20.1
Thailand	39	1,027	17.0
USA	16	652	9.6
France	3	470	7.8
Malaysia	19	462	7.6
Holland	5	238	3.9
Indonesia	4	211	3.5
Japan	13	192	3.2
Austria	2	73	1.2
South Korea	12	70	1.2
Hong Kong	17	64	1.1
Australia	11	40	0.7
Total Asian countries	172	3,283	54.3
Total Western countries	75	2,469	45.7
Total	247	6,052	100.0

*Including UK-based investors who come from Bermuda and the Caribbean islands.
Source: Myanmar Investment Commission (1997) as quoted in the East Asia Analytical Unit, *The New Aseans, Vietnam, Burma, Cambodia and Laos* (Canberra: Department of Foreign Affairs and Trade, 1997), p. 137.

Not all foreign investors who had received approval actually invested their money. Some of them decided not to go ahead with investing in the country. There were a number of reasons for this. First, many of them were concerned about the worsening economic situation and Burma's political uncertainty. Second, many of them were under pressure from company shareholders, governments, and human rights organisations who were concerned with the human rights violations committed by the military government, and decided not to proceed with investing in Burma (Box 8.1). Most of these companies came from the US, Canada, and Europe.[17] Some of them were Heineken, Levi Strauss, Eddie Bauer, Motorola, Hewlett-Packard, Peregrine, and Eastman Kodak. Even those who went ahead in Burma invested only in low-risk business activities, adopting a wait-and-see approach to the economic and political uncertainty.[18] Even so, the economic crisis in the Southeast Asian region had a direct impact on the Burmese economy. The flow of foreign direct investment (FDI) in 1997/98 fell dramatically by 79.1 per cent compared to the previous year, which meant a drop of $US585 million worth of investment.[19]

Box 8.1 Trade Restrictions Imposed by Western Countries[20]

Country	Type of Action
US	Economic sanction by banning all new investment in Burma by US companies. US selective purchasing laws: supported by five states and 17 cities.
EU	Withdrawal of generalised system of preferences benefits on agricultural goods.
Canada	Requiring Canadian companies wanting to export to Burma to get a permit
Australia	Selective purchasing law passed by Marrickville Council in Sydney.
Global	Consumer boycotts advocated by human rights organisations.

Unfinished Financial Reforms

Unlike Thailand and Indonesia, the financial sector in Burma was still highly regulated and restricted from foreign competition. From 1990 the government gradually deregulated this sector through new financial regulations such as the Central Bank Law and the Financial Institutions Law.[21] These reforms eased restrictions and opened the way for more private banks to be established in Burma. From 1992, about 15 private banks were established and some of them were granted the right to undertake foreign exchange transactions.[22] In mid-1996, Japan's Daiwa Institute of Research signed a joint venture agreement with the government-owned Myanma Economic Bank (MEB) to establish the first stock exchange company, the Myanmar Securities Exchange Centre Co. Ltd. in Rangoon.[23] By 1997, the number had increased to 21 private banks and 44 foreign banks (mostly from Southeast Asia) that had received licences to open branches in Burma.[24] In the same year, five joint ventures between local private banks and foreign banks were allowed to begin operation in Burma. These were the Mayflower Bank (with the Siam City Bank of Thailand), the Tun Foundation Bank (with the May Bank of Malaysia), the Asia Wealth Bank (with the Thai Farmers' Bank), the Yoma Bank (with the Japanese Fuji Bank), and the Myanmar Livestock and Fisheries Development Bank with (the Global Commercial Bank of Singapore).[25]

Nonetheless, the government still controlled the financial sector in Burma, with four government-owned banks holding about 90 per cent of kyat deposits and foreign exchange deposits.[26] These banks were the Myanmar Economic Bank, the Myanmar Investment and Commercial Bank (MICB), the Myanmar Foreign Trade Bank (MFTB) and the Myanmar Agricultural and Rural Development Bank (MARDB). The MEB was the largest of these, but it was believed to be unprofitable, despite the fact that it had branches throughout the country and it was financing all government transactions.[27] However, there was a consensus that the results of the reform in the financial sector were not impressive.[28] Myat Thein argued that a few problems such as negative real interest rates, credit restrictions, lack of "banking habits" and human resources in the country, and macroeconomic instability meant the financial sector in Burma was not expanding as it should be.[29]

The Black Market Economy

The extensive black market economy also played an important role in the failure of economic reform in Burma. Some reports suggest that the size of the black market economy was the same as the legal economy.[30] The most important factor influencing the size of the black market economy was the wide gap between the official exchange rate and the market exchange rate, which created price distortions. Another factor was the flow of smuggled goods from neighbouring countries such as China, India, Bangladesh and Thailand. According to an IMF report, the value of border trade reached about US$1091 million in 1995, but according to an unofficial source, the real figure was three times higher than this.[31] In Burma there are a few border towns such as Lashio on the Chinese-Burmese border, and Mae Sai and Myawaddy on the Thai-Burmese border where smuggling has been established for decades. Even in Mandalay, the second largest city in Burma, many goods smuggled from China are traded openly in markets and shops.[32]

In addition, money laundering from the heroin trade also hampered the Burmese economy. This kind of money could not easily be traced to its origins.[33] Consequently, the government lost a great deal in revenue collection. According to a US Embassy report, the size of heroin-related business activities almost equalled Burma's total legal goods and services exports.[34] This was due mainly to an increase in opium production in Burma. In 1989 the government signed peace agreements with several ethnic rebel groups (including the Wa and the Kokang) who controlled the opium-growing areas along the China-Burma border, an area which had long been the territory of the Communist Party of Burma (CPB). After this, opium production increased rapidly.[35] Despite government rhetoric about suppressing the opium trade, Burma remained one of the biggest opium exporters in the world.

The magnitude of this issue is illustrated through examining money laundering activities in Burma's capital, Rangoon. One source has suggested that heroin money was the main source of funds for economic activity in Rangoon over the past few years.[36] It is believed that well-known heroin producers like Khun Sa and Lo Hsing-han are among those who invested in infrastructure projects, retail, and property.[37] For instance, the Asia World Group, one of Lo Hsing-han's business groups (headed by Lo Hsing-han's son, Steven Law) has a total investment fund of about US$200 million, and this Group invested in several top hotels including the Traders Hotel, the Shangri-La Hotel and the Equatorial Hotel in Rangoon and the Sedoan Hotel in Mandalay.[38] Also, it is believed that heroin money was laundered in joint-venture business activities involving the military-owned business group the Union of Myanmar Economic Holdings Ltd. (UMEH), which also owns the Myawaddy Bank.[39]

Political Stalemate

The political stalemate in Burma also contributed to the erosion of confidence in the Burmese economy and politics. As has been argued in the previous chapter, the political stalemate was caused by the refusal of the Burmese military to reach a political settlement with the National League for Democracy. After NLD leader Aung San Suu Kyi was released from house arrest in 1995, the military government refused to enter into dialogue with her in order to end the political impasse. A few military leaders held talks with other leaders of the NLD, but not with Aung San Suu Kyi. In July and August 1997 a new stand-off between the military government and Aung San Suu Kyi reinforced the difficulty of reaching a political settlement in Burma. This was followed by meetings between military leaders and NLD leaders, but again without with the presence of Aung San Suu Kyi.[40]

Another aspect of the political stalemate was the deadlock over the constitution-making process. In 1993 the military government formed a National Convention to oversee the drafting of the new constitution. The central issue around which the deadlock developed was the insistence of the military that its dominant role in politics be enshrined in the constitution. However, the National Convention had to be adjourned several times, before eventually collapsing when the NLD walked out in 1995. Between 1996 and 1997 the National Convention failed to reconvene and to ratify the new constitution. Meanwhile, the NLD drafted their own proposed new constitution, emphasising the importance of upholding the principle of the separation of powers.[41]

A further factor in the ongoing political uncertainty was the failure to establish a clear timetable for transition to a more stable and democratic government. The military continued to refuse to accept the results of the 1990 general elections. But it did not give any clear indication that general elections would be held again in the near future. The only signal that might be interpreted as preparation for further elections was the mobilisation of the government-sponsored Union Solidarity and Development Association (USDA). According to an official source, in 1997 the USDA gained membership of around six million people and it is believed that the USDA will be used as political vehicle for the military in contesting future general elections.[42] The on-going armed conflict between the military government and several ethnic minorities remained another major political issue in Burma. Despite the fact that the military government had entered into ceasefire agreements with most of the armed ethnic groups, the prospects for a lasting peace settlement with the ethnic minorities remained uncertain. It was in these circumstances that the economic crisis occurred in Burma.

Responses to the Crisis

Crackdown on Foreign Exchange Dealers

Clear evidence of the approaching economic crisis in Burma can be found in the depreciation of the kyat against the US dollar and FECs from June and July 1997.[43] By mid-1998 the kyat had depreciated by 45 per cent

(Figure 8.2). The fall of the currency coincided with the acceptance of
Burma as a new member of ASEAN in July 1997. In addition, the collapse
of the Thai baht caused the value of the kyat to continue to fall because
many traders along the Burmese-Thai border used both currencies in their
business activities.[44] The depreciation of the kyat, as some suggested, was
also caused by rumours about government plans to devalue the kyat and by
the inability of the policy makers to come up with sound economic
policies.[45]

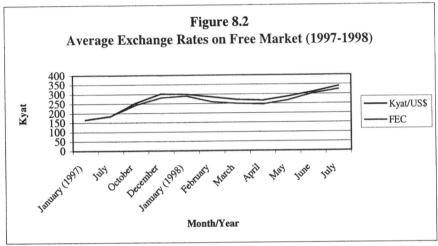

Figure 8.2
Average Exchange Rates on Free Market (1997-1998)

Source: The Economist Intelligence Unit, *A Country Report, Myanmar*, 4th quarter, 1997
and 3rd quarter, 1998.

Nonetheless, the depreciation of the kyat caused difficulty for the
military government. As people lost confidence in the kyat, rumours spread
of a government plan to abolish 200 and 500 kyat notes.[46] This was
compounded by the fact that the level of foreign reserves continued to fall.
This increased fear among the military leaders that they could lose control
of this situation, as occurred in 1987 and 1988, when the Burmese people
protested against the military government's decision to abolish several kyat
notes. At this time, the military government monitored closely the trading
of kyat and FECs in the market and at the same time, authorities detained
currency traders in Rangoon. Uncertain about how to proceed, it seemed
the military government decided to make scapegoats of the currency
dealers. From August 1997 until early January 1998 authorities carried out
widespread arrests of foreign exchange dealers operating in Rangoon.[47]

Import Restrictions

In an attempt to avoid further economic deterioration, the authorities implemented import restrictions. In the middle of 1997 they imposed restrictions by converting US$50,000 worth of FECs that were to be used for imports or transfers abroad.[48] Consequently, while those who earned FECs were not affected, this restriction made it difficult for private importers to earn and to obtain foreign currency in US dollars.[49] In March 1998, the Ministry of Commerce issued a decree imposing two categories of import restrictions.[50] The first one was the "first priority" category (known as category "A") and contained restrictions on machinery, fertiliser, transport equipment, fuel, raw materials and pharmaceuticals, while the second was the "low priority" category (known as category "B") and included radios, television, videos, rice cookers and other electrical goods. According to this decree, the import companies were allowed only to buy items from category "A" without permission from the authorities. These restrictions caused shortages of category B items, and the prices of these items rose dramatically. These restrictions made it difficult for many companies in Burma, and in Rangoon particularly, to run their businesses.[51]

The Crackdown on Border Trade

The government also responded to the deteriorating economic situation in Burma by cracking down on trading in the border areas. Without warning in November 1997 the authorities closed down the three important checkpoints of Tachilek, Myawaddy and Kawthaung along the Burma-Thailand border. According to an official source, this action was taken in order to stop smuggling but another account suggested that a shortage of foreign exchange was the main reason behind this crackdown.[52] However, by closing border trading, the government would be better able to monitor the amount of foreign currency used for imports.[53] These checkpoints were still closed at the end of January 1998.

Deregulating the Rice Sector

In November 1997 the government deregulated rice trading by abolishing the monopoly rights of Myanmar Agricultural Products Trading (MAPT), an agency under the Ministry of Commerce, to buy rice directly from farmers and sell it on the market.[54] Under the existing rule, the farmers were forced to sell their rice to the government at between 10 and 20 per cent below the market price.[55] This decision aimed to stimulate rice production, which had been in decline over the previous few years. At this time rice production was slowed by a flood which affected the Irrawady Delta in 1997, destroying rice fields and consequently reducing farmers' income and their ability to increase rice exports.

Revoking Permits for Foreign Exchange Trading

The government made another dramatic decision in response to the fall of the kyat. On 9 March 1998, the Central Bank of Myanmar revoked the licences to conduct foreign exchange trading of nine banks. These banks were the Myawaddy Bank, the Inwa Bank, the Myodaw Bank, the Myanmar Citizens Bank, the Cooperatives Bank, the Fisheries Bank, the Myanmar Industrial Development Bank, the Sibin Tharyar Yay Bank and the Myanmar Mayflower Bank.[56] This intervention meant only two government-owned banks, the Myanmar Foreign Trade Bank and the Myanmar Investment and Commercial Bank, were licensed to conduct foreign exchange transactions.[57]

Seven foreign exchange dealers were also forced to close down their offices. This measure, to some extent helped strengthen the kyat and Foreign Exchange Certificates (FECs), at least from March until May 1998.[58] However, this decision was regarded by Mya Thein as "a reversal of market-oriented reforms" and therefore ran the risk of lessening the public and business community confidence in the kyat and in Burma's financial institutions.[59]

The Privatisation Push

In order to encourage foreign investment in Burma, at the end of December 1997 the government announced the privatisation of 42 state-owned enterprises (SOEs), two farms and 72 cinemas around the country.[60] As mentioned earlier, previous efforts to privatise SOEs had been unsuccessful because so many powerful ministries resisted the plan. This time, the powerful military leader General Khin Nyunt appointed himself as the head of the Myanmar Privatisation Commission and pushed for the continuation of the privatisation policy in Burma.

Consequences of the Crisis

Inflation and Rocketing Prices

The day-to-day consequences of the economic crisis for the people in Burma were quite apparent in Rangoon. The fall of the kyat and FECs saw the inflation rate soar to 40 per cent and this was followed by an increase in the prices of basic commodities.[61] Sources estimated that between June and November 1997 the prices of basic commodities increased by between 10-40 per cent (Table 8.3). This information was confirmed by others, who pointed out that the trend to price increases continued until 1998.[62] All indicated that the economic situation had not improved despite the government's implementation of measures to respond to the economic crisis.

Table 8.3 Changes in Basic Commodity Prices in Rangoon (kyat)

Commodities	Before June 1997	November-December 1997
Ordinary rice (1 kg)	100	120
Shan rice (1 kg)	250	260
Cooking oil (1 kg)	450	550
Dry beans (1 kg)	100	150
Tomatoes (1 kg)	100	150
Potatoes (1 kg)	70	120
Onions (1 kg)	100	200
Cauliflower (1 piece)	25	125
Garlic (1 bunch)	100	70
Chicken meat (1 kg)	350	700
Butter fish (1 kg)	400	800
Prawns (1 kg)	2,000	3,000
Beef (1 kg)	200	200
Pork (1 kg)	450	800

Source: Author's observations in Rangoon (December 1997).

Slowdown in Economic Activity

The tourist industry also went into decline, particularly with respect to visitors from neighbouring Asian countries. According to Senior Minister David Abel 46 per cent of Burma's trade is with ASEAN countries and therefore the economic crisis in the region had a serious impact on the Burmese economy.[63] The economic downturn throughout the region forced tourists to stay at home. The lack of international standard accommodation, the poor infrastructure in the tourism industry, as well as the political uncertainty in Burma also resulted in tourists hesitating to go to Burma.[64]

Other sectors, such as energy sector, were also in trouble. A decision was made in July 1997 by the US-based oil company, Unocal, to delay exploration activity in the Yadana project, a pipeline gas project to supply gas to Thailand and the region.[65]

There were also signs that the agricultural sector was in trouble. This sector accounted for about 50 per cent of GDP in Burma. Meanwhile, the inflow of foreign investment was slower, with the approval of foreign direct investment in the first eleven months of the 1997/98 financial year dropping by 79.1 per cent (or US$585 million) compared with the same period in 1996/97.[66] Not a single new application for a foreign-funded project in the hotel, tourism, trade or industry sector had been made. This made it more difficult for the government to reach its official target of GDP growth of 6.4 per cent in 1997/98.[67] With the government facing both economic and political problems, an assessment from an independent source predicted that the GDP growth for 1997/98 would be about 1.1 per cent.

Searching for New Economic Policies

The government held two economic conferences in early 1998.[68] These conferences gave pessimistic assessments of the economic situation in Burma. It seemed that the government had difficulty in formulating economic policy to deal with the economic crisis.[69] It was in the context of searching for a new economic policy direction that in September 1997, the NLD had distributed a policy document explaining the party's economic platform. The NLD document advocated several courses of action: abolishing the three exchange rates currently in place and replacing these with a single, unified exchange rate which would reflect the market rate (this could be achieved by placing Burma under the supervision of the international financial agencies); privatising or selling SOEs; removing the finance of SOEs from the government budget and establishing a balanced budget system; liberalising the trade and investment climate; rescheduling external debt and inviting overseas aid; and giving the Central Bank of Myanmar more autonomy in formulating monetary policy.[70] The publication of the NLD document showed up the failure of the military government in coming up with economic policies that could avert further economic crisis. However, it remained to be seen whether the government would agree to work with the NLD in formulating economic policy.

Clearly, the difficulty of finding a solution for Burma's economic situation had been the subject of discussions between top military leaders.

But there was no clear view on what form this action should take. It is believed that the hardline faction, led by General Maung Aye, Vice-Chairman of SLORC, preferred to use trade restrictions, while the moderate faction, led by Lt. Gen. Khin Nyunt, the First Secretary of the SLORC, and the pro-reform figures, advocated further economic liberalisation.[71] General Than Shwe, Prime Minister and Chairman of the SLORC, acknowledged the seriousness of the economic situation in a public speech given to USDA members in March 1998. During his speech he acknowledged that the regional economic downturn had worsened the Burmese economy and he urged the Burmese people to prepare to face a difficult time ahead.[72]

There was, however, a consensus that the military government needed to undertake comprehensive economic reform beyond the measures which had already been implemented.[73] There was also recognition that the government could not do it on its own. It required financial and technical assistance from outside agencies such as the International Monetary Fund, the World Bank, the Asian Development Bank and individual donor countries.

The Regime Renamed

On 15 November 1997 the military government, SLORC, renamed itself the State Peace and Development Council (SPDC) (Box 8.2). According to an official source, this new name was intended to reflect the emergence of "disciplined democracy" and "a peaceful and prosperous modern state".[74] Observers suggested that this change was basically cosmetic, an attempt to improve the bad image of the military government in the eyes of the international community, particularly as Burma had formally become a member of Asean in July 1997.[75]

However, there were some other factors at work in the renaming of the regime. First, the decision was taken because of pressure from among the military leaders to implement gradual political change, within the parameters of maintaining the dominant role of the Burmese military. The decision to include new persons from both military and civilian backgrounds in the new cabinet was intended to "civilise" the military government's image both domestically and abroad. Second, the change also could be seen as the result of power struggles between the factions of General Khin Nyunt and General Maung Aye.[76] It appeared that each side had fought for control in appointing its supporters to the new cabinet. But looking at the appointment of new ministers, is suggested that it was the

Khin Nyunt faction that gained most. In order to avoid further internal tension, a few senior ministers, who were replaced as a result of the cabinet reshuffle, were given "honorary" positions in the new advisory council, which in fact did not have the power to influence the day-to-day running of the country or the formulation of government policy.

Box 8.2 The SPDC and the Cabinet Reshuffle (15 November 1997)

The State Peace and Development Council (SPDC)
- The top four generals retained their posts on the SPDC.
- Younger military commanders filled the 14 remaining SPDC posts.
- Former SLORC members were moved aside into a 14-member advisory body.

The Cabinet
- Two new ministries were formed (military affairs and electric power), expanding the size of the cabinet to 40.
- 22 new ministers appointed Cabinet members no longer had military duties (although 60 per cent of them had military backgrounds and retained their military titles).
- Senior General Than Shwe, Chairman of the SPDC, retained the post of Prime Minister and Minister of Defence.

Source: The Economist Intelligence Unit, *A Country Report, Myanmar*, 4th quarter, 1997.

Third, it was also suggested that the name change occurred as a result of an intervention by Ne Win, a former military leader who still retained influence among senior military leaders.[77] This view was based on Ne Win's stated disappointment over the failure of the Burmese military to win the "hearts and minds" of the Burmese people and to restore economic and political stability in Burma. Ne Win intervened after he visited Indonesia in September 1997, where he was confronted with many stories about corruption among senior ministers who had business dealings with Indonesian investors in Burma.[78] Lt. Gen. Khin Nyunt received similar complaints when he met Singaporean business leaders in Singapore in October 1997. The replacement of senior military officers such as the Trade Minister Lt. Gen. Tun Kyi and the Tourism Minister Lt. Gen. Kya Ba, both notoriously corrupt ministers, was seen as the result of intervention by Ne Win.[79]

The Cabinet Reshuffle

At the end of November 1997, the three former senior ministers who had lost their positions in the cabinet reshuffle, tourism minister Lt. Gen Kya Ba, trade minister Lt. Gen. Tun Kyi and agriculture minister Myint Aung, were placed under house arrest. Along with their staff and personal advisers, they were under investigation on corruption charges.[80] This action was taken after military leaders found evidence that these ministers were corrupt to a point that could altogether erode the credibility of the military government. Following this, in early December 1997, the military leaders dissolved the advisory council to which the former ministers had been appointed.[81]

Then followed another cabinet reshuffle on 20 December 1997. The main winner was Brigadier General David Abel, Minister of National Planning and Development, who was given a new position as minister of the Office of the Chairman of the SPDC.[82] David Abel was believed to be in a strong position to advise Senior General Than Shwe on economic issues. Other winners were Finance Minister Brigadier General Win Tin, who took up a new position as Communications Minister, while former Energy Minister Brigadier General Khin Maung Thein was transferred into a new position as Finance Minister. The latter was known as the only "technocrat" in the government and was better educated than other ministers. He was known for his work in encouraging foreign investors to come into Burma.[83]

Political Uncertainty in 1998

In terms of Burma's broader political situation, the economic crisis made the possibility of finding a political settlement more remote. Two important political developments in Burma during 1998 will be described. First, the government's plan to hold the National Convention and, second, the continuing political deadlock between the government and the NLD. Soon after the second cabinet reshuffle at the end of 1997, the military government decided to replace three senior military officers who had been members of the National Convention Convening Committee (NCCC), the committee overseeing the constitution drafting process.[84] These were Lieutenant General Myo Nyunt, Chairman of the NCCC, and his two vice-chairmen, Lieutenant General Maung Thint and Brigadier General Myo Thant. This was regarded as a sign that the military leaders were intending to reconvene the National Convention, which had been adjourned since 1996. By resuming the National Convention the military government might have hoped that the ratification of the proposed new constitution could take place and could be followed by a general election.[85]

It was recognised that by promising to hold a general election, the military government could satisfy demands from domestic opposition groups and the international community. This demand was reiterated by Kofi Annan, the Secretary-General of United Nations (UN), in mid-December 1997, when he met General Than Shwe at the ASEAN meeting in Malaysia, and, at this meeting, General Than Shwe promised to undertake a democratisation process in Burma.[86] This commitment was also reiterated by Deputy Prime Minister, Vice-Admiral Maung Maung Khin who said in an interview with *Asiaweek* that:

> We have not assumed the seat of power forever. We know we have to go at one time or another. We have achieved stability to a certain degree, but not 100% yet...Then, once the new Constitution is in place and elections can be held, we will hand power to whoever is elected. When, I cannot predict.[87]

However, there was little progress in ratifying the new constitution in 1998. It seemed that the military leaders were preoccupied with economic rather than political issues, although the two were related. The relationship between the military government and the National League for Democracy did not improve either, although the government allowed NLD organisers to hold meetings in 1997 and 1998.[88] Conflict between the military and the NLD occurred on several occasions throughout 1998. On one of these occasions (in May 1998) the NLD called on the government to open dialogue with them as a prerequisite for finding a political settlement in Burma. The military leaders refused to accept this demand and arrested supporters of the NLD throughout the country. On another occasion the government did not allow Aung San Suu Kyi to travel to meet her supporters in small towns outside Rangoon in July and August 1998.[89] The deadlock continued when on 21 August 1998 Aung San Suu Kyi called for NLD MPs to meet in Rangoon.[90] The military leaders cracked down on NLD meetings and continued to restrict the freedom to travel of Aung San Suu Kyi.[91] At the end of 1998 there was still no sign that the differences between the two sides could be resolved.[92]

Conclusion

This chapter has examined the economic and political consequences of the economic crisis in Burma in 1997 and 1998. It discussed the military government's response to the deterioration of the Burmese economy and the political uncertainty caused by the economic crisis. It argued that the failure of the military government to bring about economic and political stability in Burma made this country more vulnerable to changes in the neighbouring countries.

However, several other domestic factors also contributed to deepening the economic crisis. The economic reforms that were implemented by the military government after 1988 did not achieve their objectives. The government failed to establish macroeconomic stability, to create a single currency exchange system, to improve the efficiency of the state-owned enterprises (SOEs), to reform the financial sector, to attract foreign investors, and to control the black market and drug trade. Political uncertainty manifested itself in various forms such as the on-going political stalemate between the military and the National League for Democracy, the slow progress in ratifying the new constitution, the failure to establish a timetable for a democratic transition, and the ending of ethnic minority conflicts. The lack of expertise and independence of the economic policy-making institutions undermined efforts to improve the policy-making process.

The contagion effect of the economic crisis in the region upon the Burmese economy was clearly seen in the depreciation of the kyat which felt by more than 40 per cent from mid-1997 and into 1998. In contrast to Thailand and Indonesia, the military government in Burma relied very much on domestic-based resources and ad hoc measures in addressing the problems arising from the economic crisis. Responses made by the military government included arresting foreign exchange and money dealers, restricting imports, closing down check points along the border with Thailand and China, deregulating rice trading, privatising SOEs, and revoking the foreign exchange licences held by several banks. None of these measures improved Burma's economic situation. It was in this context that the NLD's views on policies to solve the economic and political crises were very significant.

Above all, the economic crisis also had political implications. The military government renamed itself in November 1997 and reshuffled the cabinet several times. This was an attempt by the government to improve its image in the international community and to ease internal rivalry among factions in the top military elite. The economic crisis in Burma forced the military government to readjust its economic and political policies, but always within the parameters of maintaining its dominant role in Burma. Seemingly, the continuity of the political stalemate and stalling in the constitution-making process during 1998 hindered attempts to formulate sound economic policies that could properly address the economic situation. Having explained this, it is then necessary to compare the economic and political changes in Burma with those of Thailand and Indonesia. The following chapter will draw together the politics of the economic reforms, booms, and crises in Thailand, Indonesia, and Burma and attempt to make sense of them in the context of the comparative economy approach which this book is suggesting.

Notes

[1] Myat Thein and Mya Than, "Transitional Economy of Myanmar: Performance, Issues and Problems" in Naya, S. F and J. L. H. Tan (eds.) *Asian Transitional Economies* (Singapore: Institute of Southeast Asian Studies, 1995), pp. 210-261; Mya Maung, "The Burmese Approach to Development", *Journal of Asian Economics*, vol. 7, no. 1, (1996), pp. 97-129; and John Wong, "Why Has Myanmar not Developed Like East Asia", *ASEAN Economic Bulletin*, vol. 13, no. 3 (March 1997), pp. 344-358.

[2] Bertil Lintner, "Deeper into the Mire", *Far Eastern Economic Review* (13 November 1997); and also Tin Maung Maung Than and Mya Than, "Myanmar, Economic Growth in the Shadow of Political Constraints", *Southeast Asian Affairs 1997* (Singapore: Institute of Southeast Asian Studies), 1997, pp. 205-230.

[3] World Bank, *Myanmar: Policies for Sustaining Economic Reform* (Washington D.C.: World Bank, 1995); International Monetary Fund, *Myanmar, Recent Economic Developments* (Washington D.C.: International Monetary Fund, 1995); and also The East Asia Analytical Unit, *The New Aseans, Vietnam, Burma, Cambodia and Laos* (Canberra: Department of Foreign Affairs and Trade, 1997).

[4] Tin Maung Maung Than and Mya Than, p. 215.

[5] It is hard to find the reliable information about military spending. This figure based on two sources, see The East Asia Analytical Unit, *The New Aseans, Vietnam, Burma, Cambodia and Laos*, p. 124; and US Embassy, *Country Commercial Guide, Burma* (Rangoon: U.S. Embassy, 1996), p. 14.

[6] The Economist Intelligence Unit, *A Country Report, Myanmar*, 4th quarter, 1997, p. 22.

[7] An interesting discussion of this can be found in David Steinberg, "Priorities for Burma's Development: the Role of International Aid" in Peter Carey (ed.) *Burma, The Challenge of Change in a Divided Society* (London: Macmillan, 1997), pp. 159-181.

[8] Ibid, p. 127.

[9] World Bank, *Myanmar: Policies for Sustaining Economic Reform*, pp. 27-30; Paul Cook and Martin Minogue, "Economic Reform and Political Conditionality in Myanmar" in Peter Carey (ed.) *Burma, The Challenge of Change in a Divided Society* (London: Macmillan, 1997), p. 204; Wong, "Why Has Myanmar not Developed Like East Asia?", p. 355; and also Myat Thein and Mya Than, "Transitional Economy of Myanmar", p. 249.

[10] Mark Mason, "Foreign Direct Investment in Burma, Trends, Determinants, and Prospects" in Robert I. Rotberg (ed.) *Burma, Prospects for a Democratic Future* (Washington D.C.: Brookings Institution Press, 1998), p. 221.

[11] Their economic activities included extraction and sale of pearls, jade and precious stones, fisheries, postal and telecommunication services, air and rail transport services, banking and insurance, broadcasting, exploration and sale of metals, electricity generation and distribution services, and military industries, World Bank, *Myanmar, Policies for Sustaining Economic Reform*, p. 93.

[12] Ibid, p. 144.

[13] Myat Thein and Mya Than, "Transitional Economy of Myanmar", pp. 224.

[14] World Bank, *Myanmar: Policies for Sustaining Economic Reform*, p. 145.

[15] The East Asian Analytical Unit, *The New Aseans, Vietnam, Burma, Cambodia and Laos* (Canberra: Department of Foreign Affairs and Trade, 1997), p. 136.

[16] Central Statistical Organization, *Selected Monthly Economic Indicators* (Yangon: Ministry of National Planning and Economic Development, July-August 1997), pp. 46-50.

[17] Mason, "Foreign Direct Investment in Burma", p. 224.

[18] Interview with Chris Poole-Johnson, Rangoon, 2 December 1997.

[19] The Economist Intelligence Unit, *A Country Report, Myanmar*, 3rd quarter, 1998, p. 19.

[20] The Economist Intelligence Unit, *A Country Report, Myanmar*, 1st quarter, 1998, p. 21; also The Economist Intelligence Unit, *A Country Report, Myanmar*, 4th quarter, 1998, p. 19..

[21] World Bank, *Myanmar, Policies for Sustaining Economic Reform*, p. 3.

[22] Myat Thein and Mya Than, "Transitional Economy of Myanmar", p. 228.

[23] The East Asia Analytical Unit, *The New Aseans, Vietnam, Burma, Cambodia and Laos*, p. 129.

[24] Ibid.

[25] Tin Maung Maung Than and Mya Than, "Myanmar, Economic Growth in the Shadow of Political Constraints", p. 224.

[26] The East Asia Analytical Unit, p. 130.

[27] International Monetary Fund, *Myanmar, Recent Economic Developments*, pp. 12-13.

[28] Interview with a Burmese banker, Rangoon, 7 August 1997.

[29] Mya Thein, "Some Aspects of Economic Reforms of Economic Reforms in Myanmar", a paper presented to Roundtable on Interaction between Myanmar and ASEAN-ISIS organised by Myanmar Institute of Strategic And International Studies, Ministry of Foreign Affairs, Rangoon, 27-30 October 1997; and also interview with a Singaporean banker, Rangoon, (3 December 1997).

[30] See US Embassy, *Country Commercial Guide, Burma*, p. 7; and The East Asia Analytical Unit, *The New Aseans, Vietnam, Burma, Cambodia and Laos*, p. 146.

[31] The East Asia Analytical Unit, p. 134.

[32] After the authorities legalised the border trade with China in 1992, more and more Chinese goods and investors entered into Burma. This is also increased the size of Chinese investment in the country. The growth of the Mandalay economy in the past few years has been fuelled by Chinese investment. This was also confirmed by the author's observation when the author visited Mandalay in December 1997. Also see Mya Maung, "On the Road to Mandalay, A Case Study of the Sinonization of Upper Burma", *Asian Survey*, vol. xxxiv, no. 5 (May 1994), pp. 455-456.

[33] For an interesting account on the politics of heroin trade in Burma, see Andre and Louis Boucaud, *Burma's Golden Triangle, On the Trail of the Opium Warlords*, revised edition (Bangkok: Asia Books, 1992).

[34] US Embassy, *Country Commercial Guide, Burma*, p. 9.

[35] For further discussion on the causes of the downfall of the Communist Party of Burma, see, Bertil Lintner, *The Rise and Fall of the Communist Party of Burma (CPB)* (Ithaca: Southeast Asia Program, Cornell University, 1990); and for the role of the ethnic groups in opium business, see Bertil Lintner, "The Politics of Drug Trade in Burma", a paper presented at *The State, Order and Prospects for Change in Burma*, Grifith University, Brisbane, 3-4 December 1992.

[36] Interview with an Australian diplomat, Rangoon, 5 December 1997.

[37] The East Asia Analytical Unit, *The New Aseans, Vietnam, Burma, Cambodia and Laos*, p. 146.

[38] Bertil Lintner, "Drugs and Economic Growth, Ethnicity and Exports" in Robert I. Rotberg (ed.) *Burma, Prospects for a Democratic Future* (Washington D.C.: Brookings Institution Press, 1998), pp. 179.

[39] Ibid.

[40] One of the meetings was held by Lt. Gen. Khin Nyunt and U Aung Shwe. See David Steinberg, "Myanmar, Regional Relationship and Internal Concerns", *Southeast Asian Affairs 1998* (Singapore: Institute of Southeast Asian Studies, 1998), p. 190.

[41] This happened in September 1998 when the NLD set up a "People's Parliament" comprised of ten members who were elected in the 1990 general election. The Economist Intelligence Unit, *A Country Report, Myanmar*, 4th quarter, 1998, p. 4.

[42] For further discussion on this, see David I. Steinberg, "The Union Solidarity and Development Association, Mobilization and Orthodoxy", *Burma Debate*, vol. 4, no. 1 (January-February, 1997), pp. 4-11.

[43] Roger Mitton, "Hard Times in Yangon", *Asiaweek*, 3 April 1998.

[44] Interview with a Burmese banker, Rangoon, 4 December 1997.

[45] The Economist Intelligence Unit, *A Country Report, Myanmar*, 4th quarter, 1997, p. 32 and Bertil Lintner, "Paper Tiger", *Far Eastern Economic Review*, 7 August 1997.

[46] Interview with an Indonesian diplomat, Rangoon, 5 December 1997; and *The Irrawaddy*, vol. 5, no. 8 (January 1998).

[47] The Economist Intelligence Unit, *A Country Report, Myanmar*, 2nd quarter, 1998, p. 27; and also Shawn W. Crispin, "Heading for a Fall", *Far Eastern Economic Review*, 27 August 1998.

[48] Roger Mitton, "Hard Times in Yangon" , *Asiaweek* (3 April 1998).

[49] The Economist Intelligence Unit, *A Country report, Myanmar*, 4th quarter, 1997, p. 32.

[50] The Economist Intelligence Unit, *A Country Report, Myanmar*, 2nd quarter, 1998, p. 18-19.

[51] Interview with Chris Poole-Johnson, Rangoon, 2 December 1997.

[52] The Economist Intelligence Unit, *A Country Report, Myanmar*, 1st quarter, 1998, p. 30.

[53] Roger Mitton, "Hard Times in Yangon", *Asiaweek* (3 April 1998).

[54] Ibid, p. 23.

[55] Steinberg, "Myanmar, Regional Relationship and Internal Concerns", p. 192.

[56] Ibid, pp. 27-28.

[57] Shawn W. Crispin, "Heading for a Fall", *Far Eastern Economic Review* (27 August 1998).

[58] The Economist Intelligence Unit, *A Country Report, Myanmar*, 1st quarter, 1998, p. 26; and David Steinberg, "Myanmar, Regional Relationship and Internal Concerns", p. 191.

[59] Myat Thein, *Improving Domestic Resource Mobilization in Myanmar*, unpublished paper, 1999, p. 35.

[60] The Economist Intelligence Unit, *A Country Report, Myanmar*, 1st quarter, p. 18.

[61] Crispin, "Heading for a Fall".

[62] The Economist Intelligence Unit, *A Country Report, Myanmar*, 3rd quarter, 1998, p. 21; and Roger Mitton, "Country in Limbo", *Asiaweek* (13 February 1998).

[63] "Don't Be So Impatient", an interview with David Abel, *Asiaweek* (3 April 1998).

[64] Interview with Chris Poole-Johnson, Rangoon, 2 December 1997.

[65] The Economist Intelligence Unit, 3rd quarter, *op.cit.*, p. 23.

[66] The Economist Intelligence Unit, *A Country Report, Myanmar*, 3rd quarter, 1998, p. 19.

[67] Ibid, p. 18.

[68] The Economist Intelligence Unit, *A Country Report, Myanmar*, 2nd quarter, 1998, p. 18.

[69] "Don't Be So Impatient", an interview with David Abel, *Asiaweek* (3 April 1998).

[70] The Economist Intelligence Unit, p. 20; and also see The East Asia Analytical Unit, *The New Aseans, Vietnam, Burma, Cambodia and Laos*, p. 148.

[71] The Economist Intelligence Unit, 1998, pp. 12-13; and also Shawn W. Crispin, "Internal Matter", *Far Eastern Economic Review* (13 August 1998).

[72] The Economist Intelligence Unit, ibid.

[73] This point was made in a length article written by Roger Mitton, "Country in Limbo", *Asiaweek* (13 February 1998).

[74] Quoted from *The Irrawady*, vol. 5, no. 8, (January 1998).

[75] Bertil Lintner, "Just as Ugly", *Far Eastern Economic Review*, 27 November 1997.

[76] Roger Mitton, "Country in Limbo", *Asiaweek* (13 February 1998).

[77] Interview with Chris Poole-Johnson, Rangoon, 2 December 1997.

[78] "A Man of Some Influence", *Asiaweek* (13 February 1998).

[79] Interview with an Australian diplomat, Rangoon, 5 December 1997; and also "A Man of Some Influence", *Asiaweek* (13 February 1998).

[80] The Economist Intelligence Unit, *A Country Report, Myanmar*, 1st quarter, 1998, p. 11.

[81] Shawn W. Crispin, "Posing a Problem", *Far Eastern Economic Review* (27 August 1998).

[82] The Economist Intelligence Unit, 1st quarter, 1998, *op.cit*, p. 12.

[83] Ibid.

[84] The Economist Intelligence Unit, *A Country Report, Myanmar*, 1st quarter, 1998, p. 12.

[85] Roger Mitton, "Country in Limbo", *Asiaweek* (13 February 1998).

[86] Ibid, p. 13.

[87] "We Know We Have to Go", an interview with *Asiaweek* (17 July 1998).

[88] Steinberg, "Myanmar, Regional Relationships and Internal Concerns", p. 190.

[89] Shawn W. Crispin, "Internal Matter", *Far Eastern Economic Review* (13 August 1998).

[90] The Economist Intelligence Unit, *A Country Report, Myanmar*, 3rd quarter, 1998, p. 11; and also "Ten Years On", *Asiaweek* (28 August 1998).

[91] Roger Mitton, "A Chance for Dialogue", *Asiaweek* (4 September 1998).

[92] Donald M. Seekins, "Burma in 1998, Little to Celebrate", *Asian Survey*, vol. xxxix, no. 1 (January-February 1999), pp. 12-19.

Chapter Nine

Conclusion:
Thailand, Indonesia and Burma
Compared

The main focus of this book has been to examine the rapid economic and political changes that have occurred in contemporary Thailand, Indonesia and Burma. The preceding chapters have provided a great deal of empirical evidence for study. This chapter compares the similarities and differences of these countries. It is divided into three sections. The first part makes a comparison of the politics of economic reform and boom in these countries. Then follows a comparison of the causes of, responses to, and consequences of the economic crisis in these countries. Finally, the arguments and empirical findings presented in this book are drawn together.

Before proceeding further, it is necessary to mention briefly the points that were made in Chapter Two. It was noted there that the growing number of studies of the Southeast Asian political economy have been influenced by the political economy approaches applied to the East Asian region.[1] Both the neo-classical and the East Asia developmentalist political economy models are commonly applied in understanding the economic success of the East Asian region. The former model suggests that economic growth can be achieved when a country implements market-based policies, limiting the role of government as the provider of public goods and allowing market forces to operate freely in the economy, while the latter model argues that strong and effective state intervention combined with insulated and credible policy-making institutions contribute to this success.

Both approaches have been criticised on different grounds. The neo-classical political economy sees economic development in a linear way and fails to acknowledge the impact of diverse social and political settings on national economies. This approach argues that the implementation of market-based economic policies would bring about the emergence of a democratic political system. This is not always the case and it does not adequately explain why the economic success of the East

Asian countries was accompanied by the authoritarian political systems. Such an approach is also inadequate to explain why although Thailand, Indonesia and, to a lesser extent, Burma, embarked upon economic reform in the 1980s and the 1990s, these countries operated under different political systems. Democratic political systems did not necessarily emerge in these countries following the implementation of economic reforms. The East Asia developmentalist political economy, which features the presence of a strong state and insulated policy-making institutions in the economy, also falls short in recognising, and taking account of, the reality of states in the Southeast Asian region. Generally the states in this region are weak, and they do not have effective institutions of the calibre of those in the East Asian countries of Japan, Korea and Taiwan.[2]

The rapid economic changes in the Southeast Asian region in the 1980s led to the emergence of the state and society-based political economy approaches to economic development. Both approaches recognise the role of the state and society-based actors in the economy and according to these approaches the economic success of the Southeast Asian countries resulted from the work of both state and non-state actors. Because the Southeast Asian states are generally weak, the role of non-state actors is important in overcoming state failures in the economic arena. The economic boom that took place in the Southeast Asian countries during the 1990s was seen by many as the "Asian miracle". This "miracle" was achieved because the countries in the region (with the exception of Burma) implemented "market-friendly" policies; policies that bridged the gap between the role of the market and the state in the economy. Although this "miracle" created rapid economic growth, it raised a serious question as to whether such growth could be sustained in these countries' economies in the long-term. The rapid economic changes in the 1990s embedded the Southeast Asian region more deeply into the world economy. These changes resulted not only from the ways in which the world economy operated, but also from changes in the global political environment and the development of new information technology. This became known as globalisation, and inevitably it changed the economic outlook of the region, while simultaneously making the region more vulnerable economically. The devastating impact of the recent economic crisis upon the economies of the region was evidence of this new vulnerability.

As noted in Chapter Two, globalisation and its impact on the region must be thoroughly understood. This book proposed a comparative political economy perspective in furthering this area of study. It takes into account the insights of relevant approaches and it uses a comparative historical and political economy analysis. It incorporates historical factors, the role of political institutions, domestic politics, economic policies, capital mobility, good governance, civil society, and external environment in understanding the political economy of contemporary Thailand, Indonesia and Burma.

The Politics of the Economic Reforms and Booms

Historical Legacies

What is the significance of this historical legacy when studying the economic reform and boom period of the 1980s and 1990s? In contrast to Indonesia and Burma, Thailand was never colonised by a foreign country. The colonisation of Indonesia and Burma strongly influenced their respective post-independence periods. There was, for instance, both widespread nationalist and populist sentiment and support for free market policies in these countries in the post-independent period. These differing sentiments influenced the process of formulating economic or other policies that suited Indonesia and Burma. In Indonesia, there was constant rivalry between the nationalist or populist camp and the pro-market camp over the direction of economic policies after Independence. In Burma the obsession with establishing a socialist state under Ne Win must be understood in the context of the colonial experience of the imposition of free market policies which excluded the majority of the population from the economy.[3]

Nationalist-populist sentiment also gained support in Thailand under the Phibun regime in the 1930s and 1940s, despite the fact that Thailand had had no foreign masters. However, the nationalist sentiment did not last long after the Phibun regime was overthrown. Also because Thailand had not been colonised and because Bangkok was one of most important trading centres in the region, nationalist sentiment did not develop as strongly as it did in Indonesia and Burma. In Indonesia and in Thailand the nationalist-populist camp did not greatly influence the direction of economic policy during the 1980s. In these countries, the pro-market camp was able to lead the reform process, making the economies of these countries more open and competitive internationally. In contrast, anti-market sentiments dominated the thinking of the Burmese military leaders and the reform process in that country failed.

The Ethnicity Factor

The politics of ethnicity in Thailand, Indonesia and Burma also varied. At independence Indonesia and Burma were multi-ethnic societies. This was a dimension of these societies which created both opportunities and problems in the nation-building process. The most important issue in this respect is that of the economic role of the ethnic Chinese in each country. In Indonesia and Burma a situation developed during colonisation where the ethnic Chinese minority occupied a stronger economic position than the local people. This created not only inter-ethnic tension in these countries but also meant that the ethnic Chinese became politically vulnerable, easy scapegoats in times of economic and political crisis. In contrast, despite strong anti-Chinese sentiment during the 1930s and 1940s in Thailand, the role of the ethnic Chinese in the Thai economy did not create inter-ethnic tension. Thailand has seen the successful integration of the ethnic Chinese into Thai society and culture over the past five decades. This may be due in part to the religious factor. The ethnic Chinese in Thailand are mostly Buddhist and consequently the government did not discriminate against the ethnic Chinese in all aspects of life, while in predominantly Muslim Indonesia they were a minority group in terms of both religion and ethnicity and thus became the subject of discriminative government policy which allowed them only to be active in the economic sector.[4]

But despite their political and social vulnerability, the ethnic Chinese played a crucial role during the economic reform and boom period of the 1980s and 1990s. In Indonesia and Thailand, and to a lesser degree in Burma, the ethnic Chinese were major players in stimulating economic growth. Their success was based not only on sound business skills, which were recognised widely, but also on their ability to create political patronage to enhance and protect their economic interests. Evidence of this is found in the successful domination of the banking sector in Thailand by a small number of ethnic Chinese families and the domination of the private sector by a number of ethnic Chinese in Indonesia. The domination of the economies of Thailand and Indonesia by the ethnic Chinese was significant, as they became the engine which drove the economic boom in Thailand and Indonesia.[5]

The Military Factor

It is useful, too, to compare the political history of the civilian-military relationships in Thailand, Indonesia and Burma. The Thai military was from the early twentieth century more politicised and more adventurous than those of Indonesia and Burma. The way in which the military groups have been involved in civilian affairs in each country has varied, of course. The Thai military made frequent use of the military coup. They launched a coup for the first time in 1932, abolishing the absolute monarchy in Thailand. After that, military coups became virtually commonplace in Thai politics and this considerably influenced the dynamics of the civilian-military relationship. In Indonesia, the military institutionalised a concept known as the dual function (*dwi fungsi*) role, allowing the military to be involved in both military and political affairs. In Burma, the military used the military coup and was also involved directly in running the day-to-day affairs of state and this certainly meant the involvement of the Burmese military in non-military affairs was from the outset much deeper than that of Thailand and Indonesia. However, military institutions and their leaders influenced the course of political change in all these countries. The primacy of the military over civil society in these countries influenced the way in which the governments carried out economic development, and to some extent shaped their successes and failures in this. The military leaders (Generals Sarit and Prem of Thailand, General Suharto of Indonesia, and Generals Ne Win, Saw Maung and Than Shwe in Burma) and their supporters took the leading roles in this process. There was popular resentment against the military in these countries, but among military leaders there was a common belief that in recent history they had intervened in national politics at a point where the civilian leaders had failed, and that therefore they were the ones who were responsible for the direction of development.[6]

Regimes Types and State Capabilities

Based on empirical evidence, this study has aimed to demonstrate that economic reforms and booms in Thailand, Indonesia, and Burma resulted from a wide variety of factors, and were not just the result of market forces or state intervention. In the case of Burma, it was the state that was responsible for the failure of the reform process. In this comparison of the similarities and differences between these countries, it is necessary to look closely at the influence of the various states and their regime types during the reform and boom period. The developmentalist approach holds that a strong state is an important factor in ensuring that economic policies can be implemented without being captured by the interests of rent seekers and other politically connected business groups.[7]

In Thailand, the state was relatively strong during the Sarit period in the early 1960s. During this period, General Sarit created the so-called "bureaucratic polity", through which he concentrated the decision-making process in his own hands, and those of his economic advisers, the military leaders and the bureaucracy. In this way, the policy-making process was insulated from political pressure from other groups. This was good for the economy, but it certainly was not good for Thai politics. The state in Thailand started to weaken after the democratic period began in the mid-1970s and it weakened even further during the Prem period in the 1980s.

This occurred because in the democratic climate civilian politicians and non-state groups emerged in national politics and challenged the domination of the state. General Prem initiated a gradual process of reform of the authoritarian Thai political system. In this study it is suggested that the economic reform process in Thailand was accompanied by political liberalisation, which allowed the parliament, media, and other non-state actors to play a greater role in national politics. This democratic transition also drew the decision-making process away from the technocrats to elected politicians and thereby diminished the power of the policy-making institutions which had played an important role prior to the Prem period.

Interestingly, it was when the state began to weaken in the 1980s and 1990s that the Thai economy grew rapidly. It may be the case that this was due to the fact that during the Prem period the state relied on the cooperation of non-state actors, in this case big business groups, to stimulate economic activity in Thailand. The establishment of the Joint Public and Private Sector Consultative Committees (JPPCCs) as a forum where government and business representatives could exchange views on economic policies and business opportunities played an important role in this process. In this respect, the implementation of economic reforms was based on the principles of neo-classical economics advocated by the Thai technocrats, but ultimately it was not market forces alone that stimulated economic growth in Thailand. The government still controlled the major part of the economic sector during this period and there is no evidence that the state deliberately intervened in the market, as was the case in East Asia. While it is true that the Prem regime's policy-making process was insulated, there is evidence that business groups were nonetheless able to influence economic policy in Thailand. As Anek Laothamatas suggests, the close cooperation between the state and business groups is what matters most here and this became possible as Thailand gradually became more democratic and pluralist during the 1980s.[8]

Indonesia is an interesting example of what appeared to be a "strong" state, but was actually weak in the sense that it had long been captured by interest groups, rent seekers, and politically connected business groups.[9] Similar to Thailand during the Sarit period, the policy-making process in Indonesia was controlled by President Suharto, his advisers, the military, and the bureaucracy, but this did not guarantee that economic policy formulation was insulated from non-state actors. This was particularly true during the deregulation period in the 1980s when politically connected conglomerate groups, including the Suharto family-owned business groups, influenced economic policy for their own benefit. In Indonesia, the state was also weak internally due to the constant rivalry between the technocrat and the nationalist-populist camps over the formulation and implementation of economic policies.[10] This explains why, in some cases, the implementation of economic policies which were based on the neo-classical economics advocated by the technocrat camp often did not achieve their goals, either they did not get support from within, or there was strong resistance from the anti-technocrat camp. The rise of the technologist camp in the 1980s also weakened the role of the technocrats in the policy-making process.

How did Indonesia achieve economic boom? The answer is that, during the deregulation period of the 1980s and the 1990s, the state was forced to readjust its role, allowing the private sector to play a greater role in the economy. As the state desperately needed to diversify its revenue base, which was drying up after the collapse of the oil price, it gradually reduced its leading role in the economy. But the readjustment process, or in MacIntyre's words the "strategic retreat" by the state, was not easy; it involved power struggles and bargaining between policy makers, political elites, and the interests of conglomerates.[11] Consequently, the implementation of deregulation policies was carried out in a gradual way and involved "trade-offs" between competing groups, and, in some cases, relatively modest state interventions to ensure the policies were correct and on track. However, the deregulation period did not actually reduce the state role in the economy because of constitutional constraints on the creation of a free-market economy such as those of the Western countries. As was the case with Thailand, it was during this state readjustment process that non-state actors such as business representatives in the Indonesian Chamber of Commerce and Industry began to play a part in influencing the policy-making process in Indonesia. It was through this readjustment of the role of the state and the emergence of business groups in the 1980s that the reform process occurred in Indonesia.

In contrast to Thailand, the period of economic reform and boom in Indonesia was not accompanied by political liberalisation. This was due to the authoritarian political system created by President Suharto, in which he was powerful above all others and the military and bureaucracy were in a dominant position in national politics. Despite the fact that deregulation had forced the state to readjust its role, this did not reduce the power of Suharto. This was possible because national decision making was centralised in his hands. This made him a stumbling block in the path to a more democratic political system in Indonesia. Nonetheless, as has been shown in this study, the emergence of non-state actors in Indonesia's national politics in the 1980s and 1990s meant Suharto's domination of Indonesian politics was subject to increasing domestic challenge.

In contrast to the cases of Thailand and Indonesia, the state failed to bring about economic development in Burma. This was the case during the rule of General Ne Win and under the subsequent military governments. The state capacity to create economic growth in Burma was handicapped by a lack of credible policy institutions and economic policies, such as those that existed in Thailand and Indonesia. The implementation of the "Burmese way to socialism"-based economic policies created a situation where the state played a dominant role in the economy and the private sector disappeared altogether. This led to economic stagnation, which eventually forced the military leaders to abandon socialist economic strategies in 1988 and to replace them with more market-based economic policies.[12] The implementation of economic reform in Burma in the 1980s and 1990s was not a simple process and did not lead to economic boom as it did in Thailand and Indonesia. Although the economic reforms opened Burma to foreign investors, the state continued to monopolise the Burmese economy. Overall, the economic reforms failed to force the state to readjust its role (as in Indonesia) or to allow partnership with the private sector (as in Thailand). The inability of the state to carry out far-reaching economic reforms was due to the fact that reforms would threaten the interests of the Burmese military and political elites. Indeed, in contrast to Thailand and Indonesia, Burma is a case of the failure of a weak state (in terms of its capacity) to foster economic development.

As with Indonesia, economic reform in Burma was not accompanied by political liberalisation, although pressure from non-state actors increased, especially when it appeared that the dominant role of the Burmese military was unsustainable. It is true that in Indonesia economic development was achieved under Suharto's authoritarian political system, while a similar type of regime failed to create economic growth in Burma. The point to be made here is that both democratic and authoritarian political regimes can succeed or fail in bringing about economic development, but the fact of Burma's three decades of economic isolation may be significant in understanding this difference. The experiences of Thailand, however, suggest that the economic development process is most effective when carried out within a democratic political system because it can gain the support of the population.

Economic-Policy Institutions and Policy Makers

The East Asian developmentalist approach holds that cohesiveness within economic policy-making institutions and competent policy makers are important during the economic reform period. The evidence from this study points to a parallel between Thailand and Indonesia. In both these countries it was the precepts of neo-classical economics or the free-market that influenced policy making. In Thailand, especially during the Sarit and Prem periods, the neo-classical economic policies were formulated by a group of technocrats from important institutions such as the National Economic and Social Development Board (NESDB), the Prime Minister's Office's Bureau of Budget (BOB), the Ministry of Finance (MOF) and the Bank of Thailand (BOT). In Indonesia, the technocrats played an important role in the formulation of neo-classical economic policies and many of them controlled institutions like the National Development Planning Board (*Bappenas*), the Ministry of Finance, and the Bank of Indonesia (BI). Both in Thailand and Indonesia, many of these technocrats were educated in American universities and maintained strong connections with them. Some worked closely with the International Monetary Fund (IMF), the World Bank and the Asian Development Bank (ADB).

It is also true that the transmission of a set of policies that Williamson called the "Washington Consensus" (from international institutions to technocrats) arose in Thailand and Indonesia in the 1990s.[13] This influenced the economic reform policies in Thailand and the deregulation policies in Indonesia, which centred on the importance of making the Thai and Indonesian economies more export-oriented and competitive internationally. The two countries differed in that in Thailand a few technocrats transformed themselves into what Williamson called "technopols", occupying political positions and acting as politicians, either by joining existing political parties or creating new ones, whereas in Indonesia, President Suharto appointed technocrats to ministerial positions. As a consequence of this, the influence of Indonesia's technocrats was limited. Indeed, from the beginning the Indonesian technocrats were a non-political group, many of whom came from academia and held no political ambitions. Moreover, in contrast to the case of the Thai technocrats, whose role began to diminish because of the emerging power of the elected politicians, in Indonesia the technocrats found themselves under challenge from within the state. This challenge came from what was known as the technologist camp, led by B. J. Habibie, who argued that the state should intervene in or play a major role in the economy by financing strategic industries which could accelerate the industrialisation process in Indonesia.[14] This camp had its own institutions which played an increasingly significant role in the economy during the latter years of the Suharto era.

Overall, these institutions were relatively insulated from political pressure from social groups. But this did not mean that they did not receive input or ideas from outside. In fact, as mentioned earlier, as Thai politics gradually became more pluralistic during the 1980s and 1990s, non-state actors started to gain more influence over the policy-making process. The strengthening of civil society also meant the policy-making process was no longer centralised among the technocrats, but was spread among a number of political groups and institutions. To some extent, in Indonesia non-state actors and institutions also began to participate in the policy-making process. But the centralisation of the decision-making process in the hands of President Suharto and the authoritarian political system that operated during the New Order period greatly limited this participation.

In Burma, the situation was very different. Compared to Thailand and Indonesia, this country had no cohesive policy institutions or competent policy makers. This study has described how the military government relied on its own resources in the policy-making process, especially on those who were attached to the Ministry of National Planning and the Office of the Prime Minister. Indeed, the lack of human resources and expertise (economists, engineers, respected bureaucrats) due to the departure of many talented people from Burma in the 1960s and 1970s, made it even more difficult for the military government to establish cohesive policy-making institutions like those in Thailand and Indonesia. This partly explains the failure of the reform process in Burma.

Domestic Coalitions

The success or failure of economic reform may also depend on the ability of a government and its leadership to create domestic coalitions or to gain broad-based support from domestic groups or, in Mackie's words, a "growth coalition".[15] Doner in his study on the automobile industry in Southeast Asian countries also stressed the importance of this type of coalition.[16] This study shows that the governments of Thailand and Indonesia created domestic coalitions and there are similarities with respect to those who initiated and were involved in this. In Thailand during the Sarit period in the 1960s, the military, the bureaucracy, and the ethnic Chinese business leaders formed a domestic coalition, with the aim of creating common strategies for economic development in Thailand. During the Prem period of the 1980s, this coalition was broadened to include politicians and it was also institutionalised through the creation of a consultative forum through which government and business representatives could work together in shaping the reform process. Surin Maisrikrod pointed out that this domestic coalition created economic and political problems in Thailand.[17] Excluded from the coalition were the Thai workers and farmers. As shown in Chapter Three, the share of the agricultural sector in Thailand's gross domestic product (GDP) decreased over the past three decades, while the manufacturing and financial sectors grew rapidly. This is evidence that the economic boom in Thailand has mainly benefited the urban middle class, especially those in Bangkok. The emergence of the civil society and non-state actors who were critical of this economic development process in the 1980s and 1990s indicated that the existing domestic coalition was no longer sustainable.

In Indonesia, a similar domestic coalition was formed after Suharto gained power in the mid 1960s. This involved the military, the bureaucracy, the political elites, and the ethnic Chinese business leaders. Through the coalition, Suharto was able to extend political patronage to political contenders and the ethnic Chinese business leaders, who depended on Suharto for political survival and also protection. This domestic coalition expanded during the deregulation period in the 1980s, when new economic actors emerged and began to demand a share in the national economy. Many of them were native Indonesians (*pengusaha pribumi*) and Suharto family members. This expansion not only brought its own internal business conflicts, but also increased the resentment against the ethnic Chinese-owned conglomerates, which, according to those new economic actors, had long dominated economic activity in the private sector in Indonesia. Anti-ethnic Chinese sentiment in Indonesia was so pronounced that it weakened the foundations of this domestic coalition. As in Thailand, the Indonesian workers, and to a great degree farmers too, were not included in this domestic coalition. Suharto's New Order government deliberately excluded and demobilised union organisations from the start.[18] This weakened the bargaining position of union groups in Indonesia, but did not beat them. Rather it heightened the radicalism of the urban workers, and led to the establishment of several new independent union organisations in the early 1990s, which began to challenge government restrictions on workers' right to organise and to strike.

In Burma, the kinds of domestic coalition described above have never existed. As mentioned earlier, the government has dominated all economic activity in Burma through the operation of the state-owned enterprises (SOEs). There were a handful of small business groups, which operated mostly through protection and facilities provided by the military government. However, this study suggests that the resistance of the military government to the creation of a broad coalition involving different groups was an important factor in the failure of the economic reform process in Burma.

External Support

The role of external support is significant, and especially in the areas of ideas, technical capacity, and finance. As mentioned earlier, in both Thailand and Indonesia the role of the IMF, the World Bank, and donor countries (mainly the Western countries) was crucial in the economic development process. In Thailand, external financial support began during the Sarit period, while in Indonesia it was initiated after Suharto took power in the mid 1960s. This external support continued during the implementation of reform policies in both countries in the 1980s. This study shows that the involvement of these institutions was facilitated by their representatives, who often worked as advisers in policy institutions in Thailand and Indonesia. Economic policies based on the neo-classical economics approach were transmitted through those foreign advisers to policy makers in these countries. Besides this, the increase in Japanese and US investment in the 1980s also contributed to the economic growth that occurred in Thailand and Indonesia. The manufacturing sector grew rapidly, especially as the Japanese automotive and electronic industries dominated the domestic markets in these countries.

In contrast Burma received very little external support. The Western countries imposed economic sanctions against the military government in 1988, making it impossible for Burma to receive external support from the IMF, the World Bank and most donor countries. Although a few countries (mainly the neighbouring Asian countries) did invest in various sectors, this did not greatly assist in the creation of economic growth in Burma. This country needed not just short-term investment, but the same long-term and comprehensive external financial support that was given to Thailand and Indonesia.

The main points of similarity and difference in the politics of the economic reforms and booms in Thailand, Indonesia, and Burma can be seen in Table 9.1.

Table 9.1   The Politics of the Economic Reforms and Booms in Thailand, Indonesia and Burma

	Thailand	Indonesia	Burma
Similarities:			
Domestic factors	• open economy • strong state up to the 1970s • "bureaucratic polity" • ethnic Chinese in economy • existence of domestic business groups • economic policy institutions • comprehensive economic reforms	• colonial economy • strong military but weak state under the New Order • ethnic Chinese in economy, • existence of domestic business groups • "Berkeley Mafia" and technocratic policy-making institutions • deregulation policies • weak civil society with limited political participation	• colonial economy • dominant military • weak civil society with authoritarian politics
External factors	• foreign investors • the US and international agencies (IMF and World Bank) • Japanese investors	• foreign investors • western donor countries • international agencies (IMF, World Bank, Asian Development Bank) • Japanese investors	
Differences:			
Domestic factors	• never colonised • frequent change of political leaders and governments • rise of civil society in the 1990s	• former Dutch colony • political stability under the New Order • ethnicity issue • rivalry between policy makers	• former British colony • legacy of political instability and ethnic conflict • social and economic isolation • lack of technocrats • failed economic reforms
External factors			• limited foreign investments • economic sanctions since 1988
Political Outcomes	• gradual political liberalisation in the 1980s and consolidation of a parliamentary democracy in the 1990s	• limited political openness in the 1980s and growing pressure for political change in the 1990s	• authoritarian political system

The Politics of the Economic Crises

Financial Liberalisation

As has been argued, the globalisation that occurred in the Asian region during the 1990s brought rapid economic and political change to Thailand, Indonesia, and Burma. The roots of the economic crisis in these countries can be traced to the impact of the financial liberalisation that took place in these countries during the 1980s and 1990s as a result of globalisation of their financial sectors. It is true that this liberalisation modernised these financial sectors. The increase in capital inflow into these countries also helped to stimulate economic activity in the private sector and to improve the economic fundamentals of both countries. This process was accelerated through the introduction of new information technology (IT), which made the movement of global capital into and out of Thailand and Indonesia easier than ever before. At the same time, the rapid increase in capital inflow also had negative impacts in Thailand and Indonesia; it increased each country's external debt (especially the US dollar denominated short-term debt) and increased the current account deficit to a dangerous level.

The rapid increase in capital inflow in Thailand and Indonesia, and to a lesser extent, Burma, cannot be separated from the larger process of the transfer of global capital from the industrial countries into the developing countries that took place in the course of the 1990s. The movement of global capital was made possible by the expansion of the activities of new market players such as fund managers, or hedge fund managers who traded in the capital market (bonds, stocks or portfolios) and in foreign exchange trading.[19] These new market players traded vast amounts of money; in some cases more than the annual trade figures of many developing countries. Their access to global capital gave them powerful influence over the economic policies of individual countries. The magnitude of the impact of the sudden withdrawal of global capital during concerted attacks on a number of Asian currencies was keenly felt during the economic crisis in 1997.

Economic Fundamentals

The decline in Indonesia's exports in 1994 and in Thailand's in 1996 made the export products of these countries less competitive internationally and this slowed down the growth of both economies. Most incoming foreign capital was invested in the property sector and activities such as foreign exchange or stock exchange trading made this situation worse. It can be argued that the excessive capital inflow into Thailand and Indonesia, and the inability of those who borrowed the foreign capital to use it productively was one of the causes of the economic crisis in these countries. The failure of policy makers in both Thailand and Indonesia to improve supervision and regulatory measures in their financial sectors also played a part in this crisis.

Although the Burmese economy was not as internationalised as those of Thailand and Indonesia, Burma was still affected by the economic crisis. The causes were domestic, however, rooted in the failure of the military government to implement far reaching economic reforms that could make the Burmese economy more open and competitive internationally. The military government failed above all in the area of improving Burma's macroeconomic performance and in areas such as reducing the budget deficit, reforming the exchange rate policy and the financial sector, improving the productivity of the state-owned enterprises, and eliminating the black market economy and money laundering. Evidence presented in this study shows that even a country like Burma, which had not yet fully opened its economy to foreign capital, could be affected by contagion from the economic crisis in its neighbouring countries.

Currency Speculators

In Thailand and Indonesia, both domestic and international currency speculators played an important role in bringing about the collapse of the baht and the rupiah in 1997. In Thailand currency speculators had already started to attack the baht in 1996 when they discovered that Thailand's economic fundamentals were not as sound as many believed. Repeated attacks finally forced the Thai government to float the baht in July 1997. Events in Indonesia were similar. The currency speculators launched their attack on the rupiah in July and August 1997 and Indonesian policy makers used band intervention in response, before finally giving up in mid-August 1997, and floating the rupiah. In both Thailand and Indonesia, the new market players participated in public debates on economic policy, particularly influencing policy makers in moving to implement the free floating exchange rate system. By contrast, currency speculators did not attack the kyat in Burma, but the contagion effect from neighbouring countries had a significant impact on the depreciation of the kyat in 1997. This happened simply because the great volume of trade along the Thai-Burma border made the value of the kyat dependent on the value of the baht in Thailand.

Policy Responses

Policy formulations and responses to the economic crisis in these countries became the responsibility of the technocrats in Thailand and Indonesia. The failure of technocrats and policy makers to come up with sound economic policies responses contributed to the crisis. In Thailand, the focus was on the failure to replace the fixed exchange rate system, which had been used by the Bank of Thailand (BOT) since the mid-1980s. With the increase in capital inflow in the 1990s, the baht became overvalued against the US dollar. Instead of instituting a more flexible exchange rate system, the BOT refused to act, even when the baht was under attack from currency speculators in 1996. The independence and credibility of the BOT deteriorated with the indecisiveness of its policy makers in formulating the exchange rate policy, and this deepened the crisis of confidence among domestic and foreign investors.

In Indonesia, it was a different story. Although the rapid increase in capital inflow also put pressure on the rupiah, the Bank of Indonesia (BI) adjusted its exchange rate policy by using band intervention (by adjusting the rupiah-US dollar band as the rupiah became overvalued or undervalued). However, this approach could not be sustained after the rupiah came under attack from currency speculators. The BI had no choice except to institute a flexible exchange rate system in August 1997. The crisis in Indonesia was also affected by rivalry between the technocrat and the technologist/nationalist camps over economic policy, making the smooth implementation of deregulation policies difficult. This sent negative signals to domestic and foreign investors and led to a crisis of confidence in the Indonesian economy.

In Burma, the military government also failed to come up with sound economic policies in response to the crisis. This was due to the absence of policy institutions and policy makers to formulate economic policies. The failure to replace the overvalued exchange rate made business operations in Burma more costly and also discouraged domestic and foreign investors from investing in the country over long-term periods.

Governance Factor and Bad Politics

Good governance and non-economic factors contributed to each country's economic profile. In Thailand, corruption and credibility issues were major factors in the crisis of confidence among domestic and foreign investors in the Thai economy. This began when the Banharn coalition government was in power from 1995 to 1996. But the situation did not change after the Banharn coalition government was replaced by the Chaovalit coalition, which governed until November 1997. The indecisiveness of Chaovalit's leadership, combined with internal disunity among the parties in his coalition, created confusion over the direction of economic policies, and this became an important factor in the intensifying attack by currency speculators on the baht.

In Indonesia, the so-called "KKN" (*korupsi, kolusi* and *nepotisme* [corruption, collusion, and nepotism]) factor also contributed to the crisis of confidence in the Indonesian economy. Manifestations of the "KKN" factor can be found in special treatment given to companies owned by the Suharto family business groups. The uncertainty of the political succession and the widespread political unrest across Indonesia during 1996 and 1997 were also significant contributing factors to the economic crisis. In Burma, the failure of the Burmese military to reach a political settlement with the National League for Democracy (NLD) contributed to the economic crisis. As with Thailand and Indonesia, widespread corruption in Burma also weakened the ability of the government to implement economic policies and, more importantly, increased the cost of business operations.

External Intervention

Interaction between the process of globalisation and domestic economic and political changes can be found in the way in which the affected countries responded to the economic crisis. In Thailand and Indonesia there are similarities in respect of the initial responses to the economic crisis. The initial response was to readjust economic policies along the lines of neo-classical economics theory, aiming to restore confidence among market actors. Measures were implemented, such as the free floating exchange rate, the imposition of tight monetary policies, rescheduling government spending, restructuring private debt, closing down troubled financial institutions and widening tax revenue bases. However, when it appeared that those measures were not adequate, and also that the extent of the problems was actually much greater than the policy makers had first thought, both Thailand and Indonesia decided to call for external assistance from the IMF and other countries.[20]

It is in the context of the involvement of the IMF in both countries that the interaction of external and domestic factors helped to shape their political dynamics. In Thailand, this process was relatively smooth because there was a strong consensus among political leaders and policy makers in support of the IMF reform package. In contrast, in Indonesia, despite early support for the intervention of the IMF, it later created tensions among political elites and economic actors in Indonesia. The economic policies advocated by the IMF and the Indonesian technocrats were primarily aimed at dismantling the monopoly rights given to those who owned the conglomerate groups (many of these including the children of President Suharto) as well as similar ones given to the state-owned enterprises. In Indonesia, domestic power struggles over the involvement of the IMF deepened the economic and political crises and meant that the IMF economic programmes and policies were revised several times.[21]

Table 9.2   The Politics of the Economic Crises in Thailand, Indonesia and Burma

	Thailand	Indonesia	Burma
Similarities:			
Domestic factors	• financial liberalisation • fixed exchange rate • oversupply in property sector • bad politics • conflict among policy makers	• financial liberalisation • fixed exchange rate with band intervention • oversupply in property sector • deregulation fatigue	• overvalued exchange rate • slow progress in financial liberalisation
External factors	• private capital inflow • short-term private debt • exports declining • IMF intervention	• private capital inflow • short-term private debt • exports declining • IMF intervention • international pressure	• foreign direct investment (FDI) in the 1990s
Differences:			
Domestic factors	• coalition politics • Chaovalit leadership	• Suharto's personal rule, • "KKN" factor • political unrest • resistance against economic reforms • elite conflicts	• dual economy • failed economic reforms • political stalemate
External factors	• currency speculators	• currency speculators and IMF	
Political Outcomes	• constitutional reform • downfall of Chaovalit Yongchaiyut • relatively peaceful resolution	• political reform • downfall of Suharto • deepening economic and political crises	• regime renamed • cabinet reshuffled • deepening political stalemate

In Burma, there were no external actors involved in responding to the economic crisis. The response of the military government was not to readjust economic policies. Instead, they imposed tough measures aimed at stopping the depreciation of the kyat and foreign exchange certificates

(FECs). These measures included crackdowns on foreign exchange dealers, restricting imports, closing down border checkpoints, and revoking permits for foreign exchange trading.

The main points of similarity and difference in the politics of the economic crises in Thailand, Indonesia and Burma can be found in the Table 9.2.

Globalisation, Domestic Politics and Political Change

How can we make sense of these findings in the broader context of the interrelationship between globalisation, domestic politics and political change? The evidence presented in this book shows that the economic and political changes in these countries resulted from a complex process which involved both external and domestic factors. In this respect, it is worth mentioning the comparative political economy study conducted by Rueschemeyer *et al.* which argues that there is a strong relationship between capitalism and democracy, but this cannot be explained in a simple argument that economic progress necessarily leads to political democracy.[22] Instead, the authors of the study suggest that a democratic political system is a product of the complex economic, social and political changes that are associated with capitalist development, including changes in the balance of power between political groups, the relationship between the state and civil society, and changes in the external or international environment.[23]

This study has argued that the economic reform and boom periods in Thailand, Indonesia, and to a lesser extent, Burma in the 1980s and 1990s, had profound political consequences. This study provides evidence that Thailand and Indonesia experienced different degrees of political change as a consequence of the economic changes put into place. When General Prem implemented economic reforms in the 1980s, he also opened up the Thai political arena which eventually led to democratic elections in 1988, bringing Prime Minister Chatichai Choonhavan to power. The arrival of the Chatichai coalition government brought with it an economic boom period that lasted until 1997. It was during this period that Thai politics changed enormously, with political pluralism becoming a feature of contemporary Thai politics.

The situation of Thailand deserves further attention. The 1990s saw the emergence of "coalition politics", in which political groups often changed and shifted alliances, causing the rise and fall of coalition governments. Thai politics in the 1990s also saw power no longer in the hands of the military, the bureaucracy or political parties, but distributed and shared between many political actors. Although this country experienced a military coup in 1991, parliamentary democracy continued to be upheld as the dominant form in politics in Thailand. This strengthened the influence of elected politicians, and, at the same time, eroded the Thai military and bureaucrats' domination of the decision-making process in Thailand. The most remarkable transformation in Thai politics in the 1990s was arguably the way the consolidation of parliamentary democracy created fertile ground for the birth of the civil society. Autonomous organisations outside the formal political institutions (with memberships of these organisations drawn from among businesspeople, journalists, and academics) as well as NGOs, unions and think tanks were formed, and they exerted considerable influence over national politics. On this issue, Rueschemeyer *et al.*, make the point that the role of civil society is crucial in the progress of democracy. Anek Laothamatas also points out that economic progress cannot itself determine the progress of democracy in the Southeast Asian and East Asian region, but that it arises as " a direct result of the strength of civil society".[24] Therefore, it can be argued that the civil society has already played an important role in not only blocking the return of authoritarianism (through the military coup in 1991), but also in creating a wider coalition through which to strengthen the democratic institutions in Thailand.

By comparison, the political changes which occurred in Indonesia in the 1980s and the 1990s were not as "liberal" as those in Thailand. During the reform and boom period, Suharto's New Order government maintained an authoritarian political system, although it came under increasing pressure into the latter stages. The uncertainty of the political succession, the future role of the Indonesian military, and the weak parliament were stumbling blocks on the path to the establishment of a more representative political system in Indonesia. The evidence in this study shows that pressure for political change grew rapidly in the early 1990s, with the emergence of non-state actors at elite, middle class and grassroots levels. These actors continuously challenged the domination of the New Order government in national politics and called for the establishment of a democratic political system in Indonesia. In Burma, the failure of economic reform was accompanied by continuity in political authoritarianism. The main reason for this is that the Burmese military continued to resist pressure to relinquish power, even after they lost the 1990 general election. The military insistence on maintaining its authoritarian political rule was enforced using military and bureaucratic structures to repress the opposition and resistance groups both inside Burma and along its borders and the country remained relatively isolated within the region.

Based on this evidence, it can be argued that the recent economic crisis brought about different types of political change in these countries. In this respect, Gourevitch points out that the economic crisis creates "political debate and political controversy" which force the government and its leader to respond.[25] However, every country's response is different. Gourevitch writes:

> Economic crises shape countries, but crises also express what is happening within those countries. Both crises and countries change over time, so that relationships change as well. And every country faces each crisis differently.[26]

In Thailand, the economic crisis in 1997 created political tension both within and outside the government, generating growth in the movement for political reform and in the support for a new constitution. As parliamentary democracy and civil society in Thailand had already been strengthened during the 1990s, public debate on strategies to end the economic crisis was very broad. The involvement of the Thai public in this relatively peaceful political process was remarkable in the sense that both state and non-state actors were involved in influencing the decision-making process. As a result the political elite and the public came to a broad consensus in favour of removing Chaovalit's government as a precondition to restoring domestic and international confidence in the Thai economy. In November 1997 the Chuan coalition government took over and embarked upon the task of ending the economic crisis in Thailand.

In Indonesia, there is evidence that the economic crisis opened up public debate on the need for further economic and political reform. As a result of this debate, there arose a broad-based coalition of former government officers, political elites, academics, religious leaders, non-government organisations and students; all of whom called for political change. In contrast to Thailand, the events that led to the downfall of President Suharto were marked by political struggles which deepened the economic and political crises in Indonesia. This was due to the fact that at the beginning there was no clear consensus between political leaders and the Indonesian public on strategies to end the economic crisis. The opposition groups were weak and failed to come up with alternative strategies for rebuilding the Indonesian economy. Therefore, the main factor forcing President Suharto to resign was the loss of support from the political and military elites surrounding him. In May 1998, Suharto's protégé, B. J. Habibie, was appointed the new President and faced the task of restoring the economy and addressing the political crisis in Indonesia.[27] In Burma, the economic crisis created further economic downturn as the economy had already been in trouble and the country was in the grip of political crisis. The deterioration of the economy widened the political gap between the military government and the NLD, as the former contemplated disassociating the Burmese economy from the regional and international economies, while the latter advocated far-reaching economic reform as a precondition for improving the economy. Although the economic crisis did not force the downfall of General Than Shwe, it caused the military government to rename itself and to reshuffle the cabinet several times. More importantly, the economic crisis also meant that political uncertainty continued to overshadow Burmese politics throughout 1998.

If we return to Reuchemeyer's argument: changes in the international arena are important factors in the process of the establishment of democracy, it is relevant then to draw on the evidence of this presented in this study. Globalisation has not occurred in "a vacuum" and it has implications for any country, in economic and social policy debates, and even in politics.[28] Therefore, it is clear that the economic crises which occurred in Thailand, Indonesia and Burma in 1997 and 1998 were a result of globalisation in the region. However, it can be argued that differences in the domestic political economies of the three countries meant each country responded to the process of globalisation in a different way. It can be suggested that for Thailand, Indonesia and Burma, globalisation has created a "window of opportunity" in the sense that they have been pushed to engage with economic and political change.[29] As this study shows, Thailand proved able to take up this opportunity, while Indonesia and Burma are still coming to grips with it. The experiences of reforming the economy in the 1980s, and managing the economic boom of the 1990s, together with the relative maturity of parliamentary democracy and political leaders in dealing with the crisis and the stronger civil society, put Thailand in a better position to handle the impact of globalisation.

The progress that Thailand achieved in its domestic political economy in the 1980s meant this country could use the experience of the economic crisis as a learning process in many areas. Despite the fact that the economic crisis caused not only economic difficulties but also human misery, the Thai economic crisis also gave this country a new opportunity to reform its economic and political sectors.[30] The change of political leaders, and the arrival of a new economic team led by the Finance Minister Dr. Tarrin Nimmanhaeminda and Dr. Supachai Panitchpakdee, successfully restored confidence in the Thai economy. The crisis also convinced the Thai public of the need to continue the efforts to reform Thai politics, institutions of governance, and overall economic policies. Although the success of the Chuan coalition government in ending the economic crisis was still not certain in late 1998, it was widely accepted that the Thai economy was in much better shape than in the previous year.[31]

Although Indonesia reformed its economy in the 1980s and enjoyed an economic boom in the early 1990s, the failure of Suharto to reform his authoritarian political system, combined with the weakness of civil society and the inability of non-state actors to create political change, resulted in Indonesia experiencing much more difficulty in dealing with the impact of globalisation. Slow progress in reforming the domestic political economy during the 1980s and 1990s meant this country suffered more than Thailand during the economic crisis period in 1997 and 1998. In contrast to the Thai case, the change in political leadership from Suharto to B. J. Habibie eased the political tension in Indonesia, but did not resolve the economic and political crises. In 1998 the economy was in contraction, while the pressure for political reform continued to have broad support from the Indonesian public. There were indications that the Indonesian economy had begun to recover in the last quarter of 1998, with the rupiah more stable and the real economy experiencing modest growth.[32] However, political uncertainty was the main obstacle to the recovery of the Indonesian economy.[33] Political reform had become the key factor in restoring the confidence of domestic and international economic actors. In this respect, the failure of Burma to undertake adequate reforms in both the economic and political arenas in the 1980s and 1990s, arguably put this country in the worst position to deal with the economic crisis. The continuing economic deterioration and political stalemate in Burma made it very difficult for the military government and the opposition to reach a political settlement that could place Burma in a stronger position to deal with the economic and political crises which assailed it.

Against this backdrop, it is clear that the strengthening of democratic institutions and civil society had helped Thailand to be more responsive and adaptable to the economic crisis of 1997/98. Indonesia's efforts to deal with it were hampered by the unworkable and undemocratic nature of Suharto's New Order political system and the weak civil society. Burma also faced serious economic and political crisis simultaneously. The effect of decades of isolation from the global economy and community were clearly seen in the lack of any civil society structures and the ability of the regime to increase its level of authoritarianism rather than be forced to respond to the calls for change. The rapid economic and political change that occurred in these countries must be seen in the context of the globalisation that took place in the Asian region during the 1990s. The integration of Thailand and Indonesia, and, by association, Burma, into the world economy made them more vulnerable to external change and, at the same time, it changed the course of domestic politics in these countries.

Finally, how can we make sense of these findings in the context of current intellectual debates on the post-Asian crisis? A lot has been written on the causes and consequences of the crisis, but there are some important points worth reiterating.[34] First of all, this study has confirmed the arguments put forward by Asian specialists that the Asian crisis has indeed rocked the economic and political structures of the Asian region. Although there had been efforts to address the consequences of the crisis by restructuring and reforming the domestic economic and political institutions of the affected countries, there is a consensus that the Asian crisis was a crisis of Asian capitalism which in many ways was also a symbol of the crisis of the global capitalism.[35] This study has emphasised the importance of the configuration of domestic factors in the way in which an individual country responded to the crisis. The crisis exposed the real picture of domestic economy and politics. In this respect, the crisis pressured political leaders and policy makers to reconcile their efforts to find domestic resources and external assistance to bring about economic recovery in countries such as Indonesia and Thailand.[36] This study also has reaffirmed the critical examination of the economic development and political strategies adopted by the affected Asian countries in particular and the Asian region in general. Economic strategies that relied heavily on foreign capital proved unsustainable in the long-term. Some scholars argue for the need to establish the so-called "post-Washington consensus" or a "new Asian miracle", incorporating people-centred economic strategies in a larger economic and political framework for the post-crisis period.[37] The study also has underlined the problematic nature of the external supports in influencing economic and political developments in the affected countries. The crisis increased the anti-Western sentiments and it has brought about the need to re-examine the roles of multilateral institutions such as the IMF and the World Bank which, in many ways, worsened the Asian crisis.[38] There are good reasons for reforming those institutions giving a more even balance of power between the Western industrial countries as the lenders and the developing countries as the borrowers.[39] The need to reassess the benefits of globalisation for the Asian region as a whole has also been raised. Although overall many countries suffered from the economic crisis, a few managed to use the crisis as a step towards deepening their economies. As far as this study is concerned, it can be argued that globalisation has brought both crisis and opportunity to these countries. The manner in which they have been able to take up the challenges presented by globalisation is determined by the unique combination of domestic and external factors affecting each country. Indeed, the diversity of the Asian region has shaped the way in which the Asian countries responded to the crisis.

Notes

[1] Compared to research on the East Asian political economy, studies on the comparative political economy of the Southeast Asian countries are still limited in numbers. A few scholars are just beginning to explore this kind of research. A few of them, for instance, Richard Doner, "Approaches to the Politics of Economic Growth in Southeast Asia", *Journal of Asian Studies*, vol. 50, no. 4 (November 1991), pp. 818-849; Andrew MacIntyre, "Indonesia, Thailand and the Northeast Asian Connection" in Richard Higgott, Richard Leaver and John Ravenhill (eds.) *Pacific Economic Relations in the 1990s* (Sydney: Allen and Unwin, 1993), pp. 250-270; and also Arief Budiman, *Negara dan Pembangunan, Studi tentang Indonesia dan Korea* Selatan [State and Development, A Study on Indonesia and South Korea] (Jakarta: Yayasan Padi dan Kapas, 1991).

[2] MacIntyre, p. 260.

[3] Robert Taylor, *The State of Burma* (Honolulu: The University of Hawaii Press, 1987), p. 297.

[4] The importance of this issue was mentioned in a recent study conducted by Alasdair Bowie and Danny Unger, *The Politics of Open Economies, Indonesia, Malaysia, the Philippines, and Thailand* (Cambridge: Cambridge University Press, 1997), pp. 185-186.

[5] For an interesting comparison of the role of the ethnic Chinese in Southeast Asia, see Jamie Mackie's, "Business Success Among Southeast Asian Chinese, The Role of Culture, Values, and Social Structure", in Robert W. Hefner (ed.) *Market Cultures, Society and Morality in the New Asian Capitalism* (Boulder: Westview, 1998), pp. 129-146.

[6] Further discussion on this issue can be found in Eric A. Nodlinger, *Soldier in Politics: Military Coup and Governments* (New Jersey: Prentice Hall, 1977).

[7] For further discussion on the comparison of state capacity, see Stephan Haggard, "Business, Politics and Policy in Northeast and Southeast Asia" in Andrew MacIntyre (ed.) *Business and Government in Industrialising Asia* (Sydney: Allen and Unwin, 1994), pp. 268-301.

[8] Anek Laothamatas, "From Clientelism to Partnership: Business-Government Relations in Thailand" in Andrew MacIntyre (ed.) *Business and Government in Industrialising Asia* (Sydney: Allen and Unwin, 1994), pp. 195-215.

[9] MacIntyre, "Indonesia, Thailand and the Northeast Asian Connection", p. 258.

[10] Andrew MacIntyre, "Politics and the Reorientation of Economic Policy in Indonesia" in Andrew MacIntyre and Kanishka Jayasuriya (eds.) *The Dynamics of Economic Policy Reform in South-east Asian and the South-west Pacific* (Singapore: Oxford University Press, 1992), p. 142; Richard Robison, "Politics and Markets in Indonesia's Post-oil Era" in Garry Rodan, Kevin Hewison and

Richard Robison (eds.) *The Political Economy of South-East Asia* (Melbourne: Oxford University Press, 1997), p. 33.

[11] Andrew MacIntyre, "Power, Prosperity and Patrimonialism: Business and Government in Indonesia" in Andrew MacIntyre (ed.) *Business and Government in Industrialising Asia* (Sydney: Allen and Unwin, 1994), pp. 244-267.

[12] This has been examined extensively in, Myat Thein and Mya Than, "Transitional Economy of Myanmar: Performance, Issues, and Problems" in Seiji F. Naya and Joseph L. H. Tan (eds.) *Asian Transitional Economies, Challenges and Prospects for Reform and Transformation* (Singapore: Institute of Southeast Asian Studies, 1995), pp. 210-261.

[13] John Williamson, "In Search of a Manual for Technopols" in John Williamson (ed.) *The Political Economy of Policy Reform* (Washington D.C.: Institute for International Economics, 1994), pp. 26-28.

[14] See "Pengembangan Tehnologi Canggih" [The Development of High-Tech] in B. J. Habibie, *Ilmu Pengetahuan, Tehnologi and Pembangunan Bangsa* [Science, Technology and Nation Building] (Jakarta: Center for Information and Development Studies, 1995), pp. 89-125.

[15] Jamie Mackie, "Economic Growth in the Asean Region: The Political Underpinnings" in Helen Hughes (ed.) *Achieving Industrialisation in East Asia* (Cambridge: Cambridge University Press, 1988), p. 293.

[16] Richard Doner, *Driving a Bargain, Automobile Industrialisation and Japanese Firms in Southeast Asia* (Berkeley: University of California Press, 1991), pp. 242.

[17] Surin Maisrikrod, "The Making of Thai Democracy, A Study of Political Alliances among the State, the Capitalists, and the Middle Class" in Anek Laothamatas (ed.) *Democratisation in Southeast and East Asia* (Singapore: Institute of Southeast Asian Studies, 1997), pp. 155-156.

[18] Vedi R. Hadiz, *Workers and the State in New Order Indonesia* (London and New York: Routledge, 1997), especially chapter four.

[19] An interesting discussion on this issue can be found in Mary Ann Haley, "Emerging Market Makers: The Power of Institutional Investors" in Leslie Elliot Armijo (ed.) *Financial Globalisation and Democracy in Emerging Markets* (London: Macmillan, 1999), pp. 74-90.

[20] For a critical examination of the role of the IMF in the affected countries in the region, see Nicola Bullard *et al.*, "Taming the Tigers: the IMF and the Asian Crisis", *Third World Quarterly*, vol. 19, no. 3 (1998), pp. 505-555.

[21] Ross McLeod, "Indonesia" in Ross McLeod and Ross Garnaut (eds.) *East Asia in Crisis, From Being a Miracle to Needing One?* (London and New York: Routledge, 1998), pp. 40-41.

[22] D. Rueschemeyer, E. H. Stephens, and J. D. Stephens, *Capitalist Development and Democracy* (Cambridge: Polity Press, 1992).

[23] Ibid, pp. 6-8.

[24] Anek Laothamatas, "Development and Democratisation, A Theoretical Introduction with Reference to the Southeast Asian and East Asian Cases" in

Democratisation in Southeast and East Asia (Singapore: Institute of Southeast Asian Studies, 1997), p. 17.

[25] Peter Gourevitch, *Politics in Hard Times, Comparative Responses to International Economic Crises* (Ithaca: Cornell University, 1986), p. 19.

[26] Ibid, p. 221.

[27] There has been an upsurge of analyses following the downfall of Suharto in May 1998. For instance, see Edward Aspinal, Herb Feith and Gerry van Klinken (eds.) *The Last Days of President Suharto* (Clayton: Monash Asia Institute, Monash University, 1999); Arief Budiman, Barbara Hatley and Damien Kingsbury (eds.), *Reformasi, Crisis and Change in Indonesia* (Clayton: Monash Asia Institute, Monash University, 1999); and also Musa Kashim (ed.) *Menuju Indonesia Baru: Menggagas Reformasi Total* [Towards a New Indonesia: Arguing for Total Reformation] (Bandung: Pustakan Hidayah, 1998).

[28] Dani Rodrik, *Has Globalisation Gone Too Far?* (Washington D.C.: Institute for International Economics, 1997), pp. 69-85.

[29] This point made by Jeffrey Garten, "Lessons for the Next Financial Crisis", *Foreign Affairs*, vol. 78, no. 2 (March-April 1999), pp. 76-92.

[30] Walden Bello, Shea Cunningham and Li Kheng Poh, *A Siamese Tragedy, Development and Disintegration in Modern Thailand* (London and New York: Zed Books, 1998).

[31] Suchitra Punyaratabandhu, "Thailand in 1998, A False Sense of Recovery", *Asian Survey*, vol. xxxix, no. 1 (January-February 1999), pp. 80-88.

[32] Badan Pusat Statistik, *Ringkasan Statistik Ekonomi Makro* [A Summary of Macro Economic Statistic], no., 8 (31 December 1998); and also Bank Indonesia, *Monetary Policy Review*, Economic Research and Monetary Policy Department (November 1998).

[33] Judith Bird, "Indonesia in 1998, The Pot Boils Over", *Asian Survey*, vol. xxxix, no. 1 (January-February 1999), pp. 27-37.

[34] The recent debates on the Asian crisis can be found in, for instance, T. J. Pempel (ed.) *Politics of the Asian Crisis* (Ithaca and London: Cornell University Press, 1999); Karl D. Jackson (ed.) *The Causes and Consequences of a Financial Crisis* (Singapore: Institute of Southeast Asian Studies, 1999); William C. Hunter, George G. Kaufman and Thomas H. Krueger (eds.) *The Asian Financial Crisis: Origins, Implications, and Solutions* (Boston: Kluwer Academic, 1999); Gregory W. Noble and John Ravenhill (eds.) *The Asian Financial Crisis and the Architecture of Global Finance* (New York: Cambridge University Press, 2000); Richard Robison, Mark Beeson, Kanishka Jayasuriya and Hyuk-Rae Kim (eds) *Politics and Markets in the Wake of the Asian Crisis* (London and New York: Routledge, 2000); and Tran Van Hoa (ed.) *The Asia Crisis: The Cures, Their Effectiveness and the Prospects After* (New York: St. Martin's Press, 2000).

[35] See Mark Beeson and Richard Robison, "Introduction, Interpreting the Crisis" in *Politics and Markets in the Wake of the Asian Crisis* (London and New York: Routledge, 2000), pp. 3-24.

[36] Kevin Hewison, *Nationalism, Populism, Dependency: Old Ideas for a New Southeast Asia?*, Working Paper Series no. 4 (May 2001).

[37] Stephan Haggard, *The Political Economy of the Asian Financial Crisis* (Washington D.C.: Institute for International Economics, 2000), especially chapter six; and also Kanishka Jayasuriya and Andrew Rosser, "Economic Orthodoxy and the East Asian Crisis", *Third World Quarterly*, vol. 22, no. 3 (2001), pp. 381-396.

[38] See Richard Higgott, "The International Relations of the Asia Economic Crisis: A Study in the Politics of Resentment" in Richard Robison, Mark Beeson, Kanishka Jayasuriya and Hyuk-Rae Kim (eds.) *Politics and Markets in the Wake of the Asian Crisis* (London and New York: Routledge, 2000), pp. 261-282.

[39] Robert Wade, "Showdown at the World Bank", *New Left Review*, no. 7 (January-February, 2001), pp. 124-137.

Bibliography

Books, Articles in Books and Academic Journals, Unpublished Papers, Theses and Documents

Abimanyu, Anggito, "Recent Economic Events in Indonesia: From Rapid Economic Growth to National Car Policy" in Gavin W. Jones and Terence H. Hull (eds.) *Indonesia Assessment 1996, Population and Human Resources* (Singapore and Canberra: Institute of Southeast Asian Studies and Research School of Pacific and Asian Studies, Australian National University, 1997), pp. 39-56.

Adas, Michael, *The Burma Delta: Economic Development and Social Change in An Asian Rice Frontier, 1852-1941* (Madison: University of Wisconsin Press, 1974).

Akira, Suehiro, *Capital Accumulation in Thailand, 1885-1985* (Tokyo: The Centre of East Asian Cultural Studies, 1989).

Alamgir, Jalal, "Against the Current: The Survival of Authoritarianism in Burma", *Pacific Affairs*, vol. 70, no. 3 (Fall 1997), pp. 333-350.

Allen, Roy E., *Financial Crises and Recession in the Global Economy* (Aldershot: Edward Elgar, 1994).

Ammar Siamwalla, "Can a Developing Democracy Manage Its Macroeconomy? The Case of Thailand" in Ammar Siamwalla (ed.) *Thailand's Boom and Bust* (Bangkok: Thailand Development Research Institute, 1997), pp. 63-75.

Amsden, Alice, *Asia's Next Giant: South Korea and Late Industrialization* (New York: Oxford University Press, 1989).

--- , J. Kochanowicz, and L. Taylor (eds.) *The Markets Meets Its Match: Restructuring the Economics of Eastern Europe* (Cambridge, Mass.: Harvard University Press, 1994).

Ananya Bhuchongkul, "Thailand in 1991, The Return of the Military", *Southeast Asian Affairs 1992* (Singapore: Institute of Southeast Asian Studies, 1992), pp. 313-333.

Anderson, Benedict, *Imagined Communities, Reflections on the Origin and Spread of Nationalism*, revised edition (London and New York: Verso, 1991).

--- , "Murder and Progress in Modern Siam" in *The Spectre of Comparisons, Nationalism, Southeast Asia and the World* (London and New York: Verso, 1998), pp. 174-191.

--- , "Cacique Democracy in the Philippines" in *The Spectre of Comparisons, Nationalism, Southeast Asia and the World* (London and New York: Verso, 1998), pp. 192-226.

--- and Ruth McVey, *A Preliminary Analysis of the October 1, 1965 Coup in Indonesia* (Ithaca: Cornell Modern Indonesia Project, Cornell University, 1971).

Anek Laothamatas, *Business Associations and the New Political Economy of Thailand, From Bureaucratic Polity to Liberal Corporatism* (Boulder: Westview Press, 1991).

--- , "The Politics of Structural Adjustment in Thailand: A Political Explanation of Economic Success" in Andrew MacIntyre and Kanishka Jayasuriya (eds.) *The Dynamics of Economic Policy Reform in South-east Asia and the South-west Pacific* (Singapore: Oxford University Press, 1992), pp. 32-49.

--- , "From Clientelism to Partnership: Business-Government Relations in Thailand" in Andrew MacIntyre (ed.) *Business and Government in Industrialising Asia* (Sydney: Allen and Unwin, 1994), pp. 244-267.

--- , "A Tale of Two Democracies: Conflicting Perceptions of Elections and Democracy in Thailand" in Robert H. Taylor (ed.) *The Politics of Elections in Southeast Asia* (New York and Melbourne: The Woodrow Wilson Center Press and Cambridge University Press, 1996), pp. 201-223.

--- , "Development and Democratization, A Theoretical Introduction with Reference to the Southeast Asian and East Asian Cases" in *Democratization in Southeast and East Asia* (Singapore: Institute of Southeast Asian Studies, 1997), pp. 1-20.

--- (ed.) *Democratization in Southeast and East Asia* (Singapore: Institute of Southeast Asian Studies, 1997).

Asia Pacific Economics Group, *Asia Pacific Profiles 1998, Overview* (Singapore: Financial Times, 1998).

Asia Year Book 1991 (Hongkong: Far Eastern Economic Review Publisher, 1991).

Asfar, Muhammad, "Kekerasan Politik dan Demokrasi di Seputar Pemilu 1997" [Political Violence and Democracy around the 1997 General Election], *Prisma*, no. 1 (1998), pp. 17-31.

Aspinall, Edward, "The Broadening Base of Political Opposition in Indonesia" in Garry Rodan (ed.) *Political Oppositions in Industrialising Asia* (London and New York: Routledge, 1996), pp. 215-240.

--- , Herb Feith and Gerry van Klinken (eds.) *The Last Days of President Suharto* (Clayton: Monash Asia Institute, Monash University, 1999).

Aung San Suu Kyi, "Towards a True Refuge", a paper delivered by Dr. Michael Aris at *the Eighth Joyce Pearce Memorial Lecture*, the University of Oxford, England, 19 May 1993.

Aung-Thwin, Michael, "The Role of Sasana Reform in Burmese History: Economic Dimensions of a Religious Purification", *Journal of Asian Studies*, vol. xxxviii, no. 4 (August 1979), pp. 671-688.

--- , "The British 'Pacification' of Burma: Order Without Meaning", *Journal of Southeast Asian Studies*, vol. xvi, no. 2 (September 1985), pp. 245-261.

--- , *Pagan: The Origins of Modern Burma* (Honolulu: University of Hawaii Press, 1985).

Azis, Iwan J., "Indonesia" in John Williamson (ed.) *The Political Economy of Policy Reform* (Washington D.C.: Institute for International Economics, 1994), pp. 385-416.

Badan Pusat Statistik, *Ringkasan Statistik Ekonomi Makro* [Indonesian Macro Economic Statistics], no. 8 (31 December 1998).

Bandyopadhaya, K., *Burma and Indonesia: Comparative Political Economy and Foreign Policy* (New Delhi and Madras: South Asia Publishers, 1983).

Bangkok Bank Monthly Review (published by Bangkok Bank), 1997.

Bank Indonesia, *Monetary Policy Review*, Economic Research and Monetary Policy Department (November 1998).

Bank of Thailand, "Analysing Thailand's Current Account Deficit", *Bank of Thailand Economic Focus*, vol. 1, no. 1 (January-March 1996).

--- , "Analysing Thailand's Short-Term Debt", *Bank of Thailand Economic Focus*, vol. 1, no. 3 (July-September 1996).

--- *Annual Economic Report 1996* (Bangkok: Bank of Thailand, 1997).

Basri, M. Chatib, "Indonesia: The Political Economy of Policy Reform" in Arief Budiman, Barbara Hatley and Damien Kingsbury (eds.) *Reformasi, Crisis and Change in Indonesia* (Clayton: Monash Asia Institute, Monash University, 1999), pp. 27-37.

Bates, Robert H. and Anne O. Krueger (eds.) *Political and Economic Interactions in Economic Policy Reform* (Cambridge: Blackwell Publishers, 1993).

Batson, Benjamin A., *The End of Absolute Monarchy in Siam* (Singapore: Oxford University Press, 1984.

Bell, Stephen, *Ungoverning the Economy, The Political Economy of Australian Economic Policy* (Melbourne: Oxford University Press, 1997).

--- , "Globalisation, Neoliberalism and the Transformation of the Australian State", *Australian Journal of Political Science*, vol. 32, no. 3 (November 1997), pp. 345-367.

Bellasa, Bella, *The Newly Industrialising Countries in the World Economy* (New York: Pergamon, 1981).

Bello, Walden, *Addicted to Capital: The Ten-Year High and Present-Day, Withdrawal Trauma of Southeast Asia's Economies*, mimeograph (Manila and Bangkok: The Philippine Center for Policy Studies, Focus on the Global South, and the Campaign Against Poverty 2000, 1997).

--- and Stephanie Resenfeld, *Dragons in Distress: Asia's Miracle Economies in Crisis* (London: Penguin, 1992).

--- , Shea Cunningham, and Li Kheng Poh, *A Siamese Tragedy, Development and Disintegration in Modern Thailand* (London and New York: Zed Books, 1998).

Bhagwati, Jagdish, *Foreign Trade Regimes and Economic Development: Anatomy and Consequences of Exchange Control Regimes* (Cambridge: Ballinger, 1978).

--- , "The Capital Myth, the Difference between Trade Widgets and Dollars", *Foreign Affairs*, vol. 77, no. 3 (May/June 1998), pp. 7-12.

Bhattacharya, Amar and Mari Pangestu, *Indonesia, Development Transformation and Public Policy* (Washington D.C.: The World Bank, 1993).

Bird, Judith, "Indonesia in 1997, The Tinderbox Year", *Asian Survey*, vol. 38, no. 2 (February 1998), pp. 168-176.

--- , "Indonesia in 1998, The Pot Boils Over", *Asian Survey*, vol. xxxix, no. 1 (January-February 1999), pp. 27-37.

Boucaud, Andre and Louis, *Burma's Golden Tringle, On the Trails of the Opium Warlords*, revised edition (Bangkok: Asia Books, 1992).

Bowie, Alasdair and Danny Unger, *The Politics of Open Economies, Indonesia, Malaysia, the Philippines and Thailand* (Cambridge and Melbourne: Cambridge University Press, 1997).

Bray, John, "Burma: Resisting the International Community", *The Pacific Review*, vol. 5, no. 3 (1992), pp. 291-296.

Bresnan, John, *Managing Indonesia, The Modern Political Economy* (New York: Columbia University Press, 1993).

Brown, Colin, "Political Developments, 1990-91" in Hal Hill (ed.) *Indonesia Assessment 1991* (Canberra: Department of Political and Social Change, Research School of Pacific Studies, Australian National University, 1991), pp. 38-52.

Brown, Ian, *The Elite and the Economy in Siam, c. 1890-1920* (Singapore: Oxford University Press, 1988).

Brown, Robin, "Globalisation and the End of the National Project" in Andrew Linklater and John MacMillan (eds.) *Boundaries in Question: New Directions in International Relations* (London: Pinter, 1995), pp. 54-68.

Budiman, Arief, "Introduction: From Conference to a Book" in Arief Budiman (ed.) *State and Civil Society in Indonesia* (Clayton: Centre of Southeast Asian Studies, Monash University, 1990), pp. 1-14.

--- , *Negara dan Pembangunan, Studi tentang Indonesia dan Korea Selatan* [State and Development, A Study on Indonesia and South Korea] (Jakarta: Yayasan Padi dan Kapas, 1991).

--- , "Indonesian Politics in the 1990s" in Harold Crouch and Hal Hill (eds.) *Indonesia Assessment 1992, Political Perspectives on the 1990s* (Canberra: Department of Political and Social Change, Research School of Pacific Studies, Australian National University, 1992), pp. 130-139.

--- , Barbara Hatley and Damien Kingsbury (eds.) *Reformasi, Crisis and Change in Indonesia* (Clayton: Monash Asia Institute, Monash University, 1999).

Bullard, Nicola *et al.*, "Taming the Tigers: the IMF and the Asian Crisis", *Third World Quarterly*, vol. 19, no. 3 (1998), pp. 505-555.

Cady, John F., *A History of Modern Burma* (Ithaca: Cornell University Press, 1960).

Callahan, Mary P., "Burma in 1994, New Dragon or Still Dragging?", *Asian Survey*, vol. xxxv, no. 2 (February 1995), pp. 201-208.

--- , "Burma in 1995, Looking Beyond the Release of Aung San Suu Kyi", *Asian Survey*, vol. xxxvi, no. 2 (February 1996), pp. 158-164.

Caouette, Therese, "Burmese Refugees in Thailand", a paper presented at *the Burma (Myanmar): Challenges and Opportunities for the 1990s Conference*, organised by FCO/ASIAN Studies Centre Conference, Oxford, England, 13-15 December 1991.

Carey, Peter, *From Burma to Myanmar: Military Rule and the Struggle for Democracy* (London: Research Institute for the Study of Conflict and Terrorism, 1998).

Catley, Bob, *Globalising Australian Capitalism* (Cambridge: Cambridge University Press, 1996).

--- , "Hegemonic America: The Arrogance of Power", *Contemporary Southeast Asia*, vol. 21, no. 2 (August 1999), pp. 157-175.

--- and Priyambudi Sulistiyanto, "The 1998 Indonesian Crisis and Australia's Strategic Interests", *Current Affairs Bulletin*, vol. 75, no. 1 (June-July, 1998), pp. 11-20.

Central Statistical Organization, *Selected Monthly Economic Indicators* (Yangon: Ministry of National Planning and Economic Development, July-August 1997).

Chai-anan Samudavanija, *The Thai Young Turks* (Singapore: Institute of Southeast Asian Studies, 1982).

--- , "Thailand: Economic Policy-Making in a Liberal Technocratic Polity" in John W. Langford and K. Lorne Brownsey (eds.) *Economic Policy-Making in the Asia-Pacific Region* (Halifax: The Institute for Research on Public Policy, 1990), pp. 181-202.

--- , "Old Soldiers Never Die, They are just Bypassed: The Military, Bureaucract and Globalisation" in Kevin Hewison (ed.) *Political Change in Thailand, Democracy and Participation* (London and New York: Routledge, 1997), pp. 42-57.

--- and Sukhumband Paribatra, "Thailand: Liberalization without Democracy" in James W. Morley (ed.) *Driven by Growth, Political Change in the Asia-Pacific Region* (London and New York: M. E. Sharpe, 1993), pp. 119-141.

Chao-Tzang Yawnghwe, *Ne Win's Tatmadaw Dictatorship*, MA thesis, The University of British Columbia, 1990.

--- , "Burma, The Depoliticization of Political" in Muthiah Alagappa (ed.) *Political Legitimacy in Southeast Asia; the Quest for Moral Authority* (Stanford: Stanford University Press, 1995), pp. 170-192.

Chalmers, Ian, "Introduction" in Ian Chalmers and Vedi R. Hadiz (eds.) *The Politics of Economic Development in Indonesia, Contending Perspectives* (London and New Zealand: Routledge, 1997), pp. 1-35.

Chang, H. J., *The Political Economy of Industrial Policy* (London: St. Martin's Press, 1994).

Chattip Nartsupha, Suthy Prasartset and Montri Chenvidyakarn, *The Political Economy of Siam, 1910-1932* (Bangkok: The Social Science Association of Thailand, 1981).

Chew, Ernest C.T., "The Fall of the Burmese Kingdom in 1885: Review and Reconsideration", *Journal of Southeast Asian Studies*, vol. x, no. 2 (September 1979), pp. 372-380.

Chowdhury, Anis and Iyanatul Islam, *The Newly Industrialising Economies of East Asia* (London and New York: Routledge, 1993).

Christensen, Scott R., *Coalitions and Collective Choice: The Politics of Institutional Change in Thai Agriculture*, Ph.D thesis, The University of Wisconsin, Madison, 1993.

Chu, Yun-han, *Authoritarian Regime under Stress: The Political Economy of Adjustment in the East Asian Newly Industrializing Countries*, Ph.D thesis, University of Minnesota, 1987.

Cole, David D. and Betty F. Slade, *Building a Modern Financial System, The Indonesian Experience* (Cambridge: Cambridge University Press, 1996).

Cook, Paul and Martin Minogue, "Economic Reform and Political Change in Myanmar (Burma)", *World Development*, vol. 21, no. 7 (1993), pp. 1151-1161.

--- , " Economic Reform and Political Conditionality on Myanmar" in Peter Carey (ed.) *Burma, The Challenge of Change in a Divided Society* (London: Macmillan, 1997), pp. 183-208.

Corder, Max, *The Asian Crisis, Is there a Way Out?* (Singapore: Institute of Southeast Asian Studies, 1999).

Cox, Robert, "Civil Society at the Turn of the Millennium: Prospects for an Alternative World Order", *Review of International Studies*, vol. 25, no. 1 (January 1999), pp. 3-28.

Cribb, Robert (ed.) *The Indonesian Killings of 1965-1966: Studies from Java and Bali* (Clayton: Monash University Centre of Southeast Asian Studies, 1990).

Crouch, Harold, *The Army and Politics in Indonesia* (Ithaca: Cornell University Press, 1978).

--- , "An Ageing President, An Ageing Regime" in Harold Crouch and Hal Hill (eds.) *Indonesia Assessment 1992, Political Perspectives on the 1990s* (Canberra: Department of Political and Social Change, Research School of Pacific Studies, Australian National University, 1992), pp. 43-62.

--- , "Masalah Dwifungsi ABRI" [On the Dwifungsi of the ABRI] in Syamsuddin Haris and Riza Sihbudi (eds.) *Menelaah Kembali Format Politik Orde Baru* [Rethinking on the Political Format of the New Order] (Jakarta: Gramedia Pustaka Utama, 1996), pp. 97-114.

--- and Hal Hill (eds.) *Indonesia Assessment 1992, Political Perspectives on the 1990s* (Canberra: Department of Political and Social Change, Research School of Pacific Studies, Australian National University, 1992).

Dapice, David, "Development Prospects for Burma, Cycles and Trends" in Robert I. Rotberg (ed.) *Burma, Prospects for a Democratic Future* (Washington D.C.: Brookings Institution Press, 1998), pp. 153-164.

Deyo, Frederic C. (ed.) *The Political Economy of the New Asian Industrialism* (Ithaca and London: Cornell University Press, 1987).

--- (ed.) *Beneath the Miracle: Labour Subordination in the New Asian Industrialism* (Berkeley: University of California Press, 1989).

Dickens, Paul, *Global Shift, The Internationalisation of Economic Activity*, 2nd Edition (London: Paul Chapman Publishing, 1992).

Diller, Janelle M., "Constitutional Reform in a Repressive State: The Case of Burma", *Asian Survey*, vol. xxxiii, no. 4 (April 1993), pp. 393-407.

--- , "The National Convention: An Impediment to the Restoration of Democracy" in Peter Carey (ed.) *Burma, The Challenge of Change in a Divided Society* (London: Macmillan, 1997), pp. 27-54.

Doner, Richard, *Driving a Bargain, Automobile Industrialisation and Japanese Firms in Southeast Asia* (Berkeley: University of California Press, 1991).

--- , "Approaches to the Politics of Economic Growth in Southeast Asia", *Journal of Asian Studies*, vol. 50, no. 4 (November 1991), pp. 818-849.

--- and Daniel Unger, "The Politics of Finance in Thai Economic Development" in Stephan Haggard, Chung H. Lee and Sylvia Maxfield (eds.) *The Politics of Finance in Developing Countries* (Ithaca and London: Cornell University Press, 1993), pp. 93-122.

Dutt, Amitava K. and Kwan S. Kim, *The States, Markets and Development, Beyond the Neoclassical Dichotomy* (Aldershot and Brookfield: Edward Elgar, 1994).

Eldridge, Philip, "Non-government Organizations, the State, and Democratization in Indonesia" in Jim Schiller and Barbara Martin-Schiller (eds.) *Imagining Indonesia, Cultural Politics and Political Culture* (Athens: Ohio University Center for International Studies, 1997), pp. 198-228.

Elliot, David L., *Thailand: Origins of Military Rule* (London: Zed Press Ltd., 1978).

Emmerson, Donald K., "Exit and Aftermath: The Crisis of 1997-98", in Donald K. Emmerson (ed.) *Indonesia Beyond Suharto* (Armonk and London: M. E. Sharpe, 1999), pp. 295-343.

Evans, Peter, "The State as Problem and Solution: Predation, Embedded Autonomy, and Structural Change" in Stephan Haggard and Robert R. Kaufman (eds.) *The Politics of Economic Adjustment, International Constraints, Distributive Conflicts, and the State* (Princeton: Princeton University Press, 1992), pp. 139-181.

Feith, Herbert, *The Decline of Constitutional Democracy in Indonesia* (Ithaca: Cornell University Press, 1962).

Felker, Greg, "Malaysia in 1998, A Cornered Tiger Bares Its Claws", *Asian Survey*, vol. xxxix, no. 1 (January-February 1999), pp. 43-54.

Forrester, Geoff, "Towards March 1998, With Determination" in Hal Hill and Thee Kian Wie (eds.) *Indonesia's Technological Challenge* (Singapore and Canberra: Institute of Southeast Asian Studies and Research School of Pacific and Asian Studies, Australian National University, 1998), pp. 55-73.

--- and R. J. May (eds) *The Fall of Soeharto* (Bathrust: Crawford House Publishing, 1999).

Furnival, J. S., *Colonial Policy and Practice: A Comparative Study of Burma and Netherlands India* (New York: New York University Press, 1947).

Garnaut, Ross, "The Financial Crisis: A Watershead in Economic Thought about East Asia", *Asian Pacific Economic Literature*, vol. 12, no. 1 (May 1998), pp. 1-11.

Garran, Robert, *Tigers Tamed, The End of the Asian Miracle* (Sydney: Allen and Unwin, 1998).

Garten, Jeffrey E., "Lessons for the Next Financial Crisis", *Foreign Affairs*, vol. 78, no. 2 (March-April 1999), pp. 76-92.

Gerschenkorn, Alexander, *Economic Backwardness in Historical Perspective* (Cambridge, Mass.: Harvard University Press, 1962).

Gills, Barry and George Philip, "Toward Convergence in Development Policy?, Challenging the 'Washington Consensus' and Restoring the Historicity of Divergent Trajectories", *Third World Quarterly*, vol. 17, no. 4 (1996), pp. 585-591.

Girling, John, *Thailand, Society and Politics* (Ithaca and London: Cornell University Press, 1981).

Goeltom, Miranda S., *The Financial Liberalisation in Indonesia* (Singapore: Institute of Southeast Asian Studies, 1994).

--- , "Perubahan Struktural Sektor Keuangan di Indonesia: Visi dan Tantangan" [Structural Changes in Indonesia's Financial Sector: Vision and Challenges] in Mari Pangestu and Ira Setiawati (eds.) *Mencari Paradigma Baru Pembangunan Indonesia [Searching for a New Paradigm of Indonesia's Development]* (Jakarta: Centre for Strategic and International Studies, 1996), pp. 51-91.

Gourevitch, Peter, *Politics in Hard Times, Comparative Responses to International Economic Crises* (Ithaca and London: Cornell University Press, 1986).

Guyot, James J., "Burma in 1988: Perestroika with a Military Face", *Southeast Asian Affairs 1989* (Singapore: Institute of Southeast Asian Studies, 1989), pp. 107-133.

--- , "Myanmar in 1990, The Unconsummated Election", *Asian Survey*, vol. xxxi, no. 2 (February 1991), pp. 205-211.

Habib, Hasnan, "The Role of the Armed Forces in Indonesia's Future Political Development" in Harold Crouch and Hal Hill (eds.) *Indonesia Assessment 1992, Political Perspectives on the 1990s* (Canberra: Department of Political and Social Change, Research School of Pacific Studies, Australian National University, 1992), pp. 83-94.

Habibie, B. J., "Pengembangan Tehnologi Canggih" [The Development of High-Technology] in B. J. Habibie, *Ilmu Pengetahuan, Tehnologi and Pembangunan Bangsa* [Science, Technology and Nation Building (Jakarta: Center for Information and Development Studies, 1995), pp. 89-125.

Hadiz, Vedi R., "Workers and Working Class Politics in the 1990s" in Chris Manning and Joan Hardjono (eds.) *Indonesia Assessment 1993, Labour: Sharing in the Benefits of Growth?* (Canberra: Department of Political and Social Change, Research School of Pacific and Asian Studies, 1993), pp. 186-200.

--- , *Workers and the State in New Order Indonesia* (London and New York: Routledge, 1997).

Haggard, Stephan, *Pathways from the Periphery, The Politics of Growth in the Newly Industrialising Countries* (Ithaca and London: Cornell University Press, 1990).

--- , "Business, Politics and Policy in Northeast and Southeast Asia" in Andrew MacIntyre (ed.) *Business and Government in Industrialising Asia* (Sydney: Allen and Unwin, 1994), pp. 268-301.

--- , *The Political Economy of the Asian Financial Crisis* (Washington D.C.: Institute for International Economics, 2000).

--- and Robert Kaufman (eds.), "Economic Adjustment and the Prospects for Democracy" in *The Politics of Adjustment, International Constraints, Distributive Politics and the State* (Princeton: Princeton University Press, 1992), pp. 319-350.

--- (eds.) *The Political Economy of Democratic Transitions* (Princeton: Princeton University Press, 1995).

--- and Steven B. Webb, "What Do We Know about the Political Economy of Economic Policy Reform", *The World Bank Research Observer*, vol. 8, no. 2 (July 1993), pp. 143-168.

--- (eds.) *Voting for Reform, Democracy, Political Liberalization, and Economic Adjustment* (New York: Oxford University Press, 1994).

Haley, Mary Ann, "Emerging Market Makers: The Power of Institutional Investors" in Leslie Elliot Armijo (ed.) *Financial Globalization and Democracy in Emerging Markets* (London: Macmillan, 1999), pp. 74-90.

Hall, Peter, *The Political Power of Economic Ideas: Keynesianism across Nations* (Princeton: Princeton University Press, 1990).

Handley, Paul, "More of the Same?, Politics and Business, 1987-96" in Kevin Hewison (ed.) *Political Change in Thailand, Democracy and Participation* (London and New York: Routledge, 1997), pp. 94-113.

Haseman, John, "Burma in 1987", *Asian Survey*, vol. xxviii, no. 2 (February 1988), pp. 223-228.

Hawes, Garry and Hong Liu, "Explaining the Dynamics of the Southeast Asian Political Economy, State, Society and the Search for Economic Growth", *World Politics*, no. 45 (July 1993), pp. 629-660.

Hefner, Robert W., "Islam, State, and Civil Society: ICMI and the Struggle for the Indonesian Middle Class", *Indonesia*, no. 56 (1993), pp. 1-35.

Held, David and Anthony McGrew, "The End of the Old Order?, Globalization and the Prospects for World Order", *British International Studies Association*, vol. 24, special issue (December 1998), pp. 219-243.

Heryanto, Ariel, "Indonesian Middle-Class Opposition in the 1990s" in Garry Rodan (ed.) *Political Oppositions in Industrialising Asia* (London and New York: Routledge, 1996), pp. 241-271.

Hewison, Kevin, "National Interests and Economic Downturn: Thailand" in Richard Robison, Kevin Hewison, and Richard Higgott (eds.) *Southeast Asia in the 1980s: The Politics of Economic Crisis* (Sydney: Allen and Unwin, 1987), pp. 52-79.

--- , *Bankers and Bureaucrats, Capital and the Role of the State in Thailand* (New Heaven: Yale University Southeast Asian Studies, 1989).

--- , "The Development of Industrial Capital, Its Situation in the 1980s" in Kevin Hewison (ed.) *Power and Politics in Thailand: Essays in Political Economy* (Manila: Journal of Contemporary Asia Publishers, 1989), pp. 142-167.

--- , "Of Regimes, State and Pluralities: Thai Politics enters the 1990s" in Kevin Hewison, Richard Robison and Garry Rodan (eds.) *Southeast Asia in the 1990s, Authoritarianism, Democracy and Capitalism* (Sydney: Allen and Unwin, 1993), pp. 161-189.

--- , "Political Oppositions and Regime Change in Thailand" in Garry Rodan (ed.) *Political Oppositions in Industrialising Asia* (London and New York: Routledge, 1996), pp. 72-94.

--- , "Thailand's Capitalism Before and After the Economic Crisis", a paper presented at the *Asian Studies Association of Australia Conference*, organised by the University of New South Wales, Sydney, 27 September – 3 October 1998.

--- , *Nationalism, Populism, Dependency: Old Ideas for a New Southeast Asia?*, Working Papers Series, no. 4 (May 2001).

--- , Richard Robison and Garry Rodan (eds.) *Southeast Asia in the 1990s Authoritarianism, Democracy and Capitalism* (Sydney: Allen and Unwin, 1993).

Higgott, Richard, "The International Relations of the Asian Economic Crisis: A Study in the Politics of Resentment" in Richard Robison, Mark Beeson, Kanishka Jayasuriya and Hyuk-Rae Kim (eds.) *Politics and Markets in the Wake of the Asian Crisis* (London and New York: Routledge, 2000), pp. 261-282.

--- and Richard Robison (eds.) *Southeast Asia: Essays in the Political Economy of Structural Change* (London: Routledge and Kegan Paul, 1983).

--- and Richard Stubbs, "Competing Conceptions of Economic Regionalism: Apec versus EAEC in the Asia Pacific", *Review of International Political Economy*, vol. 2, no. 3 (Summer 1995), pp. 516-535.

Hikam, Muhammad AS, *Demokrasi dan Civil Society* [Democracy and Civil Society] (Jakarta: LP3ES, 1996).

Hill, David, *The Press in New Order Indonesia* (Perth: Asia Research Centre, Murdoch University, 1994).

Hill, Hal, "Industrialization in Burma in Historical Perspective", *Journal of Southeast Asian Studies*, vol. xv, no. 1 (March 1984), pp. 134-149.

--- , *Southeast Asia, Southeast Asian Economic Development: An Analytical Survey* (Canberra: Economic Division, Research School of Pacific and Asian Studies, Australian National University, 1993).

--- , *The Indonesian Economy since 1966* (Melbourne: Cambridge University Press, 1996).

Hirch, Phillip, "The Politics of Environment, Opposition and Legitimacy" in Kevin Hewison (ed.) *Political Change in Thailand, Democracy and Participation* (London and New York: Routledge, 1997), pp. 179-194.

Hirst, Paul and G. Thomsom, *Globalisation in Question* (Cambridge: Polity Press, 1996).

Hughes, Helen (ed.) *Achieving Industrialization in East Asia* (Melbourne: Cambridge University Press, 1988).

Hunter, William C., George G. Kaufman, and Thomas H. Krueger (eds.) *The Asian Financial Crisis: Origins, Implications, and Solutions* (Boston: Kluwer Academic, 1999).

Huntington, Samuel P., *The Third Wave: Democratization in the Late Twentieth Century* (Norman: University of Oklahoma Press, 1991).

Hutchison, Jane, "Class and State Power in the Philippines" in Kevin Hewison, Richard Robison and Garry Rodan (eds.) *Southeast Asia in the 1990s, Authoritarianism, Democracy and Capitalism* (Sydney: Allen and Unwin, 1993), pp. 193-212.

Ingram, James C., *Economic Change in Thailand 1850-1970* (Stanford: Stanford University Press, 1971).

Institute of Public Policy Studies, *Policies of Thai Political Parties in the 1995 General Election* (Bangkok: Institute of Public Policy Studies, 1995).

International Monetary Fund, *Myanmar, Recent Economic Developments* (Washington D.C.: International Monetary Fund, 1995).

--- , *World Economic Outlook, Interim Assessment* (Washington D.C.: The International Monetary Fund, 1997).

--- , *Developing Countries and the Globalization of Financial Markets* (Washington D.C.: International Monetary Fund, 1998).

--- , *The Relative Importance of Political and Economic Variables in Creditworthiness Ratings* (Washington D.C.: International Monetary Fund, 1998).

Jackson, Karl D. (ed.) *The Asian Contagion: The Causes and Consequences of a Financial Crisis* (Singapore: Institute of Southeast Asian Studies, 1999).

Jayasuriya, Kanishka and Andrew Rosser, "Economic Orthodoxy and the East Asian Crisis", *Third World Quarterly*, vol. 22, no. 3 (2001), pp. 381-396.

Jenkins, David, *Soeharto and his Generals: Indonesian Military Politics 1975-1983* (Ithaca: Cornell Modern Indonesia Project, Cornell University, 1984).

Ji Ungpakorn, *The Struggle for Democracy and Social Justice in Thailand* (Bangkok: Arom Pongpangan Foundation, 1997).

Johnson, Chalmers, *MITI and the Japanese Miracle: The Growth of Industrial Policy, 1925-1975* (Stanford: Stanford University Press, 1982).

--- , "Political Institutions and Economic Performance: The Government-Business Relationship in Japan, South Korea and Taiwan" in Frederic Deyo (ed.) *The Political Economy of the New Asian Industrialism* (Ithaca and London: Cornell University Press, 1987), pp. 136-164.

Johnson, Colin, "Survey of Recent Developments", *Bulletin of Indonesian Economic Studies*, vol. 34, no. 2 (August, 1998), pp. 3-60.

Jomo, Kwame Sundaram, *A Question of Class: Capital, the State and Uneven Developments in Malaysia* (New York: Monthly Review Press, 1988).

Kahin, George McT., *Nationalism and Revolution in Indonesia* (Ithaca: Cornell University Press, 1952).

Kang, David C., "South Korean and Taiwanese Development and the New Institutional Economics", *International Organisation*, vol. 49, no. 3 (Summer 1995), pp. 555-587.

Kazhim, Musa (ed.) *Menuju Indonesia Baru: Menggagas Reformasi Total* [Towards a New Indonesia: Arguing for Total Reformation] (Bandung: Pustaka Hidayah, 1998).

Kennedy, Paul, *Preparing for the Twenty-First Century* (London: Harper Collins Publishers, 1993).

Keohane, Robert O. and Helen V. Milner, *Internationalization and Domestic Politics* (Cambridge: Cambridge University Press, 1996).

Keputusan Menteri Keuangan Republik Indonesia Nomor 455/KMK 01/1997 tentang Pembelian Saham oleh Pemodal Asing Melalui Pasar Modal [The Finance Ministerial Decree Number 455/KMK 01/1997 about Purchasing Stock by Foreign Investors through Capital Market].

Kesorn Chantarapootirat, *Thai Export-Oriented Growth Performance and Industrial Development*, Ph.D thesis, Fordham University, 1991.

Keterangan Pemerintah Mengenai Gejolak Rupiah dan Upaya untuk Mengatasinya [Government Explanation about the Fluctuation of the Rupiah and Efforts to Overcome with it], Finance Minister Mar'ie Muhammad's speech at the House of Representatives, Jakarta, 16 September 1997.

Khin Maung Kyi, "Will Forever Flow the Ayeyarwady?", *Southeast Asian Affairs 1994* (Singapore: Institute of Southeast Asian Studies, 1994), pp. 209-230.

--- , "In His Own Words", *Burma Debate*, vol. iv, no. 2 (March-June 1997).

Khin Yi, *The Dobama Movement in Burma, 1930-1938* (Ithaca: Southeast Asia Program, Cornell University, 1988).

King, Daniel E., "Thailand in 1996, Economic Slowdown Clouds Year", *Asian Survey*, vol. xxxvii, no. 2 (February 1997), pp. 160-166.

Kobkua Suwannathat-Pian, *Thailand's Durable Premier, Phibun through Three Decades, 1932-1957* (Kuala Lumpur: Oxford University Press, 1995).

Koenig, Willam J., *The Burmese Polity, 1752-1819: Politics, Administration and Social Organisation in the Early Kon-baung Period* (Michigan: Centre for South and Southeast Asian Studies, The University of Michigan, 1990).

Krueger, Anne, *Foreign Trade Regimes and Economic Development: Liberalization Attempts and Consequences* (New York: National Bureau of Economic Research, 1978).

--- (ed.) *Political economy of Policy Reform in Developing Countries* (Cambridge: The Massachusetts Institute of Technology Press, 1993).

Krugman, Paul, "The Myth of Asia's Miracle", *Foreign Affairs*, vol. 73, no. 6 (November-December 1994), pp. 62-78.

Kunio, Yoshihara, *The Rise of Ersatz Capitalism in Southeast Asia* (Singapore: Oxford University Press, 1987).

--- , *The Nation and Economic Growth, the Philippines and Thailand* (Singapore: Oxford University Press, 1994).

Laird, John, *Proposal for Constitutional Reform* (Bangkok: Craftsman Press Co., Ltd., 1997).

Lane, Max, *'Openness', Political Discontent and Succession in Indonesia: Political Developments in Indonesia, 1989-91* (Brisbane: Centre for the Study of Australia-Asia Relations, Griffith University, 1991).

Langford, John W. and K. Lorne Brownsey (eds.) *Economic Policy-Making in the Asia Region* (Halifax: The Institute for Research on Public Policy, 1988).

Lev, Daniel S., *The Transition to Guided Democracy: Indonesian Politics, 1957-1959* (Ithaca: Southeast Asia Program, Cornell University, 1966).

Liang, Chi-shad, "Burma's Relations with the People's Republic of China: From Delicate Friendship to Genuine Co-operation" in Peter Carey (ed.) *Burma, The Challenge of Change in a Divided Society* (London: Macmillan, 1997), 71-93.

Liddle, R. William, "Indonesia in 1996, Pressures from Above and Below", *Asian Survey*, vol. xxxvii, no. 2 (February 1997), pp. 167-174.

Lieberman, Victor, *Burmese Administrative Cycles: Anarchy and Conquest, c.1580-1760* (Princeton University Press, 1984).

Lim, Linda, "The Southeast Asian Currency Crisis and its Aftermath", *Journal of Asian Business*, vol. 13, no. 4 (1997), pp. 65-83.

Lindblad, J. Thomas, "Survey of Recent Developments", *Bulletin of Indonesian Economic Studies*, vol. 33, no. 3 (December 1997), pp. 3-33.

Lintner, Bertil, *Outrage: Burma's Struggle for Democracy*, revised edition (London and Bangkok: White Lotus, 1990).

--- , *The Rise and Fall of the Communist Party of Burma (CPB)* (Ithaca: Southeast Asia Program, Cornell University, 1990).

--- , *Aung San Suu Kyi and Burma's Unfinished Renaissance* (Bangkok: Peacock Press, 1990).

--- , "Burma and its Neighbours", *China Report*, vol. 28, no. 3 (1992), pp. 225-259.

--- , "The Politics of Drug Trade in Burma", a paper presented to *the State, Order and Prospects for Change in Burma Conference*, organised by Griffith University, Brisbane, 3-4 December 1992.

--- , "Burma, Struggle for Power", *Jane's Intelligence Review*, vol. 5, no. 10 (October 1993), pp. 466-471.

--- , *Burma in Revolt, Opium and Insurgency Since 1948* (Boulder: Westview Press, 1994).

--- , "Drugs and Economic Growth, Ethnicity and Exports" in Robert I. Rotberg (ed.) *Burma, Prospects for a Democratic Future* (Washington D.C.: Brookings Institution Press, 1998), pp. 165-183.

LIPI, "Menuju Reformasi Politik Orde Baru: Beberapa Usulan Perbaikan" [Toward the Political Reform under the New Order: Some Proposal for Changes] in Syamsudin Haris and Riza Sihudi (eds.) *Menelaah Kembali Format Politik Orde Baru* [Rethinking on the Political Format of the New Order] (Jakarta: Gramedia Pustaka Utama, 1996), pp. 182-191.

Lissak, Moshe, *Military Roles in Modernization: Civil-Military Relations in Thailand and Burma* (Beverly Hills and London: Sage Publications, 1976).

Lucas, Anton, *One Soul One Struggle, Region and Revolution in Indonesia* (Sydney: Allen and Unwin, 1991).

Luwarso, Lucas (ed.) *Jakarta Crackdown* (Jakarta: Alliance of Independence Journalists,1997).

MacIntyre, Andrew, *Business and Politics in Indonesia* (Sydney: Allen and Unwin,1990).

--- , "State-Society Relations in New Order Indonesia: The Case of Business" in Arief Budiman (ed.) *State and Civil Society in Indonesia* (Clayton: Centre of Southeast Asian Studies, Monash University, 1990), pp. 369-394.

--- , "Politics and the Reorientation of Economic Policy in Indonesia" in Andrew MacIntyre and Kanishka Jayasuriya (eds.) *The Dynamics of Economic Policy Reform in South-east Asia and the South-west Pacific* (Singapore: Oxford University Press, 1992), pp. 138-157.

--- , "Indonesia, Thailand and the Northeast Asian Connection" in Richard Higgott, Richard Leaver and John Ravenhill (eds.) *Pacific Economic Relations in the 1990s, Cooperation or Conflict?* (Sydney: Allen and Unwin, 1993), pp. 250-270.

--- , "The Politics of Finance in Indonesia: Command, Confusion, and Competition" in Stephan Haggard, Chung H. Lee and Sylvia Maxfield (eds.) *The Politics of Finance in Developing Countries* (Ithaca and London: Cornell University Press, 1993), pp. 123-164.

--- , "Business, Government and Development: Northeast and Southeast Asian Comparisons" in Andrew MacIntyre (ed.) *Business and Government in Industrialising Asia* (Sydney: Allen and Unwin, 1994), pp. 1-28.

--- , "Power, Prosperity and Patrimonialism: Business and Government in Indonesia" in Andrew MacIntyre (ed.) *Business and Government in Industrialising Asia* (Sydney: Allen and Unwin, 1994), pp. 244-267.

--- and Kanishka Jayasuriya (eds.) *The Dynamics of Economic Policy Reform in Southeast Asian and Southwest Pacific* (Singapore: Oxford University Press, 1992).

Mackie, Jamie, "Economic Growth in the ASEAN region: the Political Underpinings" in Helen Hughes (ed.) *Achieving Industrialization in East Asia* (Melbourne: Cambridge University Press, 1988), pp. 283-326.

--- , "Indonesia: Economic Growth and Depoliticization" in James Morley (ed.) *Driven by Growth, Political Change in the Asia-Pacific Region* (London: East Gate, 1993), pp. 69-96.

--- , "Business Success Among Southeast Asian Chinese, The Role of Culture, Values, and Social Structure" in Robert W. Hefner (ed.) *Market Cultures, Society and Morality on the New Asian Capitalism* (Boulder: Westview, 1998), pp. 129-146.

--- and Andrew MacIntyre, "Politics" in Hal Hill (ed.) *Indonesia's New Order, The Dynamics of Socio-economic Transformation* (Sydney: Allen and Unwin, 1994), pp. 1-53.

Majidi, Nasyith, *Mega Skandal, Drama Pembobolan dan Kolusi Bapindo* [Mega Scandal, The Drama of the Closure and Collusion of Bapindo] (Bandung: Mizan, 1994).

Malik, J. Mohan, "Sino-Indian Rivalry in Myanmar: Implications for Regional Security", *Contemporary Southeast Asia*, vol. 16, no. 2 (September 1994), pp. 137-156.

Marzouk, G. A, *Economic Development and Policies, Case Study of Thailand* (Rotterdam: Rotterdam University Press, 1972).

Mason, Mark, "Foreign Direct Investment in Burma, Trends, Determinants, and Prospects" in Robert I. Rotberg (ed.) *Burma, Prospects for a Democratic Future* (Washington D.C.: Brookings Institution Press, 1998), pp. 209-229.

Matthews, Bruce, "Buddhism Under a Military Regime, The Iron Hell in Burma", *Asian Survey*, vol. xxxiii, no. 4 (April 1993), pp. 408-423.

McCargo, Duncan, *Chamlong Srimuang and the New Thai Politics* (London: Hurst and Company, 1997).

--- , "Thailand's Political Parties: Real, Authentic and Actual" in Kevin Hewison (ed.) *Political Change in Thailand, Democracy and Participation* (London and New York, Routledge, 1997), pp. 114-131.

McLeod, Ross H. (ed.) *Indonesia Assessment 1994, Finance as a Key Sector in Indonesia's Development* (Singapore and Canberra: Institute of Southeast Asian Studies and Research School of Pacific Studies, Australian National University, 1994).

--- , "Postcript to the Survey of Recent Developments: On Causes and Cures for the Rupiah Crisis", *Bulletin of Indonesian Economic Studies*, vol. 33, no. 3 (December 1997), pp. 35-52.

--- , "Some Comments on 'The Funding of PT DSTP: A High-Technology Project'" in Hal Hill and Thee Kian Wie (eds.) *Indonesia's Technological Challenge* (Singapore and Canberra: Institute of Southeast Asian Studies and Research School of Pacific and Asian Studies, Australian National University, 1998), pp. 234-237.

--- , "Indonesia" in *East Asia in Crisis, From Being a Miracle to Needing One?* (London and New York: Routledge, 1998), pp. 31-48.

--- , "Indonesia's Crisis and Future Prospects" in Karl D. Jackson (ed.) *Asian Contagion, The Causes and Consequences of a Financial Crisis* (Singapore: Institute of Southeast Asian Studies, 1999), pp. 209-240.

McVey, Ruth, "The Materialization of the Southeast Asian Entrepreneur", in *Southeast Asian Capitalists* (Ithaca: Southeast Asian Program, Cornell University, 1992), pp. 7-33.

Mendelson, Michael, *Sangha and State in Burma* (Ithaca: Cornell University Press, 1973).

Milner, Helen V. and Robert O. Keohane (eds.) *Internationalization and Domestic Politics* (Cambridge: Cambridge University Press, 1996).

Moertopo, Ali, *The Acceleration and Modernization of 25 Years' Development* (Jakarta: Centre for Strategic and International Studies, 1973).

Mommen, Andrew, "The Asian Miracle, A Critical Reassessment" in A. E. Jilberto and Andrew Mommen (eds.) *Liberalization in the Developing World, Institutional and Economic Changes in Latin America, Africa and Asia* (London and New York: Routledge, 1996), pp. 28-50.

Montes, Manuel F., *The Currency Crisis in Southeast Asia*, update version (Singapore: Institute of Southeast Asian Studies, 1998).

Moore, Barrington, *Social Origins of Dictatorship and Democracy: Lord and Peasant in the Making of the Modern World* (Boston: Beacon Press, 1966).

Morell, David and Chai-anan Samudavanija, *Political Conflict in Thailand, Reform, Reaction, Revolution* (Cambridge, Mass.: Oelgeschlager, Gunn and Hain, Publishers, Inc., 1981).

Morley, James W. (ed.) *Driven by Growth, Political Change in the Asia-Pacific Region* (New York: An East Gate Book, 1993).

Murray, David, *Angels and Devils: Thai Politics from February 1991 to September 1992, A Struggle for Democracy* (Bangkok: White Orchid Press, 1996).

Muscat, Robert J., *Development Strategy in Thailand, A Study of Economic Growth* (New York: Frederick A. Praeger, 1966).

--- , *Thailand and the United States, Development, Security, and Foreign Aid* (New York: Columbia University, 1990).

--- , *The Fifth Tiger, A Study of Thai Development Policy* (New York: United Nations University Press, 1994).

Mya Maung, *Burma Road to Poverty* (New York: Praeger, 1991).

--- , *Totalitarianism in Burma: Prospects for Economic Development* (New York Paragon House, 1992).

--- , "On the Road to Mandalay, A Case Study of the Sinonization of Upper Burma", *Asian Survey*, vol. xxxiv, no. 5 (May 1994), pp. 447-459.

--- , "The Burmese Approach to Development", *Journal of Asian Economics*, vol. 7, no. 1 (1996), pp. 97-129.

Mya Than and Joseph L. H. Tan (eds.) *The Myanmar Economy at the Crossroads: Options and Constraints* (Singapore: Institute of Southeast Asian Studies, 1990).

Myat Thein, "An Assessment of the Measures taken for the Proper Evolution of the Market-oriented Economic System" in Office of Strategic Studies, *Symposium on Socio-Economic Factors Contributing to National Consolidation* (Rangoon: Office of Strategic Studies, Ministry of Defence, 1997), pp. 3-14.

--- , "Some Aspects of Economic Reforms in Myanmar", a paper presented to *Roundtable on Interaction between Myanmar and ASEAN-ISIS*, organised by Myanmar Institute of Strategic and International Studies, Ministry of Foreign Affairs, Rangoon, 27-30 October 1997.

--- , "Improving Domestic Resource Mobilization in Myanmar", mimeograph, no date and year.

--- and Mya Than, "Transitional Economy of Myanmar: Performance, Issues and Problems" in S. F. Naya and Joseph L. H. Tan (eds.) *Asian Transitional Economies* (Singapore: Institute of Southeast Asian Studies, 1995), pp. 210-161.

Myo Myint, *The Politics of Survival Burma: Diplomacy and Statecraft in the Reign of King Mindon, 1853-1878*, Ph.D thesis, Cornell University, 1987.

Naris Chaiyasoot, "Industrialization, Financial Reform and Monetary Policy" in Medhi Korngkaew (ed.) *Thailand's Industrialization and Its Consequences* (London: St. Martins's Press, 1995), pp. 160-182.

Nasution, Adnan Buyung, *The Aspiration for Constitutional Government in Indonesia: A Socio-legal Study of the Indonesian Konstituante 1956-1959* (Den Haag: CIP-Genevans Koninklijke Bibliotheek, 1992).

Nasution, Anwar, "Banking Sector Reforms in Indonesia, 1983-93" in Ross H. McLeod (ed.) *Indonesia Assessment 1994, Finance as a Key Sector in Indonesia's Development* (Singapore and Canberra: Institute of Southeast Asian Studies and Research School of Pacific and Asian Studies, Australian National University, 1994), pp. 130-157.

Neher, Clark D., "Thailand in 1987, Semi-Successful, Semi-Democracy", *Asian Survey*, vol. xxviii, no. 2 (February 1988), pp. 192-201.

--- , "The Transition to Democracy in Thailand", *Asian Perspective*, vol. 20, no. 2 (Fall-Winter 1996), pp. 301-321.

--- *Southeast Asia, Crossroads of the World* (DeKalb: Southeast Asia Publications, Northern Illinois University, 2000).

Nelson, Joan M. (ed.) *Fragile Coalitions: The Politics of Economic Adjustment* (Washington D.C.: The Overseas Development Council, 1989).

Niksch, Larry A., "Thailand in 1988, The Economic Surge", *Asian Survey*, vol. xxix, no. 2 (February 1989), pp. 165-173.

Noble, Gregory W. and John Ravenhill (eds.) *The Asian Financial Crisis and the Architecture of Global Finance* (New York: Cambridge University Press, 2000).

Nordlinger, Eric A., *Soldier in Politics: Military Coup and Governments* (New Jersey: Prentice Hall, 1977).

Ockey, James Soren, *Business Leaders, Gangsters, and the Middle Class: Societal Groups and Civilian Rule in Thailand*, Ph.D thesis, Cornell University, 1992.

--- , "Political Parties, Factions, and Corruption in Thailand", *Modern Asian Studies*, vol. 28, no. 2 (1994), pp. 251-277.

--- , "Thailand, The Crafting of Democracy", *Southeast Asian Affairs 1997* (Singapore: Institute of Southeast Asian Studies, 1997), pp. 301-316.

Ohmae, Kenichi, *The End of the Nation State: The Rise of Regional Economics* (London: Harpercollins, 1996).

Oman, Charles, *Globalisation and Regionalisation: The Challenge for Developing Countries* (Paris: Development Centre of the Organisation for Economic Cooperation and Development, 1994).

Pakorn Vichyanond, *Thailand's Financial System: Structure and Liberalization* (Bangkok: Thailand Development Research Institute, 1994).

Pangestu, Mari, "Financial Markets and Policies" in *Economic Reform, Deregulation and Privatization, The Indonesian Experience* (Jakarta: Centre for Strategic and International Studies, 1996), pp. 133-149.

--- , "Managing Economic Policy Reforms in Indonesia" in *Economic Reform, Deregulation and Privatization, The Indonesian Experience* (Jakarta: Centre for Strategic and International Studies, 1996), pp. 1-29.

Pasuk Phongpaicit, "Technocrats, Businessman, and Generals: Democracy and Economic Policy-Making in Thailand" in Andrew MacIntyre and Kanishka Jayasuriya (eds.) *The Dynamics of Economic Policy Reform in South-east and the South-west Pacific* (Singapore: Oxford University Press, 1992), pp. 10-31.

--- , "Among Dragons, Geese and Tigers: The Thai economy in Global and Local Perspective", a paper presented to the *6th International Conference on Thai Studies*, Chiangmai, Thailand, 14-17 October 1996.

--- , "Power in Transition: Thailand in the 1990s" in Kevin Hewison (ed.) *Political Change in Thailand, Democracy and Participation* (London and New York: Routledge, 1997), pp. 21-41.

--- , *Thailand's Crisis* (Singapore: Institute of Southeast Asian Studies, 2000).

Patcharee Siroros and Sylvia Maxfield, "The Politics of Central Bank in Thailand", a paper presented at *the Annual Meeting of the Association for Asian Studies*, Washington D.C., 2-5 April 1992.

--- and Chris Baker, *Thailand, Economy and Politics* (Singapore: Oxford University Press, 1997).

--- and Sungsidh Piriyarangsan, *Corruption and Democracy in Thailand* (Bangkok: Silkworm Books, 1994).

Pempel, T. J., *Regime Shift, Comparative Dynamics of the Japanese Political Economy* (Ithaca and London: Cornell University Press, 1998).

--- (ed.) *Politics of the Asian Economic Crisis* (Ithaca and London: Cornell University Press, 1999).

Phatra Research Institute, "The Impact of Liberalization on Thailand's Financial Market", a paper presented at the *5th Convention of the East Asian Economic Association*, Bangkok, 25-26 October 1996.

Prudhisan Jumbala, "Thailand, Constitutional Reform amidst Economic Crisis", *Southeast Asian Affairs 1998* (Singapore: Institute of Southeast Asian Affairs, 1998), pp. 265-291.

--- and Maneerat Mitprasat, "Non-governmental Development Organisations: Empowerment and Environment" in Kevin Hewison (ed.) *Political Change in Thailand, Democracy and Participation* (London and New York: Routledge, 1997), pp. 195-216.

Przeworski, Adam, *Democracy and the Market: Political and Economic Reforms in Eastern Europe and Latin America* (New York: Cambridge University Press, 1991).

Putnam, Robert D., *Making Democracy Work, Civic Traditions in Modern Italy* (Princeton: Princeton University Press, 1993).

Radelet, Steven and Jeffrey Sachs , "Asia Reemergence", *Foreign Affairs*, vol. 76, no. 6 (November-December 1997), pp. 56-59.

--- , "The East Asian Financial Crisis: Diagnosis, Remedies, Prospects", a paper presented to *Brooking Panel*, Washington D.C., 26-27 March 1998.

Ramsay, Ansil, "Thialand 1979: A Government in Trouble", *Asian Survey*, vol. xx, no. 2 (February 1980), pp. 112-122.

Rana, P., "Globalization and Currencies", *Far Eastern Economic Review* (11 September 1997).

Rhee, Jong-Chan, *The State and Industry in South Korea: The Limits of the Authoritarian State* (London: Routledge, 1994).

Rice, Robert C., "The Habibie Approach to Science, Technology and National Development" in Hal Hill and Thee Kian Wie (eds.) *Indonesia's Technological Challenge* (Singapore and Canberra: Institute of Southeast Asian Studies and Research School of Pacific and Asian Studies, Australian National University, 1998), pp. 185-198.

Ricklefs, M. C., *A History of Modern Indonesia Since c. 1300*, second edition (London: Macmillan Press Ltd., 1993).

Riggs, Fred W., *Thailand, The Modernization of a Bureaucratic Polity* (Honolulu: East-West Center Press, 1966).

Rimmer, Peter J. (ed.) *Pacific Rim Development, Integration and Globalisation in the Asia-Pacific Economy* (Canberra and Sydney: Department of International Relations and the Department of Human Geography, Australian National University and Allen and Unwin, 1997).

Robinson, Court, *The War is Growing Worse and Worse: Refugees and Displaced Persons on the Thai-Burmese Border* (Washington D.C.: United States Committee for Refugees, 1990).

Robinson, David, Yango Byeon and Ranjit Teja, *Thailand: Adjusting to Success, Current Policy Issues* (Washington D.C.: International Monetary Fund, 1991).

Robison, Richard, *Indonesia: The Rise of Capital* (Sydney: Allen and Unwin, 1986).

--- , "Indonesia: Tensions in State and Regime" in Kevin Hewison, Richard Robison and Garry Rodan (eds.) *Southeast Asia in the 1990s, Authoritarianism, Democracy and Capitalism* (Sydney: Allen and Unwin, 1993), pp. 41-74.

--- , "The Middle Class and the Bourgeoisie in Indonesia" in Richard Robison and David S. G. Goodman (eds.) *The New Rich in Asia, Mobile Phones, McDonalds and Middle-Class Revolution* (London and New York: Routledge, 1996), pp. 77-101.

--- , "Politics and markets in Indonesia's Post-oil Era" in Garry Rodan, Kevin Hewison and Richard Robison (eds.) *The Political Economy of South-East Asia* (Melbourne: Oxford University Press, 1997), pp. 29-63.

--- , Mark Beeson, Kanishka Jayasuriya and Hyuk-Rae Kim (eds) *Politics and Markets in the Wake of the Asian Crisis* (London and New York: Routledge, 2000).

Rodan, Garry, *The Political Economy of Singapore's Industrialization: National State and International Capital* (London: Macmillan, 1989).

Rodrik, Dani, *Has Globalization Gone Too Far?* (Washington D.C.: Institute for International Economics, 1997).

Rosenberger, L. R., "Southeast Asia's Currency Crisis: A Diagnosis and Prescription", *Contemporary Southeast Asia*, vol. 19, no. 3 (December 1997), pp. 223-251.

Rosser, Andrew, "Surviving the Meltdown: Liberal Reform and Political Oligarchy in Indonesia", a paper presented at *the Asian Studies Association of Australia Conference*, organised by the University of New South Wales, Sydney, 27 September-3 October 1998.

Rueschemeyer, D., E. H. Stephens, and J. D. Stephens, *Capitalist Development and Democracy* (Cambridge: Polity Press, 1992).

Said, Salim, *Genesis of Power: General Sudirman and the Indonesian Military in Politics, 1945-1949* (Jakarta: Pustaka Sinar Harapan, 1992).

Samego, Indria, "Politik Pembangunan Orde Baru: Beberapa Interpretasi Teoritik Mengenai Peran Negara dalam Mengembangkan Pengusaha Nasional" [The Politics of the New Order's Development: Some Theoretical Interpretations on the Role of the State in the Development of National Entrepreneur] in Syamsuddin Haris and Riza Sihbudi (eds.) *Menelaah Kembali Format Politik Orde Baru* (Reinterpreting the Political Format of the New Order (Jakarta: LIPI and Gramedia, 1995), pp. 115-141.

Sanit, Arbi, "Transformasi Partai dan Reformasi Sistem Kepartaian Indonesia" [Transformation of Political Parties and the Reform of the Political Party System in Indonesia] in Rustam Ibrahim (ed.) *Mempertimbangkan Kembali Format Orde Baru* [Rethinking the Format of the New Order] (Jakarta: Centre for the Study of Democracy, 1997), pp. 83-95.

Sarkisyanz, E., *Buddhist Backgrounds of the Burmese Revolution* (The Hague: Martinus Nijhoff, 1965).

Sato, Yuri, "The Astra Group: A Pioneer of Management Modernization in Indonesia", *The Developing Economies*, vol. xxxiv, no. 3 (September 1996), pp. 247-280.

Schmidt, Johannes Dragsbaek, "Paternalism and Planning in Thailand: Facilitating Growth without Social Benefits" in Michael J. G. Parnwell (ed.) *Uneven Development in Thailand* (Aldershot: Avebury Publishing Ltd., 1996), pp. 63-81.

Schwarz, Adam, *A Nation in Waiting, Indonesia in the 1990s* (Sydney: Allen and Unwin, 1994).

Schwarz, Herman M., *States versus Markets: History, Geography, and the Development of the International Political Economy* (New York: St. Martin's Press, 1996).

Seekins, Donald M., "Burma in 1998, Little to Celebrate", *Asian Survey*, vol. xxxix, no. 1 (January-February 1999), pp. 12-19.

Selth, Andrew, "The Myanmar Army Since 1988: Acquisitions and Adjustment", *Contemporary Southeast Asia*, vol. 17, no. 3 (December 1995), pp. 237-264.

--- , *Transforming the Tatmadaw: the Burmese Armed Forces since 1988* (Canberra: Strategic and Defence Studies, Research School of Pacific and Asian Studies, Australian National University, 1996).

--- , "Burma's Intelligence Apparatus", *Burma Debate*, vol. iv, no. 4 (September/October 1997), pp. 4-18.

Shiraisi, Takashi, "The Military in Thailand, Burma and Indonesia" in R. A. Scalapino, S. Sato, and Jusuf Wanandi (eds.) *Asian Political Institutionalization* (Berkeley: Institute of East Asian Studies, University of California, 1989), pp. 157-180.

--- , "Rewiring the Indonesian State" in Daniel S. Lev and Ruth McVey (eds.) *Making Indonesia* (Ithaca: Southeast Asian Program, Cornell University, 1996), pp. 164-179.

Sidel, John T., "Macet Total: Logics of Circulation and Accumulation in the Demise of Indonesia's New Order", *Indonesia*, no. 66 (October 1998), pp. 159-194.

Silcock, T. H., "Money and Banking" in T. H. Silcock (ed.) *Thailand, Social and Economic Studies in Development* (Canberra: Australian National University Press, 1967), pp. 170-205.

Silverstein, Josef, "First Steps on the Burmese Way to Socialism", *Asian Survey*, vol. iv, no. 2 (February 1964), pp. 716-722.

--- , *Military Rule and the Politics of Stagnation* (Ithaca: Cornell University Press, 1977).

--- , "The Military and Foreign Policy in Burma and Indonesia", *Asian Survey*, vol. xxii, no. 3 (March 1982), pp. 278-291.

--- , "Civil War and Rebellion in Burma", *Journal of Southeast Asian Studies*, vol. xxi, no. 10 (October 1990), pp. 1007-1019.

--- , "Burma in An International Perspective", *Asian Survey*, vol. xxxii, no. 1 (October 1992), pp. 951-963.

--- , *The Political Legacy of Aung San*, revised edition, (Ithaca: Southeast Asian Program, Cornell University, 1993).

--- , "The Civil War, the Minorities and Burma's New Politics" in Peter Carey (ed.) *Burma, The Challenge of Change in a Divided Society* (London: Macmillan, 1997), pp. 129-156.

Sirilaksana Khoman, "The Asian Financial Crisis and Prospects for Trade and Business with Thailand", *Thammasat Review*, vol. 3, no. 1 (June 1998), pp. 64-86.

Sjahrir, "The Indonesian Deregulation Process: Problems, Constraints and Prospects" in John W. Langford and K. Lorne Brownsey (eds.) *Economic Policy-Making in the Asia-Pacific Region* (Halifax: The Institute for Research on Public Policy, 1990), pp. 321-339.

Skocpol, Theda, *States and Social Revolution, A Comparative Analysis of France, Russia, and China* (Cambridge: Cambridge University Press, 1979).

Smith, Heather, "Industrial Policy in East Asia", *Asian-Pacific Economic Literature*, vol. 9, no. 1 (May 1995), pp. 17-39.

Smith, Martin, *Burma: Insurgency and the Politics of Ethnicity* (London and New Jersey: Zed Books Ltd., 1991).

--- , "Burma's Ethnic Minorities: A Central or Peripheral Problem in the Regional Context?" in Peter Carey (ed.) *Burma, The Challenge of Change in a Divided Society* (London: Macmillan, 1997), pp. 97-128.

So, Alvin Y. and Stephen W. K. Chiu, *East Asia and the World Economy* (London and New Delhi: Sage Publications, 1995).

Soemitro, "Tempat dan Peran Abri dalam Politik" [Place and the Role of Abri in Politics] in Rustam Ibrahim (ed.) *Mempertimbangkan Kembali Format Politik Orde Baru* [Rethinking the Political Format of the New Order] (Jakarta: Center for the Study of Democracy, 1997), pp. 113-121.

Soesastro, Hadi and M. Chatib Basri, "Survey of Recent Developments", *Bulletin of Indonesian Economic Studies*, vol. 34, no. 1 (April 1998), pp. 3-54.

Spiro, Melford, *Buddhism and Society: A Great Tradition and Its Burmese Vicissitudes* (Berkeley: University of California Press, 1982).

Steinberg, David I., *Burma's Road Toward Development, Growth and Ideology under Military Rule* (Boulder: Westview Press, 1981).

--- , *Burma: A Socialist Nation of Southeast Asia* (Boulder: Westview Press, 1982).

--- (ed.) *In Search of Southeast Asia, A Modern History*, revised edition (Sydney and Wellington: Allen and Unwin, 1987).

--- , *The Future of Burma: Crisis and Choice in Myanmar* (Lanham: The University Press of America, 1990).

--- , "Democracy, Power and the Economy in Myanmar, Donor Dilemmas", *Asian Survey*, vol. xxxi, no. 8 (August 1991), pp. 729-742.

--- , "Myanmar as Nexus: Sino-Indian Rivalries on the Frontier", *Terrorism*, vol. 16 (1993), pp. 1-8.

--- , "The Union Solidarity and Development Association, Mobilization and Orthodoxy", *Burma Debate*, vol. 4, no. 1 (January-February, 1997), pp. 4-11.

--- , "Priorities for Burma's Development: the Role of International Aid" in Peter Carey (ed.) *Burma, The Challenge of Change in a Divided Society* (London: Macmillan, 1997), 159-181.

--- , "The Road to Political recovery, The Salience of Politics in Economics" in Robert I. Rotberg (ed.) *Burma, Prospects for a Democratic Future* (Washington D.C.: Brookings Institution Press, 1998), pp. 269-286.

--- , "Myanmar, Regional Relationship and Internal Concerns", *Southeast Asian Affairs 1998* (Singapore: Institute of Southeast Asian Studies, 1998), pp. 179-195.

Suchit Bunbongkarn, "Thailand in 1991, Coping with the Military Guardianship", *Asian Survey*, vol. xxxii, no. 2 (February 1992), pp. 131-139.

--- , "Elections and Democratization in Thailand" in Robert H. Taylor (ed.) *The Politics of Elections in Southeast Asia* (New York and Melbourne: The Woodrow Wilson Centre Press and Cambridge University Press, 1996), pp. 184-200.

Suchitra Punyaratabandhu, "Thailand in 1998, A False Sense of Recovery", *Asian Survey*, vol. xxxix, no. 1 (January-February 1999), pp. 80-88.

Suehiro, Akira, "Capitalist Development in Postwar Thailand: Commercial Banks, Industrial Elite, and Agribusiness Groups" in Ruth McVey (ed.) *Southeast Asian Capitalists* (Ithaca: Southeast Asia Program, Cornell University, 1992), pp. 35-63.

Sulistiyanto, Priyambudi, *Burma: The Politics of Uncertain Transition, 1988-1994*, MA thesis, Flinders University of South Australia, 1995.

--- , "The Urban Riots that Rocked Jakarta", *Current Affairs Bulletin*, vol. 73, no. 1 (June-July, 1996), pp. 26-28.

--- , "The May 1997 General Election in Indonesia, What Went Wrong?", *Current Affairs Bulletin*, vol. 74, no. 2 (August-September, 1997), pp. 13-19.

Sundhaussen, Ulf, "Indonesia's New Order: A Model for Myanmar?", *Asian Survey*, vol. xxxvi, no. 8 (1995), pp. 768-780.

Surin Maisrikrod, *Thailand's Two General Elections in 1992, Democracy Sustained* (Singapore: Institute of Southeast Asian Studies, 1992).

--- , "Thailand 1992: Repression and Return of Democracy", *Southeast Asian Affairs 1993* (Singapore: Institute of Southeast Asian Studies, 1993), pp. 327-349.

--- , "The Making of Thai Democracy, A Study of Political Alliances Among the State, the Capitalists, and the Middle Class" in Anek Laothamatas (ed.) *Democratization in Southeast and East Asia* (Singapore: Institute of Southeast Asian Studies, 1997), pp. 141-166.

Suthad Setboonsarng, "Asean Economic Co-operation, Adjusting to the Crisis", *Southeast Asian Affairs 1998* (Singapore: Institute of Southeast Asian Studies, 1998), pp. 18-36.

Suthy Prasartset, "The Rise of NGOs as Critical Social Movement in Thailand" in *Thai NGOs: The Continuing Struggle for Democracy* (Bangkok: Thai NGO Support Project, 1995), pp. 97-134.

Suu Kyi, Aung San, *Freedom From Fear and Other Writings* (London: Penguin Books, 1991).

Taylor, Robert H., *The State of Burma* (Honolulu: The University of Hawaii Press, 1987).

--- , "Burma's Ambigious Breakthrough", *Journal of Democracy*, vol. 1, no. 1 (Winter 1990), pp. 62-72.

--- , "Myanmar, New, but Different?", *Southeast Asian Affairs 1995* (Singapore: Institute of Southeast Asian Studies, 1995), pp. 241-256.

Thailand Government Office, a pocket guide (Bangkok: Alpha Research Co. Ltd., 1996).

The East Asia Analytical Unit, *The New Aseans, Vietnam, Burma, Cambodia and Laos* (Canberra: Department of Foreign Affairs and Trade, 1997).

Thitinan Pongsudhirak, "Thailand's Media, Whose Watchdog?" in Kevin Hewison (ed.) *Political Change in Thailand, Democracy and Participation* (London and New York: Routledge, 1997), pp. 217-232.

Tienchai Wongchaisuwan, *The Political Economy of Thailand: The Thai Peripheral State, 1958-1988*, Ph.D thesis, State University of New York at Binghamton, 1993.

Tin Maung Maung Than, "Burma's National Security and Defence Posture" *Contemporary Southeast Asia*, vol. 11, no. 1 (June 1989), pp. 40-59.

--- , "Neither Inheritance nor Legacy: Leading the Myanmar State since Independence", *Contemporary Southeast Asia*, vol. 15, no. 3 (June 1993), pp. 24-63.

--- and Mya Than, "Myanmar, Economic Growth in the Shadow of Political Constraints", *Southeast Asian Affairs 1997* (Singapore: Institute of Southeast Asian Studies, 1997), pp. 205-230.

Tran, Van Hoa, *The Asia Crisis: The Cures, Their Effectiveness and the Prospects After* (New York: St. Martin's Press, 2000).

Tun Wai, U, "The Myanmar Economy at the Crossroads, Options and Constraints" in Mya Than and Joseph L. H. Tan (eds.) *The Myanmar Economy at the Crossroads: Options and Constraints* (Singapore: Institute of Southeast Asian Studies, 1990), pp. 18-52.

Unger, Danny, *Building Social Capital in Thailand, Fibers, Finance, and Infrastructure* (Cambridge: Cambridge University Press, 1998).

--- , "Government and Business in Thailand" in Young C. Kim (ed.) *The Southeast Asian Economic Miracle* (New Brunswick and London: Transaction Publishers, 1995), pp. 137-158.

U.S. Embassy, *Country Commercial Guide, Burma* (Rangoon: U.S. Embassy, 1996).

Vatikiotis, Michael, *Indonesian Politics under Suharto, Order, Development and Pressure for Change* (London and New York: Routledge, 1993).

Wade, Robert, *Governing the Market: Economic Theory and the Role of Government in East Asian Industrialization* (Princeton: Princeton University Press, 1990).

--- , "Globalization and Its Limits: Reports of the Death of the National Economy are Greatly Exaggerated" in Suzanne Berger and Ronald Dore (eds.) *National Diversity and Global Capitalism* (Ithaca and London: Cornell University Press, 1996), pp. 60-88.

--- , "Showdown at the World Bank", *New Left Review*, no. 7 (January-February, 2001), pp. 124-137.

--- and Frank Veneroso, "The Asian Crisis: the High Debt Model Versus the Wall Street-Treasury-IMF Complex", *New Left Review*, vol. 22, vol. 8 (March-April 1998), pp. 3-23.

Ward, Ken, *The 1971 Election in Indonesia: An East Java Case Studies* (Clayton: Monash University Centre of Southeast Asian Studies, 1974).

Warr, Peter G., "The Thai Economy: From Boom to Gloom?", *Southeast Asian Affairs 1997* (Singapore: Institute of Southeast Asian Studies, 1997), pp. 317-333.

--- and Bhanupong Nidhiprabha, *Thailand's Macroeconomic Miracle, Stable Adjustment and Sustained Growth* (Washington D.C.: The World Bank, 1996).

Waters, Malcolm, *Globalisation* (London: Routledge, 1995).

Weiss, Linda, "Governed Interdependence: Rethinking the Government-Business Relations in East Asia", *The Pacific Review*, vol. 8, no. 4 (1995), pp. 589-616.

Weiss, Linda, *The Myth of the Powerless State, Governing the Economy in a Global Era* (Oxford: Polity Press, 1998).

Weller, Mark (ed.) *Democracy and Politics in Burma* (Manerplaw: The National Coalition Government of the Union of Burma, 1993).

Williamson, John, "In Search for a Manual for Technopols" in John Williamson (ed.) *The Political Economy of Policy Reform* (Washington D.C.: Institute for International Economics, 1994), pp. 11-28.

Winarto, Jasso (ed.) *Pasar Modal Indonesia, Retrospeksi Lima Tahun Swastanisasi BEJ [Indonesia's Capital Market, Restrocpection of Five Years' Privatization of Jakarta Stock Exchange]* (Jakarta: Pustaka Sinar Harapan dan Jakarta Stock Exchange, 1997).

Winters, Jeffrey, *Power in Motion: Capital Mobility and the Indonesian State* (Ithaca: Cornell University Press, 1996).

Wong, John, "Why Has Myanmar not Developed Like East Asia", *ASEAN Economic Bulletin*, vol. 13, no. 3 (March, 1997), pp. 344-358.

World Bank, *World Development Report 1991, The Challenge of Development* (Washington D.C.: The World Bank, 1991).

--- , *The East Asian Miracle, Economic Growth and Public Policy* (Washington D.C.: The World Bank, 1993).

--- , *Myanmar: Policies for Sustaining Economic Reform* (Washington D.C.: The World Bank, 1995).

--- , *Indonesia, Sustaining High Growth with Equity* (Washington D.C.: The World Bank, 1997).

--- , *Statistical Report, 1997* (Washington D.C.: The World Bank 1997).

--- , *Statistical Report, 1999* (Washington D.C.: The World Bank, 1999).

Yam, Joseph, "The Impact of Technology on Financial Development in East Asia", *Journal of International Affairs*, vol. 51, no. 2 (Spring 1998), pp. 539-553.

Young, Kenneth and Richard Tanter (eds.) *The Politics of Middle Class Indonesia* (Clayton: Centre of Southeast Asian Studies, Monash University, 1990).

Interviews

Professor Loekman Soetrisno, Director of Rural and Regional Studies, Gajah Mada University, Yogyakarta, 15 August 1997.

Umar Juoro, Lembaga Pengkajian Pembangunan Nasional (Institute for National Development Studies), Jakarta, 2 September 1997.

Dr. Indria Samego, Senior Reseacher, The Institute of Indonesian Sciences, Jakarta, 4 September 1997.

Hadimulyo, the United Development Party, Jakarta, 16 September 1997.

E. Shobirin Nadj, Centre for the Study of Democracy, Jakarta, 19 September 1997.

Dr. Alex Irwan, Bisnis Indonesia, Jakarta, 23 September 1997.

Dr. Dennis de Tray, World Bank's Representative, Jakarta, 24 September 1997.

Dr. Didik Rachbini, Dean of the Faculty of Economics, Mercu Buana University, Jakarta, 24 September 1997.

Dr. Anek Laothamatas, Vice-Rector of Thammasat Universirty, Bangkok, 28 October 1997.

Desmond Holmes, ANZ Group Representative, 6 November 1997.

Australian banker, the National Australia Bank, Bangkok, 7 November 1997.

Dr. Chareonchai Lengsiriwat, Divison Chief of Office of Capital Market Research and Development, Bangkok, 11 November 1997.

Ji Ungpakorn, Political Scientist, Faculty of Political Science, Chulalongkorn University, Bangkok, 11 November 1997.

James C. Roe, Vice President/Manager, Global Markets and Treasury, Chase Manhattan Bank, Bangkok, 13 November 1997.

Dr. Patcharee Siroros, Director of School of Business Administration, Thammasat University, Bangkok, 13 November 1997.

Somchai Sakulsurarat, President of Bank of Ayudhya, Bangkok, 18 November 1997.

Pornchanok Watunyuta, Senior Economist, Phatra Research Institute, Bangkok, 21 November 1997.

Professor Krirkkiat Phipatseritham, Rector of Thailand Chamber Commerce and Industry, Bangkok, 22 November 1997.

Nitaya Pibulratagit, Bank of Thailand (BOT), 26 November 1997.

Chris Poole-Johnson, General Manager, Bates Advertising, Rangoon, 2 December 1997.

Singaporean banker, United Overseas Bank Group (Singapore), Rangoon, 3 December 1997.

Burmese banker, Hana Bank, Rangoon, 4 December 1997.

Australian diplomat, Australian Embassy, Rangoon, 5 December 1997.
Indonesian diplomat, Embassy of the Republic of Indonesia, Rangoon, 5 December 1997.

Internet Sources

Asean Secretariat, <http://www.asean.or.id/>
Center for Information and Development Studies (CIDES), <http://www.cides.org.id/>
Chalongphob Sussangkarn, "Thailand's Debt Crisis and Economic Outlook", *Thailand Development Research Institute's Homepage*, <http://www.tdri.or.th>
Econit, *Kinerja Kabinet Pembangunan VII: Dibawah Bayang-Bayang Keraguan [The Performance of the 7th Development Cabinet: Under the Shadow of Doubt]*, Econit's Homepage, <http://www.indoexchange.com/econit/
Kompas Homepage, <http://www.kompas.com
Republika Homepage, <http://www.republika.co.id
Solidaritas Perempuan's Homepage, <http://www.angelfire.com/or/soliper>

Newspapers, News Magazines, Monthly and Quarterly Reports

Adil (weekly, Jakarta).
Asiaweek (weekly, Hong Kong).
Bangkok Post (daily, Bangkok).
Bisnis Indonesia (daily, Jakarta).
Burma Debate (bi-monthly, Washington D.C.).
Business Day (daily, Bangkok).
Burma Focus (bi-monthly, Bangkok).
Detektif dan Romantika (daily, Jakarta).
Far Eastern Economic Review (weekly, Hong Kong).
Forum Keadilan (weekly, Jakarta).
Gatra (weekly, Jakarta).
Infobank (weekly, Jakarta).
Kompas (weekly, Jakarta).
Panji Masyarakat (weekly, Jakarta).
Prospek (weekly, Jakarta).
Republika (daily, Jakarta).
The Australian (daily, Sydney).
The Australian Financial Review (daily, Sydney).
The Economist (weekly, London).
The Economist Intelligence Unit, *Indonesia, Country Report*, 1996-1998.
--- *Myanmar, Country Report*, 1996-1998.
--- *Thailand, Country Report*, 1995-1998.

The Irrawaddy (bi-monthly, Chiangmai).
The Jakarta Post (daily, Jakarta).
The Nation (daily, Bangkok).
The New Light of Myanmar (daily, Rangoon).
The Weekend Australian (weekly, Sydney)
Warta Ekonomi (weekly, Jakarta).

Index

ADB 4, 32, 103, 175, 197, 223, 224,
  236, 254, 258
AFTA 24, 33, 82, 160
APEC 24, 33, 160
approach 7-10, 14-22, 26, 27, 36,
  37, 69, 70, 94, 137, 145, 205,
  227, 241, 246, 247, 250, 254, 257
    comparative political
      economy 7-10, 14, 21, 26,
      36, 37, 241, 246, 247
    developmentalist 16-22, 36,
      37, 246, 247, 250, 254
    neo-classical economies 14-
      17, 20, 22, 36, 246, 254, 257
    society-based 19-22, 37, 247
    state-based 20-22, 37, 247
ASEAN 33, 160, 177, 205, 231,
  234, 236, 239
ASEAN Free Trade Agreement. *See*
  AFTA
Asia Pacific Economic Cooperation.
  See APEC
Asian 14, 22-26, 30, 32-34, 37, 45,
  103, 175, 197, 203, 223, 226,
  234, 236, 247, 254, 257-259,
  268-270
    miracle 14, 22, 23, 37, 247,
      269
    region 2, 6, 14, 22, 24-26,
      30, 32-34, 37, 45, 259, 268,
      270
Association of Southeast Asian
  Nations. *See* ASEAN
Aung San 187, 194, 195, 199
Aung San Suu Kyi 199, 208-210,
  214, 229, 230, 239

Badan Penelitan dan Penerapan
  Technologi. *See* BPPT

Badan Pengelola Industri-Industri
  Strategis. *See* BPIS
Badan Perencana Pembangunan
  Nasional. *See* BAPPENAS
baht 9, 34, 49, 52, 55, 63, 83, 84,
  86, 88, 90, 95-102, 107-111, 168,
  184, 231, 260-262
    devaluation 52, 86, 88, 96,
      98, 99, 110
    float 9, 86, 95, 98, 99, 101,
      102, 108, 110, 111, 168, 184,
      260
balance of payments 26, 28, 49, 61,
  86, 127, 135
Bangkok International Banking
  Facilities. *See* BIBF
bank 46, 47, 49-51, 54-58, 70, 71,
  81-83, 85, 86, 90, 95, 97-103,
  107, 108, 110, 111, 125, 127,
  129-132, 134, 156-161, 167-177,
  179, 180, 184, 196, 197, 201,
  202, 205, 223, 225, 227-229,
  233, 235, 236, 240, 249, 254,
  257, 258, 261, 269
    commercial 49-51, 54, 81,
      82, 85, 90, 99, 205
    deposits 49, 50, 170, 176,
      228
    foreign 46, 50, 82, 86, 101,
      127, 157, 196, 227, 228
    private 71, 97, 157, 159, 176,
      180, 201, 227, 228
Bank Indonesia. *See* BI
Bank of Thailand. *See* BOT
Bank Rakyat Indonesia. *See* BRI
BAPPENAS 129-131, 161, 254
Berkeley Mafia 31, 121, 123-125,
  127, 170, 174, 258

BI 129, 130, 152, 156-158, 160,
    168-170, 172, 173, 176, 179,
    180, 254, 261
BIBF 82-85, 110
BOB 55, 56, 59, 90, 254
boom 1, 4, 8, 9, 10, 14, 19, 22, 23,
    28, 32, 33, 37, 45, 52, 54, 56, 59,
    60, 67, 71, 83, 86, 121, 126, 128,
    129, 132, 134, 145, 147, 148,
    158, 193, 212, 241, 246-250,
    252, 253, 256-258, 264, 265,
    267, 268
BOT 48, 49, 54-57, 64, 71, 81-88,
    90, 91, 95-103, 109, 110, 254,
    261
BPIS 130
BPPT 130
BRI 157
BUMN 170
Bureau of Budget. *See* BOB
bureaucratic 48, 54, 71, 124, 143,
    250, 258, 265
    polity 48, 54, 71, 250, 258
Burmese Way to Socialism 196,
    200, 253

capital 2, 20, 22, 24, 25, 29, 32-34,
    37, 49, 66, 81-88, 95, 102, 110,
    122, 123, 131, 157-159, 169,
    173, 176, 178, 183, 184, 197,
    202, 248, 259-261, 263, 269
    foreign 2, 49, 81-83, 86, 88,
        95, 123, 159, 178, 183, 197,
        259, 260, 269
    inflow 33, 34, 49, 82, 84-88,
        95, 110, 158, 159, 184, 259,
        261, 263
    market 34, 66, 169, 173, 259
    mobility 24, 25, 33, 37, 86,
        248, 259
    outflow 33, 82, 84, 173, 178,
        184
Capital Adequacy Ratio. *See* CAR
capitalism 57, 264, 269
CAR 82, 86, 157, 176

central bank 55, 56, 102, 129, 156,
    157, 168, 170, 171, 201, 202,
    205, 223, 227, 233, 235
Chart Pattana Party. *See* CPP
Chart Thai Party. *See* CTP
Chinese 27, 33, 46, 47, 49, 55, 57,
    59, 71, 122, 126, 128, 132, 134,
    135, 147, 148, 161, 164, 167,
    178, 182, 183, 194, 249,255, 256,
    258
Choonhavan, Chatichai 60, 61, 64,
    65, 67, 72, 86, 87, 89, 93, 94, 96,
    97, 109, 264
collusion 2, 34, 164, 177, 181, 184,
    262
colonization 5, 27, 45, 121-123,
    139, 193, 194, 248, 249, 258
    British 5, 193, 194, 258
    Dutch 5, 121-123, 139, 147,
        258
comparative 1, 5, 6, 8, 10, 14, 26,
    37, 241, 247, 264
    political economy 5, 8, 10,
        14, 26, 37, 241, 247, 264
    study 1, 5, 8, 10, 247, 264
conglomerates 17, 60, 102, 128,
    132-134, 157, 161, 163, 164,
    171, 173, 175, 203, 252, 256, 263
corruption 2, 23, 34, 63, 67, 72, 105,
    126, 128, 164, 181, 184, 197,
    225, 237, 238, 261, 262
coup 34, 46, 51, 59-62, 67-70, 72,
    87, 183, 195, 198-201, 205, 206,
    213, 250, 265
CPP 65, 89, 94, 96, 98, 105, 107,
    109, 111
crisis 1-10, 14, 15, 22, 23, 25-28,
    30, 32-34, 45, 47, 50, 52, 62, 69,
    81, 86, 88, 92, 93, 95-97, 101-
    103, 107, 110, 111, 124, 126,
    127, 131, 135, 139, 147, 148,
    156, 164, 168, 170-181, 183,
    184, 193, 195, 198, 199, 213,
    214, 222, 227, 230, 234, 235,
    238-241, 246, 247, 249, 259-264,
    266-270

causes 2, 4, 5, 7-9, 22, 25,
  81, 127, 148, 156, 222, 246,
  260, 269
consequences 2, 5, 7-9, 22,
  27, 81, 102, 148, 156, 179,
  234, 239, 246, 269
economic 1-4, 6, 8, 10, 15,
  22, 23, 25-28, 30,32-34, 45,
  52, 81, 93, 96, 97, 102, 107,
  110, 126, 131, 139, 147,
  148, 156, 168, 172, 173,
  175, 178, 179, 183, 184,
  198, 214, 222, 227, 230,
  234, 235, 238-241, 247, 249,
  259-264, 266-268
financial 81, 93, 95, 103,
  110, 111, 127, 183
political 3, 10, 45, 47, 50, 52,
  62, 124, 126, 139, 147, 181,
  183, 193, 195, 198, 199,
  213, 222, 249, 263, 266-268
impact 3, 172, 181, 183, 247
cronyism 177, 182
CTP 52, 59, 60, 62-65, 87-94, 106
currency 2, 6, 8, 26, 28, 33-35, 52,
  60, 82, 86, 88, 96-102, 108, 109,
  111, 158, 168-171, 173, 180,
  181, 184, 198, 205, 223, 231,
  232, 240, 259-263
  crisis 8, 100, 101, 102, 168,
    171, 181, 184
  depreciation 2, 101, 169,
    170, 173, 231
current account 2, 6, 52, 82-84, 88,
  103, 110, 158, 159, 179, 184,
  223, 259
  deficit 2, 52, 83, 84, 88, 103,
    110, 159, 184, 223, 259

debt 2, 6, 28, 33, 52, 82, 84, 85, 88,
  90, 91, 95, 99, 101, 110, 127,
  128, 159, 170, 174, 175, 183,
  184, 223, 235, 259, 262, 263
  external 6, 52, 82, 84, 85, 88,
    101, 110, 159, 184, 235, 259
  private 81, 84, 101, 159, 174,

  175, 184, 262, 263
Democrat Party (Prachathipat) 50,
  62, 64, 65, 67, 89, 92-94, 105,
  109, 110
deregulation 7, 14, 16, 31, 127, 128,
  134-136, 147, 160, 161, 166,
  171, 175, 184, 227, 232, 240,
  252, 254, 256, 258, 261, 263
devaluation 51-53, 88, 98-100, 110,
  127, 168, 224, 231
Dewan Perwakilan Rakyat. *See*
  DPR
Dewan Riset National. *See* DRN
DPR 136, 140-143, 172
DRN 130

East Asia 1, 5, 7, 14-23, 26, 28, 35-
  37, 135, 246, 247, 251, 254, 265
EOI 14, 16, 21, 30, 49, 50, 127
exchange rate 2, 14, 22, 31, 52, 81,
  83, 85-90, 99-101, 110, 157, 158,
  169, 170, 184, 205, 222-225,
  228, 231, 235, 260-263
Export-oriented Industrialization.
  See EOI
external 8, 9, 26, 28, 32, 33, 37, 45,
  52, 59, 84, 85, 88, 101, 110, 111,
  121, 130, 135, 158, 159, 174,
  175, 184, 193, 202, 205, 207,
  213, 223, 235, 248, 257-259,262-
  264, 268, 269
  factors 8, 9, 32, 37, 45, 52,
    59, 121, 135, 193, 258, 263,
    264, 269
  shocks 26, 28, 33, 84, 158,
    184

FDI 31, 53, 60, 159, 226, 227, 235,
  263
FEC 201, 224, 230-234, 263, 264
financial 18, 22, 25, 27, 30-33, 46,
  47, 49, 51, 56, 61, 71, 81, 82, 84,
  86, 88, 90, 91, 93, 95-99, 101-
  103, 107-111, 123, 125, 127,
  129-131, 135, 156-158, 170, 172,
  174, 175, 180, 183, 196, 200,

201, 205, 224, 225, 227, 228,
233, 235, 236, 240, 256, 257,
259, 260, 262, 263
   crisis 81, 93, 95, 103, 110,
      111, 127, 183, 222
   institutions 4, 31, 81, 82, 86,
      90, 95-99, 103, 107, 111,
      156, 157, 174, 201, 205,
      227, 233, 235, 262
   liberalization 9, 13, 31, 33,
      49, 81, 82, 88, 90, 91, 110,
      157, 158, 183, 259, 263
float 9, 81, 86, 95, 98-102, 108, 110,
   111, 168-170, 180, 184, 260, 262
   baht 9, 81, 86, 95, 98-102,
      108, 110, 111, 168, 184, 260
   rupiah 9, 168-170
foreign 1, 2, 4, 5, 14, 22, 31-34, 45,
   46, 48-55, 60, 61, 71, 81-83, 86,
   88, 91, 92, 94-97, 99, 100, 102,
   107, 109-111, 123-127, 135, 136,
   156, 157, 159, 161, 167-170,
   172-174, 178, 183, 184, 193,
   195-197, 200-203, 205, 212, 213,
   222, 224-228, 230-233, 235, 238,
   240, 248, 253, 257-261, 263,
   264, 269
   capital 2, 49, 81-83, 86, 88,
      95, 123, 159, 178, 183, 197,
      259, 260, 269
   exchange 44, 46, 54, 82, 97,
      168, 172, 201, 224, 227,
      228, 230-233, 240, 259, 264
   investment 48, 53, 60, 127,
      159, 200, 202, 222, 226,
      227, 233, 235, 263
   investor 1, 4, 14, 32, 34, 48,
      61, 71, 81, 88, 91, 92, 96,
      99, 102, 110, 111, 125, 126,
      136, 156, 157, 161, 167,
      168, 170, 172, 173, 183,
      193, 201-203, 205, 213, 225,
      226, 238, 240, 253, 258, 261
   policy 5, 48, 94, 124
Foreign Direct Investment. *See* FDI

Foreign Exchange Certificates. *See*
   FEC
Functional Groups. *See* Golkar

GDP 3, 6, 49, 53, 82, 83, 97, 107,
   110, 129, 158, 159, 179, 196,
   223, 224, 235, 256
   growth 3, 83, 129, 158, 223,
      235
globalization 2, 7-10, 14, 16, 20, 22-
   27, 32, 33, 35, 37, 71, 72, 81,
   110, 156, 172, 247, 259, 262,
   264, 267-269
   economic 9, 16, 71, 172
   impact 9, 16, 26, 72, 156,
      172, 247, 259, 267, 268
   result 7, 33, 35, 37
Golkar 125, 131, 141, 142, 166,
   167, 183, 208
governance 2, 4, 23, 27, 34, 37, 248,
   261, 267
Gross Domestic Product. *See* GDP

Habibie, B. J. 126, 130, 131, 160,
   161, 171, 178-180, 182-184, 254,
   266, 268
Hartarto 126, 131, 161, 165
Hassan, Bob 126, 132, 133, 182
House of Representatives. *See* DPR

IMF 4, 16, 31, 32, 34, 59, 71, 91,
   102, 103, 107, 111, 125, 130,
   131, 170, 174-177, 179-184, 223,
   228, 236, 254, 257, 258, 262,
   263, 269
   reform package 102, 103,
      107, 111, 175-177, 179, 180,
      182, 184, 262
   rescue package 103, 174, 175
Import Substitution Industrialization.
   See ISI
Indonesian Democratic Party. *See*
   PDI
International Monetary Fund. *See*
   IMF

internationalization 23-27, 33, 194, 195

investor 1, 4, 14, 32-34, 48, 53, 60, 71, 81, 88, 91, 92, 96-99, 102, 107, 110, 111, 125, 126, 135, 136, 156, 157, 161, 167, 168, 170-173, 178, 180, 183, 193, 195, 201-205, 213, 224-226, 237, 238, 240, 253, 258, 261
  domestic 85, 88, 91, 92, 96, 102, 110, 111, 156, 161, 167, 168, 170, 171, 183, 201, 261
    foreign 1, 4, 14, 32, 48, 85, 88, 91, 92, 96, 99, 102, 110, 111, 125, 126, 136, 156, 157, 161, 167, 168, 170-173, 183, 193, 195, 201-203, 205, 213, 225, 226, 238, 240, 253, 261
    Japanese 53, 58, 60, 71, 126, 135, 258

ISI 14, 48-50, 52, 57, 126

joint-venture 59, 135, 165, 203, 220, 225, 227-229

judiciary 27, 34, 60, 198

Khin Nyunt 207, 233, 236, 237

KKN 164, 181, 184, 262

kyat 198, 218, 223-225, 228, 230, 231, 233, 234, 240, 260, 263

Leekpai, Chuan 62-67, 82, 87, 90, 92, 93, 109, 110, 266, 267

liberalization 9, 14, 31-33, 45, 49, 61, 72, 81, 82, 88, 90, 91, 110, 121, 156-158, 183, 206, 225, 235, 236, 251-253, 258, 259, 263
  financial 9, 31, 33, 49, 81, 82, 88, 90, 91, 110, 156-158, 183, 259, 263
  political 9, 45, 121, 206, 251-253, 258
  trade 14, 31, 61, 235

macroeconomic 2, 14, 22, 25, 55, 86, 101, 130, 158, 170, 179, 222-224, 228, 240, 260
  performance 9, 179, 223, 224, 260
  policy 14, 25, 55, 130, 158, 170
  stability 22, 55, 130, 222, 223, 228, 240

Mandalay 207, 211, 228, 229

Mar'ie, Mohammad 155, 165, 167, 169, 170, 172-174, 176, 180

market 1, 2, 7, 9, 14, 15, 17-19, 21, 22, 27, 29, 30, 32-34, 36, 50, 52, 66, 67, 81, 82, 84, 88, 95, 96, 99, 102, 107, 110, 111, 125, 127, 128, 130, 131, 156, 158, 165, 168-173, 175, 177, 179, 180, 182, 184, 194, 197, 198, 200, 202, 222-225, 228, 231-233, 235, 240, 246-248, 250-253, 257, 259, 260, 262
  black 197, 198, 221, 222, 228, 240, 260
  economy 1, 9, 15, 17, 29, 197, 202, 222, 225, 228, 246, 252, 260
  failure 14, 17, 18, 36
  free 9, 17, 125, 131, 200, 202, 231, 248, 252
  intervention 13, 21, 36, 96, 102, 158, 168
  players 27, 33, 34, 67

martial law 48, 51, 123, 199

middle class 35, 54, 62, 65, 89, 105, 107, 108, 142, 144, 145, 166, 179, 196, 256, 265

Minister 55, 56, 60-65, 68, 87-100, 102-111, 123, 126, 127, 129, 130, 131, 134, 137, 156, 160, 161, 165, 169-174, 176, 177, 179-181, 183, 195, 198, 199, 202, 206, 236-239, 254, 255, 264, 267
  Commerce 87, 94, 108, 165
  Defence 65, 93, 198, 199,

237
Economy 97, 110, 155, 160,
170, 180
Finance 4, 47, 64, 87, 90, 94-
100, 102, 107, 108, 111,
156, 160, 165, 169, 170,
172, 174, 176, 177, 180,
238, 267
Industry 94, 98, 126, 131,
161, 165, 170
Interior 93, 105, 106, 108
Prime 4, 9, 47, 54-56, 60-65,
68, 87-94, 96, 98, 99, 102-
110, 127, 173, 179, 199,
202, 206, 237, 239, 254,
255, 264
Research and Technology
126, 130, 161, 171
MOF 48, 53-56, 59, 61, 71, 81, 91,
95, 128-130, 157, 158, 202, 254
MOI 55, 59, 61, 63, 91, 104, 106
monarchy 45-47, 69, 71, 104, 193,
250
monetary policy 9, 14, 46, 55, 103,
125, 129, 157, 158, 169, 175,
179, 235, 262
money 34, 46, 60, 63, 66, 83, 86,
88, 89, 96, 97, 103, 104, 111,
126, 127, 156, 157, 169, 173,
176, 223, 224, 226, 229, 240,
259, 260
politics 50, 60, 89, 104, 111
speculators 34, 88, 96, 169

NAP 62-65, 89, 91-94, 104, 109
National Development Planning
Board. *See* BAPPENAS
National Economic and Social
Development Board. *See*
NESDB
National League for Democracy.
See NLD
Ne Win 195-198, 200, 202, 210,
213, 237, 248, 250, 253
nepotism 2, 34, 164, 181, 184, 262
NESDB 49, 56, 87, 254

New Aspiration Party. *See* NAP
New Order 1, 30, 121, 124, 125,
127, 128, 131, 134, 135, 138,
140-145, 147, 148, 166, 167,
170, 255, 256, 258, 265, 268
NGO 59-62, 66, 68, 72, 137, 144-
146, 166, 181, 265, 266
Nitisastro, Widjojo 125, 128, 130,
170, 174, 180
NLD 199, 200, 206, 208-214, 229,
230, 235, 238-240, 262, 267
non-state actors 7-9, 19, 21, 22, 24,
26, 54, 136, 137, 143, 148, 247,
251-253, 255, 256, 265, 266, 268

Panyarachun, Anand 61, 62, 64, 82,
87, 104
Partai Demokrasi Indonesia. *See*
PDI
patronage 6, 20, 21, 49, 66, 123,
164, 249, 256
PDI 141, 142, 146, 166, 167
Peoples' Representative Council.
See DPR
pluralist 15, 60, 72, 124, 251, 255,
264
populist 27, 32, 50, 248, 252
privatization 9, 31, 61, 157, 200,
225, 233, 235, 240
protection 19, 22, 29, 30, 32, 49, 57,
72, 126, 156, 157, 165, 256

Rangoon 203, 210, 227, 229, 231,
232, 234, 239
reform 1, 2, 4, 7-10, 14, 16, 26, 28-
32, 37, 45, 46, 52, 54, 56, 57, 59,
61, 66, 70, 72, 95-97, 102-104,
106, 107, 109, 111, 122, 137,
142, 143, 156, 157, 172, 174-
177, 179-182, 184, 193, 198,
200-203, 205, 206, 213, 222,
223, 225-228, 233, 236, 240,
241, 246-258, 260, 262-269
economic 1, 2, 4, 7-9, 16, 29,
30, 37, 45, 52, 54, 56, 57,
59, 61, 66, 70, 72, 97, 107,

111, 172, 175, 177, 179,
181, 182, 184, 193, 198,
200-203, 206, 213, 222, 223,
228 ,236, 240, 241, 246-255,
257, 258, 260, 263-269
  exchange rate 31, 52, 260
  financial sector 9, 61, 95-97,
    102, 109, 157, 222, 227,
    228, 240, 260
  political 4, 7, 26, 29, 103,
    104, 106, 107, 137, 142,
    143, 181, 184, 213, 251,
    263, 266-269
  tax 31, 52, 61
rent-seeking 23, 123, 171, 203, 225,
  250, 251
rupiah 9, 34, 127, 158, 167-170,
  172-174, 177-181, 182, 184, 260,
  261, 268

Saw Maung 191, 198, 206, 250
SET 82, 91, 97, 99, 108, 109
Silpaa-archa, Barnharn 63-65, 68,
  88-93, 97, 104, 110, 111, 261
SLORC 193, 198-200, 202, 205,
  207-209, 213, 236, 237
Social Action Party 50, 52, 55-57,
  62, 65, 89, 94
SOE 47, 124, 126-128, 140, 161,
  162, 170, 197, 201, 203, 204,
  213, 222, 225, 226, 233, 235,
  240, 256, 260, 263
Songram, Phibun 47-49, 57, 248
Soros, George 34, 96, 173
SPDC 236-238
state 6, 8, 14, 15, 17-23, 26-29, 35-
  37, 47, 51, 108, 122-124, 128,
  131, 132, 134, 138, 147, 159,
  161, 162, 171, 180, 183, 193,
  194, 196, 198, 200, 203, 206,
  207, 236, 237, 246-248, 250-254,
  258, 264,266
    authoritarian 18, 29, 120,
      124
    capacity 19, 20, 21, 250, 253
    failure 19, 20, 21, 37, 247,

250, 253
    intervention 17-21, 26, 246,
      250-252, 254
    strong 17-20, 36, 247, 250,
      251, 258
    weak 21, 36, 247, 251-253,
      258
State Law and Order Restoration
  Council. *See* SLORC
State Peace and Development
  Council. *See* SPDC
state-owned 47, 90, 124, 126-128,
  130, 140, 156, 157, 159, 161,
  170, 180, 197, 201, 203, 204,
  213, 222, 225, 233, 240, 256,
  260, 263
    enterprise. *See* SOE
stock exchange 67, 81, 157, 170,
  172, 173, 227, 259
Suharto 4, 8, 9, 16, 121, 124-133,
  135-141, 143, 144, 147, 148,
  156, 161, 164-167, 170, 173,
  176-184, 250-257, 262, 263, 265,
  266, 268
    Bambang Trihatmodjo
      (second son) 132-134, 164-
      166, 176, 177
    family 126, 128, 132, 139,
      164, 173, 176, 182, 262, 263
    Hutomo "Tommy" Mandala
      Putra (youngest son) 132,
      133, 163, 165, 166
    resignation 4, 8, 9, 139, 143,
      183, 266
    Siti Harjati Rukmana or
      "Tutut" (eldest daughter)
      132, 180, 182
Sukarno 123-125, 139, 146, 147
Sukarnoputri, Megawati 146, 166,
  178, 181

tariffs 9, 61, 98, 127, 165
technocrats 14, 16, 32, 49, 50, 53,
  55, 56, 59, 61, 71, 72, 83, 85-88,
  125-128, 130, 131, 147, 160,

161, 171, 175, 184, 202, 238,
251, 252, 254, 255, 258, 261, 262
Thai Farmers' Bank 45, 49, 50, 57,
58, 70, 81, 228
Than Shwe 207, 236-239, 250, 267
Thanarat, Sarit 16, 47-49, 55, 56,
59, 71, 86, 124, 126, 250, 251,
254, 255, 257
Tinsulanonda, Prem 46-48, 50, 52-
54, 56, 57, 59-61, 65, 66, 68-72,
86, 89, 97, 99, 104, 109, 124,
250, 251, 254, 255, 264
transparency 4, 104, 105, 164, 165,
179

U Nu 194, 195, 199, 210
UN 197, 198, 206, 212, 239

USDA 203, 208, 230, 236

vote 63-65, 68, 72, 89, 92, 93, 104,
106, 111, 181, 199
buying 63, 64, 68, 72, 89, 93,
104, 111

World Bank 4, 6, 16, 22, 23, 25, 31,
32, 34, 56, 59, 71, 103, 107, 125,
130, 131, 158, 159, 168, 173,
174, 197, 223, 225, 236, 254,
257, 258, 269
World Trade Organisation 160, 166

Yongchaiyuth, Chaovalit 4, 8, 9, 63-
65, 68, 81, 92-99, 102-111, 201,
261-263, 266